The 2010s

A Decade of Contemporary British Fiction

Titles in *The Decades Series*

The 1930s: A Decade of Modern British Fiction, edited by Nick Hubble, Luke Seaber and Elinor Taylor

The 1940s: A Decade of Modern British Fiction, edited by Philip Tew and Glyn White

The 1950s: A Decade of Modern British Fiction, edited by Nick Bentley, Alice Ferrebe and Nick Hubble

The 1960s: A Decade of Modern British Fiction, edited by Philip Tew, James Riley and Melanie Seddon

The 1970s: A Decade of Contemporary British Fiction, edited by Nick Hubble, John McLeod and Philip Tew

The 1980s: A Decade of Contemporary British Fiction, edited by Emily Horton, Philip Tew, and Leigh Wilson

The 1990s: A Decade of Contemporary British Fiction, edited by Nick Hubble, Philip Tew and Leigh Wilson

The 2000s: A Decade of Contemporary British Fiction, edited by Nick Bentley, Nick Hubble and Leigh Wilson

The 2010s: A Decade of Contemporary British Fiction, edited by Nick Bentley, Emily Horton, Nick Hubble and Philip Tew

In preparation:

The 1920s: A Decade of Modern British Fiction, edited by Tamás Bényei, Shené Boskani and Nick Hubble

The 2010s

A Decade of Contemporary British Fiction

Edited by
Nick Bentley, Emily Horton,
Nick Hubble and Philip Tew

BLOOMSBURY ACADEMIC
LONDON • NEW YORK • OXFORD • NEW DELHI • SYDNEY

BLOOMSBURY ACADEMIC
Bloomsbury Publishing Plc, 50 Bedford Square, London, WC1B 3DP, UK
Bloomsbury Publishing Inc, 1385 Broadway, New York, NY 10018, USA
Bloomsbury Publishing Ireland, 29 Earlsfort Terrace, Dublin 2, D02 AY28, Ireland

BLOOMSBURY, BLOOMSBURY ACADEMIC and the Diana logo are trademarks of
Bloomsbury Publishing Plc

First published in Great Britain 2024
Paperback edition published 2025

Copyright © Nick Bentley, Emily Horton, Nick Hubble, Philip Tew and contributors, 2024

The editors and contributors have asserted their right under the Copyright,
Designs and Patents Act, 1988, to be identified as Authors of this work.

For legal purposes the Acknowledgements on p. xiv constitute an extension
of this copyright page.

Cover design: Rebecca Heselton

All rights reserved. No part of this publication may be: i) reproduced or transmitted in any form, electronic or mechanical, including photocopying, recording or by means of any information storage or retrieval system without prior permission in writing from the publishers; or ii) used or reproduced in any way for the training, development or operation of artificial intelligence (AI) technologies, including generative AI technologies. The rights holders expressly reserve this publication from the text and data mining exception as per Article 4(3) of the Digital Single Market Directive (EU) 2019/790.

Bloomsbury Publishing Plc does not have any control over, or responsibility for, any third-party websites referred to or in this book. All internet addresses given in this book were correct at the time of going to press. The author and publisher regret any inconvenience caused if addresses have changed or sites have ceased to exist, but can accept no responsibility for any such changes.

A catalogue record for this book is available from the British Library.

A catalog record for this book is available from the Library of Congress.

ISBN: HB: 978-1-3502-6821-0
PB: 978-1-3504-4089-0
ePDF: 978-1-3502-6822-7
eBook: 978-1-3502-6823-4

Series: The Decades Series

Typeset by RefineCatch Limited, Bungay, Suffolk

For product safety related questions contact productsafety@bloomsbury.com.

To find out more about our authors and books visit
www.bloomsbury.com and sign up for our newsletters.

Contents

Series Editors' Preface	vii
Contributors	xi
Acknowledgements	xiv
Introduction: Fiction of the 2010s in the Context of a Country in Transition *Emily Horton, Nick Hubble, Nick Bentley and Philip Tew*	1
1 Fictions of the Break-Up *Nick Hubble*	23
2 Fiction in the Age of Distraction: Reading and Attention in the 2010s *Alice Bennett*	51
3 Border Crossings: Diasporic British Fiction of the 2010s *Emily Horton*	79
4 'Defining it is a Struggle': Working-Class Fiction in the 2010s *Matti Ron*	107
5 What's To-day? Politics and Typography in Ali Smith's Decade *Tory Young*	137
6 The 'Teenie' Novels of Jonathan Coe: Intertextuality, Satire, Parody, Farce and Irony *Philip Tew*	153
7 'The English Problem': Reading the Body Politic in Post-Brexit Fictions *Kristian Shaw*	183
8 Inexhaustible Literature? Contemporary Experimental Approaches in Literature *Mark P. Williams*	209
9 Speculative Fiction of the 2010s *Anna McFarlane*	239
10 The Neo-mythological Novel: Re-writing the Epic in Contemporary British Fiction *Nick Bentley*	263

Timeline of Works	291
Timeline of National Events	295
Timeline of International Events	303
Biographies of Writers	307
Index	315

Series Editors' Preface

Nick Hubble, Philip Tew and Leigh Wilson

The series began with a focus on Contemporary British fiction published from 1970 to the present, an expanding area of academic interest, becoming a major area of academic study in the last twenty-five years and attracting a seemingly ever-increasing global scholarship. However, that very speed of the growth of research in this field has perhaps precluded any really nuanced analysis of its key defining terms and has restricted consideration of its chronological development. This series addresses such issues in an informative and structured manner through a set of extended contributions combining wide-reaching survey work with in-depth research-led analysis. Naturally, many older British academics assume at least some personal knowledge in charting this field, drawing on their own life experience, but increasingly many such coordinates represent the distant past of pre-birth or childhood not only for students, both undergraduate and postgraduate, but also younger academics. Given that most people's memories of their first five to ten years are vague and localized, an academic born in the early to mid-1980s will only have real first-hand knowledge of less than half these forty-plus years, while a member of the current generation of new undergraduates, born in the early 2000s, will have no adult experience of the period at all. The apparently self-evident nature of this chronological, experiential reality disguises the rather complex challenges it poses to any assessment of the contemporary (or of the past in terms of precursory periods). Therefore, the aim of these volumes, which include timelines and biographical information on the writers covered, is to provide the contextual framework that is now necessary for the study of the British fiction of these four decades and beyond.

The first nine volumes in this Decades Series emerged from a series of workshops hosted by the now vanished Brunel Centre for Contemporary Writing (BCCW) located in the now vanished School of Arts at Brunel University London, UK. These events assembled specially invited teams of leading internationally recognized scholars in the field, together with emergent younger figures, in order that they might together examine critically the periodization of initially contemporary British fiction (which overall chronology was later expanded by adding previous decades) by dividing it into its four constituent decades: the 1970s symposium was held on 12 March 2010; the 1980s on 7 July 2010; the 1990s on 3 December 2010; and the 2000s on 1 April 2011. Subsequent seminars expanding the series included the 1960s on 18 March 2015; the 1950s on 22 April 2015; the 1930s on 21 June 2017; the 1940s on 6 June 2018; and the 2010s on 8 July 2021. During workshops, draft papers were offered and discussions ensued, exchanging ideas and ensuring both continuity and also fruitful interaction (including productive dissonances) between what would become chapters of volumes that would hopefully exceed the sum of their parts.

The division of the series by decade could be charged with being too obvious and therefore rather too contentious. In the latter camp, no doubt, would be Ferdinand Mount, who in a 2006 article for the *London Review of Books* concerned primarily with the 1950s, 'The Doctrine of Unripe Time', complained 'When did decaditis first strike? When did people begin to think that slicing the past up into periods of ten years was a useful thing to do?' However, he does admit still that such characterization has long been associated with aesthetic production and its relationship to a larger sense of the times. In *The Sense of an Ending: Studies in the Theory of Fiction*, published in 1967, Frank Kermode argued that divisions of time, like novels, are ways of making meaning. And clearly both can also shape our comprehension of an ideological and aesthetic period that seem to co-exist, but are perhaps not necessarily coterminous in their dominant inflections. The scholars involved in our BCCW symposia discussed the potential arbitrariness of all periodizations (which at times is reflected by contributors by extending the parameters of the decade under scrutiny), but nevertheless acknowledged the importance of such divisions, their experiential resonances and symbolic possibilities. They analysed the decades in question in terms of not only leading figures, the cultural zeitgeist and socio-historical perspectives, but also in the context of the changing configuration of Britishness within larger, shifting global processes. The volume participants also reconsidered the effects and meaning of headline events and cultural shifts such as the Great Depression, Proletarian Literature, the Popular Front, the Second World War, the emergence of the Welfare State, the Cold War, Neoliberalism and the Thatcher Government to name only a very few. Perhaps ironically to prove the point about the possibilities inherent in such an approach, in his *LRB* article Mount concedes that 'For the historian ... if the 1950s are famous for anything, it is for being dull', adding a comment on the 'shiny barbarism of the new affluence'. Hence, even for Mount, a decade may still possess certain unifying qualities, those shaping and shaped by its overriding cultural mood.

After the various symposia had taken place at Brunel, guided by the editors of the particular volumes, the individuals dispersed and wrote up their papers into full-length chapters (generally 10,000–12,000 words but in some cases longer), revised in the light of other papers, the workshop discussions and subsequent further research. These chapters form the core of the book series, which, therefore, may be seen as the result of a collaborative research project bringing together initially twenty-four academics from Britain, Europe and North America. Five further seminars and volumes have now added scholars to this ongoing project, which is approaching completion.

Each volume shares a common, although not necessarily identical, structure. Following a critical introduction shaped by research, the first chapter of each volume provides a perspective on the 'Literary History of the Decade'. The next two chapters are generally themed around topics that have been specially chosen for each decade, and which also relate to themes of the preceding and succeeding decades, enabling detailed readings of key texts to emerge in full historical and theoretical context. The tone and context having been set in this way, the remaining chapters fill out a complex but comprehensible picture of each decade. In certain volumes a 'Colonial/Postcolonial/Ethnic Voices' chapter addresses the ongoing experience and legacy of Britain's Empire and the rise of a new globalization, which is arguably the most significant long-term influence on contemporary British writing. A chapter will focus on women's writing and gendered forms of voice, perception and written response to both literary impulses and historical eventfulness. Various other chapters with a variety of focuses are added according to the dynamics and literary compulsions of each particular decade, which may feature international contexts or a specific sub-genre of the novel form, for instance. Each decade is different, but common threads are seen to emerge.

In its final form, the Decades Series will extend from 1920 to 2020, in effect reconnecting Contemporary British Fictions with their modern precursors from the aftermath of the First World War, and showing through detailed and forensic analysis how the literary landscape has been transformed over a century of unprecedented social change.

Works cited

Kermode, Frank. *The Sense of an Ending: Studies in the Theory of Fiction*. Oxford: Oxford University Press, 1967.

Mount, Ferdinand. 'The Doctrine of Unripe Time.' *London Review of Books* 28 (22) (16 November 2006): 28–30, http://www.lrb.co.uk/v28/n22/ferdinand-mount/the-doctrine-of-unripe-time: n.p.

Contributors

Alice Bennett is Senior Lecturer in English Literature at Liverpool Hope University. She is the author of *Contemporary Fictions of Attention* (Bloomsbury, 2018) and *Alarm* (Bloomsbury, 2022).

Nick Bentley is Senior Lecturer in English literature at Keele University, UK. He is author of *Contemporary British Fiction: A Reader's Guide to the Essential Criticism* (2018); *Martin Amis* (2015); *Contemporary British Fiction* (2008); *Radical Fictions: The English Novel in the 1950s* (2007); and co-editor of *The 2000s: A Decade of Contemporary British Fiction* (2015), *The 1950s: A Decade of British Fiction* (2018) and *Teenage Dreams: Youth Subcultures in Fiction, Film and Other Media* (2018). He is currently writing a monograph entitled *Making a Scene: Youth Subcultures in Postwar and Contemporary Fiction*.

Emily Horton is a Senior Lecturer in English Literature at Brunel University. Her research focuses on contemporary world literature, specializing in trauma fiction, genre and popular fiction, and fictional explorations of globalization and transnationalism. Her first monograph, *Contemporary Crisis Fictions*, was published in 2014. She has also co-edited two volumes: *The 1980s: A Decade in Contemporary British Fiction*, with Philip Tew and Leigh Wilson (Bloomsbury, 2014); and *Ali Smith*, with Monica Germanà (Bloomsbury, 2013).

Nick Hubble is Professor of Modern and Contemporary English at Brunel University London, UK. They are the author of *Mass-Observation and Everyday Life: Culture, History, Theory* (2006/2010) and *The Proletarian Answer to the Modernist Question* (2017); and one of the series editors of Bloomsbury Academic's 'British Fiction: The Decades Series'. Nick was a judge for the Arthur C. Clarke Award for Best Science Fiction Novel published in Britain in 2021 and 2022.

Anna McFarlane is a Lecturer in Medical Humanities at the University of Leeds. Her British Academy Postdoctoral Fellowship, 'Products of Conception: Science Fiction and Traumatic Pregnancy, 1968–2015', looks at fantastic literature (including science fiction, fantasy, and horror) and cinema alongside medical advice literature and women's memoirs about pregnancy to argue that the fantastic constitutes a valuable way of approaching reproductive trauma. She is the co-editor of *The Routledge Companion to Cyberpunk Culture* (2020), *Fifty Key Figures in Cyberpunk Culture* (2022), and *The Edinburgh Companion to Science Fiction and the Medical Humanities* (forthcoming). Her first monograph is a study of William Gibson's novels, *Cyberpunk Culture and Psychology: Seeing Through the Mirrorshades* (2021).

Matti Ron completed his PhD at the University of East Anglia in 2020 with a thesis on the relationship between working-class fiction, the avant-garde and political representation in the twentieth century. In 2018, he won the Raymond Williams Society's Simon Dentith Memorial Prize for an essay on modernism and 1930s proletarian fiction. The essay was subsequently published in the 2020 issue of *Key Words: A Journal of Cultural Materialism*. He has also published two book chapters on class and race in postwar Caribbean literature.

Kristian Shaw is Associate Professor in English Literature at the University of Lincoln. He is the author of *Cosmopolitanism in Twenty-First Century Fiction* (2017) and *Brexlit: British Literature and the European Project* (Bloomsbury 2021). He is series co-editor of the Manchester University Press series *Twenty-First Century Perspectives* and co-editor of *Hari Kunzru* (2023, with Sara Upstone) and *Kazuo Ishiguro* (2023, with Peter Sloane). He is currently working on the forthcoming *Routledge Handbook to Literature and Globalization*.

Philip Tew is Professor Emeritus at Brunel University London and a fellow of the Royal Society of Arts. His main publications include *B.S. Johnson: A Critical Reading* (2001); *The Contemporary British Novel* (2004; rev. 2nd edn 2007); *Zadie Smith* (2010); *Ageing, Narrative and Identity: New Qualitative Social Research* (2013, with Nick Hubble); *Reading Zadie Smith: The First Decade and Beyond* (2013); and with Jonathan Coe and Julia Jordan *Well Done God! Selected Prose and Drama of B.S. Johnson* (2013). He completed a second doctorate in Creative Writing at Brunel in 2016 and has since published the following fiction: *Afterlives: A Novel* (2019); *Fragmentary Lives: Three Novellas* (2019); and a second novel *Clark Gable and his Plastic Duck* (2020). A third novel, *Heroes and Villains*, will come out in 2023.

Mark P. Williams's main areas of research are on the relationships between fantastic fiction, avant-garde writing, and politics, and he previously contributed to the Decades series for *The 1970s* and *The 1990s*. He now teaches English and Politics at a bilingual High School having previously taught at universities in Germany, the UK, and Aotearoa New Zealand. This includes teaching at the Universität Duisburg-Essen and Johannes-Gutenberg Universität, Mainz; at the University of East Anglia in Norwich; and at Victoria University of Wellington/ Te Herenga Waka. He has also worked as a Political Reporter in the New Zealand Parliamentary Press Gallery and as web editor and reviewer for the *Scoop Review of Books*.

Tory Young is an Associate Professor of English Literature at Anglia Ruskin University, Cambridge, where she teaches 20th–21st-century literature. At the start of her career, she combined research into modernist women writers especially Nancy Cunard (founder of the Hours Press) with Writing in the Disciplines. Her 2008 guide for undergraduates *Studying English Literature: A Practical Guide* has sold around the world. In 2013, she was awarded a British Academy Grant to study feminist narratology which resulted in a symposium, a special edition of *Textual Practice* (2018), and a book *Queer and Feminist Theories of Narrative* (2021). In 2021, she began a collaboration with the National Centre for Writing, developing a series of life-writing seminars for participants aged 70+ entitled 'A Life Written' (https://www.youtube.com/watch?v=83H8MW3NDkc) and is currently researching intergenerational friendships in contemporary fiction, and the impact of writing on wellbeing.

Acknowledgements

We would like to thank all our contributors for their expertise, patience and generosity when responding to our queries and guidance as this book has gradually taken shape. We have enjoyed excellent support throughout from the editorial team at Bloomsbury, especially David Avital, Mark Richardson, Clara Herberg, Lucy Brown, Ben Doyle, and Laura Cope, who have been instrumental in bringing this series and book to fruition.

We gratefully acknowledge the support of the Brunel University Research and Knowledge Transfer Committee for providing the funding which enabled the Brunel Centre for Contemporary Writing, before its untimely cancellation, to host various events in the 'British Fiction Decades Seminar Series' during 2010, 2011, 2015, 2017, 2018, and 2021, which have led to the publication of the volumes in this book series. Without the support of administrative and catering staff at Brunel these events could not have taken place. We would also like to thank all the academics and postgraduate students who attended and contributed to the discussions at these events. We would also like to acknowledge gratefully the staff at Brunel University Library, the British Library, the National Library of Scotland, the National Library of Wales and other research libraries who have provided support to the contributors to this volume.

Introduction: Fiction of the 2010s in the Context of a Country in Transition

Emily Horton, Nick Hubble, Nick Bentley and Philip Tew

From the aftermath of the 2008 global financial crash to the Covid-19 pandemic of 2020, the 2010s have been a decade of crisis, in which every area of everyday life has been affected. Internationally, the intensification of what is now a fierce rivalry between the US and China has led to a redistribution of the global balance of power and a heightened tension. Flooding, wildfires and other catastrophic consequences of climate change are now recurrent annual events. Political phenomena such as the election of Donald Trump as US President in 2016 and the rise of the populist right across Europe seem to mark a decisive political shift in postwar Western democracies. The relentless presence of social media and 24-hour digital news has brought about the transformation of people's lives ranging from, on the one hand, spreading awareness of social movements, such as Black Lives Matter and #MeToo, to, on the other hand, undermining democracy through misinformation and the spread of fake news.

Nationally, there has been a decade of austerity economics punctuated by divisive referendums on Scottish independence and whether Britain should leave or remain in the EU. This volume relates the British fiction of the decade to these contexts in order to examine and explain contemporary trends, such as the rise of a new working-class fiction, the ongoing development of separate national literatures of Scotland and Wales, and shifts in modes of attention and reading. However, in chronological terms, *The 2010s* is also the concluding volume of the Decades Series, which charts the history of British fiction since the First World War. 'A Century of Transformational Change for British Fiction', the foreword to the forthcoming *The 1920s: A Decade of Modern British Fiction* will set out the trends identified across the series and make a provisional assessment of how these 100 years of British fiction are likely to be seen by cultural historians of the future. Although, novels will continue to be written and read in the UK, there are good reasons for thinking that a historical watershed has been passed so that future fiction written in Britain is unlikely to have the same cultural signification within national life as it has over the past century. In the first half of this introduction, we explore some of the distinctive aspects of national identity in the 2010s and suggest some of the ways in which it might turn out to be a transitional decade.

Cultural, political and social changes in Britain during the 2010s

Britain in 2023, at the time of the writing of this introduction, feels a very different country to the Britain at the beginning of 2010, when the New Labour Government was in its thirteenth year of power. It is true that it was not long before the General Election of 6 May 2010 gave rise to a hung parliament and, after agreement was reached between David Cameron's Conservative Party and Nick Clegg's Liberal Democrats, the formation of the first coalition government since 1945. However, rather than a constitutional oddity, this seemed to some to be the long-awaited introduction of mature European politics to the UK. Among the early acts of the coalition were the introduction of fixed-term parliaments of five years' duration and legislation for a referendum on changing the electoral system from 'first past the post' (FPTP) to the 'alternative vote' (AV). While AV was decisively rejected in the referendum on 5 May 2011 by 68 per cent to 32 per cent, the coalition held firmly together and went on to legislate to introduce same-sex marriages, the first of which took place on 29 March 2014. At the same time, however, the coalition were following an economic programme of austerity, which cut public spending, including welfare payments, in order to reduce the national debt. When the fixed term of the parliament came to an end, automatically leading to a General Election on 7 May 2015, opinion polls suggested the result would be similar to the one of five years earlier. The most likely outcome seemed to be another five years of coalition government. Few suspected that parliamentary politics in the closing years of the decade would in fact become characterized by instability, chaos and the abandonment of parliamentary procedure to an extent hitherto unimaginable even in the fraught years of the late 1970s (see the 'Timeline of National Events' at the end of this volume for details of these events). Even fewer would have foreseen the UK's formal withdrawal from the European Union at 23:00 GMT on 31 January 2020, marking both an epochal shift in foreign policy and the most significant change to Britain's internal political landscape since the implementation of devolution at the end of the 1990s.

It is easy enough to say that the cause of both the parliamentary instability and Brexit was the narrow and divisive outcome of the United Kingdom European Union membership referendum of 23 June 2016, in which 17,410,742 (51.89%) people voted to leave the EU and 16,141,241 (48.11%) voted to remain. However, in the years since, it has become clear that this result did not just reflect a simple division over a binary choice but represents a more complex fragmentation of social and political values that have totally undermined any remaining sense of a British common culture. This fragmentation was not caused by the referendum, which merely brought it to light, but was the result of processes of divergence within British society dating back to at least the 1960s and probably earlier than that. The immediate reason for the referendum taking place was as a consequence of the surprise outcome of the 2015 General Election, which saw Cameron's Conservative Party take power on its own after winning a majority of ten seats. The unexpected result of which was that Cameron therefore found himself having to honour a manifesto commitment to holding an in-out referendum on Britain's place in the EU, which might otherwise have been vetoed by the Liberal Democrats in renewed coalition talks. However, to explain why the Conservatives won the 2015 election requires examining trends and events that were already gathering pace in the opening years of the decade, and, as suggested above, whose roots lie further back. There is a good case for arguing that the 2010s as a whole were characterized by unprecedented and potentially irreversible changes to British culture and identity, the ultimate consequences of which remain profoundly uncertain.

One of the key long-term changes in British society was the persistent and ongoing rise in the levels of social inequality. The introduction to the previous volume in this series, *The 2000s*, noted that not only was the UK the only country in the G7 to have recorded rising inequality in the twenty-first century but also, as compellingly set out in the 2009 bestselling work of popular social science *The Spirit Level* by Richard Wilkinson and Kate Pickett, that this trend had begun in the Thatcherite 1980s (see Bentley, Hubble and Wilson 2015: 4–5). According to the Equality Trust, by 2022, UK households in the bottom 20 per cent of the population had on average an equivalized disposable income of £13,218, whilst the top 20 per cent had £83,687.[1] However, these figures do not show the true extent of income inequality because they disguise the fact that the incomes of the top 1 per cent are significantly higher than anyone else's. Wealth is even more unequally divided than income: in 2020, the Office of National Statistics (ONS) calculated that the richest 10 per cent of households hold 43 per cent of all wealth, while the poorest 50 per cent own just 9 per cent. For the UK as a whole, the World Inequality Database found that the total wealth share of the top 0.1 per cent doubled between 1984 and 2013 by reaching 9 per cent of all wealth: in other words, the wealth of the top 0.1 per cent of UK society is equivalent to that of the bottom 50 per cent. However, these overall UK figures only tell part of the story of inequality in the UK, which is complicated by regional and generational factors. One area in which the redistributive effect of taxes and benefits, characteristic of how the British Welfare State used to function, still has a significant effect is in the case of retired households, in which disposable income inequality is lower than non-retired households. Therefore, pensioners are more likely to have a degree of insulation from inequality than the general public as a whole. The biggest disparities in inequality within the overall UK figures, however, relate to national and regional variations. The median household total wealth of £503,400 in the South East is more than twice the comparable amount for Scotland (£214,000) and three other English regions, the North East (£168,500), the North West (£237,500) and Yorkshire and the Humber (£214,900), with the equivalent figures for Wales, the East Midlands and the West Midlands not much higher.

These national and regional variations are broadly in alignment with the breakdown of the 2016 EU referendum vote, some of the details of which can be found in the 'Timeline of National Events' at the end of this book. However, there were some crucial differences. In particular, Scotland voted heavily to remain in the EU despite having a very similar median household wealth to the three Northern English regions, which tended to vote heavily to leave. While the East and West Midlands of England voted by the biggest margins of all to leave, Wales, with almost identical median household wealth voted to leave by a much narrower margin that was more or less in line with the narrow overall UK vote, as did the much wealthier South East of England. Aside from Scotland and Northern Ireland, the only remain-voting region of the UK was London, with a household median income of £340,300. This result was indicative of a divide in England between remain-voting metropolitan areas and leave-voting rural communities and small towns. However, outside England, the rural areas of Scotland and the Welsh-speaking rural counties of Ceredigion and Gwynedd voted for remain alongside the metropolitan centres of Edinburgh, Glasgow and Cardiff. Thus, it can be seen that national identity played a huge role in shaping the distribution of the leave and remain votes in the EU referendum.

These national variations within the Brexit vote were anticipated in the 2015 General Election, when, as Ailsa Henderson and Richard Wyn-Jones (2021) note, 'for the first time in the UK's democratic history (but repeated twice since), four different parties topped the polls in the state's four different constituent territories' (13). In contrast, when serious academic studies of election voting behaviour began in 1964, 'in political terms at least the United Kingdom could be viewed as forming "one nation" – one nation with two dominant political parties, each deeply entrenched on either side of a class divide and enjoying the loyal support of most members of "their" respective classes' (12). That situation began to change almost immediately following famous by-election victories by Plaid Cymru in Carmarthen in 1966 and by the Scottish National Party (SNP) in Hamilton 1967. Over the intervening half century, one 'national' electorate became four national electorates. By 2015, following the devolution of various powers from 1999 onwards, campaigns were being framed in nationally distinctive terms with direct reference to specific national divisions, but this was taken to a different level when the Conservatives became the first major party to produce a manifesto explicitly targeted at voters in England. In David Cameron's introduction to this English manifesto, he specifically referred to his speech on the morning after the Scottish Independence Referendum of 2014 when he declared the Conservative Party to be the party of the Union. But he also declared that 'Our great National Health Service, our education system, our support to help first time buyers – all these policies are effectively devolved to England, just as they are devolved to Scotland and Wales' (qtd. Henderson and Wyn Jones 2021: 15).

In particular, the Conservatives focused their campaign on what they saw as the dangerous prospect of Ed Miliband leading a Labour Government dependent on SNP support; a threat that they embodied in an iconic Saatchi-produced poster depicting Miliband in the pocket of former SNP leader Alex Salmond (see Perraudin and Mason 2015: n.p.). This campaign was especially targeted at potential Liberal Democrat and UK Independence Party (UKIP) voters and proved extremely effective at eating into those parties' support. The Liberal Democrat leader Nick Clegg later complained that:

> Conservative central office was posting letters from David Cameron to tens of thousands of Lib Dem voters in the South-West of England that essentially said, 'I know you're a Lib Dem, that's okay, we've worked with them very well for five years, but if you really don't want Ed Miliband in charge, with Alex Salmond pulling the strings. Then on this occasion please lend us your vote.' It was a devastatingly effective tactic.
>
> qtd. Henderson and Wyn Jones 2021: 19

There is a strong case for arguing, therefore, that the decisive factor enabling the Conservatives to win a surprise majority at the 2015 General Election was their exploitation of an antipathy amongst English voters towards not just the SNP but also the Scottish people and Scotland more generally. The reasons behind this are more complicated than simple prejudice and result from the evolution of Englishness as a 'political force' in the phrase used in the subtitle of Henderson and Wyn Jones's book, *Englishness*. On the one hand, they note the rise of 'devo anxiety' in England since 1999: 'a perception that England is unfairly treated within the territorial settlement that now exists in the UK' (65). On the other hand, the transition between people in England describing themselves as English rather than British predates the establishment of the devolved administrations. As Henderson and Wyn Jones discuss, the growth of English national identity is a different kind of phenomenon to Welsh, Scottish or Irish nationalism, which all entail a definition against Britishness and a rejection of the legacy of the British Empire. In contrast, their research through the Future of England Survey (FoES), first run in 2011 and regularly repeated since, shows Englishness to be a more fluid identification, which embraces England for internal purposes but a particular traditional version of Britain for external ones. By 2016, those who identified as primarily English saw little or no benefits to Britain's membership of the EU and also strongly tended to see the EU as having more influence than the UK Government over how Britain was run, leading them to support leaving the EU by a margin of three to one (see Henderson and Wyn Jones 2021: 80–102).

The idea of the Brexit vote being a specifically English revolt informs Kristian Shaw's chapter in this volume, '"The English Problem": Reading the Body Politic in Post-Brexit Fictions'. After mentioning the emergence of a 'Brexlit' movement, Shaw specifically discusses the ways a nostalgic and potentially self-destructive nativist English identity is represented across a range of novels including Sarah Moss's *Ghost Wall* (2018), Sam Byers's *Perfidious Albion* (2018), and Anthony Cartwright's *The Cut* (2017). This development was not widely anticipated: Henderson and Wyn Jones note that when they initially set up the FoES, they didn't anticipate that it would lead to a monograph-length study of English nationalism. Previously, most commentators had treated any mention of nationalism within an English context as incongruous. Nevertheless, the political development of Englishness within the 2010s has clear parallels with some of the paradigms set out in nationalist literature. For example, Miroslav Hroch (1985) describes three stages to nationalist agitation: the forging of a national past through a focus on tradition, the persuasion of the target population that they belong to this national tradition, and the development of the resultant national consciousness into a mass social phenomenon. It is possible to map the transition from the second of these stages to the third – typically achieved by linking the national cause to the material interests of the target audience – on to the events surrounding the 2015 General Election and the 2016 EU referendum:

> ...on this reading, the fear that 'undue' Scottish influence over a UK Labour government would lead to Scotland being given even more favourable (and therefore unfair) treatment in terms of public spending, and so on, made concrete more abstract concerns about the role of non-English members of Parliament in legislative votes for England, creating the conditions for successfully nationalist mobilization by the Conservatives. Similarly, a precondition for nationalist success in 2016 was a belief – justified or not – that leaving the European Union would release additional funding for and capacity in public services by stopping the transfer of 'billions of pounds' to Brussels and putting an end to 'uncontrolled' immigration.
>
> Henderson and Wyn Jones 2021: 198

Therefore, the Leave victory was mainly due to neither cultural nor economic reasons but to the 'success [...] of campaigners in persuading voters that they are linked to each other in ways that demand a nationalist response' (198).

In this manner, the phenomenon of rising identification with Englishness that had been gradually emerging into the public sphere since the 1990s became a major determinant of political outcomes in the 2010s. Of course, there were other events in which national consciousness rose to the fore during the decade, notably the Scottish Independence Referendum of 18 September 2014, which itself came about as a result of the SNP winning a majority, despite the electoral system of proportional representation, in the Scottish Parliament Election of 5 May 2011. As discussed in the introduction to *The 2000s*, although Scots voted by a ratio of 55 per cent to 45 per cent to stay in the UK, the net result was a political surge for the SNP, who won 56 seats in the 2015 UK General Election and remain the dominant political force in Scotland at the time of writing. National differences within British fiction long precede the 2010s, being discussed in previous volumes within the Decades Series including *The 1930s* (see Hubble 2021), *The 1970s* (see Hubble 2014) and *The 1980s* (see Germanà 2014), but as Nick Hubble discusses in the first chapter of this volume, 'Fictions of the Break-Up' – which includes analysis of some Scottish and Welsh fiction[2] – to continue treating British fiction as a meaningful category in the face of increasingly divergent national traditions has become an ideological operation. While, formerly, even resolutely Scottish novels such as William McIlvanney's *Docherty* (1975) might still be discussed in a British context due to shared elements of class experience, it no longer makes sense to consider, for example, James Robertson's *And the Land Lay Still* (2010) under the rubric of British fiction, other than as an example of why the term no longer works. Nor is this divergence simply a product of upbringing. Nina Allan, one of the writers discussed in Anna McFarlane's chapter, 'Speculative Fiction of the 2010s', recently stated in public that while she used to consider herself as belonging to the post-New-Wave alongside writers such as M. John Harrison, that since moving to Scotland she has found herself questioning that British anti-novel tradition and writing in a more Scottish speculative style.[3] Both Hubble's and McFarlane's chapters in this volume cast light on this ongoing national and regional divergence within British fiction.

The cultural, political and social shifts transforming the space of what was once a relatively uniform Britain became once again reconfigured in the new landscape revealed by the UK General Election of 12 December 2019, when the Conservative Party under Boris Johnson won a resounding parliamentary majority of 80 seats on a platform of ending the political chaos in the UK Parliament by getting 'Brexit done'. Key to Johnson's achievement was winning 34 of the 48 so-called northern 'Red Wall' constituencies, which were defined through the four factors of not having returned a Conservative MP since at least 1997, having a high vote to leave the EU (63 per cent on average), having a substantial Labour majority during the 1990s, but also a substantial minority Conservative vote even during these Labour majority years (see Payne 2022: 20). In some quarters, this was explained as evidence of something that the Labour Party was failing to come to terms with: that 'the working class has changed beyond recognition' (388). However, this was only true at the level of symbolism because there was nothing new in the working class being more than unionized men in blue-collar jobs. Nevertheless, the fact that this was now publicly undeniable, suddenly stripped class of its magical status as the all-purpose explainer of British social and cultural life. While some enterprising social entrepreneurs have tried to take advantage of this opportunity for alternative theories by proclaiming that the real class divide in modern Britain is between those with and without a university education (Skelton 2021; Goodwin 2023), the new reality is rather more complicated as became apparent from analysis of the findings from the BBC's 'Great British Class Survey', which was launched in 2011.

A team of sociologists led by Mike Savage responded to 161,000 responses to the survey and the way in which 'spiralling levels of inequality are remaking social classes' by redrawing the traditional hierarchical British model of upper, middle and working classes to produce a non-hierarchical set of seven new categories: 'elite', 'established middle class', 'new affluent workers', 'technical middle class', 'traditional working class', 'emerging service workers' and a 'precariat' (Savage et al. 2015: 3, 174). In turn, the BBC incorporated these categories into an interactive 'Class Calculator',[4] which allowed members of the public to input their personal data for an informal self-assessment: 'Within a week seven million people – roughly one in five of the British adult population – clicked on the Class Calculator to find out which "new" class they were in' (Savage et al. 2015: 6). Savage concluded that social class was once again a very powerful force in the popular imagination. As we have seen, while class had certainly returned to political attention, it was playing out differently within the fragmented state of twenty-first century Britain, and subject to fierce contestation, which is still ongoing. In a previous decade of intense uncertainty, the 1930s, George Orwell jokingly comforted fellow members of the sinking middle class that falling into the working class 'will not be so dreadful as we feared, for, after all, we have nothing to lose but our aitches' (1986: 204). There is more than one reason why the same joke would not have worked in the 2010s, but the chief one was that of the bleakness of the condition of precarity afflicting 15 per cent of British society in 2015 (probably more by 2023) and haunting the lives of many more who were just about getting by. The second half of this introduction focuses on precarity and its consequences.

Precarity, affect, and embodiment

Looking back on the 2010s from the perspective of ongoing austerity and widespread illness, and from a wealth of new fictions centred specifically on dystopian predicaments, one consideration that emerges as salient to this decade is just how vulnerable the period imagined itself from the very beginning, immediately framing its identity and values in terms of a pervasive precarity. As Liam Connell reflected in 2021, 'Looking across the collection of books [in the British Library] that contain the word precarious in their title, more than two-thirds were published this century, and more than half were published in the last decade' (27). These statistics echo a visible literary critical, cultural and sociological rise in interest around this topic, which is nevertheless interpreted in notably different ways depending on how and to what it is applied. Emily Hogg comments on how precarity has come to stand in for a range of contemporary socio-political anxieties, including 'temporary work contracts', 'environmental catastrophe', 'state violence', and 'pervasive anxiety', all of which reflect global capitalist 'insecurity and instability' (2021: 1). She continues by arguing that widespread experiences of 'precarity, precariousness and the precariat' come through 'in lack of access to state benefits and healthcare, in housing crisis, and in brutal anti-migrant policies', reinforcing the 'urgent' need to examine and investigate this topic (2).

From one angle, this anxiety can be connected back to (still prescient) pre-millennial concerns regarding class divisions built into local British economies, explored by such twentieth-century authors as James Kelman, Alan Sillitoe, Alasdair Gray and Pat Barker, and more recently, by Niall Griffiths, Sarah Moss, Jon McGregor, Tim Maughan, and Daisy Johnson. As Griffiths's *Broken Ghost* (2019) reflects, 'what was once a welfare state now seems to see it as a duty not to give poor children enough to live on and [. . .] this attitude has come to be seen as good' (74). This understanding recalls Thatcherite socioeconomic policy and its unapologetic dismantling of social services, but also to more recent austerity measures which seeks to cut 'the state's budget, debts and deficits' through further reductions to public sector wages and public spending (Blyth 2013: 2). As Linnie Blake and Agnieszka Soltysik aptly express, such policies, particularly in the wake of the financial crisis, 'effectively forced the public to pay for the mistakes of the banking sector', setting in place 'a kind of "voluntary deflation"', which sought 'to restore competitiveness' through 'measures that targeted the poorest and most vulnerable members of society' (2017: 5). In other words, the State's embrace of neoliberal policy authorized measures wholly indifferent to social destitution and inequality, centred instead on the well-being of the finance sector and the health of the market.

As Richard Seymour comments, 'the banks didn't merely shape the narrative; they partially manufactured the reality that the narrative described' (2014: 19). This was done through a governmental approbation of the banking sector's accumulation of debt, authorized on the part of 'the Technical Debt Management Committee and the Board of Directors of the Citizen Budget Commission' – as well as by a strategic disinvestment in the city's own arrears and an encouragement of 'small investor clients to purchase large of amounts of this precarious debt' (Seymour 2014: 19). More generally, the government was complicit in constructing a narrative suggesting that the financial sector was inherently stable and independent of State decisions, even as it increasingly drew on the prospect of State intervention to achieve its objectives. The result was that a range of public sector services and utilities have been increasingly privatized, including sizable sectors of the NHS, education and policing, while unions and community organizations repeatedly took the blame for market instability, seen as unruly aggressors intent to disrupt the status quo. As Seymour reflects, 'the bankers' effective coup d'état took power away from elected officials deemed too sensitive to popular constituencies', even as 'the job losses began' and the poor increasingly took the brunt of the so-called '"rescue" plan' (20).

The monstrous cruelty of this governmental agenda emerges in a range of politically invested literature in the 2010s, awash with dystopic and Gothic scenarios, but also darkly comic satires, gritty realism, and politically minded experiment, or a mix of the above, as visible in different ways in the writing of Jonathan Coe, Anthony Cartwright, Zadie Smith, James Kelman, and Ali Smith. As Philip Tew reflects in his chapter in this collection, 'The "Teenie" Novels of Jonathan Coe: Intertextuality, Satire, Parody, Farce and Irony', Coe's most recent, politically charged novels 'chart the lives of the lower middle classes set against in each case a political and an economic crisis, Blair's dodgy Iraq dossier and its fallout in *Number 11*' and the 'social divisions caused by the Brexit campaign' in *Middle England*. In both novels, as well as in *The Terrible Privacy of Maxwell Sim* (2010) and *Expo 58* (2013), Coe develops previously rehearsed comic strategies, combining pastiche, satire and parody, to comment on contemporary British State corruption and callousness, while also negotiating routine decisions and dilemmas tied to working-class experience. As Tew explains, 'there exists an overarching perspective on larger issues to be gleaned from mundane people and scenarios, foregrounding the opinions and perspectives of those whose existences are defined by humdrum, often uneventful lives'. In this way, despite Coe's interest in bizarre and darkly comedic scenarios, his writing repeatedly comes back to private working-class uncertainties, and to concerns with day-to-day unease, boredom, and precarity.

Matti Ron's chapter on 2010s working-class fiction, '"Defining it is a Struggle": Working-Class Fiction in the 2010s', also explores this daily reality, while at the same time recognizing notable formal and stylistic 'heterogeneity' across this writing. Examining such texts as Anthony Cartwright's *How I Killed Margaret Thatcher* (2012), James Kelman's *Mo Said She Was Quirky* (2012), and Zadie Smith's *NW* (2012), he indicates a move away from postwar realist modalities, stressing how the 'all-too-frequent equation of working-class writing with realist aesthetics, though always an overgeneralization, is now surely untenable'. Indeed, for Ron, this generation of writers diverges not only in terms of style, but also ideology and focus, shifting beyond twentieth century understandings of class based on employment or wealth to those founded on upbringing, identity and culture. As he explains, 'this emphasis on class as identity rooted in a sense of geographic space or community [...], must also be understood in relation to the lack of emphasis [...] on contemporary waged work', such that 'it makes sense that in a period of diminished struggle what we are left with to understand class are largely its signifiers of culture and identity'. In this way, Ron stresses a reimagining of class in notably non-antagonistic terms, while also recognizing the State's continued negligence in addressing working-class needs and preoccupations.

These readings again frequently reinforce twentieth-century anxieties still alive within the present day, while at the same time reframing these for a twenty-first-century readership perhaps in some ways distracted from class politics or only newly awakened to its importance following the 2008 financial crash. Thus, for Pierre Bourdieu, writing across the late twentieth century, precarity more largely encapsulates the global capitalist dismantling of the post-war welfare state, especially as this impacts on (in)secure employment and casualization, and there is a sense in which this apprehension returns in 2010s fiction in renewed form. In 1998, Bourdieu comments on how:

> It has emerged clearly that job insecurity is now everywhere: in the private sector, but also the public sector, which has greatly increased the number of temporary, part-time or casual positions [...]. In all these areas it produces more or less identical effects, which become particularly visible in the extreme case of the unemployed: the destructuring of existence [...] and the ensuing deterioration of the whole relationship to the world, time and space.
>
> Bourdieu 1998: 82

This unabashedly catastrophic socioeconomic assessment highlights the radical destabilization produced by a global capitalist system, not only in terms of general morale, but also, the ability of workers 'to project themselves into the future' and in this way, to mobilize collective action in pursuit of change (83). Precarity impacts, in other words, both personal subjectivity and socio-political investment, as it reorients temporality to undercut organized insurgency. As the homeless narrator of McGregor's *Even the Dogs* (2010) affirms, sitting outside a local wet clinic and lamenting his destitution, 'We've got the time. All the time in the world' (113).

In this collection, this critical preoccupation with a defunct contemporary temporality is reiterated by Tew and Ron in the above chapters, as well as by Anna McFarlane in her account of a regionally specific speculative fiction in 'Speculative Fictions of the 2010s'. Ron's reading sees this as encompassing a repeated emphasis on 'passivity' and 'a sense of impotence' in contemporary life, wherein working-class fiction betrays a 'difficulty in imagining historical progress'. Similarly, for McFarlane, the texts assessed – including work by Adam Roberts, Dave Hutchinson, M. John Harrison, and Nina Allan, amongst others – reinforce a damning picture of neoliberal austerity, while also toying with moments of utopian hope produced by locally based solidarities or grass-roots organizations, especially on social media. As McFarlane explains, 'a greater focus on rural settings, or at least settings beyond the metropoles, became more commonplace as writers tackled the perceived polarization between the concerns of the urban "cultural elites" and working-class concerns largely associated with people living in ex-mining communities and rural economies'. Echoing John Lanchester's aptly named *Capital* (2012) as it voices the 'relentless, remorseless pounding solitude' (268) of corporate finance and the disabling temporality that this produces, these fictions overtly comment on how precarity and unemployment, especially following the financial crisis, only further augment this reality, creating social desperation with often brutal consequences.

Drawing on the theoretical writing of Mark Fisher, McFarlane notes how the particular combination of hope and despair in these fictions echoes a dawning perception of growing conservatism within left-wing culture, as it enters into an American-led 'culture war' intent to undercut class-based solidarities. Here, McFarlane explains, Fisher identifies the fracturing of the British socialist movement into multiple identities put to work policing each other as serving the interests of capitalism, because 'call-out culture acts as a deflection from solidarity and class struggle'. Under this Marxist critical outlook, Fisher is seen to lament Britain's failure to become the society it might have been, registering the precarity of the State and calling on speculative writing to articulate 'a hauntology of alternative affects and ways of being' never fully achieved.

This is, of course, only one element of Fisher's prolific production, which as McFarlane notes, stretches across the 2010s, ending with a 2020 collection of posthumous essays following Fisher's suicide in 2017. Nevertheless, in its focus on the limits of 'capitalist realism' and the corresponding necessity of speculative reimagining, it speaks to a conjoint temporal and generic preoccupation alive across 2010s writing. Another prominent theoretical voice articulating this anxiety is the American art critic Jonathan Crary, whose understanding of precarity clearly informs a variety of 2010s writing, both speculative, realist and more experimental, highlighting a distinctly 'disenchanted' contemporary temporality, in this case connected to the '24/7' infrastructure of the global market (2014, 19). As Crary explains, 'A 24/7 environment has the semblance of a social world, but it is actually a non-social model of machinic performance and a suspension of living that does not disclose the human cost required to sustain its effectiveness' (9). More specifically, the experience of precarity described by Crary is one of sleeplessness and dysphoria, as extended work shifts and the requirement to balance multiple employments culminate in an ongoing 'sleep mode', involving 'insensibility' and 'insomnia' (13). This ultimately impacts not only on humans, but also the planet, as the earth is 'reimagined as a non-stop work site or an always open shopping mall of infinite choices, tasks, selections, and digressions', and as the resultant wastefulness and the 'depletion of resources' then circles back to affect all living creatures and their natural habitats (15, 17).

Here again, both of these concerns – regarding capitalist insomnia and the adjacent destruction of the environment – are readily visible in 2010s fiction. Writings such as Lanchester's *Capital*, Tom McCarthy's *Satin Island* (2015), and Sunjeev Sahota's *The Year of the Runaways* (2015), all in very different ways and for different demographics, highlight a contemporary experience of non-stop work and fatigue, at once recalling and reframing John Barth's notion of 'literature of exhaustion' in notably more material terms. Likewise, across 2010s literature, a repeated anxiety to link global capitalist modes of life to environmental destruction – and to an ongoing, unstoppable 'slow violence' happening beyond the media's cameras (Nixon 2011) – registers in a desire to re-read precarity in distinctly planetary terms and to challenge dominant Anthropocene – or perhaps better, 'Capitalocene' – ideologies and values (Moore 2016). As Adam Trexler reflects in 2015, one of the 'most striking feature of novels written in the last several years is that they have sought to explore the complex economic and social adaptations necessary in a period of anthropogenic global warming', often through defamiliarizing tactics that unsettle 'familiar systems' and reconfigure 'human ecology' in more critical terms (202, 173). On a similar note, Amitav Ghosh, in 2016, highlights the particular value of genre fiction in approaching this task, where, by contrast to the 'moderate and orderly' view of 'Nature' put forward by mainstream realism, – always eager to conceal the planet's 'uncanny' dimensions – genre writing allows for the improbable, the unpredictable and the catastrophic (22). He continues,

> To introduce such happenings into a novel is in fact to court eviction from the mansion in which serious fiction has long been in residence; it is to risk banishment to the humbler dwellings that surround the manor house – those generic out-houses that were once known by names such as 'the Gothic,' 'the romance,' or 'the melodrama,' and have now come to be called 'fantasy,' 'horror,' and 'science fiction.'
>
> Ghosh 2016, 24

Turning this eviction around to proudly claim popular writing's contemporary importance, Ghosh's writing sets the stage for fictions of the 2010s, implicitly explaining why recent writers look to genre to negotiate ecology.

One way in which this concern comes through in 2010s British literature specifically, notably even before the events of the Covid-19 pandemic, is in literary engagements with capitalist encroachments producing widespread disease and/or contagion, or conversely with readings of capitalism itself as a parasitic illness. As Robert Castel reflects in 2003, 'like a virus that permeates everyday life, dissolving social ties and undermining the physical structures of the individuals, [capitalist insecurity] has a demoralizing effect as a principal of social dissolution' (27). Such an analysis, with its central metaphor of viral contagion, informs the register of numerous 2010s texts, which often move fluidly between a critique of corporate politics and pandemic governance. M.R. Carey's *The Girl with All the Gifts* (2014), Alex Scarrow's *Plague Land* (2016), R.R. Haywood's *The Undead* series (2012–2021) offer perhaps some of the more overt (pre-pandemic) generic instances of this literature, incorporating Gothic zombie and plague narratives to navigate illness and to tie this to capitalist institutions and Capitalocene practices. Similarly, more recent and less overtly Gothic works, such as Ali Smith's *Summer* (2020), Kazuo Ishiguro's *Klara and the Sun* (2021), and Sarah Moss's *The Fell* (2021) can also be read to connect neoliberal thinking to monstrous viral epidemics and diseased societies, in this way reinforcing the deathly implications of global capitalist government. As *The Fell*'s character Kate reflects, 'One of the things we're learning, we of the end times, is that humanity's ending appears to be slow, lacking in cliffhangers or indeed any satisfactory narrative shape; characterized, for the lucky, by the gradual vindication of accumulating dread' (115). In this way, Gothic horror, in the shape of unnarratable apocalypse, articulates the violence of global capitalist institutions, which gradually eek away at humanity and the planet's capacity for survival.

As McFarlane again explains in her chapter, this eco-critical concern is also visible in 2010s speculative fiction, not only in its above-mentioned engagement with rural landscapes – themselves often defined by 'the weird' or 'the eerie' – but also in its repeated concern to relate patriarchal violence both to the planet and to women's bodies. As she explains, 'Ken MacLeod's *Intrusion* (2012) shows the use of biopolitics via healthcare as a means of controlling the public [...], while Paul McAuley's *Austral* (2016) uses miscarriage as a metaphor for an uncertain future in the face of climate change'. Indeed, numerous texts McFarlane explores – including, Joanna Kevenna's *The Birth of Love* (2010), Ann Smith's *Baby X* (2016), Helen Sedwick's *The Growing Season* (2017), and Anne Charnock's *Dreams Before the Start of Time* (2017) – all likewise engage this eco-critical feminism in poignant ways, repeatedly connecting a patriarchal medical establishment to Anthropocene violence, and likewise looking to environmentally based solutions to women's oppression.

This said, what is perhaps different for some of these authors, including many from speculative or Gothic traditions, is that rather than simply despairing of global capitalist institutions or affirming an anarchic detachment from sociopolitical realities, precarity can also (perhaps ironically) be seen to offer a foundation for protest, as for example in the acts of rebellion explored by Carey's *The Girl with All the Gifts*, Griffiths's *Broken Ghost*, Tim Maughan's *Infinite Detail*, and Smith's *Autumn*. As Guy Standing sees it, these events (and he focuses specifically on the EuroMayDay protests stretching from 2001 into the 2010s) describe a widespread, visible resistance to capitalism set in place on account of precarity's violence, which has become increasingly obvious and socially unacceptable, at least among the so-called working-class 'precariat'. As he puts it (in 2011), 'a politics of paradise will be built on respect for principles of economic security and all forms of work and leisure, rather than the dour labourism of industrial society. The precariat understands that, and politicians on the left should listen' (n.p.). On a somewhat different note, Smith's 'mother' character in *Autumn* responds to the brutality of contemporary right-wing policy by indicating that she is ready 'to go and get herself arrested', proceeding then to throw objects at a government fence to invoke 'less cruel and more philanthropic times' (2020, 255). Likewise, Carey's zombie ('hungry') protagonist refuses to save humanity from apocalypse, opting instead to assist a spreading fungal plague on behalf of the planet. In these texts, these scenarios identify modes of anti-neoliberal activism at once alarming and topically relevant, incorporating both realist and fantasy narratives (respectively) to underline insurgency's urgency. As Castel stated in his last interview, 'fortunately, we cannot state with any certainty that "everything is going to the dogs". The worst of the future remains uncertain' (Chaillan 2013, n.p.).

These above theorists (including Bourdieu, Castel and Standing) are not without problems in their approach to precarity, tending to promote improved 'security' as a response to socioeconomic anxieties in ways that can exclude and even threaten certain minority populations, focusing on employment conditions and 'on the relationship between capital and labour as the primary site for the emergence of new political subjectivities' (Hogg 2021, 6). Correspondingly, the 'solutions' they offer to precarity, while in some ways radical in their Marxism, nevertheless sometimes overlook issues of difference and intersectionality, ignoring 'more multidimensional views of politics, struggle and identity that have developed from gender and race studies over the past thirty years' (6). As Hogg continues, global capitalist regimes of precarity seek to ensure not only neoliberal 'flexibilization', but also more traditional, Western-centred 'valorizations of security, noting the way that ideals of protection could be invoked to support nationalist, anti-migrant politics and reinforce normative conceptions of wage labour' (4). In this way, prominent demonstrations of protest and re-theorization in the 2010s can also said to seek a wider view on contemporary precarity, seeing this not (or not only) in terms of white, male, working-class disadvantage, but rather a whole spectrum of systematic inequalities and exploitations in need of new (non-security-oriented) solutions.

The works of Mohsin Hamid, Kamila Shamsie and Guy Gunaratne, explored in Emily Horton's chapter in this collection, 'Border Crossings: Diasporic British Fiction of the 2010s', reaffirm this anxiety expressly and in critical terms, tying it to post-9/11 society, Brexit, and migration. In these texts, rather than prioritizing inequality at an economic level, precarity is stretched to encompass a range of socio-political concerns, including experiences of systematic racism and vulnerability specific to diasporic South Asian and Islamic communities, as well as modes of urban exclusion and stigmatizing often misread within the popular media. Amongst other preoccupations, this includes a post-9/11 anti-immigrant politics gradually more reactionary within the 2010s, as well as increased religious extremism and radicalization in inner-city environments. In both cases, the emphasis throughout these texts – including Hamid's *Exit West* (2017), Shamsie's *Home Fire* (2017), and Gunaratne's *In Our Mad and Furious City* (2018) – on disparities between distinct UK ethnic demographics and related government policies, underlines how suffering itself is unequally distributed within the 2010s, disadvantaging especially those who, as Judith Butler puts it, 'fall outside the human' due to their skin colour, ethnicity, and/or religion (1990, 111).

These concerns are echoed across a range of 2010s literature, which repeatedly draws attention to corporeal materiality and to emotions and affects reflective of systematic exclusion and institutional marginality. In texts such as Sahota's *The Year of the Runaways* (2015), Tahmima Anam's *The Bones of Grace* (2016), Bernadine Evaristo's *Girl, Women, Other* (2019), and Courttia Newland's *A River Called Time* (2021), following Butler's own critical distinction between precariousness and precarity, emphasis is placed not simply on universal experiences of grief and suffering, but rather specific historical relations defined by amplified vulnerability: for example, the refugee crisis, the Afghan War, the #MeToo movement, BlackLivesMatter, and the 2018 Windrush Scandal – situations wherein precariousness is made 'more acute under certain social policies' (Lloyd 2015, 173). In this distinction, precarity comes to identify an uneven distribution of 'modes of "unliveability"' (174), or increased 'risk, jeopardy and threat for specific populations' (175) – in these novels specific to diasporic Asian and Black British populations.

In fact, this understanding is influential in shaping the 2010s both in terms of its literature and theory, which in each case explores precarity's cultural valences and the affective and temporal dimensions of social precarity's experience. These concerns resonate in different ways in the chapters of Tory Young and Alice Bennett in this collection, which again read 2010s writing through its engagement with emotional disorder, distraction and violence. In Young's 'What's to-day? Politics and Typography in Ali Smith's Decade', this emerges in the 'affective economy' of Ali Smith's *Seasonal Quartet* (2016–2020), alongside her other 2010s writing, which incorporates puns, hyphens, and other typological play to challenge strategic political jargon intended to demonize certain minority communities. As she puts it, 'For Smith, everything is meant, and metonymic slide is far from being a non-intentional abuse of argument. It is a kind of play that exposes adherences and associations as a form of enquiry into the affective political resonances of written and spoken words.'

More specifically, working with Sara Ahmed's (2014) idea of an affective 'stickiness', Young identifies the playfulness of Smith's politicized experiment, connecting this both to activist commentary and aesthetic experiment within her writing. Emphasizing an attentive and topical 'today-ness' in Smith's writing, Young considers how this author's investment in particularly 'sticky' affects marks her own critique of prevalent contemporary right-wing discourse, with a focus on how Conservative politicians distribute these 'sticky' feelings, making them adhere to certain marginalized communities (for example, migrants). This appraisal then buttresses a reading of Smith's work as juxtaposing 'the Political' and 'the political': recent current events and socio-political ideologies. Put differently, for Young, Smith underlines experiment's importance in confronting problematic State rhetoric, this then offering a means to upending State deception at its ideological core.

This reading, then, expressly underlines recent 2010s events and governmental discourses appearing in Smith's work, even as it spotlights the author's fascination with language and creative experiment. As Young writes, 'At a fundamental level, the continual focus on puns and idioms invites the reader to consider not just meaning but how meanings change, using novelty to draw attention to the fact that words are a record of a historical moment, one that will change like language itself does.' On a similar note, Alice Bennett's chapter, 'Fiction in the Age of Distraction: Reading and Attention in the 2010s' focuses on popular media misreadings of attention and distraction, considering how the writing of Will Self, Adam Thirlwell and Olivia Sudjic both identifies and rewrites these popular narratives. As Bennett writes, 'This work would question some of the foundational understanding of attention itself that underpinned these popular accounts of the decade as an age of distraction', in some cases in ways that move beyond these writers' own non-fictional writing. In both chapters, then, affect is seen as socially and politically significant, as it emerges as a basis for critical commentary, often in ways that disrupt mainstream discourse and hegemonic institutions.

Finally, as both Nick Bentley's 'The Neo-mythological Novel: Re-writing the Epic in Contemporary British Fiction' and Mark Williams's 'Inexhaustible Literature? Contemporary Experimental Approaches in Literature' demonstrate, from different ends of the scale so to speak, even when all else fails, both narrative and literature remain. In the midst of political crisis and cultural anxiety, as Bentley argues, the neo-mythological novel – such as Pat Barker's *The Silence of the Girls* (2018) or Natalie Haynes's *A Thousand Ships* (2019) – does not simply offer the reassurance of the familiar but also the promise of a new genre, fuelled through an alliance of writers, readers, publishers, booksellers, literary prize culture, and literary festivals. On the one hand, such work appeals to the cultural capital of classical studies, while on the other it delivers the plot-driven sensationalism of fantasy, adventure, violence, heroes, gods and monsters. At the same time, however, it allows the working through of the cultural and political preoccupations of the twenty-first century, including gender, sexuality, the politics of age and youth, marginalized identities, class, race, human rights, war and migration.

In other words, grand narratives are back with a vengeance. Conversely, as Williams explains by ingenious reference to the '[B.S.] Johnson–[Terry] Pratchett problem', such narratives are not necessarily incompatible with experiment because although 'experiment can break a story [...] sometimes that breakage is precisely what makes a better story'. In other words, worrying about the apparent divide between narrative and experimental fiction blinds us to a material understanding of what fiction itself does: sometimes it works, 'sometimes breaking the story makes the text do something more powerful, and sometimes it needs to be broken again, a different way, next time'. Maybe this has always been the case, but what has changed according to Williams is that it is no longer practical to separate avant-garde work (or, indeed, most fiction) from the life of the author (or the contexts they live in), nor is it critically appropriate. By a similar token, it is not clear for how much longer it will be practical to separate critical work from the life of the critic. The theory-centred regime of criticism that began to emerge in the late 1960s and 1970s, and became dominant during the course of the 1990s, is now indubitably on the wane as demonstrated by the growing number of books reassessing the role of critics and criticism (see, for example, Felski 2015; North 2017; Guillory 2022). However, given that most of these books are written from the perspective of elite US institutions, such analysis is not always especially applicable to the working conditions experienced by the majority of UK literature academics today, an increasing number of whom no longer even work from within universities. For this reason, and others such as the fact that impersonal 'academic' criticism is liable to find itself overtaken by machine intelligence within the very near future, we are going to see a rapid growth in autobiographical criticism over the coming years, such as that demonstrated in this volume by Williams. The advent of this transformed criticism, and the likelihood that it will increasingly originate from outside the institution, is another reason why this volume marks the endpoint of the current series. The literary history of the 2020s will be written to a different beat.

Notes

1 Figures for this paragraph are taken from an article 'The Scale of Economic Inequality in the UK', which takes its figures from the Office for National Statistics and the World Inequality Database, on the website of the Equality Trust: https://equalitytrust.org.uk/scale-economic-inequality-uk (accessed 7 May 2023).
2 Although the Decades Series has discussed some Irish fiction in previous volumes, it has tended, rightly or wrongly, to focus on writing within Great Britain itself. One of the factors in halting the series at this point is that with a universal British outlook no longer hegemonic, it no longer makes sense to talk of British fiction. A more pluralistic 'Isles' based approach would provide a better framework for discussing Irish fiction alongside English, Welsh and Scottish writing.
3 Speaking on a panel, 'Thirty-four Years, and An Interim Survey', at the British National Science Fiction Convention, Birmingham, 8 April 2023.
4 The 'Great British Class Calculator' is still available online: https://www.bbc.co.uk/news/special/2013/newsspec_5093/index.stm (accessed 7 May 2023).

Works cited

Ahmed, Sara. *The Cultural Politics of Emotion*. Edinburgh: Edinburgh University Press, 2014.
Bentley, Nick, Nick Hubble and Leigh Wilson. 'Introduction: Fiction of the 2000s: Political Contexts, Seeing the Contemporary, and the End(s) of Postmodernism'. In *The 2000s: A Decade of Contemporary British Fiction*. Nick Bentley, Nick Hubble and Leigh Wilson (eds). London: Bloomsbury, 2015: 1–26.

Blake, Linnie and Monnet, Agnieszka Soltysik. 'Introduction: Neoliberal Gothic'. In *Neoliberal Gothic: International Gothic in the Neoliberal Age*. Linnie Blake and Agnieszka Soltysik Monnet (eds). Manchester: Manchester University Press, 2017: 1–18.

Blyth, Mark. *Austerity: The History of a Dangerous Idea*. Oxford: Oxford University Press, 2013.

Bourdieu, Pierre. *Acts of Resistance: Against the New Myths of Our Time*. Richard Nice (trans.). Oxford: Polity, 1998.

Butler, Judith. *Gender Trouble: Feminism and the Subversion of Identity*. New York: Routledge, 1990.

Castel, Robert. *L'insécurité sociale, Qu'est-ce qu'etre protégé?* Paris: Seiul, 2003.

Chaillan, Pierre. 'Robert Castel, 1933–2013: Last Interview with the thinker who studied the "social question" most deeply', *transform!europe*, 18 March 2013: https://www.transform-network.net/en/blog/article/robert-castel-1933-2013/ (accessed 5 May 2023)

Connell, Liam. 'Anxious Reading: The Precarity Novel and the Affective Class'. In *Precarity in Contemporary Literature and Culture*. Emily J. Hogg and Peter Simonsen (eds). London: Bloomsbury, 2021: 27–41.

Crary, Jonathan. *24/7*. London: Verso, 2014.

Felski, Rita. *The Limits of Critique*. Chicago, IL: University of Chicago Press, 2015.

Germanà, Monica. 'The Awakening of Caledonias? Scottish Literature in the 1980s'. In *The 1980s: A Decade of Contemporary British Fiction*. Emily Horton, Philip Tew and Leigh Wilson (eds). London: Bloomsbury, 2014: 51–74.

Ghosh, Amitav. *The Great Derangement: Climate Change and the Unthinkable*. Chicago, IL: University of Chicago Press, 2016.

Goodwin, Matthew. *Values, Voice and Virtue: The New British Politics*. London: Penguin, 2023.

Griffiths, Niall. *Broken Ghost*. London: Vintage, 2019.

Guillory, John. *Professing Criticism: Essays on the Organization of Literary Study*. Chicago, IL: University of Chicago Press, 2022.

Henderson, Ailsa and Richard Wyn Jones. *Englishness: The Political Force Transforming Britain*. Oxford: Oxford University Press, 2021.

Hogg, Emily J. 'Introduction'. In *Precarity in Contemporary Literature and Culture*. Emily J. Hogg and Peter Simonsen (eds). London: Bloomsbury, 2021: 1–24.

Hroch, Miroslav. *Social Preconditions of National Revival in Europe: A Comparative Analysis of the Social Composition of Patriotic Groups among the Smaller European Nations*. Ben Fowkes (trans.). Cambridge: Cambridge University Press, 1985.

Hubble, Nick. 'The Ordinariness of the Extraordinary Break-Up of Britain'. In *The 1970s: A Decade of Contemporary British Fiction*. Nick Hubble, John McLeod and Philip Tew (eds). London: Bloomsbury, 2014: 43–67.

Hubble, Nick. '"You're Not in the Market at Shielding, Joe": Beyond the Myth of the "Thirties"'. In *The 1930s: A Decade of Modern British Fiction*. Nick Hubble, Luke Seaber and Elinor Taylor (eds). London: Bloomsbury, 2021: 17–57.

Lanchester, John. *Capital*. London: Faber and Faber, 2012.
Lloyd, Moya 'The Ethics and Politics of Vulnerable Bodies'. In *Butler and Ethics*. Moya Lloyd (ed.). Edinburgh: Edinburgh University Press, 2015: 167–192.
McGregor, Jon. *Even the Dogs*. London: Bloomsbury, 2010.
Moore, Jason. *Anthropocene or Capitalocene?: Nature, History, and the Crisis of Capitalism*. Oakland, CA: PM Press, 2016.
Moss, Sarah. *The Fell*. London: Picador, 2021.
Nixon, Rob. *Slow Violence and the Environmentalism of the Poor*. Cambridge, MA: Harvard University Press, 2011.
North, Joseph. *Literary History: A Concise Political History*. Cambridge, MA: Harvard University Press, 2017.
Orwell, George. *The Road to Wigan Pier*. Harmondsworth: Penguin, 1986.
Payne, Sebastian. *Broken Heartlands: A Journey through Labour's Lost England*. London: Pan Books, 2022.
Perraudin, Frances and Rowena Mason. 'Tory election campaign poster depicts Ed Miliband in pocket of SNP'. *The Guardian*, 9 March 2015: https://www.theguardian.com/politics/2015/mar/09/tory-election-poster-ed-miliband-pocket-snp-alex-salmond (accessed 7 May 2023).
Savage, Mike et al. *Social Class in the 21st Century*. London: Penguin, 2015.
Seymour, Richard. *Against Austerity: How We Can Fix the Crisis They Made*. London: Pluto Press, 2014.
Skelton, David. *The New Snobbery: Taking on Modern Elitism and Empowering the Working Class*. London: Biteback Publishing, 2021.
Smith, Ali. *Autumn*. London: Penguin, 2020.
Standing, Guy. 'Who will be the voice for the emerging precariat?' *The Guardian*, 1 June 2011: https://www.theguardian.com/commentisfree/2011/jun/01/voice-for-emerging-precariat (accessed 5 May 2023)
Trexler, Adam. *Anthropocene Fictions: The Novel in the Time of Climate Change*. Charlottesville: University of Virginia Press, 2015.

1

Fictions of the Break-Up

Nick Hubble

Introduction: Beyond the cosy catastrophe

In the early days of the 2020 Covid pandemic, during a period in which we now know that the UK Government and Local Authorities had resigned themselves to hundreds of thousands of fatalities, there was a kind of uncanny familiarity to what was happening. For example, half the car park at my local hospital in Aberystwyth was barriered off to install a triage-station portacabin that looked like a set from the film *28 Days Later*. I found myself recalling a passage from J.G. Ballard's *The Wind from Nowhere* (1962):

> They had the Dunkirk mentality, had already been defeated and were getting ready to make a triumph out of it, counting up the endless casualty lists, the catalogues of disaster and destruction, as if these were a measure of their courage and competence.
>
> Ballard [1962] 1974: 57

The uncanniness of the situation was due to the recognition that we, on this increasingly fractured island, found ourselves living within a version of one of the most dominant and persistent postwar British genres, the 'cosy catastrophe'. According to Brian Aldiss, in the classic form of this genre – John Wyndham's 1951 novel *The Day of the Triffids* for example – 'the hero should have a pretty good time (a girl, free suites at the Savoy, automobiles for the taking) while everyone else is dying off' (Aldiss and Wingrove 2001: 280). But other versions, such as those written by Ballard have been darker in tone. Over the years, the form has attenuated to something more similar to the zombie apocalypse, but the basic idea still has a key place within the British, or perhaps we should say English, imaginary.

The reason for this became blindingly obvious during the pandemic when everyone with a house and a garden and a professional job that could be done from home had an opportunity to feel like the hero while others, disproportionately those poorer or from BAME backgrounds, were dying off. In this respect, the pandemic was just a more intense version of what has passed for normal life in Britain since at least the 1970s. However, for once, nobody could ignore that daily mortality rate which headlined every news broadcast. It became apparent that 'cosy catastrophes' are not so much a popular cultural form as social realism in our class-based unequal country, where the heroes do get to have a pretty good time while everyone else is slowly dying off.

Of course, one might argue that, to a greater or lesser extent, all countries are affected by social inequality. However, what distinguishes England from many other European countries, including Scotland and Wales, is that it is ruled by an ideology that values 'inequality' above the 'social'. As Margaret Thatcher famously said in 1987: 'There's no such thing as society. There are individual men and women and there are families' (Keay 1987: 10).[1] Therefore, in England it was initially possible for Boris Johnson to say repeatedly of Covid that he would prefer to let it 'rip' while the 'bodies pile high' rather than have any more lockdowns (Morrison 2021: n.p.) – a policy which has been followed in England since 19 July 2021 (Allegretti and Geddes 2021: n.p.) – while retaining popularity because a big enough percentage of the population were primarily motivated by defending their position as cosy heroes in the slow catastrophe that has been unfolding since the 1970s.

As Raymond Williams noted in *Towards 2000* (1983), the replacement of the term Britain with the United Kingdom, a term which had not been widely used before the 1970s, marked an ideological transformation to '"the Yookay", no longer a society but a market sector' (191). I summarized his argument in my chapter in *The 1970s: A Decade of Contemporary British Fiction*:

> What had been Britain was no longer 'a whole lived order but a willed and selective superstructure' merely sufficient to maintain the necessary level of social and economic order for the international market to function.
>
> Hubble 2014: 44

This transformation had been very sudden. During the years 1977–8, the Gini coefficient measuring income inequality reached its lowest ever level for British households, the number of Britons living below the poverty line also reached its lowest ever level, and social mobility peaked (see Beckett 2009: 409–410). It's a measure of how fast that has unravelled, that Williams was already bemoaning the destruction of the social-democratic values of postwar Britain only a few years afterwards. However, concentrating on the destructive effect of Thatcherite neoliberalism obscures a less intuitive insight, which is that this mid-late 1970s period of social equality and social mobility was itself destructive to the postwar British social order. The result of everyone no longer knowing their place led to chaos and existential angst as reflected in what is arguably the most significant condition-of-England novel written in the 1970s, Margaret Drabble's *The Ice Age* (1977). The title of the novel refers to the three-year recession and economic freeze that began late in 1973 as a result of the oil crisis and brought an abrupt end both to the long period of rising incomes that had lasted for nearly twenty years and to any social certainty:

> Not everyone in Britain that night in November was alone, incapacitated, or in jail. Nevertheless, over the country depression lay like fog, which was just about all that was missing to lower spirits even further, and there was even a little of that in East Anglia. All over the nation, families who had listened to the news looked at one another and said, 'Goodness me,' or 'Whatever next,' or 'I give up,' or 'Well, fuck that,' before embarking on an evening's viewing of colour television, or a large hot meal, or a trip to the pub, or a choral society evening. All over the country, people blamed other people for all the things that were going wrong— the trades unions, the present government, the miners, the car workers, the seamen, the Arabs, the Irish, their own husbands, their own wives, their own idle good-for-nothing offspring, comprehensive education.
>
> Drabble 1977: 59

Read today, it is difficult to see beyond the novel's registration of horror at the very idea of working-class mobility and the decentring of its own narrative voice from a position of unquestioned privilege. However, it has historical value for the way it captures the sudden implosion of what had appeared to be a stable postwar British society. A related version of the same reaction to equality and mobility can be see in Eric Hobsbawm's 1978 article 'The Forward March of Labour Halted', which blames consumerism and the women's movement for the collapse of a male-centric, cloth cap and football 'common style of proletarian life' that it posits to have been steadily progressing towards socialism since the 1880s.

But although that working-class structure of feeling might no longer be dominant it still remains a residual component of English social and political life as can be seen from the instance of 'Len', one of the subjects of James Hinton's *Seven Lives from Mass Observation* (2016). Despite widespread belief that Mass Observation skews unrepresentatively left and liberal, three of Hinton's subjects from the contemporary post-1981 project, including Len, turned out to be UK Independence Party (UKIP) voters. Those like Len were people who hated both the social liberalization of the 1960s and the economic disruption of the Thatcher years (despite often benefitting financially from them in the long run) and therefore 'felt themselves and what they stood for marginalized, excluded, and politically unrepresented' (Hinton 2016: 93). Hinton suggests that Len can be 'seen as a man who had internalized a narrow and life-denying subaltern consciousness' (108). However, rather than seeing him as a passive adherent of supposedly common proletarian values, it makes more sense to view Len as actively drawing on an idealized version of working-class masculinity from his 1930s childhood in order to construct social values opposed to what he saw as a progressive establishment. For Len, these values took the form of active misogynist statements concerning the undermining of masculinity by female teachers and 'wayward wives', which he supported with an unwavering belief in binary gender essentialism: 'Nature has equipped women to fulfil some functions in life and men others' (102). Therefore, Len's ideas for achieving a restoration of the social cohesion of postwar British society are predicated on the adoption of fixed gender roles, which would in fact be far more essentialist than those that existed in either the early postwar decades or, indeed, the interwar period preceding that.

While Len's specific views on the role of women in social and public life would still probably be considered extreme by the majority of the British public, his general stance of antipathy to both Thatcherite economic disruption and social liberalization is much more representative of the current dominant political outlook in the UK. It is exactly those voters 'who lean left on spending and public services but are culturally conservative' (Shipman 2021: n.p.), who were considered decisive in the December 2019 landslide election victory of Boris Johnson's Conservative Party. There has been much discussion of whether there has been a political shift in class alignment in Britain resulting in the Conservative party gaining working-class support from Labour, while losing middle-class voters – especially younger graduates and professionals – to them (see, for example, Kellner 2021: 7). This has now become a moot point because Johnson's political downfall in 2022 and the Conservative Party's disastrous return to the pure neoliberalism during Liz Truss's short-lived premiership has put paid to any such realignment that might have happened. However, at the time of writing, rather than advance alternative politics, the Labour Party have chosen to occupy the ideological position vacated by Johnson's departure by promising to 'make Brexit work'.[2]

While the specificities of such current political positionings are liable to shift in response to changing contexts, the wider discussion around them raises significant and enduring questions about the British state and British identity.

The default understanding of postwar Britain is that its values were set by the landslide election of the 1945 Labour Government and the establishment of the Welfare State, which has been significantly eroded since. However, the fact that substantial elements of that Welfare State still remain in place today, despite the privatization, deregulation and spending cuts introduced by all governments since 1979, suggests that there has always been a considerable degree of cultural consensus between the Conservative and Labour parties. Although the Thatcherite years are portrayed as the period when consensus broke down, in many ways it probably makes more sense to see this as one of a number of moments when the political consensus underwent a realignment rather than a collapse. From this perspective, electoral British politics is rarely a choice between genuinely opposed values. Tellingly, when something like such a choice was offered by the radical manifesto of Labour under Jeremy Corbyn in 2019, voters rejected it decisively. Instead, UK general elections are usually a contest between the main parties as to who can best lay claim to a very narrowly prescribed set of policies. Since 2010, the parties have competed on questions such as who would most credibly reduce net immigration, who can best enforce law and order and who can ensure Scotland stays in the UK; all arguably culturally conservative positions that are shared across the mainstream political landscape. Despite not on the whole being primary concerns in 1945, none of these objectives are out of keeping with the founding impulse of the postwar political settlement. There is nothing coincidental about this because, as David Edgerton convincingly demonstrates in *The Rise and Fall of the British Nation* (2018), the defining feature of the state that emerged to replace the ruins of empire under the national coalition governments of the 1930s and 1940s was British nationalism, and the resultant 'actual post-Second World War United Kingdom was in some ways better prefigured in the programme of the Tories and the British Union of Fascists (BUF) than that of the Liberals or the Labour party' (Edgerton 2019 [2018]: xxxiv).

When Williams, as discussed above, protested against the erosion of 'a whole lived order' in the interests of an international market economy, he was writing in defence of values that ran deeper than the 'Britain' which had been born within his own lifetime. A few years earlier he had told his interviewers from *New Left Review*, 'I want the Welsh people – still a radical and cultured people – to defeat, override or bypass bourgeois England' (1979: 296). In this manner he gave testament to what had already been described by Tom Nairn as 'The Break-Up of Britain': the collapse of the British state 'in the form of territorial disintegration rather than as the long awaited social revolution' (2021: 14).

I wrote about Nairn, Williams and 'The Ordinariness of the Extraordinary Break-Up of Britain' in *The 1970s*. In particular, I noted how subsequent devolution has created a situation where the identities represented in the fiction of William McIlvanney, Jennifer Johnston and Williams himself have become more representative of lives in the nations they wrote about – respectively Scotland, Northern Ireland and Wales – than the alternatives they contested. In what follows, I assess the ongoing progress of that 'territorial disintegration' in relation to, first, Scotland and then Wales. I am not on this occasion going to write specifically about Northern Ireland because I think the situation there transcends the limits of the British state – a fact that has been reinforced by the political and legal complexities involved in keeping the Irish border open following the UK's departure from the EU. Moreover, as noted in the Introduction to this book, it would probably make more sense today to read fiction from the island of Ireland in relation to the fiction of the island of England, Scotland and Wales within an 'Isles' framework – in this respect, the current volume is a coda to an earlier period.

However, Britain is not just disintegrating territorially, it is also breaking up psychologically: splintering across a number of binary fault lines as discussed in the second half of this chapter. Such fragmentation of the supposedly common culture that binds the British people together is typically demonized in a variety of ways. Len, discussed above, railed against the influence of the 'crackpot theories' of 'trendy progressives' (Hinton 2016: 95), while the Conservative Party and the right-wing British Press are currently obsessed with the threat posed by 'woke ideology' (see, for example, Shipman 2021; Forrest 2022; Strimpel 2022). But more generally the challenge posed to social norms since the 1960s by, for example, the various waves of feminism and the LGBTQ+ movement has been dismissed as 'identity politics'. Indeed, according to some accounts, any form of deviation from the norm or even excessive individualism is inherently unBritish.

A major part of the appeal of those cosy catastrophes written in the early postwar decades by science fiction authors such as Wyndham and John Christopher was that they gave expression to an individualism which was repressed within a British society structured tightly around deference and hierarchy. It is true that there was a class-war aspect to these novels, which were fictions of middle-class escape with working class characters represented stereotypically, in the case of Wyndham, or even contemptuously, in the case of Christopher. However, writers of the 1960s New Wave, such as Aldiss and Ballard, adapted the sub-genre to a satirical counter-cultural stance opposed to the officer class and the authorities in general. Ballard went on to push the form to its logical limits in *Millennium People* (2003), in which whole sections of the West London middle class opt out of British society *en masse*, and then beyond those limits in the prophetic *Kingdom Come* (2006), which anticipates an English revolution taking place across a sprawling landscape of suburban edgelands and out-of-town shopping malls:

> Consumer fascism provides its own ideology, no one needs to sit down and dictate *Mein Kampf*. Evil and psychopathology have been reconfigured into lifestyle statements. It is a fearful prospect, but consumer fascism may be the only way to hold a society together.
>
> Ballard 2006: 168

In this respect, Ballard pushed the cosy catastrophe beyond the pleasure principle, the Freudian concept of the ego's primary defence mechanism for keeping the level of excitement resulting from stimuli to as low and stable a level as possible. In a consumer society, the resultant sense of satisfaction from making a shopping purchase provides the perfect example of the pleasure principle in action, but in Freudian terms this is an infantile mechanism that is supposed to be superseded by adherence to the reality principle and the deeper satisfaction of deferring pleasure in order to pursue long-term objectives. However, as Freud explained in 'Beyond the Pleasure Principle' (1920), the developmental jump necessary to make the transition to reality principle is by means of compulsively repeating distressing actions as part of a cycle of minimally deferred satisfactions, such as when a child endlessly throws a toy out of the pram each time that it is given back. The problem is that this stage itself may be preferable by many to the subsequent developmental stages that are supposed to succeed it. Rather than the passive experience of immediate satisfaction, the compulsion to repeat offers an active sense of agency and perhaps mastery over the immediate environment. From a Freudian perspective this is a form of psychopathology but, as Ballard understood, it also has the essential ambiguity that it could be the means of escape from a repressive society, such as a class-bound hierarchy in which the available long-term goals are strictly limited for the majority of the population, or it could form the basis for an imposed social lifestyle that is designed to hold an otherwise fragmenting society together.

Ballard's charting of such ambiguous psychopathologies can be seen as his distinctive contribution to the post-New-Wave British anti-novel, which is still continuing with major works such as Christopher Priest's *The Evidence* (2020), and M. John Harrison's *The Sunken Land Begins to Rise Again* (2020). As well as discussing these novels, the second half of this chapter will consider how Justina

Robson's *The Switch* (2017) and Simon Ings's *The Smoke* (2018) reflect the social and psychological break-up of Britain and imagine the possibility, or otherwise, of escape from the collapsing ruins.

Territorial disintegration Part 1: 'This was the land'

Robert Crawford has noted that:

> the development of the subject 'English Literature' has constantly involved and reinforced an oppressive homage to centralism. As such, English Literature is a force which must be countered continually by a devolutionary momentum. Creative writers have been more alive to these needs than have most critics.
>
> Crawford 1992: 7

While this is true of many creative writers from everywhere except England, it seems particularly true of Scotland whose writers have predominantly been countering oppressive English centralism since at least the mid-twentieth-century Scottish Renaissance. As noted above, devolution and the foundation of a new Scottish Parliament in 1999, created a political jurisdiction to match the distinctive identities expressed by Scottish writers. In 2012, the SNP politician Stephen Maxwell noted that 'while the novels of Alasdair Gray, James Kelman, Irvine Welsh and Andrew Greig reference political themes, James Robertson is the only contemporary Scottish writer to have put the dramas of Scotland's public life at the centre of a novel' (qtd. in Hames 2020: 211). Robertson's huge panoramic *And the Land Lay Still* (2010) charts the trajectory of this history up to the present, beginning from 1950; a year which is described to us by means of an amazing documentary montage sequence that extends for several pages in the following manner:

> This was Scotland in 1950: land of 250 pits and 80,000 colliers, 100,000 farmworkers and four universities; land of Singer sewing machines in Clydebank, the Saxone Shoe Company in Kilmarnock, Cox Brothers jute mills in Dundee and the North British Locomotive Company in Springburn, every town and city and every part of every city with its own industries and hard-won skills; land of textiles and paper, hydraulic pumps and valves, carpets and linoleum and twenty-eight shipyards employing 60,000 workers on the Clyde. This was the land recovering from war, the land of nationalization and council-house building, its old grease-thick, reeking, clanging heavy industries reinjected with life and a grim, tired kind of hope, the grinding last surge of steel and shipbuilding before

Japan and Germany got up off their knees; this was the land that had change coming to it, like it or not, the closure of factories and the shedding of skills.

Robertson 2011 [2010]: 200

Critics of *And the Land Lay Still*, such as Scott Hames, have noted how 'frequently the novel reverts to journalism' (2020: 214) and tried to suggest that Robertson's fictional reconstruction of the historical trajectory of Scotland since the heyday of the postwar British state is flawed because

> Robertson cannot count on his readership – even his Scottish readership of the optimal vintage, born around 1950 – recognising the basic timeline and dramatis personae [...] so that the novel must produce as it goes the 'memory' it seems to be recounting. [...] Thus, we have a novel forced to laboriously produce the basic story-stuff it wants to recover and recollect.
>
> Hames 2020: 213

Leaving aside the fact that this criticism would invalidate huge swathes of historical fiction, it also rather prejudges the historical-knowledge levels of readers, who tend to be both educated about and interested in these areas by definition. Hames describes *And the Land Lay Still* as 'mainly realist' with some 'forays into the folkloric, the paranoid-conspiratorial, and the alcoholically surreal' (2020: 213), which makes it sound like a whimsical conspiracy theory. He develops this argument to complain about the novel often being far from 'lived experience or natural speech' (214), implying that it is not authentic in the same way that, for example, the work of Kelman is. While Robertson's work is different to Kelman's, this is not in itself a critical judgement unless Kelman is taken to be some sort of canonical benchmark for Scottish literature, which in this case would have started to take on some of the oppressive centralism Crawford identified in English literature. Who is to judge what is authentic to lived experience, which surely comes in infinite variation, unless the term is really functioning as a signifier for a universalizing ideological hegemony?

An alternative reading of *And the Land Lay Still* might consider the fantastical 'forays' as framing the apparently realist historical narrative, which rather than being 'produced' in order to 'recover' it, is being rewritten in order to move beyond it. Key in this respect are the punctuating short italicized semi-stream-of-consciousness second-person sections, reminiscent of similar passages in Lewis Grassic Gibbon's *A Scots Quair* (1932–4), one of which opens the novel:

> *The source of stories and legends was in those long mutual observations, those reachings for the unreachable, yearnings for the unobtainable. But that was what*

they were, unobtainable, and so you turned and came away from the edge, and there was the land again, the earth – rich poor red black brown – and grass flowers trees crops grew the earth and were nourished by it. And farmers broke the earth and turned it, and that was humankind's relationship with the land, to need it and love it and break it into giving.

Robertson 2011 [2010]: 1, original italics

Here, the land, as in Gibbon's writing, exists as a separate plane of reality to that of mundane capitalist everyday life and therefore as the possibility of alternate forms of living. In this respect, land is not merely a designation of territory but also expresses an epochal temporal dimension far in excess of industrial clock time. The 'stillness' of the land in Robertson's title does not indicate a lack of movement but a fluid sense of the past, the present and the future combined. A conversation early in the novel between the central protagonist, Michael Pendreich and the older and wiser Jean Barbour, explicitly sets out a criticism of 'chronological order' as unimaginative and instead makes the case for telling 'a story with no beginning, no middle and no end' (40). The implication is that like the land itself, the story should not be finite and therefore *And the Land Lay Still* needs to find mechanisms of evading the closure which is characteristic of the novel form. It does this, in the main, through precisely the journalistic, documentary style that Hames criticizes.

If we return again to the passage quoted above describing Scotland in 1950, we can see there is an almost-rhythmic counterpointing of the land and the timebound specific social context, subject to change. The passage as a whole, sandwiched between descriptions of a mining disaster and the disappearance of one of the main characters, Jack Gordon, serves not to create a reality effect but rather to emphasize the ephemerality of this apparently stable social order. The emotional charge of the novel is not directed towards nostalgia for, and the recovery of, a lost Scotland subsequently destroyed by Thatcherism but towards the escape from this false, limiting 'reality' that is sought by Gordon, who we come to realize is also the subject of the second-person stream-of-consciousness passages. Gordon returns to the land in a manner that again recalls the ending of *A Scots Quair*, but *And the Land Lays Still* ends instead with Pendreich taking the responsibility for making the connections which will bring past, present and future into new alignment and thereby enable new social configurations for Scotland. Within a year of the novel's publication the SNP won a majority in the Scottish Parliament elections, paving the way to the Independence referendum of 2014. While the matter of Scotland's future is not yet settled, the temporal shift registered by Robertson has undoubtedly taken effect.

Territorial disintegration Part 2: Cofiwch Aberystwyth

A story in the magazine *Interzone*, 'Cofiwch Aberystwyth' (2020), by the Welsh-based Irish writer Val Nolan, is set some years after the mutiny of the English petty officers and sailors of a Trident submarine on manoeuvres in the Irish Sea, and their subsequent nuclear strike on the Welsh National Eisteddfod in Aberystwyth, killing 150,000 people. We learn that the mutineers 'were English nationalists radicalized by one of the fractured Brexit Party's far-right daughter factions' (18). The story thereby expresses the fear that the peaceful break-up of Britain will not be accepted by the English. The title is a reference to the famous slogan, 'Cofiwch Dryweryn' (Remember Tryweryn), originally painted on a wall beside the A487 a few miles south of Aberystwyth to commemorate and protest the 1965 flooding of the Tryweryn valley, which involved the evacuation and loss of several villages and small communities, to create a reservoir to provide a water supply for Liverpool. This event played a key role in the rise of Welsh nationalism, contributing to the famous 1966 Carmarthen by-election victory of Gwynfor Evans, the president of Plaid Cymru. More recently, in the aftermath of the EU referendum, the slogan – which still exists in palimpsestic form at its original location – has been reproduced across Wales by supporters of Welsh independence. Aberystwyth, fortunately from my point of view, does not yet need commemoration but Nolan's story captures something of the sense of branching temporal possibilities lying ahead of Welsh-speaking Wales. These possibilities are raised differently by two different novels responding in different ways to the aftermath of the Brexit vote: John Osmond's *Ten Million Stars Are Burning* (2018) and Niall Griffiths's *Broken Ghost* (2019).

Broken Ghost captures a period that, caught between the EU referendum and the Covid pandemic, already feels historically distinct. Even though set in Aberystwyth, where Griffiths lives, and therefore 'in part of Wales ... [that has] stayed half way resistant to the darkness that's taken over much of [Britain]' (74), it is still part of the UK in which, as one of the three protagonists, Adam, considers telling his table companions, when visiting the residential centre in which he got over his addictions, but in the end does not say aloud:

> out there people are killing themselves, in this isolated, inward-looking, mean country that its populace voted for it to become; that as the support they need is eroded away so they fall out of life. I'll tell them that anyone who needs state support is now regarded as a scrounging parasite to be ostracised, and persecuted, to death if needs be.
>
> Griffiths 2019: 74–75

The novel begins when Adam, Emma and Cowley witness a vision of a huge woman in the sky above a ridge they have walked up to after an all-night party in the wilderness to the east of Aberystwyth. The novel then follows the three characters as they disintegrate in parallel across the coming days – for example, simultaneously experiencing hostile attitudes in the Job Centre – before they all find their way back to the ridgetop, which in the meantime has become the centre of a millennial pilgrimage to the site of the vision that they experienced.

Comparisons are often made between the times we are living through and the 1930s, including in the relevant volume in this book series (see Hubble, Seaber and Taylor 2021). In that respect, the portrayal in *Broken Ghost* of individuals struggling with personal issues against a larger social context is the equivalent of novels such as Graham Greene's *Brighton Rock* (1938) and Patrick Hamilton's *Hangover Square* (1941), which also includes scenes set in Brighton. The fact that Aberystwyth can function in this way as the locus for the moral examination of our social and cultural collapse suggests the extent to which the spatial imagination of Britain has shifted since the Second World War. Rather than an hour on the train from London, it is now necessary to travel five or five and a half hours by train winding through the Cambrian mountains and alongside the Dyfi estuary (if you are lucky enough not to find yourself on a replacement bus service) to reach a location sufficiently different to provide moral perspective. Although the countercultural encampment that springs up at the site of the vision's appearance is brutally raided and destroyed by the police at the end of *Broken Ghost*, in a prescient foreshadowing of the 2023 Public Order Act giving the police unprecedented authority to stop public protest, the novel registers a resistance whose time has not yet come. Because, at some point in the not-too-distant future, the British state will find places like Aberystwyth just too far away to bother with and so they will be left, in the same way as coastal settlements are beginning to be abandoned to erosion and flooding, to find their own alternative values.

In contrast, *Ten Million Stars*, which is an even more explicitly documentary novel than Robertson's *And the Land Lay Still*, does not have so many jokes as *Broken Ghost* about nearby Tregaron but instead offers historical perspective in its retelling of Welsh history between the UK's entry into the Common Market in 1973 and the aftermath of the disastrously unsuccessful devolution referendum in 1979, when establishing a Welsh Assembly was rejected by a ratio of 80:20. The scene of the action moves backwards and forwards across Wales, and to and from Westminster, but, due to geography and the limited road and rail networks, repeatedly comes through Aberystwyth and its pubs (although not the same ones as featured in *Broken Ghost*). Therefore, rather than a marginal location, the town is represented as central to a temporal and spatial version of Wales, which is entirely distinct to the British State despite notionally forming part of it.

Raymond Williams appears as a principal character in the novel, amongst a huge cast of historical figures, Here, Williams's real-life declaration to his interviewers from *New Left Review* that he wanted the Welsh people to defeat bourgeois England is inserted into a conversation with the (autobiographical) journalist protagonist, Owen James, as part of the former's attempt to convince the latter that while they, as Welsh comrades, are 'living through a hard, fierce, disputacious and bitterly contested time', they are also part of 'an expression of a remarkable vitality' (Osmond 2018: 578). Thus, while the novel charts a series of what were often seen at the time as a series of political defeats culminating in the humiliation of the referendum loss, it presents them as a part of a wider shift of consciousness. For example, although the attachment of the need for a referendum to the devolution bill was a measure designed to thwart devolution imposed by hostile Welsh Labour MPs under the leadership of Leo Abse, James explains to a colleague on the *Western Mail* that although this is another battle lost on one level, it nonetheless will establish a precedent for transcending 'the so-called sovereignty of [the Westminster] parliament' (383–384) and establishing the Welsh people as the ultimate power in determining how Wales is governed. As James's colleague perceptively points out, this is implicitly an argument for independence; such a future affirmation would potentially overcome the differences highlighted in the 'Three Wales hypothesis' (10) – the divide between Y Fro Gymraeg (the Welsh-speaking west and north), Welsh Wales (the Valleys), and British Wales (the British-identifying eastern marches, south coast and Pembrokeshire). The ideas of both a Welsh people and Welsh independence are therefore as much predicated on the future than any sense of the past, which is more a source of divisions to be overcome.

The second main fictional protagonist of the novel, Rhiannon Jones-Davies, is an activist in Cymdeithas yr Iaith Gymraeg (the Welsh Language Society), who is imprisoned at different times in Holloway and Risley as a result of occupying television transmitters in the ultimately successful campaign for a Welsh language channel. As she realizes, while attending a Catalan nationalist summer school, and therefore outside the confines of the British State, the function of Cymraeg (Welsh) is both to be a repository of Welsh culture but also crucially to hold open for the future 'a separate identity of the Welsh as a people' within the land, 'our space of earth between England and the Irish sea' (564). The struggles of the 1970s, while not always successful, are thereby shown to have provided their protagonists with an expanded sense of space and time, able to imagine Wales from a perspective beyond both the narrow concerns of the present and the parochial territory of Great Britain. This perspective remains in place, like the land itself, waiting for the moment that the British state does eventually recede or finally break up.

Binary faultlines

Griffiths's choice to depict the EU flag flying as a protest to the authorities over the countercultural camp in *Broken Ghost* indicates the difficulty of interpreting the significance of the outcome of what on the face of it had seemed a completely binary choice in the referendum held on 23 June 2016. As discussed in the introduction to this volume, this choice is partly determined by the territorial divisions in the UK. Aberystwyth, although historically a bilingual town, is in the Welsh-speaking rural areas of Wales that voted for remain, and therefore supports a perspective that sees Brexit as imposed by mainstream British politicians against the popular will. In contrast, viewed from the Midlands or the North of England, Brexit itself appears to be an English revolt against the London authorities (see Kristian Shaw's chapter in this volume). Despite the 52:48 ratio of the vote lending itself to interpretations of a central divide in British society, 'remain' and 'leave' do not represent two distinct homogenous halves of the population that can be easily mapped in terms of factors such as social class, educational attainment and generational difference, or simply explained by reference to racism and xenophobia and attitudes to immigration. This is not to say that these factors were not relevant, as social scientists have shown that they clearly were (see, for example, Sobolewska and Ford 2020), but rather that they intersected in a number of complex ways which means that, even taking national difference within the UK into account, it is difficult to provide any definitive account of what was at stake in the referendum beyond the headline question of what people were voting for and against.

At a political level, leaving the EU did not represent an end in itself but rather opened up existential questions concerning how British society should be organized and what its relationship to the rest of the World should be. It is not an exaggeration to say that the radical uncertainty generated by these questions completely destabilized the society, economy and political institutions of Britain. In particular, as can be seen from the 'Timeline of National Events' at the end of this book (see also Russell and James 2023), the UK Parliament descended into unprecedented chaos from 27 January 2017, when the Supreme Court ruled that the Article 50 process of withdrawal from the EU could not be invoked by the Government without an Act of Parliament. There followed nearly two years of seemingly endless late-night knife-edge votes that often stretched parliamentary conventions beyond breaking point. In particular, a series of extraordinary votes occurred in late March and early April 2019, when backbench MPs wrested control of the Commons agenda from the Government but failed to find a majority for any of the various options for future relations with the EU that they set out. They did, however, manage to extend the Article 50 period so that Britain was not forced into a no-deal exit from the EU by the parliamentary impasse. Subsequently, after Theresa May's replacement as Conservative Party leader by Boris Johnson (the second of four sudden changes in Conservative leader and Prime Minister that have so far occurred since the EU referendum), the Supreme Court was forced to intervene in the political realm again by ruling Johnson's prorogation (suspension) of Parliament, which was probably intended to facilitate a no-deal Brexit, unlawful. When, following this setback, Johnson did manage to agree a withdrawal deal by temporarily accepting exactly the different arrangements for Northern Ireland which he had earlier opposed (and would oppose again later), it is not surprising that he won the December 2019 General Election with a landslide majority from an English public who were by now just desperate to 'get Brexit done' in the hope that this would bring an end to all the uncertainty. However, despite these hopes, and the repeated attempts of the two mainstream political parties to firmly state that Brexit is over, the uncertainty has very much not ended, and 56 per cent of the British public now consider leaving the EU to have been a mistake (Smith 2023: n.p.).

The problem is not just that Britain has been, perhaps irretrievably, economically damaged by Brexit but that what formerly appeared to be its common culture has been splintered into a multiplicity of differences. In this sense, Brexit has had a similar effect on Britain as 9/11 had on the USA and is perhaps best understood through some of the critical responses to that earlier event. In *Welcome to the Desert of the Real* (2002), Slavoj Žižek took his title from a line in the Wachowski sisters' film, *The Matrix* (1999) and used it to explain the realization in the USA following 9/11, that the stable consensual shared understanding that people used to take for 'real life' is an illusion. The complete destabilization of British everyday life since Brexit should be understood as a similar revelation that how we used to understand our society as bound by shared values was really just a collective fantasy, which we uncritically accepted. As Žižek argues, the only way to fully overcome such an illusion (rather than go on kidding ourselves that things will go 'back to normal') is to constantly remind ourselves that we live in a kind of fiction: 'we should be able to discern, in what we experience as fiction, the hard kernel of the Real which we are able to sustain only if we fictionalize it' (Žižek 2002: 19). Much of the analysis within this book bears out how the British fiction of the 2010s fictionalizes and estranges aspects of social life in the UK that just used to be taken for granted and thereby enables readers to see through the illusoriness of 'real life'. In the remainder of this section, I want to discuss how speculative science fiction in particular enables us not only to see the incompatibilities and differences fissuring our illusory common culture but also provides us with future-orientated approaches for moving beyond those multiple binary divisions of class, generation, gender, sexuality and ethnicity.

In Simon Ings's *The Smoke* (2018), a new technological boom has led to Huddersfield, one of the former hubs of the industrial revolution, once again booming with 'spaceship yards and bomb manufactories' (20). The industries might be unfamiliar, but the northern experience represented by Stuart Lanyon's trip with his dad, Bob, for fish and chips by the canal—and then on for five pints in the pub – is straight out of postwar British kitchen-sink drama. But soon Stuart must return to London, divided between the rundown inner-city areas served by the tube and new technologically transformed zones, where he is trying to pick up the pieces following the break-up of his relationship with girlfriend, Fel, a posthuman descended from members of the early twentieth-century Jewish Labour Bund. This racial othering of financial and technological development as semi-alien Jewishness is uncomfortable for the reader but forces us to confront how Stuart's inability to overcome his resistance to Fel, even as he is overwhelmed by desire both for her and to be like her, has blighted his life. The plot is complicated by the existence of another posthuman species, the nonbinary 'chickies', who are trying to intervene in and thereby transform the gendered sexual violence of male human beings. Ings has stated in an interview that the chickies are left over from an earlier version of the novel explicitly focused on gender: 'One of the versions of the story was about gender invention. It was going to be a society in which only men existed, so femininity had to be manufactured' (Thornton 2018: n.p.). However, the end result of the evolution of the novel is a complex intersectional text, in which one chickie's sustained attempts to save Stuart from the British cycle of toxic masculinity represented by his older brother, bring home to the reader that perhaps it will require a posthuman revolution to drag Britain out of its addiction to both the social values of the 1950s and the sexual politics of the *Carry On* films.

The Smoke is also an alternate history – there is no America and the Second World War has not happened – in which Britain is trying to hang on as a global power in the face of globalization and rapid technological change. Therefore, the set-up of *The Smoke* illuminates all the fantasies surrounding Brexit and the internal barriers between the post-industrial North and metropolitan liberal London. This strange blend of gender politics, British social realism, alternate history, and futuristic technology does not dovetail into a neatly unified whole but generates a messily fragmented approach which enables the novel to represent more effectively than realist novels, the full humiliating awfulness of what it was like to have go through the Brexit process for anyone with more than an insular awareness. *The Smoke* captures exactly what it feels like to be trapped within a backward-looking, jingoistic, introverted British culture while it lurches drunkenly forward, trousers round ankles, slap-bang into the relentlessly onrushing future of climate catastrophe, technological singularity, post-binary genders, and transhumanism.

One of the ways in which *The Smoke* tries to move beyond the binaries still residually governing twenty-first century Britain is by relating personal development to spatial experience; the mechanism that Fredric Jameson identifies as providing a solution to the structural problem 'of closure generally in SF' (2005: 312). As Jameson notes, the novel is a bourgeois literary form, which is structurally dependent on formal resolution, but science fiction is a genre that desires to move beyond closed thinking and social constraints. He argues that Vonda McIntyre's 1975 novel *The Exile Waiting* transcends this problem by reformulating the relationship between personal subjectivity and social intersubjectivity into an interplay between inside and outside, which scales up from the protagonist, Mischa, hiding in a cave from the people of Center to her looking down on the planet from a departing spaceship, with a whole galaxy spreading before her. Therefore, *The Exile Waiting* does not provide the formal resolution typical of the novel form but moves beyond the constrictions and binary divides of its hierarchical planet-bound context through a switch of perspective that opens up an exploration of individual and social possibility without limits. In its overdetermined complexity, *The Smoke* demonstrates narrative recognition of the link between personal development and spatial experience, while showing the consequences of Stuart's unwillingness to commit to its inherent possibilities. In denial of the fact that he is afraid to take the step from his proletarian roots to a transformed future, Stuart instead ascribes his break-up from Fel to *her* difference from him. As a result, he condemns himself to being left behind, and the novel leaves us with a sobering perspective in which we look back on the emotional ruins of British life in the late 2010s from an extraterrestrial transhuman vantage point.

A different variation on the same relation of personal development to spatial experience structures Justina Robson's *The Switch* (2017), set on the ironically named Harmony, which appears to be a planet but is in fact a section of a giant space Orbital similar to those portrayed in Iain Banks's *Culture* novels,[3] which is cut off from the rest of the universe by 'the wall':

> a massive, grey cliff, a klick high, of billions of panels that cut straight up from the sandy ground in a perfectly straight line that ran for thousands of miles in both directions. High on its summit a field blurred the edges of the sky. Drones patrolled in groups of three, no cluster ever out of sight of its comrades. Nothing had ever passed through or over this structure.
>
> Robson 2017: 189

People know there is an 'offworld', but they cannot see it or get to it. The structural situation described by the novel, in which a country is deliberately separated off from a larger territory in order to isolate it socially and culturally for political purposes, is entirely applicable to what has been happening in Britain since 2016. Rather than a decaying monarchy characterized by class stratification and social deference, Harmony, is an alchemical, religious utopia, in which perfectly engineered gene lines result in adherents of the faith effectively having superpowers. Despite these specific differences, it is nonetheless, like Britain, a failed patriarchal order artificially preserved by the maintenance of a closed society. This link is made clear in *The Switch* by the explanation that Tecmaten, the 300+ years old founder of Harmony, has specifically revived the long-forgotten concepts of heteronormativity and cisnormativity from old Earth sociology of 10,000 years in the past and made them the structuring components of the rigid hierarchy he has socially engineered. As Nico, the queer protagonist of the novel, comments at a stage when he is beginning to understand fully the nature of the oppressive society he lives within, '[cisnormativity] shouldn't even be an idea, it's so ruinously ugly in every way' (171), before going on to explain how 'In the Alchemy, it was essential that one's gender matched one's physical form but, as with my particular variant, this was something that even the most refined Alchemist had yet to assure' (172). *The Switch* shows not only that these binaries are maintained precisely because they enable a hierarchical social structure but also that such rigid binaries can only be maintained within a hermetically sealed-off society with closed borders. As part of this process, Harmony, which is based on the pretence that there is no outside society, has to create an 'other' internally – the slum, Chaontium – in order to show its faithful adherents what bad things will happen to them if they deviate from the narrow path of orthodoxy. Nico, who lives variously on the streets, as a gang member and then part of a crime cartel in Chaontium after escaping from the orphanage in which he grew up, understands perfectly well that 'people like me walk the plank to keep the ship straight' (9).

The Switch unfolds with a delirious pulp sensibility – at one point a pink-haired Nico with lotus tattoo on inner thigh is working as a no-holds-barred Arena fighter under the stage name of Pretty Flower – and plays on the various possible meanings of 'switch'. At one level, Nico himself is clearly the 'switch' of the title but also he becomes the possessor of a 'pilot Switch', a piece of offworld 'transcendent wetware' that is surgically implanted and which enables him to sync with a starship (and thereby ultimately escape from Harmony). This is not the *deus ex machina* it appears and raises all sorts of questions of where Tashin, the girlfriend of Twostar – Nico's 'sister' from the orphanage, whom he has protected on the streets and in the gangs – has got this amazing piece of tech from. In fact, Tashin turns out to an offworlder with an agenda not dissimilar to those of Special Circumstances agents in Banks's Culture novels in that she wants to overthrow the failed patriarchal order of Harmony for committing 'choice theft' on its people. Tashin can also override Nico's consciousness and take control of his body through the switch but as the relationship between the two becomes more complex, Nico has to take over Tashin's body at one point. Therefore, while 'switch' can connote taking advantage, or a con as in 'bait and switch', it also suggests a mutuality and interdependence that transcends the rigidly binary thinking of Harmony and Chaontium (and Britain). Through his interaction with others, Nico learns to adjust his street thinking to this new mutuality over the course of the novel. In particular he develops a relationship with the privileged Isylon, while infiltrating the elite seminary at the centre of Harmony in order to find proof that the Alchemy is dependent on offworld tech for its genetic engineering.

At the end of *The Switch*, Harmony and Chaontium are revealed to be functioning as a 'storefront display' for gene-tailored perfect human forms made by the Alchemy to be bought and occupied (by other conscious beings) via the trading post at Skyline Orbital on the other side of the wall. Nico realizes that 'everything I had lived in as absolute reality was a lie' (317). This realization relates back to an earlier conversation between Nico and Isylon in which the former disagrees with the latter's insistence that 'reality is very much a matter of interpretation' (216). The essential point here is not a realization that people on

Harmony have been confusing a fiction with reality, but rather that only by understanding reality as functioning like fiction, in the manner suggested by Žižek, is it possible to comprehend the real possibilities open to people. Ultimately for Nico, Twostar and Isylon, this point is reached at the moment they finally escape off world and find they have a whole universe to discover. One of their first stops is the Harmony shop where they find their various body types in the catalogue and Nico's is described as 'model still under test' (355). As with *The Exile Waiting* and *The Smoke*, the combination of personal development with a spatial switch of perspective in *The Switch* is shown to open up perspectives beyond the limiting binaries that have been used to structure social reality.

Amidst the flotsam and jetsam of the postwar state

While escape from the planet into outer space is not yet widely available as a means of widening perspective, it is important to remember that science fiction writers since the New Wave have also explored what Ballard famously described as 'inner space' (1963: n.p.), which provides a different route to enabling an inside-outside interplay of personal subjectivity and social intersubjectivity. Such interplay occurs in the oblique social commentaries of Priest and Harrison, two writers who began their careers in the 1960s by publishing New Wave stories. Priest, in particular, has been exceptionally productive in recent years. *The Evidence* (2020) was the fifth novel that he had published since 2010. It is set in the Dream Archipelago, a fictionalized combination of the Greek Islands with a drowned British landscape, which he originally introduced as a setting in several short stories written in the 1970s but has subsequently grown into the backdrop for a loosely linked sequence of novels.

In recent years, Priest's work has come to resemble an ironic commentary on the relationship between genre conventions and literary writing, which he is well placed to experience. In the 1970s, he was a Faber and Faber author, who went on to be included in 1983 in the inaugural *Granta* list of Best of Young British Novelists list. In 2023, an article in *The Times* marking the publication of the fourth such list, rather dismissively described him as a 'sci-fi writer [...] still plugging away in [his] genre' (Millen 2023: n.p.). Against this sort of ignorant and hostile background, it seems appropriate that *The Evidence* begins with crime writer, Todd Fremde, on his way to the island of Dearth to give, as requested, a keynote lecture to a conference organized by the University of Dearth Literary and Historical Society, on 'The Role of the Modern Crime Novel in a Crime-Free Society'. Obviously, Dearth is not a crime-free society and so the specification of such a title is an ideological manoeuvre typical of a state in which the acceptable parameters of thought are controlled. The real-life British equivalent would be a university asking Priest to give a keynote on 'The Problem of the Modern Science Fiction Novel in a Stable Society Not Subject to Social and Technological Change'. The point being that we very much live in an unstable society completely subject to social and technological change and therefore the wilful marginalization of science fiction writers from a literary perspective as 'pluggers' is the equivalent of the ideological posturing of a totalitarian state.

Fremde has accepted this academic invitation against his better judgement, swayed by the promise of top cuisine, a suite at the hotel, and being driven around in a university car. Needless to say, as anyone familiar with UK universities could have told Fremde, the amenities on Dearth fail to match up to their billing. However, the real trouble arises from Fremde's inability to align his inner experience of space and time with what happens on Dearth. As a result he falls foul of 'seignioral mutability regulations' (Priest 2020: 16) with the consequences that his watch stops, the electrical equipment in his room (not suite) takes on a life of his own, letters disappear from his emails and texts, and he incurs hefty fines for 'electrical mutability abuse' (46). Fortunately, he is able to offset some of the cost of these by cashing in the return half of his rail ticket and accepting the offer of a lift back across the island from a woman, Frejah Harsent, who attended his talk. But this has unforeseen consequences, as Harsent turns out to be a semi-retired detective in the 'Transgression Investigation Department, Dearth Seignioral Police' (59). On the journey it becomes evident that she is incredibly prejudiced against serfs, which forces Fremde to make the heartfelt response: '"That's just your assumption," I said. "Don't feel sorry for me. I'm a writer. All writers are serfs."' (66).

This opposition to the authorities, which we take to be the author's attitude, becomes more starkly apparent from the drop-down menu of 'social level' options that Fremde is later forced to select from: 'Serf, Citizen Serf, Villein, Squire, Vassal, Corvée Provider, Cartage Provider, Demesne Landed, Knight, Manorial Landed, Baron, Seignior' (179). In having Fremde comment 'I knew my place' while selecting 'Citizen Serf' (180), Priest reminds us of the well-known 'Class System' comedy sketch first broadcast in an episode of David Frost's satirical comedy television programme *The Frost Report* on 7 April 1966,[4] which imagines a simple tripartite hierarchy of upper, middle, and lower class. In *The Evidence*, this outdated class system, which exists in the mind despite not existing in reality, is linked with financial collapse as a manifestation of mutability, which is clarified as both a real and unreal process that happens or is thought to happen: 'best understood as existing somewhere between quantum physics and psychology' (72). Events in the novel start to turn when Fremde realizes that he can adapt mutability through his own writing in order to negotiate the difference between 'the outer perception of material reality' and 'the inner perception of change without memory' (171). This is a more subtle version of those forms of Ballardian psychopathology that are shown to reshape how reality is perceived with frequently ambiguous consequences.

The unexpected reappearance of the medieval term 'Vassal' in British political discourse of the 2010s presents a real-world example of this kind of simultaneously real and unreal existence. It resurfaced following the EU referendum to express the concern of Brexiteers, such as Boris Johnson, warning against the danger of the UK becoming a 'vassal state' of the EU (Stewart 2017). On one level, this is a psychopathological analysis with no basis in the historical reality of the near half-century that the UK had spent in the EU, but at the same time it helped create the new political reality in which Johnson was able to become Prime Minister. That this kind of psychopathology was able to impose social consensus on the UK for long enough that Johnson could win a landslide election supports William Davies's argument that, with the advent of unlimited data which can be framed in multiple ways, UK news and politics has fallen prey to 'escalating opportunities for conflict over the nature of reality' (2020: 202–203). Priest fictionalizes instability of this sort as mutability and therefore simultaneously estranges it as absurd while making it tangible as a force operating within the World. Fremde might have been tasked with the seemingly paradoxical task of talking about the role of the modern crime novel in a crime-free society but through speculative fictional framing Priest tackles the even more difficult problem of writing about the relationship between illusion and reality in a world in which the distinction between them has collapsed.

Harrison's *The Sunken Land Begins to Rise Again* appears to represent a stage of decay beyond even that registered by Priest. While Priest's protagonists nearly always manage to find their way back to some form of meaningful existence even as the ruins of consensus reality collapse around them, Harrison's characters eventually succumb to the chaos around them and stay lost, although maybe losing themselves is their only hope of escape. Therefore, we find fifty-something protagonist Shaw going through a 'rough patch' (2020: 3) that isn't really a breakdown but 'too late to be a midlife crisis' (5). His desultory relationship with forty-something Victoria satisfies neither so she leaves London to take on her late mother's house in a town in the Severn Gorge in Shropshire and he moves to a new bedsit 'in a quiet suburban Badlands between East Sheen and the Thames'

(5–6). On the one hand, this dual structure allows Harrison to satirize both the contemporary suspension of life in a London where everyone is 'someone else's subtenant' (7) and in a provincial Midlands town, which Victoria variously describes as 'very Brexit' (60) and 'very English Heritage' (97).

Shaw sells print-on-demand copies of a book called *The Journey of Our Genes*, which is a badly compiled cut-and-paste selection of varied sources, which hints at a strange divergence in human evolution incorporating a kind of fish people. As he admits to Victoria, 'It's not really a job [...] it's what everyone has these days' (188). Through a series of weird encounters and transactions with the would-be entrepreneurs of 'the abandoned high streets of the post-2007 austerity', Shaw uncovers a sub-class of Thatcherite middle-class-proletarians, the products of the break-up and ongoing recalibration of the English class system:

> Their real obsession lay in the idea of commerce as a kind of politics, expression of a fundamental theology. They had bought the rhetoric without having the talent or the backing. The internet was killing them [...] They were like old-fashioned commercial travellers, fading away in bars and single rooms, exchanging order books on windy corners as if was still 1981 – denizens of futures that failed to take, whole worlds that never got past the economic turbulence and out into clean air, men and women in cheap business clothes washed up on rail platforms, weak-eyed with the brief energy of the defeated, exchanging obsolete tradecraft like Thatcherite spies.
>
> Harrison 2020: 32

On one level, this is satire directed at those Thatcherite entrepreneurs who set up their own shops and businesses in the 1980s, before ending up operating out of their garages or spare bedrooms following the 2008 financial crisis, but still voted for Brexit and the promise of free trade. However, the novel can also be seen to function as an anti-cosy catastrophe which exposes how the Thatcherite desire to become the hero profiting from social collapse is little more than a mental crutch for those without any other source of meaning. This neoliberal legacy plays out in Victoria's experience of the middle-aged builders renovating her mother's house and the various dealings she has with people whose entire value systems are purely calibrated to transactional gain and yet also think that they are 'the future now' (121), in a society in which 'now everyone will stand a chance' (121). In the face of such incomprehensible but nonetheless thinly veiled threats, Victoria is eventually seduced into slipping out of this plane of reality and the most optimistic gloss that can be put on the ending of the novel is that maybe Shaw will find his way after her.

In this respect, *The Sunken Land Begins to Rise Again* almost functions as social realism, representing the current condition of England very effectively despite, or perhaps because of, being comic and absurdist. There is also more than an element of nostalgia here for what has been lost as a result of the collapse of the common culture. However, despite these minor compensations, the novel paints a bleak vision of a country that has lost itself and now amounts to little more than a random assortment of flotsam and detritus left behind by the ebb tide of the break-up of Britain, lying scattered throughout the text: 'behaviour from the fifties and sixties' (10), 'ABBA in 1979' (100), 'a Virago book cover in 1982' (112), 'Olga Korbut' (119), and 'horrible [club] nights in Lewisham in the 1990s' (221).

Conclusion: 'Myths from a geography long forgotten or not yet invented'

The fiction of the 2010s suggest that neither the mainstream political parties or anyone else is going to be able to save Britain from terminal break-up and reinstate a common culture supported by state institutions and a stable class structure. Moreover, they also strongly suggest that even if this were possible, it would not be a desirable goal. Welsh and Scottish fictions, such as those of Osmond and Robertson, suggest that these two nations have access to temporal landscapes, which include within themselves different future possibilities from those constrained by the British state. In their reimagination of time and space, both *And the Land Lay Still* and *Ten Million Stars* have features in common with the science fiction of the decade, calling into question the continued utility of the tired genre labels still residually determining literary discourse in the UK. Furthermore, emphasizing the science-fictional nature of such scenarios, the possibility of Welsh and Scottish independence is dependent to some extent – as, of course, is the future of England itself – on whether the English can find some way of living with the break-up of Britain other than descending into Ballardian 'consumer fascism' or treating it as a cosy catastrophe offering the opportunity for the minority to survive it heroically while others die around them.

If, like Stuart Lanyon in *The Smoke*, the English find themselves unable to accept that the future will be different, then individual escape may turn out to be the best we can hope for whether territorially (and perhaps metaphorically) via outer space, as in Robson's *The Switch*, or psychologically via inner space, as in Priest's work. Either route offers perspectives beyond the limiting binaries that have been used to structure social reality and therefore those who find their way through to these positions will find themselves freed from the continual acts of 'choice theft' perpetrated by the authorities and mainstream political parties in Britain. Possibilities will open up before us once we are in a position to see them. In this respect, the title of *The Sunken Land Begins to Rise Again* is not wholly ironic, containing the merest hint of a promise that we might be able to escape the tyranny of the temporal frame of a present forever orientated to its immediate past and enter a wider landscape of the imagination, as suggested by one of Victoria's dreams:

> She was to understand [...] that she was seeing a future. People had found fresh ways to live. Or perhaps it wasn't, as far as the [Severn] Gorge was concerned, a future at all, only an intersection of possibilities, unconformable layers of time, myths from a geography long forgotten or not yet invented.
>
> Harrison 2020: 108

Notes

1. A full transcript of Thatcher's interview with Douglas Keay for *Women's Own* is available on the Margaret Thatcher Foundation website: https://www.margaretthatcher.org/document/106689 (accessed 28 May 2023).
2. As set out by Labour leader, Keir Starmer in a speech at the Centre for European Reform on Monday 4 July 2022: https://labour.org.uk/press/keir-starmer-sets-out-labours-5-point-plan-to-make-brexit-work/ (accessed 28 May 2023).
3. Robson explicitly acknowledges Banks: 'you will see that the ship names here are somewhat reminiscent of his Culture ship names and that Harmony exists on an Orbital of the type pioneered in his stories. So much of his work has such an influence on my imagination of a spacefaring world that it was impossible not to include them' (2017, 360).
4. See https://www.youtube.com/watch?v=UDIHrX-Jp2E (accessed 28 May 2023)

Works cited

Aldiss, Brian and David Wingrove. *Trillion Year Spree*. London: House of Stratus, 2001.
Allegretti, Aubrey and Linda Geddes. 'PM to confirm 19 July end to Covid rules despite scientists' warnings'. *The Guardian*, 4 July 2021: https://www.theguardian.com/politics/2021/jul/04/pm-confirm-19-july-end-covid-restrictions-scientists-warnings-england (accessed 28 May 2023).

Beckett, Andy. *When the Lights Went Out: What Really Happened to Britain in the Seventies*. London: Faber and Faber, 2009.

Ballard, J.G. *The Wind from Nowhere*. Harmondsworth: Penguin, 1974 [1962].

Ballard, J.G. 'Time, Memory and Inner Space' [1963]: https://www.jgballard.ca/non_fiction/jgb_time_memory_innerspace.html (accessed 28 May 2023).

Ballard, J.G. *Kingdom Come*. London: Fourth Estate, 2006.

Crawford, Robert. *Devolving English Literature*. Oxford: Oxford University Press, 1992.

Davies, William. *This is Not Normal: The Collapse of Liberal Britain*. London: Verso, 2020.

Drabble, Margaret. *The Ice Age*. New York: Alfred A. Knopp, 1977.

Edgerton, David. *The Rise and Fall of the British Nation: A Twentieth-Century History*. London: Penguin, 2019 [2018].

Forrest, Adam. 'Decadent "woke" ideology putting west in danger, claims Tory party chair'. *Independent*, 15 February 2022: https://www.independent.co.uk/news/uk/politics/woke-cancel-culture-oliver-dowden-b2015324.html (accessed 28 May 2023).

Freud, Sigmund. 'Beyond the Pleasure Principle'. In *On Metapsychology*, Penguin Freud Library 11. Angela Richards (ed.). Harmondsworth: Penguin, 1984 [1920]: 65–97.

Griffiths, Niall. *Broken Ghost*. London: Vintage, 2019.

Harrison, M. John. *The Sunken Land Begins to Rise Again*. London: Gollancz, 2020.

Hames, Scott *The Literary Politics of Scottish Devolution: Voice, Class, Nation*. Edinburgh: Edinburgh University Press, 2020.

Hinton, James. *Seven Lives from Mass Observation*. Oxford: Oxford University Press, 2016.

Hobsbawm, Eric. 'The Forward March of Labour Halted'. *Marxism Today*, September 1978: 279–286.

Hubble, Nick. 'The Ordinariness of the Extraordinary Break-Up of Britain'. In *The 1970s: A Decade of Contemporary British Fiction*. Nick Hubble, John McLeod and Philip Tew (eds.). London: Bloomsbury, 2014: 43–67.

Hubble, Nick, Luke Seaber and Elinor Taylor (eds). *The 1930s: A Decade of Modern British Fiction*. London: Bloomsbury, 2021.

Ings, Simon. *The Smoke*. London: Gollancz, 2018.

Jameson, Fredric. *Archaeologies of the Future: The Desire Called Utopia and Other Science Fictions*. London: Verso, 2005.

Keay, Douglas. 'Aids, Education and the Year 2000!'. *Woman's Own*, 31 October 1987: 8–10.

Kellner, Peter. *From Red Walls to Red Bridges: Rebuilding Labour's Voter Coalition*. London: Tony Blair Institute for Global Change, 2021.

Millen, Robbie. 'Death of the celebrity novelist: What the *Granta* list tells us about fiction'. *The Times*, 13 April 2023: https://www.thetimes.co.uk/article/granta-magazine-twenty-under-forty-list-best-young-british-novelists-2023-8wcvhgwdq (accessed 28 May 2023).

Morrison, Sean. 'Boris Johnson "told aides he would rather let Covid rip than impose second lockdown"'. *Evening Standard*, 27 April 2021: https://www.standard.co.uk/

news/uk/boris-johnson-let-covid-rip-bodies-pile-up-claims-b931846.html (accessed 28 May 2023).

Nairn, Tom. *The Break-Up of Britain: Crisis and Neo-Nationalism*. 3rd edn. London: Verso, 2021.

Nolan, Val. 'Cofiwch Aberystwyth'. *Interzone* 285 (Mar–Apr), 2020: 12–27.

Osmond, John. *Ten Million Stars Are Burning*. Llandysul: Gomer, 2018.

Priest, Christopher. *The Evidence*. London: Gollancz, 2020.

Robertson, James. *And the Land Lay Still*. London: Penguin Books, 2011 [2010].

Robson, Justina. *The Switch*. London: Gollancz, 2017.

Russell, Meg and Lisa James. *The Parliamentary Battle Over Brexit*. Oxford: Oxford University Press, 2023.

Shipman, Tim. 'How the Tories weaponised woke'. *Sunday Times*, 13 June 2021: https://www.thetimes.co.uk/article/how-the-tories-weaponised-woke-jlmwh0p36 (accessed 28 May 2023).

Smith, Matthew. 'Most Britons say Brexit has been "more of a failure"'. Yougov.co.uk, 22 May 2023: https://yougov.co.uk/topics/politics/articles-reports/2023/05/22/most-britons-say-brexit-has-been-more-failure (accessed 28 May 2023).

Sobolewska, Maria and Robert Ford. *Brexitland: Identity, Diversity and the Reshaping of British Politics*. Cambridge: Cambridge University Press, 2020.

Stewart, Heather. 'Boris Johnson breaks ranks with Brexit "vassal state" warning'. *The Guardian*, 17 December 2017: https://www.theguardian.com/politics/2017/dec/17/boris-johnson-breaks-ranks-with-brexit-vassal-state-warning (accessed 28 May 2023).

Strimpel, Zoe. 'The woke Left has declared war on our history – and Britain is surrendering'. *The Telegraph*, 3 December 2022: https://www.telegraph.co.uk/news/2022/12/03/woke-left-has-declared-war-history-britain-surrendering/ (accessed 28 May 2022).

Thornton, Jonathan. 'Interview with Simon Ings'. *The Fantasy Hive*, 27 March 2018 https://fantasy-hive.co.uk/2018/03/interview-with-simon-ings/ (accessed 27 May 2023).

Williams, Raymond. *Politics and Letters: Interviews with New Left Review*. London: NLB, 1979.

Williams, Raymond. *Towards 2000*. Harmondsworth: Penguin, 1985 [1983].

Žižek, Slavoj. *Welcome to the Desert of the Real: Five Essays on September 11 and Related Dates*. London: Verso, 2002.

2

Fiction in the Age of Distraction: Reading and Attention in the 2010s

Alice Bennett

The 2010s was a decade bookended by two versions of attention crisis. At the beginning of the decade, a spate of pop-science books and self-examinatory thinkpieces framed the moment as an 'age of distraction' whose cause was the internet. By the end of the decade, during the Covid-19 pandemic, similar concerns about a loss of focus and an inability to concentrate appeared in newspaper articles and other media discussion, this time framed through an analysis of how attention can be affected by stress, social isolation, and the 'brain fog' of long Covid. This chapter identifies how British fiction of the 2010s responded to these conceptions of attention in crisis by identifying why and how the decade was presented as an 'age of distraction' in its fiction. In spite of reminders from people with ADHD, autism, dyslexia, and other neurodivergence that human attention has a huge variation and diversity, popular discourses surrounding attention in the 2010s had a tendency to treat perceived shortcomings in or struggles with attention as something distinctly contemporary – indeed, a defining feature of the present.

To think about the representation of distraction in the 2010s is therefore to think about how the decade conceived of itself, and how writers represented their own moment. In what follows, I draw on fiction by Will Self, Adam Thirlwell and Olivia Sudjic to identify how fiction of the 2010s responded to the premise that literary reading ought to operate in competition with, or as a corrective to, engagement with online content, and how discourses of attention and distraction were implicated in that comparison.

Perhaps the most significant contribution to the early 2010s discourse of imperilled attention – and of digital reading and print reading, respectively, as cause and cure – was Nicholas Carr's book *The Shallows* (2010). The subtitle of the book's British edition (*How the Internet is Changing the Way We Think, Read and Remember*) identified reading as the most specific terrain that Carr's analysis would discuss. *The Shallows* opens with a lengthy self-examination that sees Carr immediately connect together concentration and the ability to read:

> My mind isn't going – so far as I can tell – but it's changing. I'm not thinking the way I used to think. I feel it most strongly when I'm reading. I used to find it easy to immerse myself in a book or a lengthy article. My mind would get caught in the twists of the narrative or the turns of the argument, and I'd spend hours strolling through long stretches of prose. That's rarely the case anymore. Now my concentration starts to drift after a page or two. I get fidgety, lose the thread, begin looking for something else to do. I feel like I'm always dragging my wayward brain back to the text. The deep reading that used to come naturally has become a struggle.
>
> Carr 2010: 6

Carr goes on to ascribe these changes in his mind to his use of the internet where, for more than a decade, he had been 'tripping lightly from link to link' (6). In contrast, Carr's 'deep reading' – with its necessary slowness and its dragging demands on his 'wayward brain' – required an effort from him that he was finding more and more difficult to muster. Crucially, he blames his 'trouble with reading' on the way 'the Net' seemed to have been 'chipping away at [his] capacity for concentration and contemplation' (6). Carr's argument in the book is not just that being online has diminished his capacity for concentration, but that print reading could bring it back again. Because the brain is plastic and can be reshaped by habit and practice (and because reading therefore does *not* come naturally), a return to reading should bring back what was lost. Reading is the diagnostic tool for attention crisis – it's what lets you 'feel it most strongly' – and, for Carr, it's also the cure.

The Shallows was only one of a number of books and thinkpieces from the 2010s – most from the United States, but with an impact across anglophone cultures – making an association between the struggles for concentration, being online, and reading offline.[1] From the end of the decade a similar concern with reading difficulties and problems with focus appears refracted through the lens of the pandemic.[2] Across these examples, we see similar language – imagery of 'broken brains', of lost focus, of the struggle to read – and a continuing sense that the 'age', the specific conditions of the moment, is to blame.

There is a broad corpus of attention writing from the long 2010s which encompasses self-help, business and productivity content. Non-fiction bestsellers from this period, such as Cal Newport's *Deep Work: Rules for Focused Success in a Distracted World* (2016) and Chris Bailey's *Hyperfocus: How to Be More Productive in a World of Distraction* (2018), represent a strain of writing that is TED-talk adjacent and associated with lifehacking, productivity maximizing and the hustle and grind culture that characterizes the neoliberal contemporary. At other times, writing about attention in the decade has been shaped more profoundly by a critique of tech culture and tends to conceive of attention as something that has been increasingly commodified. Books such as Maggie Jackson's *Distracted: The Erosion of Attention and the Coming Dark Age* (2008), Michael Crawford's *The World Beyond Your Head: How to Flourish in An Age of Distraction* (2014), Tim Wu's *The Attention Merchants: The Epic Scramble to Get Inside Our Heads* (2016), James Williams's *Stand out of Our Light: Freedom and Resistance in the Attention Economy* (2018), Jenny Odell's *How To Do Nothing: Resisting the Attention Economy* (2019), Stefan Van der Stigchel's *Concentration: Staying Focused in Times of Distraction* (2020), and Johann Hari's *Stolen Focus: Why You Can't Pay Attention* (2022), all fit loosely into this latter category. And all these books frame their present moment as one in which attention is under particularly acute strain.

There is therefore a readily available and useful story here for writers of the 2010s about the value and purpose of literary reading in developing a capacity for sustained concentration. By this account, reading is the activity that develops your powers of concentration and helps you resist digital distraction. In the quotation that opened this chapter we saw Nicholas Carr opposing the concentration of 'deep reading' to the digital action (or distraction) of 'tripping lightly from link to link' (6). Carr's argument is that the brain is plastic and so it can be reorganized by practice. To return to a capacity for deep reading is therefore as simple as spending more time reading and spending less time on the internet. It is easy to see why this might be an attractive proposition for writers, allowing them to place themselves at the vanguard, defending the human mind itself against the onslaught of digital content, most of it intended to corral and commodify your attention into deeply compelling but strictly regimented platforms. But, as I'll argue in this chapter, this story relies on setting up an oppositional and hierarchical configuration between literary text and digital media and between 'deep' concentration and 'shallow' distraction, neither of which hold up very well to critical scrutiny.

Alongside the body of popular writing that identified distraction as a danger, the late 2000s and 2010s also saw the parallel expansion of scholarship in what might now be identified as critical attention studies. This work would question some of the foundational understanding of attention itself that underpinned these popular accounts of the decade as an age of distraction. In philosophy, for example, Bernard Stiegler's work developed an argument that attention must be understood as care as well as focus or concentration. For Stiegler, attention is 'originally and irreducibly *both* psychic (as concentration, "attention span") and social (as kindness and solicitude)' (2010: 172). Moreover, the intergenerational, social care of tending to a child is what nurtures that child's individual, psychic capacity for attention; developmentally, attention as care precedes attention as concentration. Yves Citton's work on attention ecology also emphasized the social and interpersonal aspects of attention over an understanding of attention as the property of an individual (his book, *The Ecology of Attention*, was published in French in 2014 and translated into English in 2017). For Citton, the concept of attention 'ecology' replaces the conventional idea of attention as a resource that can be counted and captured – something that can function as a unit in an economy – with something joint, collective, and co-constructed. Citton's attention is something vectoral that always points elsewhere and that must therefore extend beyond the individual's willed control. Where psychological models of attention try to isolate it as a faculty in laboratory conditions, Citton's work comprehends attention in the wild, with an ecological understanding. One preoccupation that unites Citton's and Stiegler's work is a dedication to pedagogy and to thinking about the responsibility of being what Citton calls 'attention attendants' – those who, by their own practices of attention, might construct social situations that direct the attention of others (153). This is also the central concern of two essays by N. Katherine Hayles, which were influential in shaping ideas about attention within contemporary literary studies in the 2010s. Like Citton, Hayles is interested in reading, and in the scenarios in which pedagogies of reading can model attention. 'Hyper and Deep Attention: The Generational Divide in Cognitive Modes' (2007) and the article that followed it, 'How We Read: Close, Hyper, Machine' (2010), investigate the possibilities for the teaching of literature to enable other forms of attention beyond those associated with slow, sustained, deep, or close concentration. In 'How We Read', Hayles asks why literature scholars – people who, 'know how to read really well, and [...] know how to teach students to read' – aren't also teaching their students how to attend to the internet (2010: 63). These perspectives from critical attention studies challenge the famous William James dictum, 'Everyone knows what attention is', and offer a theory of attention as something that takes many forms, and that cannot be the property of an individual subject (James 1890: 1:381). Once the link between the individual and attention is broken, it becomes more difficult to simply valorize attention and to condemn distraction. Moreover, these interventions from critical attention studies also underscore how the discourses that identify the present as an 'age of distraction' are also an expression of anxieties about young people and about generational change.

Amongst these different conversations about attention there is, extremely loosely, a vein of US self-help and individualism on the one side and the legacy of continental philosophy's deconstruction of the coherent individual subject on the other. For British writers of the 2010s, situating themselves within or between these debates about distraction also means engaging with these intellectual and cultural traditions from a position that has never fully committed to either. Rather than staging a defence of reading that identifies its utility in improving concentration or undertaking a fully-fledged deconstruction of the attending subject, British fiction of the 'age of distraction' instead addresses some specifically British contexts, while also engaging with this broader field of attention-writing.

In Britain, the age of distraction was also the age of austerity, and it doesn't seem unreasonable to suggest that people experiencing an increased demand on their attention might have been feeling pressure on their time and their concentration from an intensely neoliberal 'recovery' from the 2008 financial crisis – with precarity that could plausibly have been felt as pressure to multitask, to fragment attention, to do more with less. Later in the decade, after the Brexit vote in 2016, another set of anxieties about attention began to emerge. The Cambridge Analytica scandal – in which the data analytics company was suspected of using Facebook data to target political messages during the Brexit campaign – raised questions about the extent to which attention was marshalled and commodified by social media platforms, in spite of the eventual judgement by the Information Commissioner that Cambridge Analytica had not been involved in the campaigning around the referendum. Broader concerns about the ways that online echo chambers or what Eli Pariser has termed 'filter bubbles' (2012) could emerge from the algorithmic curation of media feeds therefore also frame an understanding of attention in the 2010s. With the dominance of digital experience by a small number of social media platforms, it became increasingly clear that what might feel like distracted mind-wandering online is in actuality a highly regulated commodification of attention itself by processes that are, in turn, inaccessible to our attention.

How, then, might identifying the 2010s as a decade that thought of itself as an 'age of distraction' help us to conceive of the period *as* a period? We could certainly identify how and why distraction might have become a particularly pressing concern early in the decade: some of the themes that would often recur in the discourse of the attention crisis include references to increased ADHD diagnoses, dismay about smartphones causing people (especially young people) to be no longer fully 'present' in the places they physically inhabited, and anxiety expressed by the kinds of people who tend to write books or newspaper columns (mostly white, mostly middle-class, mostly neurotypical, mostly in jobs which give them a lot of control over their own time) that they were finding it quite difficult to resist using the internet. Often, these expressions of crisis reveal an unevenness in their distribution – because an attention crisis articulated by writers and journalists might occlude another attention crisis experienced by a young person overloaded with multiple jobs in a gig economy, or a child with ADHD trying to complete their schooling in an education system built to exclude them, or a woman trying to juggle the gendered demands of care work without an adequate infrastructure for social care.

Against this social and political backdrop, there are many paths one could take through considering attention in British fiction of the 2010s. For example, the revelation of previous inattention or ignorance appears as a trope in writing about the 2008 financial crisis, as Katy Shaw has argued in *Crunch Lit* (47, 68). In Zia Haider Rahman's *In the Light of What we Know* (2014), for instance, the novel's narrator reflects on how the 'yawning indifference of the public and press' meant that financiers were able to destabilize the economy without oversight (65). Elsewhere, the decade's nature fiction and its careful practices of attentive noticing record the slow violence of climate catastrophe unfolding in ways that are too easy to ignore. Novels like Jon McGregor's *Reservoir 13* (2017) or Melissa Harrison's *Clay* (2013) destabilize narrative attention by guiding the reader to notice aspects of the natural world that seem like a distraction or digression from their main narrative and turn the peripheral into the central. Other British fiction of the 2010s engages with various aspects of attention, from the sports psychology of focus and spiritual practices of mindfulness in Nicola Barker's *The Yips* (2012) and the idea of single-minded absorption and flow in Tom McCarthy's *Satin Island* (2015), to the caring attention that appears as a form of ethics in Zadie Smith's *NW* (2011) (see Bennett 2018, 2020). Attention is thematically intertwined with many of the decade's most profound concerns in ways that reflect changes in the conceptualization of attention itself as well as a heightened interest in understanding attention as a phenomenon that has real effects in the world.

In what follows I take one path through the 2010s' attentions and analyse the representation of attention and distraction in the context of the digital. In these readings, I consider the representation of the smartphone and the kinds of attention it calls up in order to establish how writers conceive of their own age as an age of distraction. Following the release of the iPhone in 2008, the smartphone became ubiquitous in the 2010s, and could even be considered emblematic of the decade. A device that could be carried in the pocket and which could engage its user's attention while travelling on a bus or sitting in the doctor's waiting room: the smartphone is an object that could fill the space of a book. In many of the texts I consider, however, this opposition or hierarchy between phone and print, scrolling and reading, is tested, distorted, or transformed entirely. Representing the internet's attention means that these texts are never completely separate from the digital. The smartphone, in the fiction of the 2010s, becomes the object that above all others provides a motif or physical marker for these concerns about attention, serving as the book's other – the object of attention that is turned away from the printed page.

I begin by considering Will Self's Marshall McLuhan-inflected essays about the digitally precipitated end of the 'Gutenberg mind' and the novel form it takes with it. I argue that Self's 2017 novel, *Phone*, provides a more speculative response to the idea of an 'age of distraction' than his essays, imagining modes of neurodivergent attention that could make meaning in ways that the novel has not conventionally had the forms to accommodate. The second piece of fiction I explore is Adam Thirlwell's *Kapow!* (2012), a novella that uses its experimental form to tell the story of the 'social media revolution' of the Arab Spring in Egypt. Thirlwell is acutely aware of the attention economy both online and in fiction publishing and he uses the experimental book design and layout of *Kapow!* to differentiate between digital forms and the conventions of print, and to make the case for the continuing relevance of print in an increasingly digital world. Finally, I read Olivia Sudjic's essay *Exposure* (2018) alongside her first novel, *Sympathy* (2017), which explores how the experience of understanding one's online attention as commodified, monitored and tracked can provoke responsive forms of attention in turn – whether that's a hypervigilant, resistant anxiety, or a return of the surveilling attention of online following and digital stalking in an intensified form.

The texts discussed here not only respond to the conception of the 2010s as an 'age of distraction' but also use this idea as part of an attempt to grasp the concept of periodization and of writing the present in and of itself. The problem of attention – or of attending to attention – is also the problem of being present in the present. This interest in periodization emerges through a recurrent thematic of generations and generational divides, which are also a feature of Stiegler's and Hayles's analysis of contemporary attention, perceived as a change in the relations between the young and the old. Along with the representation of digital media (via the smartphone) and the representation of generational divides, each of these novels also addresses the social or interpersonal aspects of attention – those features Citton has identified as 'attention ecology'. Ultimately, these three examples show writers of the 2010s trying to understand and convey the diversity and complexity of contemporary attention, while at the same time offering commentary on the place of fiction in the period.

The canary in the coalmine

Phone (2017) is the final novel of Will Self's 2010s trilogy, which began with *Umbrella* (2012) and *Shark* (2014). Described in the *Telegraph* as a an 'epic anti-tweet' whose length was both a challenge to concentration and a reward for those who were able to sustain the attention needed to reach the end, *Phone* is a long novel at the end of a long trilogy, spanning a century (White 2017: n.p.), and takes the story of the two previous novels to the present day of the 2010s. The phone of the novel's title is a ringing distraction that interrupts every few words of the text's opening pages with its typographically rendered alert, '........!', (1). These interruptions 'insistently persistently' require readers to tune them out in order to read the novel (1). From the start, then, the phone and the book are set at odds in their demands on readers' concentration.

Phone returns to Self's recurrent character, the (now-elderly) psychiatrist Zack Busner, who first appeared in Self's work in the stories of the 1991 collection, *The Quantity Theory of Insanity*. Highly distractible, accused by his children of 'pathological inattention' to their needs (58) and in old age prone to mind-wandering, Busner is one pole of distraction in a novel whose other extreme is the Ritalin-abusing spy with a photographic memory, Jonathan De'Ath. Busner's grandson, Ben, brings the two into a final connection by setting up Busner's phone to deliver to him a succession of '*nudges. . . alerts. . . pulses – pushes. . .*' (70) in an effort to manage his dementia-heightened distraction. In a book full of attempts to marshal and regulate attention, the smartphone is both a regulator of attention and a disruptive distraction.

During the 2010s Self would write explicitly about the status of the literary novel in an increasingly digital world. A 2014 essay in *The Guardian* titled 'The novel is dead (this time it's for real)' argues that the novel is a dying form, doomed to play an increasingly minor role in cultural life. Drawing on Marshall McLuhan's arguments about the way that new forms of media change minds and change social relations, Self outlines a transformation in thinking and living caused by the dominance of digital media. Following McLuhan and using his description of the 'Gutenberg mind' fostered by the medium of the book, Self identifies a version of subjectivity on the wane which was, for a time at least, able to think itself through the 'extended prose form' (2014a: n.p.). Words 'when arranged sequentially' could represent thinking subjects and their worlds, allowing readers to reflect on the processes of their own minds (n.p.). And if narrative fiction's central place within cultural forms is now subsiding then, as Self argues, there are modes of thinking that are also diminishing with it. In a second piece published in *The Guardian*, Self explains that he anticipates the 'solitary, silent, focused reading' that was a product of the physical codex will be replaced by new forms of consciousness which are networked, social, non-linear, and even characterized by the 'fracturing of attention and the attenuation of memory' ('Will Self: The fate of our literary culture is sealed', 2014b: n.p.). Focused reading, unbroken attention, the ability to think about thinking – these habits of mind were enabled by a vanishing medium. Digital connectivity, networked sociality, skimming, and scrolling replace the concentration that accompanies reading on paper. This division between two styles of thinking and attending are a feature of a significant strand in attention writing, from the pop science of Nicholas Carr's *The Shallows* to Sven Birkerts' *Changing the Subject* (2015) and N. Kathleen Hayles's work on hyperattention and deep attention.

Self's 'The novel is dead' essay is framed by an encounter with his teenage son, the young 'canary in the coalmine' of contemporary culture, who is not a reader but who nevertheless expresses a sincere interest in artistic and cultural questions. The same generation gap and imagery of the canary appears in *Phone*, as the novel pairs the ageing Busner with his younger grandson, Ben. It is Ben who gives Busner the phone of the novel's title and who we see, in childhood, being schooled in practices of attention by his mother and grandfather. In this context, Busner lays out a theory about how children learn to concentrate:

> But when they do focus for the first time, it's always on their mother's eyes. Little Ben will see you, Milla – and he'll see that you're seeing him, see also that you're focusing on other things, other people . . .
>
> [. . .]
>
> Ultimately perception isn't individual but collective, and the world which is its object is nothing more or less than the analogue of all those myriad moments when we look into another's eyes and see them *looking elsewhere*.
>
> Self 2017: 183–184

This description accords closely with Stiegler's *Taking Care of Youth and the Generations* (2010), in which he argues that attention is developed through proper care from an older generation: 'what creates attention in the first place is adult attention toward minors and of minors' developing attention' (14). Attention – as care – begets attention as focus, concentration and single-mindedness. Care is ultimately social attention, represented by 'kindness and solicitude' (172). However, there is more to Busner's intergenerational analysis. His description of Ben as 'a canary in the coalmine' is not just because of his age, but also because Ben is autistic. Busner muses on his theory at length:

> What they were now calling Autistic Spectrum Disorder is – he believes – a *canary in the coalmine* of the human condition, its cheeping heralding a decisive shift away from the human psyche's attempt to understand itself ... *by itself* to the conviction that enlightenment could be gained ...*from the screens*.
> Self 2017: 77–78

Busner believes that Ben and other autistic people have a quality he calls '*didginess*' (78), which seems to indicate a mode of thought closely analogous to the connectivity of the digital. Given Self's lament for the end of the Gutenberg mind in his essays, we might expect the novel to wholly endorse Busner's diagnostic stance towards Ben, and to see '*didginess*' – Busner's shorthand term for thinking that is augmented and extended by the digital – as a kind of degeneration from the codex-shaped concentration of minds made by print. It's to Self's credit that *Phone* is more open to the natural diversity of human attention than that. Instead of the polemical stance of his essays, Self's novelistic position allows for a good deal of irony at Busner's expense, undermining his credibility as a cultural prognosticator and making him into something more like a parody of Self's own position – more curmudgeonly, more out of touch, and more careless in his judgement of other people's minds.

This ironic treatment of Busner unfolds in two ways. First, we see Busner reflecting on some of his earlier specialisms later in the novel and acknowledging that he has a tendency to take his diagnostic urge too far. Recalling the early years of his career treating people with encephalitis lethargica (the subject of *Umbrella*), he realizes that he had 'begun to see symptoms of their malady *everywhere*' (466). In this commentary on extrapolation from the case study to the cultural diagnosis, the text offers a critique of Busner's tendency to use the hammer of his psychiatric expertise to turn everything into a nail. The novel's penultimate section takes the reader into Ben's consciousness, and this is where the novel undercuts Busner's confident cultural diagnosis for a second time. In

Phone's final pages, Ben tells us that at least some of his self-presentation to Busner has been a 'mask' that provided him with what he wanted to see:

> In this respect, the rise in autism diagnoses during my lifetime has played to my advantage, providing me with an off-the-peg set of characteristics – the stimming, the food-pickiness, the eye-avoidance, the palilalia – with which to play, in turn, to the gallery of my family.
>
> Self 2017: 594

Busner, Ben diagnoses, is afflicted with anosognosia – a chronic lack of self-insight – which leaves him 'unable to remove his pathologising spectacles' (595). Finally, at the end of the novel, it is Ben's ability to interpret a large dataset, and therefore to process information in a way that belongs to the digital rather than the book, which allows the plot of *Phone* to come together and for a connection to be made between Busner and Jonathan De'Ath (the nephew of one of the women he treated in *Umbrella*). While Busner pathologizes Ben's neurodivergence, the novel ultimately relies on his *didginess* for its plotting. It is therefore possible to read the novel as an investigation into and recognition of the kinds of attention and reading that emerge both from neurodivergence and from the digital. Where Self mourns the decline of the Gutenberg mind in his essays, the novel seems willing to identify an ecology of broader forms of attention that could thrive beyond the dominance of this single variety.

The epitaph given for Busner at the beginning of Self's 1994 collection, *Grey Area*, reads, 'He had no interests but interest' – a continued attention to attention which manifests in *Umbrella* as a fascination with his patients' 'fixed regard' (69, 93, 373) and in *Phone* in his diagnostic attention to Ben's 'focus' (183). Busner's interest in 'the human psyche's attempt to understand itself … *by itself* is, fundamentally, an interest in interest, and an attention to attention (2017: 78). If the novel and psychiatry both offer tools for a self-reflexive understanding of the mind, then perhaps *Phone* ultimately represents a victory for the novel over psychiatry (because the novel is able to imagine its digital other, where Busner's psychiatry tends to pathologize it). Self the novelist, unlike Busner the psychiatrist, is able to 'remove his pathologising spectacles' (595) and use the tools of the novel to imagine attentions other than his own and minds other than the Gutenburg mind.

To write a book called *Phone* is therefore to make a study of the object that is the antithesis of the physical book. In making his case for the death of the novel in the first of his two lectures on the subject in 2014, Self argues that, barring the 'kidult boywizardsroman and the soft sadomasochistic porn fantasy', the novel is in terminal decline (2014a: n.p.). These are important exceptions. The release of *Harry Potter and the Deathly Hallows* (2007), the seventh and final book of the Harry Potter series, and the publication of the *Fifty Shades* trilogy between 2011 and 2012 must shape an understanding of British fiction of the 2010s. *Phone* records this landscape of popular reading almost too pointedly, with an imagined monologue from a talking copy of *Harry Potter and the Chamber of Secrets* (chosen, perhaps, because this is the novel in the series in which an enchanted book writes back to its reader):

> I'm a real page-turner, so I am – and that's how I've got hundreds of thousands of boys like this one into reading, making them capable in due course of absorbing the entire Western canon, and along with it the values of liberality and tolerance which have underpinned our civilisation for millennia.
>
> Self 2017: 436

These claims about Western values are deeply ironic in the context of the events of this part of the plot, in which British soldiers – the boys who've read Harry Potter – are torturing a group of Iraqi detainees. *Phone* therefore stages an overt critique of the claim that all reading is good reading and that fiction is morally or ethically improving. (Self's defence of the novel as a form is that it helps us understand consciousness, not that it makes us better people.)

Self's trilogy should ultimately be considered part of an ongoing attempt to return to the tools of the modernist avant-garde to understand another age of new media and new approaches to consciousness. This is an attempt that has continued to be a hallmark of the 2010's, from Tom McCarthy's *C* at the beginning of the decade to Lucy Ellman's *Ducks, Newburyport* at the end. *Phone* represents a response to the perception of an age of distraction which was placing not just reading under threat but a whole familiar cast of mind. Modernism, with its attempts to understand and represent the mind, offers a set of literary techniques that are elastic enough to represent a diversity of attentions. In this, Self's fiction is able to be more exploratory and tentative than his provocative and polemical non-fiction writing about the state of the novel.

The politics of the attention economy

In a 2014 speech to mark the award of *The White Review* short story prize, Adam Thirlwell chose as his theme the status of literary writing and publishing in the age of the attention economy. Celebrating the form of the literary magazine, he identifies *The White Review* and its success as 'one proof that literature might still be possible in this distracted era' (2014, 'Literature in a distracted era': n.p.). Founded in 2011 to offer a British counterpart to US magazines publishing short fiction and poetry, *The White Review* is also a product of the 'distracted era' this essay discusses: the 2010s. Thirlwell cites an observation from the artist Tino Sehgal, who suggests that in the present moment and its 'attention economy' in which 'time is a bigger factor than space' art needs to adopt 'a medium that actually deals with sociality and time' (Thirlwell, 2014: n.p.). Thirlwell finds that the magazine, as a medium, does exactly this, by establishing networks and associations between its contributors and by the temporal rhythms of both its publication schedule and its reading experience. For Thirlwell, the mechanisms through which the literary magazine counters distraction also include its capacity for generating 'commercial attention' and encouraging readers to pay for writing. If the attention economy produces an unreadably large quantity of online content, paid for in attention itself, then the literary magazine represents the possibility of a different commercial proposition and therefore a different kind of attention. Ultimately, the literary magazine is a matter of 'attention to time', Thirlwell asserts – a concept that he glosses as meaning 'an attention to the reader' (2014: n.p.). Magazines make readers wait and anticipate and experience – they are 'an event [...] a fun palace [...] a show – something to be wandered through over time'. In contrast with Self's assertions in the same year that literature was facing a terminal decline in the face of a distracted age, Thirlwell suggests that literary writing has a role to play in offering an alternative to the content-driven churnover of the internet's attention economy. He also demonstrates an acute sensitivity to the properties of literary form that can enable or investigate certain kinds of attention.

Thirlwell's short novel, *Kapow!* (2012), represents an ambivalent response to the notion of a 'distracted era' produced by digital culture and its attention economy. The events of the novel are set during the Arab Spring in Egypt but narrated from London by a character who is hearing the story at third hand from a taxi-driver. Taking the events of 2011 as its subject – not just the events of Tahrir Square, but also mentioning the urban uprisings in British cities in the summer of that year and the beginning of the Occupy movement – the book responds to the debate that was happening in the culture of the early part of the decade about the role of social media in political change, and the shortcomings of a belief that digital communications were inherently liberatory.[3] The novel therefore represents a set of concerns explored by the fiction of the 2010s about the relationship between attention, digital media, and politics. By the end of the decade, the dominance of a small number of online platforms and their role in shaping political discourse would turn a conversation about the openness of the internet into one about its closedness, so that fiction from later in the decade that explores the relationship between politics, attention, and digital media turns to the idea of the filter bubble and its limiting of what is available to attention, rather than the information overload of the digital's demands on an economized attention.

Like Thirlwell's description of the literary magazine, *Kapow!* is a kind of fun palace, 'something to be wandered through over time'; its slightly gimmicky form, with its fold-out pages and inset notes, is both showy and meandering. It devotes 'an attention to the reader' through direct address to a 'you' narratee, and it constructs a reading experience that's both durational and emphatically bookish. In Jessica Pressman's use of the term, 'bookishness' describes a tendency that emerged from the 1990s onwards, as anxieties about the death of the book gained pace, for a heightened set of affective bonds towards books as objects (2020: 25–26). While the digital became the default, writers and book artists lodged feelings about reading and literary culture into both the representation of books in their writing and into the physical forms of the codex itself. *Kapow!* does more of the second than the first by using an experimental form that requires new ways of interacting with its long, folding pages. The book therefore addresses two questions about the 'distracted era' of the 2010s: what are the political implications of the attention and distraction activated by the internet? And what new literary forms are required to respond to these political questions?

Attention is a preoccupation in *Kapow!* from the outset. We meet the narrator of the novel 'in a blissful state of suspension' between the distractions of dope and the focus-inducing highs of caffeination (2012: 5). In this state, he explains that he 'kept thinking one thing, then another, then another' (5) as he is told a story about the uprisings in Egypt by a taxi-driver in London. The novel's form, the narrator explains, stems from an attempt to 'follow every thought as far as you could, into all the sad dead ends' – an endeavour that results in 'pull-out sentences, and multiple highspeed changes in direction' (18). This story, 'made up of so many digressions and evasions that in order to make it readable it would need to be divided in every direction' (18), is a narrative that depends upon a suspension between more than one state of attention. There are u-turns down caffeinated dead ends, but also long, dopey drives along one thought, then another, which run down, entropically, across extended pages.

The novel uses bifurcations or branchings – distracting sideshoots and digressions – in both its narrative and material form. Most of the pages include notes, indicated by a branched symbol which Lawrence Lenhart in one review describes as a 'wishbone [...] which intuitively means *wander*' (2012: n.p.) and according to Steven Poole in another is a 'half-finished gallows in Hangman' (2012: n.p.). To me, it looks most like the road-sign for a motorway junction or slip road (appropriate for the book's stories of Egyptian taxi-drivers), but if it is a slip road then it is a road to nowhere, with all of the notes it indicates ending at their 'sad dead ends' (Thirlwell 2012: 18). Rather than being located in the footer or in the margin, the notes indicated by the symbol are embedded inside each page's text, in blocks of various shapes and orientations, so reading the book means turning it from side to side and upside down. The book also uses fold-out pages, producing a reading motion that evokes and then shuts down the possibility of an infinitely extending page. The 2010s was the decade characterized by the infinite scroll of the constantly updated media feed – a development introduced in 2006 and adopted by Facebook, Twitter, and finally Instagram – and the fold-out pages of *Kapow!* ultimately emphasize the inevitability of the 'sad dead ends' of the printed page and of literary writing. Where the only end to reading the internet is the exhaustion of our attention, the book will (ideally) end before our attention does. Unlike the internet's infinite scroll, the book's inevitable limitations mean that it has to offer a form that is aware of filtering, selecting, choosing, and giving attention to time and to the reader as limiting factors. While it might seem that we could read the internet forever, follow every path and click every link, each of those unfolding avenues will be limited by our time and by our attention.

From its unfolding pages to its branching notes, then, *Kapow!* is non-linear and digressive. This non-linear shape contrasts with the form imposed on the events of the Arab Spring by English-language media coverage. The novel quotes the journalist Anne Applebaum, commenting on watching the events of the revolution unfold on TV: 'Television creates the illusion of a linear narrative and gives events the semblance of a beginning, a middle, and an end' (31). In contrast, the virtue that is celebrated in *Kapow!* is the ability to see many things at once, and to avoid being seduced by the illusion of linearity. The book starts with the observation, 'Everyone who was everywhere was using a videophone' (5). In contrast with the linearity of the TV news, the citizen journalists are everyone, everywhere, making 'miniature movies on the internet' of the multiple revolutions (5). From here, the book gives a series of instructions, cast in the second person, for how to extend forms of attention that are able to follow these multiple, distinct and diverging versions of events: 'You just have to keep looking, as everything splits into its infinite directions' (53); 'You have to manage this gorgeous acrobatic feat of looking in every direction' (71); 'You just have to describe in every direction and who gives a fuck about what it looks like' (78.5). Sometimes this 'you' is the reader and sometimes the writer, but what is clear is that this attention is not directed along the illusory linearity of old media narratives.

The text offers a form for a 'distracted era' by providing both the 'attention to time' and 'an attention to the reader' that Thirlwell prescribes in his piece in *The White Review*. As the narrator of *Kapow!* explains: 'It's always been about you, dear reader. If you want to know what is really a digression and what isn't, in a story, then you have to wait until the end' (71–72). *Kapow!* therefore does two things at once: it affirms that the kinds of attention activated by digital media are different from what has gone before, and offers forms which reflect on these changes, but at the same time maintains a clear distinction between the print book's 'dead ends' and the infinite directions of the digital.

Alison Gibbons makes the case that the multi-modal form of *Kapow!* conveys the mediation of world events for its 'young and fairly politically naïve London hipster' narrator (2015: 35). As a 'privileged Westerner', the narrator can only access the events of the uprising through its 'stylised' media portrayals (35). The book therefore functions as an investigation into the kinds of mediated, distant attention expected of people insulated from the events unfolding in faraway places. The early part of the 2010s was not only witnessing debate about the status of digital media reshaping democracy, protest, or the public sphere, but also about attention itself as a kind of activism. The year of *Kapow!*'s publication, 2012, was also the year of one of the most notorious examples of internet 'slacktivism', which attempted to leverage virality, by way of the digital attention economy, into political or social change: the Kony 2012 campaign. The aim of the campaign was to bring about the arrest of the Ugandan war criminal Joseph Kony by the end of 2012, through a strategy that involved as many people as possible watching a viral video about his crimes. At this moment in the early 2010s, the attention of privileged Westerners on the internet was, in and of itself, being understood as a political tool, and *Kapow!* participates in a broader critical discourse about the shortcomings of this experience of attention mediated through technology as a tool for political transformation.

This interest in depicting the mediated experience of watching terrible things happen elsewhere, and understanding the attention involved in that watching as an ethical or political resource, is a recurrent theme in 2010s British fiction. In Zadie Smith's 2013 story, *The Embassy of Cambodia*, for instance, a character wonders how to maintain a space for her own concerns in a world that is full of the overwhelming awareness of the need to attend to other people's stories:

> The fact is if we followed the history of every little country in the world – in its dramatic as well as its quiet times – we would have no space left in which to live our own lives or apply ourselves to our necessary tasks, never mind indulge in occasional pleasures, like swimming. Surely there is something to be said for drawing a circle around our attention and remaining within that circle. But how large should this circle be?
>
> Smith 2013: 23–24

There is a preoccupation here with the way that media extends attention and creates an obligation to attend. The action of 'drawing a circle around our attention' recognizes something material and direct: that the ethical attention of witnessing and caring, and the political attention of raised consciousness, has been turned (through clicks and viewing figures) into something measurable and commodifiable.

A slightly different version of the same image of the circle of attention occurs at the beginning of Ali Smith's *Autumn* (2016), the first book of her seasonal quartet. The novel begins with a character's perception posthumously extended to every horizon in a circle of attention that can focus in precisely on anything within that circle, 'as if he were using a camera zoom' (5). Inside this enhanced field of attention are both the bodies of the 'tide-dumped dead' and the oblivious holiday-makers elsewhere on the beach, 'sitting in the shade reading a little screen' (12). Smith's *Autumn* is both a Brexit novel and an exploration of the movement of people that responds to the humanitarian crisis unfolding on Europe's borders in the 2010s. In its representation of reading on the 'little screen', the novel identifies how the phone both opens up and forecloses possibilities of extended attention. On one hand, that extended attention threatens to overwhelm the 'circle' of attention with information overload, and on the other it can result in the inattentive obliviousness of the 'filter bubble'. In both Thirlwell's and Smith's work, the British reader is imagined as a person of relative privilege whose relationship with world events is mediated through the 'miniature movies' on the 'little screen' and whose most pressing concern is the management of the forms of attention that screen out or admit the ethical demands of these current events.

Kapow! and other novels like it therefore seem to address two questions. First, in the context of an attention economy in which British consumers of digital media were encouraged at every turn to understand their attention as a commodity and the act of attending to something as a form of political action in and of itself, what kinds of politics were made possible through the digital? Second, what role could literature – and especially the kinds of literature that operate in an experimental, defamiliarizing, attention-grabbing literary tradition – play in an era in which distraction itself has come to be understood as a social evil? *Kapow!* offers a rather ambivalent answer. It is a novel that emphasizes the ways in which its form is both like and unlike the internet, with its forking paths and its finite dead-ends. In the end, we can see in the fiction of this period an attempt to grapple with the relationship between commodified attention, digital media and politics. Thirlwell recognizes the position of both literature and politics within an attention economy and develops an experimental form that can view those forms of commodified attention through a long lens. Fiction, within its own sphere, separate from the internet, becomes a space for creative exploration of this contemporary concern and a place with enough distance to attend to the internet's politicized attention on its own terms.

Like, follow, ghost

In her 2018 essay, *Exposure*, Olivia Sudjic identifies a relationship between anxiety, distraction, and the digital that would come to dominate conversations about reading and attention by the end of the 2010s. She finds, with Kierkegaard, that 'anxiety is a special kind of attention' (60) and that reading the internet heightens anxiety, through a fearful superfluity of watchful attention: 'We are transfixed by the slot machine of our newsfeed. We become hypervigilant, monitoring each change in our environment for any potential threat' (42). As Sudjic explains, the algorithmic consequences of the attention economy result in a 'creeping feeling of being observed, followed, recorded, predicted' – an awareness that you are being watched over by both algorithmic and human attentions which in turn produces hypervigilant watchfulness and anxiety (64). It is this hypervigilant anxiety that becomes more prominent in Sudjic's discussions of distraction and fiction-reading. Sudjic's hypervigilance is not quite the same as the reports of 'pandemic brain' that appeared repeatedly in popular media discourses about reading being edged out by doomscrolling at the end of the decade, but it does seem to me to be closely related to it. This is a version of attention crisis that is a response to global crises that unfold in real time on the infinite scroll of a newsfeed.

In her first novel, *Sympathy* (2017), Sudjic explores a set of familiar preoccupations with attention that also appear in Self's *Phone* – including generational differences, the use of nootropics to improve focus, and difficulties with reading – but also addresses the anxieties evoked by the internet's illusion of one-way attention. If *Exposure* showed how the act of 'following' people or topics online also sees us exposing ourselves to the experience of 'being observed, followed, recorded, predicted' in return (2018: 64), Sudjic's *Sympathy* identifies the affective aspects of liking and likeness that emerge through the sympathetic resonances of digital intimacy.

Sympathy follows Alice Hare, a narrator who falls into that category of listless, directionless, lonely young women who became a staple of writing in the second half of the 2010s alongside the protagonists of Halle Butler's *The New Me* (2019), Rebecca Watson's *Little Scratch* (2020) and, perhaps the exemplar, Ottessa Moshfegh's *My Year of Rest and Relaxation* (2018). In Sudjic's novel, Alice goes to New York to stay with her grandmother and becomes obsessed with a woman, Mizuko Himura, whose Instagram she starts following through a series of chance connections. Eventually she engineers a meeting in real-life, after becoming convinced that their lives are running, sympathetically, in parallel with each other. She writes the story from a basement flat in Wood Green after being ghosted by Mizuko, torturing herself by looking through the 'porthole' of the profile picture on Mizuko's locked Instagram account (2017: 2) and receiving Google alerts from the 'million traps' she has set for Mizuko's name (6). At the end of the novel Alice gives an account of how she went from 'actively looking for her name' to being served results that related to Mizuko – 'I'd searched her name enough times by that point so that anything to do with her would seek me out without my soliciting it' – to setting up the alerts (404). Search algorithms register and repeat Alice's compulsive interest in Mizuko, conveying the sense that the attention economy's ideal form of attention is obsessive, monomaniacal and one-sided – the kind of parasocial relationship that means following someone and watching every day of their life in real time, but without them knowing anything about you in return.

The novel is also in some ways just as interested in attention and generational differences as Self's *Phone*, although its generations are micro-differentiated. Alice and Mizuko's relationship is shaped by their age gap, and Mizuko seems interested in twenty-three-year-old Alice mainly for her youth – her ability to hold the 'zeitgeist' (86). Mizuko theorizes that a change in attention has occurred which has also altered practices of reading: 'She seemed obsessed with my *generation*. She had led a class about how my *generation* couldn't physically cope with books anymore; they had been rewired and could now learn only through "gamification"' (78). Mizuko is thirty-two years old in the novel – an elder millennial, born in 1982 – so her *Shallows*-inspired comments about brain rewiring seem comically out of step with her own age. Later in the novel, Alice's uninspiring boyfriend, Dwight, explains his perspective on generational differences, with the assertion that they are living in an 'age of *connectivity*' (125). Dwight's background in 'business studies and digital marketing' find him always attempting to segment an audience and spot new trends, suggesting that generational distinctions as much about marketing as about attempting to define the present and to grapple with periodization (125).

However, despite her protestations, it is Mizuko who presents the clearest struggle with attention in the novel. Alice describes how, in spite of Mizuko's belief that she occupies the unsullied side of the 'digital divide' with a brain that has not yet been rewired, in truth 'her thoughts were nonlinear, more like a lattice', which leaves her 'predisposed [...] to getting distracted' (78). She is powerless to resist 'Wikipedia wormholes', to the point that she has to turn off her Wi-Fi or turn over her devices to her doorman in order to get any writing done. As the novel develops, Alice takes on the role of attention-monitor, instructing Mizuko to block her ex-boyfriend, keeping hold of her phone, and organizing a writing retreat to enable Mizuko to finish her book. Mizuko introduces Alice to Provigil (the brand name of Modafinil), which they both take off-label 'for days at a time' as an aid to concentration and focus (264). Alice describes the effects as producing 'selfish tunnel vision' – a rabbit hole in the novel's *Alice in Wonderland* thematics – and a 'state of deep concentration' (245, 334). Mizuko uses Provigil for writing, but Alice uses it for reading, to stop herself looking at her phone (328, 335). Alice, sure in her sympathetic looking-glass attention to Mizuko, believes that the latter thinks as she does, that 'her mind worked like mine' (78). However, as it transpires, Mizuko has been suffering from a more physical affliction: a brain parasite that, amongst its symptoms, produces difficulties with concentration and attention (345). What Alice understood to be a shared symptom of an age of distraction was, in fact, something with a very specific, material and individual cause. This illness is no longer a metaphor, and Alice's attempts to read it that way are revealed to be a mirror-image projection of her preoccupation with her own attention.

Mizuko's comments about young people's reading are significant, nevertheless, because they are the beginning of the novel's interest in the possibilities of writing fiction that can exist alongside the internet. Mizuko, teacher of creative non-fiction, argues that the novel is dead and that the internet killed it: 'Mizuko often said that novels were dead because we have the Internet everywhere we go now and we can find out anything we want to know straightaway, which tends to kill a plot. That was why she wrote just about real life' (79). This is not quite the same as Nicholas Carr struggling with concentration and 'dragging [his] wayward brain back to the text' or Will Self auguring the end of the 'Gutenberg mind', but it does directly oppose novel-reading and the internet and imply that distraction – or at least the absence of patient attention that can sustain itself through the delay that is inevitably involved in plotting – is a threat to the novel. *Sympathy* therefore sets itself the challenge of establishing modes of plotting that acknowledge they may test the concentration of a reader who can simply look up anything they want to know 'straightaway'. The book orchestrates some sly rejuvenation of old plot conventions by having Alice engineer the plot's coincidences and structuring parallels and similarities. Her belief in the sympathetic likeness of her own life and Mizuko's allows her to act as the agent of the plot inside the text by such digitally augmented means as using Instagram's location tags to orchestrate a chance meeting in a cafe.

By emulating an algorithm that serves up like for like (if you liked this, you'll like that) Alice not only participates in a broader pattern of liking and likeness that dominates the digital attention economy but intensifies it to the point where the whole feedback loop of liking and following collapses. She likes Mizuko too much, follows her too much, and her obsessive attention overflows the commodified channels that have previously kept it running. But, as Joanna Walsh reminds us in her book, *Girl Online*, the concept of likeness is not just one of repetition but also of alterity:

> We like the meme's likeness to what it is like. It is not identical but an iteration that might be surprising or funny or ironic or similar-but dissimilar, though always a bit like, and as an 'imitated thing', it is also something to imitate: an example. [...] Memes replace emotional content: they allow me to like not quite liking, not being quite like.
>
> Walsh 2022: 72

Like all mimetic art, like relatable content, we like the realist novel because it is both like and not-like life. To be able to look at something other and say, 'It me': this is also sympathy. The pattern of liking is a marker of interest and commodified attention – or even commodified care. Sudjic too observes the recirculation of likenesses and liking through 'stockpiling memes and "relatable content"' or following the 'prescribed codes of communication social media offers (hearts, emojis, follows)' (2018: 39). Both Walsh and Sudjic therefore identify a narrowing of possible responses that appears under the rubric of likeness. Likeness recurs in the image of the mirror, which appears repeatedly in 2010s responses to the digital, from the British TV series *Black Mirror* (written by Charlie Brooker and first broadcast in 2011) to Jia Tolentino's book of essays, *Trick Mirror*, from 2019.

Walsh's *Girl Online*, glimmers with references to *Alice Through the Looking Glass*, while *Sympathy*'s Alice Hare is in an even more complicated hall of Alice mirrors, looking into her phone and seeing her own reflection, but also passing through the device and into wonderland. Nicknamed Rabbit by her family and by Mizuko – a name which sees her imagined as both the self-sacrificing rabbit in the moon in the Japanese folktale and the white rabbit leading Alice down the rabbithole – Alice represents the confusion between leading and following, stalking and ghosting, which comes about when technology reshapes and reflects our attention back to us in forms that are both intensified and inverted. If Alice 'lacks an identity except that which she siphons from a woman she stalks online' (2018: 64) – the action of 'liking', 'following', observing and attending to Mizuko and her life has made Alice into her mirror or likeness.

As well as turning a fresh eye to plot and to mimesis in the age of distraction, *Sympathy* is also interested in a third new way in which attention and fiction converge in the 2010s: the way that description can record new configurations of noticing and attention to the everyday. In the novel, Alice describes how Mizuko's Instagram transforms 'ordinary pavement markings [...] slants of light, shadows on brick, foam feet' (85), making everyday things beautiful through the kind of attentive, curatorial acts of selection and observation that the app encourages. Robin, the man who, it eventually transpires, is Mizuko's father, exhibits the same talent for noticing and recording ordinary things. Later in the novel, Alice finds him photographing 'odd stuff' to produce an album of 'shadows, leaves, bricks, pipes' (232–233). Both Mizuko and Robin bring 'a very specific attention to things' (233), which Alice tries to emulate: 'I began to look at plain, ordinary-seeming things in the way I thought she might look at them and so to try to remake them like she did' (85). Before we reach this point in the text, however, we have already read Alice noticing and narrating in exactly this vein:

> The sun was low in the sky, its light arrowing straight across from one side of the island to the other, west to east, blinding us. We looked down at our feet as we walked. The spokes of light picked out each herringbone brick and made it redder. Our shadows cast us as a ludicrous double act.
>
> Sudjic 2017: 67

The shadows, the slanting light, the bricks – all the elements that Alice has taken up from Mizuko and Robin's transfigurations of ordinary objects are here, in Alice's retrospective narration. To read it the first time is to see it as an extraordinarily acute act of noticing, but to read it again, knowing that it is one of the things Alice has 'siphoned' from Mizuko, is to see this scene as a pastiche, a meme, a looking-glass reflection – something that has been liked and followed from elsewhere.

Part of this emphasis on noticing, I think, accords with the observations of Andrew Epstein, who finds that 'the contemporary "crisis of attention" is also profoundly connected to [...] a preoccupation with the everyday' that he names 'everyday hunger' (2016: 4). Epstein sees this interest in the ordinary surfacing across twentieth-century poetry, only to appear in an intensified form in the twenty-first century and to be channelled through online platforms such as Facebook and Instagram, which commodify their users' desire to record quotidian experience. But in Sudjic's writing these acts of outward attention and noticing can also be a way for characters to draw attention away from themselves: Alice replicates Mizuko's curatorial noticing as a substitute for forming an identity of her own.

Sudjic's essay, *Exposure*, is preoccupied by the risks – especially to women – of attracting attention or seeming to court attention. Sudjic quotes from an interview with Rachel Cusk in which she describes how, following the brutal reception of her memoir, *Aftermath* (2012), she became a writer whose identity – as she put it – was 'obscured' after having 'lost all interest in having a self' (Cusk 2017, 'Rachel Cusk gut-renovates the novel', n.p.). In *Exposure* Sudjic finds in Cusk's subsequent work a writer who, even as she is obscured, is '[m]ore keenly observant than ever' (2018: 112). This work, the trilogy of autofiction that includes *Outline*, *Transit* and *Kudos*, follows its writer-protagonist, Faye, who somehow disappears in her careful acts of attention to other people: '[s]trangers expose themselves to her', Sudjic comments, but she is 'over-exposing herself to the point of blankness' (2018: 116–117). The obscured author and the overexposed narrator enter into a complex dynamic of attention, in which noticing distracts from the noticing subject. Writing about Cusk's Faye, Merve Emre (2018: n.p.) describes how, in the trilogy, 'Cusk wants us to notice Faye noticing', and this noticing of noticing is a feature of *Sympathy* too, in its memeing of Alice's 'very specific attention' to the details of the everyday. But if Alice is overexposed, one of the things that seems to be bleached out in this process is her Blackness, which is hinted at in passing in the course of the novel (a question from a child here, an awkward invitation to the tennis club there) and only confirmed when she signs up to an app for threesomes and is 'inundated with messages from white men saying that their girlfriends had always wanted to have sex with a black woman' (2017: 336). As with the novel's other examples of the digital as attention-intensifier, it is only through the (unwanted, gendered and racialized) attention of others that Alice's identity is exposed.

Sympathy is an Instagram novel, which understands the phone camera as a mediator of attention and a valve for regulating the flow of attention through the looking glass of the digital interface. The 2010 iPhone 4, the first iPhone with both a front-facing camera and a back-facing camera, popularized the selfie and could be said to emblematize the division of postable subjects into the self and the everyday world of curated images of sharply noticed shadows, bricks, pavements and feet ('Apple Presents iPhone 4': 2010). If *Sympathy* conceives of the phone as an object through which attention of many kinds can flow, Sudjic also recognizes that this is not something wholly new. In *Exposure* she observes that liking and following create an 'illusory intimacy that can shadow the experience of reading or writing fiction' (2018: 39). New-old kinds of intimacy can emerge through the internet, which register lightness, distance, distraction. And we would be foolish not to recognize these as the intimacies that also draw us to reading and writing.

There are aspects of *Sympathy*'s twisting form which are close to those in *Kapow!*. Its chain-like, claustrophobic narrative structure means that we follow Alice from one location to another, as she recalls different parts of her relationship with Mizuko out of chronological order. Reading the novel is most like going down a Wikipedia rabbithole, leaving you unsure where you started and impressed by the tangential interlinking of its elements. Alice describes her narrative as tracing 'each little link in the chain' of events, each involving an unlikely coincidence bringing her closer to Mizuko (8). But, as Alice's narration reflects on the structure of her own story, she also comments on the internet's open-ended connectivity: 'That generation [boomers] tends to think in terms of beginnings and endings. They don't understand what you can do with the Internet, or how there's no end to things, no way out' (233). Alice's escalating obsession sees her – even at the novel's end – hoping that her connection to Mizuko will be restored and that there will be no end to their relationship. But novels do have to end and must put a limit on the things they include, rather than only stopping when their readers stop.

Writing about her 2020 novel, *Little Scratch*, Rebecca Watson describes how 'the pressures of an age of distraction' resulted in formal experimentation and inspired her to 'shake up form' and 'break up prose' (Watson 2019). This has been the case for all the writers considered here, whose fiction develops new approaches to novelistic conventions of plot, character and description, new kinds of physical and textual objects, and new ways of conveying thoughts and voices. The fiction of the 2010s needed new ways to tell the stories of the decade.

These novels exist in self-conscious dialogue not only with the internet in general, but with the always-on, real-time, infinite scrolling of social media platforms on a personal mobile device. I've argued here that this form of being online was understood in popular discourse as reading's Other in the 2010s. Reading – and especially the sustained reading of novels – was enlisted as both a marker of 'healthy' attention and a prescription for attention in crisis, but none of these novels seem to readily accept a role for themselves as aids to attention or cures for distraction. Their inattentive, distracted, obsessive, hypervigilant or stimulant-fuelled characters are not cautionary tales or models for our attention. Neither are their forms an exercise in self-improvement to show readers how to regulate or manage their focus. Instead, in these fictions we see attention appear as something dynamic and various, which extends between characters and outwards to their readers in ways that often run counter to the optimizing logic of the prevailing cultural attitudes to attention. It is closer to the diverse attentions described by those theorists of critical attention studies such as Stiegler, Citton and Hayles than the commodified and economized attention that came to dominate digital platforms in this decade. These fictions affirm attention not as a faculty that should be dutifully schooled through reading, but instead as a necessarily unruly force which, even as it is organized and administered through a contemporary attention economy, still emerges in unpredictable, disruptive ways.

Notes

1 For example, David L. Ulin's book *The Lost Art of Reading: Why Books Matter in a Distracted Time* (2010) and Alan Jacobs's *The Pleasures of Reading in an Age of Distraction* (2011) both emerge from the same moment at the start of the 2010s and underscore an opposition between reading and the distracted present. They incorporate a defence of reading and its concentrated, deep attention, which can correct or mitigate digital distraction. It's an argument that persists through to the end of the decade in books such as Megan Cox Gurdon's *The Enchanted Hour: The Miraculous Power of Reading Aloud in the Age of Distraction* (2019) and Maryanne Wolf's *Reader, Come Home: The Reading Brain in the Digital World* (2019). All of these examples demonstrate a broader trope that opposes spending time reading books and spending time online.

2 The number of pieces on 'pandemic brain' are too many to catalogue, but here is a representative selection of titles from 2020–21: Kelli María Korducki in *The Guardian*, 'I have 'pandemic brain': will I ever be able to concentrate again?'; Sarah Manavis in the *New Statesman*, 'Why can't we focus during the pandemic?';

Kate Morgan on the BBC, 'How Anxiety Affects your Focus'; Lizzie Thomson in the *Metro*, 'Lockdown has killed our attention span – this is why we are struggling to focus on everything and anything'.

3   Ekaterina Stepanova's (2011) article 'The Role of Information Communication Technologies in the "Arab Spring": Implications Beyond The Region' summarizes and analyses some of the debate in news and commentary from European and US media, including making reference to a popular intervention by Malcolm Gladwell in the *New Yorker* in September 2010, which sparked significant debate.

Works cited

'Apple Presents iPhone 4'. *Apple.com*, 7 June 2010: https://www.apple.com/uk/newsroom/2010/06/07Apple-Presents-iPhone-4/ (accessed 23 June 2023).

Bennett, Alice. '"Tuning into my 'awareness continuum'": Optimized Attention in *The Yips*', in *Nicola Barker: Critical Essays*. Berthold Schoene (ed.). Canterbury: Gylphi, 2020.

Bennett, Alice. *Contemporary Fictions of Attention: Reading and Distraction in the Twenty-First Century*. London: Bloomsbury, 2018.

Carr, Nicholas. *The Shallows: How the Internet Is Changing the Way We Think, Read and Remember*. London: Atlantic Books, 2011.

Citton, Yves. *The Ecology of Attention*. Barnaby Norman (trans.). London: Polity, 2017.

Cusk, Rachel. 'Rachel Cusk gut-renovates the novel'. Interview with Judith Thurman. *The New Yorker*, 31 July 2017: https://www.newyorker.com/magazine/2017/08/07/rachel-cusk-gut-renovates-the-novel (accessed 26 June 2023).

Emre, Merve. 'Of Note'. *Harpers*, June 2018: 'https://harpers.org/archive/2018/06/of-note/ (accessed 26 June 2023).

Epstein, Andrew. *Attention Equals Life: The Pursuit of the Everyday in Contemporary Poetry and Culture*. Oxford: Oxford University Press, 2016.

Gibbons, Alison. '"Take that you intellectuals!" and "kaPOW!": Adam Thirlwell and the Metamodernist Future of Style'. *Studia Neophilologica* 87, 2015: 29–43.

Hayles, N. Katherine. 'How We Read: Close, Hyper, Machine'. *ADE Bulletin*, no. 150, 2010: 62–79.

Hayles, N. Katherine. 'Hyper and Deep Attention: The Generational Divide in Cognitive Modes'. *Profession*, 2007: 187–199.

James, William. *The Principles of Psychology*. 2 vols. 1890. Cambridge, MA: Harvard University Press, 1981.

Lenhart, Lawrence. 'Review: Adam Thirlwell, *Kapow!*, Visual Editions, 2012'. *The Diagram* 12.6: https://thediagram.com/12_6/rev_thirlwell.html (accessed 26 June 2023).

Pariser, Eli. *Filter Bubble: What the Internet Is Hiding from You*. London: Penguin, 2012.

Poole, Steven. 'Kapow! by Adam Thirlwell – review'. *The Guardian*, 25 May 2012: https://www.theguardian.com/books/2012/may/25/kapow-adam-thirlwell-review (accessed 26 June 2023).

Pressman, Jessica. *Bookishness: Loving Books in a Digital Age*. New York: Columbia University Press, 2020.

Rahman, Zia Haider. *In the Light of What We Know*. London: Picador, 2014.

Self, Will. 'The novel is dead (this time it's for real)'. *The Guardian*, 2 May 2014a: https://www.theguardian.com/books/2014/may/02/will-self-novel-dead-literary-fiction (accessed 26 June 2023).

Self, Will. *Phone*. London: Penguin, 2017.

Self, Will. *Umbrella*. London: Bloomsbury, 2012.

Self, Will. 'Will Self: The fate of our literary culture is sealed'. *The Guardian*, 3 October 2014b: https://www.theguardian.com/books/2014/oct/03/fate-literary-culture-sealed-internet-will-self (accessed 26 June 2023).

Self, Will. *Grey Area*. London: Bloomsbury, 1994.

Shaw, Katy. *Crunch Lit*. London: Bloomsbury, 2014.

Shaw, Katy. *Crunch Lit*. London: Bloomsbury, 2015.

Smith, Ali. *Autumn*. London: Hamish Hamilton, 2016.

Smith, Zadie. *The Embassy of Cambodia*. London: Hamish Hamilton, 2013.

Stepanova, Ekaterina. 'The Role of Information Communication Technologies in the "Arab Spring"'. *Ponars Eurasia* 15.1, 2011: 1–6.

Stiegler, Bernard. *Taking Care of Youth and the Generations*. Stephen Barker (trans.). Stanford, CA: Stanford University Press, 2010.

Sudjic, Olivia. *Exposure*. London: Peninsula Press, 2018.

Sudjic, Olivia. *Sympathy*. London: Pushkin Press, 2017.

Thirlwell, Adam. *Kapow!* London: Visual Editions, 2012.

Thirlwell, Adam. 'Literature in a Distracted Era'. *The White Review*, August 2014. https://www.thewhitereview.org/feature/the-2014-white-review-short-story-prize-announcement-speech/ (accessed 26 June 2023).

Walsh, Joanna. *Girl Online: A User's Manual*. London: Verso, 2022.

Watson, Rebecca. 'The Art of Fiction in the Age of Social Media'. *FT*, 8 November 2019: https://www.ft.com/content/f551cc98-fefa-11e9-b7bc-f3fa4e77dd47 (accessed 26 June 2023).

White, Duncan. 'Will Self's Phone is a Brilliant, Epic Anti-Tweet – Review'. *The Telegraph*, 8 June 2017: https://www.telegraph.co.uk/books/what-to-read/will-selfs-phone-brilliant-epic-anti-tweet-review/ (accessed 9 August 2023).

3

Border Crossings: Diasporic British Fiction of the 2010s

Emily Horton

Introduction

In examining literary representations of migration published in the 2010s, a concern arises with just how much has changed socially, politically, culturally and economically since the start of the millennium, but also with how the enormous shifts in migration policy initiated with the events of September 11, 2001 have continued to impact upon cultural and literary production in familiar ways. These latter events are widely recognized to have brought about increased discrimination against South Asian, Middle Eastern, and African Muslim diasporic communities living across the West, as a governmentally sanctioned discourse of US national trauma was deployed in response to the attacks to justify retaliatory wars in Iraq and Afghanistan, and to initiate an ongoing 'War on Terror' both at home and abroad. As Deepa Kumar explains, '[i]n the months that followed [September 11], tens of thousands of Muslims were "interviewed" by the state, and thousands were imprisoned, tortured, and deported; a whole process of demonization had begun' (Kumar 2012: 5). While the initial post-9/11 novel largely ignored this persecutory experience, seeking instead to respond to 'the immediate trauma of "the day itself"' within a local New York or US context, as Daniel O'Gorman reflects, subsequent literary writers have sought to expand and alter this fiction's contextual and ideological outlook, 'reframing [...] the 9/11 genre' in more critical ways (O'Gorman 2015: 6 and 7).

Much of this work, as criticism by Sara Upstone (2010), Sadia Abbas (2014), Rehana Ahmed (2015), Peter Morey (2018), and Claire Chambers (2019) amongst others has shown, can be attributed to diasporic South Asian, Middle Eastern, and African writers themselves, often of a Muslim background, whose fiction repeatedly returns to questions of migrant identity in a post-9/11 world.

While keeping in mind the danger of laying the burden of post-9/11 literature solely on the shoulders of immigrant or Muslim writers, or otherwise promoting an ideal of immigrant or Muslim writing as necessarily more 'authentic' in its account of this experience (Morey 2018: 8), on the other hand, it remains important to recognize how such writers – whose communities have been repeatedly silenced by the dominant culture – have nevertheless spearheaded innovative post-9/11 writing in critical directions. As Pei-chen Liao writes, such works 'open up spaces for readers to reach beyond the narrow category of the "9/11" fiction and […] to recognise the uncanny fact that 9/11 is not yet over' (Liao 2013: 19). My argument in this chapter develops from this suggestion, exploring how several contemporary British South Asian diasporic writers in the 2010s continue this reframing project, confronting 9/11's ongoing prejudicial repercussions both for society and politics in the wake of 7/7 and in response to an increasingly racialized and prevention-directed policy landscape.

Of course, the 2010s themselves have witnessed considerable transformations both to migrant experience and immigration policy across the globe, which further impact on the articulation and deployment of 'War on Terror'-related policies. The Syrian Civil War, beginning in 2011, brought in its wake a refugee crisis of dramatic proportions: while for 2010, the UNHCR lists 10.5 million refugees worldwide, by 2020, the figure has nearly doubled, reaching 20.7 million, not including 48 million internally displaced persons (UNHCR 2021). This radical transmutation of numbers across the decade brought with it a shift to the right for many Western governments, perhaps most overtly reflected in the election of Donald Trump as US President in 2017, on the back of a strongly anti-immigrant agenda and followed shortly by an executive order banning entry into the United States to citizens of seven predominantly Muslim countries. In Britain, this shift is also reflected in the success of the Brexit Referendum in June 2016, determining the withdrawal of the United Kingdom from the European Union, an event which fuelled a range of literary and artistic responses from across the country, as Kristian Shaw also explores in his chapter in this volume. Importantly, this event encompasses numerous social, cultural, political and economic concerns, connected both to conservative and liberal interests, where many on the Left were also decidedly in favour of Brexit, often for reasons disconnected from race or immigration. For example, many had long identified the EU as a problematic bastion of neoliberal policies and values (see Hermann 2007; Duman 2014; Socialist Worker 2017). Nevertheless, as Ankhi Mukherjee reflects, the campaign's repeated invocations of exaggerated net migration figures, accompanied by posters 'purportedly showing migrants and refugees arriving in hordes to a Britain made borderless by the EU', unmistakably invoke an anti-immigrant outlook on cultural politics (2018: 77–78). Indeed, the racialized politics implicit in this discourse were further augmented by more extreme right-wing campaigns visibly emergent at the time, such as 'Britain First', which as Madeline-Sophie Abbas writes, quoting the TUC, 'was characterized "by highly divisive rhetoric and sensationalist appeals to racial and nation sentiment," that by conflating issues of immigration, the so-called "refugee crisis" in Europe and Islamic terrorism, encouraged resentment towards new and settled minority ethnic groups, and Muslims in particular' (2019: 2453). Given the radical impact of these events on received understandings of national identity and belonging, where this became increasingly determined by a conservative, anti-multicultural invocation of 'British values' (Chaudhury 2017: 229, 234), it seems no surprise that British South Asian fiction should make this experience a key priority for investigation, confronting and challenging what emerges as a heightened social and political antagonism towards migrant (and especially Muslim) communities, and as a broadening of state powers in the realm of surveillance and counter-terrorism (O'Toole et al. 2016: 167, 171–172).

Yet if Brexit emerges as Britain's most obvious touchstone for recent anti-immigrant feeling, it should not be forgotten that immigration policy in the country faced major changes long before June 2016, thus instancing a significant continuity between this decade and the last. As Colin Yeo points out, the notorious Hostile Environment Policy of 2012 – under which those suspected of not having a legal status are '[cut] off from the necessities of life and prevented access to public services,' as well as being made at risk of detention and deportation – can be traced back to early post-9/11 legislation, which was then revised and extended to encompass a larger immigrant population (2020: 29). As he explains, 'the idea was that it was hard to arrest, prosecute and convict actual terrorists themselves, but it might be easier to target them indirectly by cutting off financial and other support from sympathizers and donors' (28–29). When David Cameron's government in the 2010s then sought to target net migration, he (and Theresa May as Foreign Secretary) reapplied this 'same principle of indirect influence' to migrants themselves, thus setting in place a security policy that overtly criminalized these populations, including long established British migrant communities, as unlawful residents (29).

As the Windrush Scandal of 2018 subsequently illustrated, this policy, and the associated legislation set in place by the Immigration Acts of 2014 and 2016, has radically discriminatory implications not only for those unauthorized in the country, but also for many lawful British residents without access to required documentation, leading to 'thousands of people being detained, deported and denied access to housing, healthcare, education and financial services' (El-Enany 2020: 32). Amelia Gentleman, who covered this story in the *The Guardian*, aptly summarizes its damning national significance when she writes that the scandal 'came as the direct result of a government attempt to assuage the anxieties of a nation stoked up into a frenzy about immigration. [...] Ministers tackled these concerns with a brutality that had devastating consequences for many' (2019: 10). In this way, the tightening of borders set in place post-9/11 makes way for an even more aggressive anti-immigrant politics in the 2010s, effectively pulling apart established British communities in the name of national security and border control.

In this chapter, looking at works by Kamila Shamsie, Mohsin Hamid, and Guy Gunaratne, I consider these writers' critical responses to this 'hostile environment', seeing these as contributing to a larger *ongoing* contemporary literary re-reading of post-9/11 society and politics attentive to the shifting and increasingly biopolitical register of UK policy. More specifically, borrowing from postcolonial theory a concern with how imperial violence continues to shape contemporary politics, contributing to a reactionary obsession with patrolling a threatened neo-colonial state, I read these novels as partaking in a conjoint project of post-9/11 and postcolonial reimagining, directly challenging the dominant governmental and media discourses on migrants and migration in favour of a more critical cosmopolitan approach to 'security'-related issues. The fact that all these writers choose Britain as a principal setting for this exploration, in this way underlining Brexit-era governmental policy shaping immigration law, further sees these novels responding more specifically to Britain's role within this larger post-9/11 context, positioning this directly against a longer (and ongoing) imperialist agenda, and questioning how this programme impacts upon current right-wing prejudice against migrant communities. My argument thus investigates both the historical and socio-political positioning of this representation within 2010s Britain, examining how the particular generic innovations these texts employ – tragedy, for Shamsie; speculative fiction, for Hamid; realism, for Gunaratne – respond to this discriminatory politics in critical and oppositional ways.

Tragedy and the repatriation narrative in *Home Fire*

One form in which this exploration emerges, then, is through a concerted attention to contemporary discourses on security and migration, not only as these unfold in relation to new UK migrant communities, in the context of the post-Syria 'refugee crisis', but also longstanding migrant populations previously welcomed under a multiculturalist agenda, but who have since seen their rights increasingly restricted following 9/11 and 7/7. As Jago Morrison reflects, 'even in the immediate aftermath of 9/11, speculation on the risk of Islamist violence focused almost exclusively on the idea of foreign born sleeper cells waiting to inflict atrocities on Western cities' (2017: 568). By contrast, 'the bombing of the London Underground in July 2005 [...] saw a major shift of attention towards the idea of the danger posed by home-grown extremists', a concern which authorized a new focus on 'radicalization' as a governmental priority (568). This redirection of energies, as Charlotte Heath-Kelly also comments, has had major consequences for the perception of British Muslims since that date, where increasingly an outlook of 'suspicion' and 'pity' enshrouds governmental engagements with this community, requiring proof of Britishness, while at the same time portraying Muslims as 'vulnerable' or susceptible of 'becoming risky' (2013: 405, 407).

As Madeline-Sophie Abbas explains regarding the 2010s more specifically, such 'questions of Muslim loyalty' have shifted even further during the Syrian conflict, 'as British-born Muslims have travelled to fight alongside IS or Daesh in Syria', in this way invoking a concern with terrorists 'returning to enact violence at home having received training in Syria' (2019: 2454). Such narratives of invasion play on a long-enduring imperial Gothic fear of 'reverse colonisation', which situates the racial other explicitly as 'primitive', encroaching, and innately dangerous (2454), returning to the unsuspecting colonial metropolis to inflict retributive damage. Under this Gothicized discourse, as Sivamohan Valluvan explains, 'the increasingly trenchant, nigh world-historical anxieties tied to the figure of the Muslim – as patriarchal, indolent, violent, [and] fanatical' become a convenient means by which contemporary politicians reaffirm a popular 'nationalist orientation', manipulating Western cultural apprehensions 'that hinge on certain iconic figures of non-belonging' (2019: 5).

Looking to Shamsie's *Home Fire* (2017), this critical understanding directly illuminates the text's tragedy-bound reading of contemporary Britain, where, as under Home Secretaries Theresa May, Sajid Javid, Priti Patel and Suella Braverman, Muslim migrant communities have faced an increasing politics of suspicion, and where likewise, repatriation has repeatedly been denied to members of terrorist organizations who have asked to return to Britain to revoke these alignments, as for example in the well-known case of Shamima Begum (see Speckhard and Ellenberg 2020; Masters and Regilme 2020). Shamsie's choice of Sophocles' *Antigone* as inspiration for this project underlines these concerns explicitly, where Creon's post-war refusal of Antigone's plea for Polyneices' burial effectively summarizes the terrorist-cum-patriot's disenfranchised position, but also the attendant tensions placed on the terrorist's family and the larger community to declare their loyalties to the state and to decide between family and the law. Interestingly, Judith Butler also finds inspiration from *Antigone* in writing on the precarity of the post-9/11 terror suspect, where Polyneices' failed access to 'grievability', for her, stands in for the lives of such de-patriated individuals, supposedly undeserving of mourning on account of their links to extremism (2004: 34).[1] 'Violence against those who are already not quite living,' she writes, 'that is, living in a state of suspension between life and death, leaves a mark that is no mark. There will be no public act of grieving (said Creon in *Antigone*)' (2004: 36). In *Home Fire*, Shamsie extends on this understanding to confront the 'state of exception' introduced by post-7/7 British law in relation to the radicalized subject, building on Butlerian ideas of revoked 'grievability' both in her critique of terrorist networks themselves and the British state.

In accordance with the classic five-act play, the novel is divided into five parts, each focalized through a different perspective, in this way granting voice to a range of contrasting contemporary social outlooks. These viewpoints are also, importantly, the voices of Sophocles' *Antigone*, foregrounding that work's central opposition between the family and the state, and the continuing biopolitical practice of monitoring and enforcing national loyalty post-9/11 and 7/7. This focus can be seen from the start of the novel, where despite the fact that Isma (the novel's Ismene figure) frets over US customs and immigration in her travels, 'certain they would detain her or put her on a plane back to London' (2017: 7–8), in the event of flying itself, it is Heathrow security which features most prominently in the narrative, as Isma is held for extensive questioning on account of her family connections to terrorism, determinedly rehearsing in her head the appropriate response to enquiries probing 'her Britishness' (5). This opening, rather than dismiss the threat that US immigration control holds for Muslim travellers, instead turns the camera inwards, to comment specifically on UK anti-immigration politics post-7/7, exploring how British citizenship itself has become increasingly precarious on account of tightened security measures, especially in response to the figure of the 'home-grown extremist' and the correspondent threat of UK-based radicalization.

In line with the novel's Sophoclean reference-point, Isma responds to this test as Ismene would, with conformity and concession, thanking 'the woman whose thumbprints were on her underwear, not allowing even a shade of sarcasm to enter her voice' (7). In so doing, she underlines what Urzula Rutkowska identities as a central 'problem facing the British-Muslim community,' namely, 'that unless British-Muslims present themselves as an embodiment of "British values", often through the acceptance of discrimination, they will not be allowed to think of themselves as British' (2022: 9). Her conformism in this way bows to state norms on behalf of her own and her family's wellbeing, refusing to pay a higher price for the sake of personal dignity, an attitude she later reaffirms in reporting her brother Parvaiz for his connections to Syria. As she puts it to her sister, Aneeka, 'We're in no position to let the state question our loyalties. [...] if you co-operate, it makes a difference' (42). Despite this concession to state edict, however, Isma remains aware of Britain's long history of legal infringements on minority rights and conscious of the injustice of her brother's position, where this can be understood in terms of a longer (racialized) history of policing and exclusion: a 'precedent for depriving people of their rights' on account of their ethnic and/or racial background (38). 'The only difference,' Isma explains, 'is this time it's applied to British citizens [...] rhetorically being made unBritish [...,] always something interposed between their Britishness and terrorism' (38). Isma thus highlights for the reader recent state efforts to disguise Britain's terrorist connections and in this way to justify its discriminatory, rights-infringing treatment of British Muslims, connecting this to a colonial legacy of systematic oppression.

As Nira Yuval-Davis explains, these policies invoke the reassertion of a nationalist 'politics of belonging' within a post-7/7 Britain, wherein the question of 'how [it is] possible that "British" people were about to carry out such atrocities in Britain' underscores a pressing cultural anxiety that 'people's nationality [must] be more important to them than their religious and political beliefs', and indeed that supposedly *real* British citizens remain somehow '"immune" from taking part in such an attack' (2011: 1). While Isma bends to the pressure such discourses place upon her, reporting her brother and insistently positioning him as an 'enem[y] of both Britain and Islam' (197), by contrast Aneeka, the novel's Antigone figure, directly questions this compliance, affirming that, had the state not known, Parvaiz 'could have come home [...]. You've made him not able to come home' (42). Aneeka's dissent against her sister's conformity in this way predicates her refusal of a security-driven state imperative: her brother's whereabouts, she implies, are not the business of the UK government, nor must she comply with its denunciatory protocol to prove her own or his belonging.

In light of the novel's romantic sub-plot, it becomes important that this perspective informs Aneeka's relationship with Eamonn, as she seeks to manipulate his family connections to secure her brother's repatriation, but also to change his views on national belonging, gradually instilling in him a more tolerant and faith-accepting perspective. Thus, from the start of the novel, Eamonn negotiates a distinctly Islamophobic mentality, questioning in response to Isma's turban, whether 'Cancer or Islam' is 'the greater affliction' (21). Indeed, he reiterates a prominent Orientalist stereotype of Islam as 'dysfunctional and anti-modern' (Aistrope 2016: 184) as he invokes 'the need for British Muslims to lift themselves out of the Dark Ages' (59). As Debjani Banerjee reflects, 'This binary of Dark Ages and Enlightenment is one that the text borrows from the public discourses of the time. Distilled understanding from these easy binaries was that Britishness as a value had to be instilled into young men and women,' this set in distinct contrast to the supposed barbarism of Muslim culture (2020: 295). In opposing this Manichean perspective, then, the text promotes a more open-minded, postcolonial perception on national identity, 'enabled and energized by London's transcultural traffic which perpetually traverses national borders' (McLeod 2004: 18).

Also in contrast to Aneeka's open-mindedness is the character of Karamat Lone, the voice of national assimilation, and the novel's Creon figure. 'Don't set yourselves apart', he tells a group of Muslim students, '[not] in the way you dress, the way you think, the outdated codes of behaviour you cling to, [...] Because if you do, you will be treated differently [...] from everyone else' (87–87). More specifically, the novel suggests that Muslims in particular will be treated as enemies of the state, condemned for their apparel, appearance, and cultural practices as presumed terrorists. As Arun Kundnani reflects, this suspicion (what he calls 'values racism' (2012: 155–156)) has become central to Britain's Prevent programme, which since 2006 has set in place a 'wide-ranging anti-terrorist legislation' intended to identify and curtail terrorists in advance of actual terrorist activities, including by equating moderate Islamic ideological positions with extremism (2015: 162). Under this framework, 'Intelligence officials argued that the government could not wait until extremism turned into terrorism; there had to be interventions earlier in the process' (157). This shift towards prevention and surveillance thus works to fuel anti-Muslim sentiment, a phenomenon made explicit in *Home Fire* not only in Karamat's remarks, but also through a wider textual engagement with interventionary discourses. For example, in a joke Eamonn shares with his affluent liberal peers following his absence from their friendship group, the novel makes clear the dubious indicators aligned to intervention within the upper classes:

> "I don't know," Max said, "Twenty-something unemployed male from Muslim background exhibits rapidly altered pattern of behaviour, cuts himself off from old friends, moves under the radar. Also, are we sure that's an evening shadow rather than an incipient beard? I think we may need to alert the authorities."
>
> Shamsie 2017, 82

While this commentary emerges as intended humour within this context, no one actually believing Eamonn to be at risk of being radicalized, for other characters in the novel, its threat is expressly real. In effect, all members of the Pasha family are variously subjected to suspicion and intervention at some point in the text, precisely on account of their Islamic identities: for Isma, in the airport, where she is detained and interrogated (1–7); for Aneeka, on the bus, where she is spat at (90); and for Parvaiz, in unwarranted police detainments under a Stop and Search policy (132). These confrontations with British law reinforce the state's own role in alienating Muslim citizens, as well as, as Jonathan Githens-Mazer and Robert Lambert write, the way in which 'the label of "radicalization" has become a tool of power exercised by the state and non-Muslim communities against, and to control, Muslim communities in the twenty-first century' (2010: 901). Indeed, it is precisely Karamat's Prevent-intoned comments on the need for assimilation, made public via the media, that function to place Isma, Aneeka, and Parvaiz in an increasingly precarious position across the course of the text, setting them up as the focal point of government and media antagonism. As Aneeka comments to Eamonn, following Karamat's speech on assimilationism:

> What do you say to your father when he makes a speech like that? Do you say, Dad, you're making it OK to stigmatise people for the way they dress? Do you say, what kind of idiot stands in front of a group of teenagers and tells them to conform? Do you say, why didn't you mention that among the things this country will let you achieve if you're Muslim is torture, rendition, detention without trial, airport interrogations, spies in your mosques, teachers reporting your children to the authorities for wanting a world without British injustice?
>
> Shamsie 2017: 90–91

In this passage, Aneeka identifies the biopolitical surveillance mechanisms set in place by the post-9/11 British state, which include a range of human rights infringements justified in the name of state security, and which directly affect her own life on a deeply personal level. The novel's repeated attention to these exceptional practices reaffirms its critical response to War on Terror policy, where 'a broader shift to a "pre-crime", preventive paradigm in security policy' sets in place 'the development of denaturalisation as a policy tool', a supposedly acceptable, while at the same time rights-infringing, measure in preserving 'British values' (Choudhury 2017: 228).

Following the narrative arc of *Antigone*, *Home Fire*'s plot brings this reactionary state-mandate around to its tragic conclusions, as Karamat refuses to concede to Aneeka's plea for her brother's repatriation and instead condemns her too to statelessness. Karamat's wife, Terry, emerging as the voice of Sophocles' Tiresias, announces the reversal of circumstances, the *peripeteia*, that leads to Karamat's downfall: 'A few days ago your greatest rival was a man born with a diamond-encrusted spoon in his mouth, a party insider for years', she says. 'And now it's this orphaned student [...]. Look at her, Karamat: look at this sad child you've raised to your enemy and see how far you've lowered yourself in doing that' (253). With this ending, the novel underlines the tragic cruelty of the right-wing power spectacle that Karamat enacts, as underneath it lies the radical inequality dividing his family's life from that of his Muslim constituents: characterized by extreme wealth and power, contrasted with poverty and repeated exclusion from state protection. Thus, while the Pashas are forced to sell their house to allow for Isma's graduate studies, for Eamonn, America is just another stop on his leisured travels, while his family home is equipped with security guards and a basement bunker. As Karamat finally recognizes this inequality and with it the enormous privilege enshrouding his flawed decisions, the text affirms the still unlearned truths of the existing Conservative administration, where the demonization and denaturalization of British citizens on the back of their Muslim identities continues to represent a major human rights violation within the contemporary era. Negotiating a social tragedy of his own making, Karamat confronts the needlessness of death caused by the violence of his own policy, a lesson also relevant to right-wing thinking on citizenship and repatriation.

Speculative fiction and the refugee 'crisis' in Hamid's *Exit West*

The overt cultural materialist orientation of *Home Fire*'s socio-political critique, founded as it is upon a critically informed awareness of migrant difference within contemporary Britain and of the potentially tragic dimensions of this difference when it comes to contemporary policing and security policy, seems in many ways in contrast to Mohsin Hamid's optimist take on migration in *Exit West* (2017a), which insists upon imagining 'a brighter future' of universal migrancy through recourse to speculative fiction (2017b: n.p.). To borrow from

Rosi Braidotti, the novel celebrates an unabashed 'nomadism' in its approach to potential futures, prioritizing an ability 'to recreate a home base anywhere' and to relinquish 'all idea, desire, or nostalgia for fixity' as an imperative for future progress (1994: 22). It does this through an expansion of 'migrancy' to include both spatial and temporal interpretations, as well as through an awareness of how new technologies make possible new forms of rapid and instantaneous movement, carried out in both physical and virtual domains. As Hamid himself puts it, the novel looks to the future to find a necessary 'antidote' to a pervasive 'nostalgia' infecting contemporary culture (2017b), locating this in a world in which 'our reality as a migratory species' is embraced and celebrated (2019: n.p.). Even so, as with Shamsie's novel, the text is not without attention to darker, more biopolitical dimensions of contemporary post-9/11 policy, in particular as this impacts on refugee and asylum seeker precarity in a post-Syria context, instead integrating this into a notably multi-sided investigation of modern refugee experience: underlining the 'shift from human rights to security' accompanying the Arab Spring (Abbas 2019: 2457). In this way, *Exit West* approaches the so-called 'refugee crisis' by moving between universalizing and differentiating registers, invoking 'radical hopefulness' alongside a detailed register of refugee struggle and oppression (Hamid 2017b; Rask Knudsen and Rahbek 2021).

The principal vehicle for this double-edged reflection emerges through fantastic hidden doors capable of instantaneously transporting the characters from one place to another, in this way evading a popular media reduction of refugees to their perilous journeys. As Hamid reflects, 'I think we use the journeys of migrants to place them in a different category [from the rest of humanity...]. I don't intend to minimize the dangers and difficulties of migration with the doors. I intend to minimize the strength of our instinct to treat our fellow humans as "other"' (Brice 2020). The underlying benefit of this speculative invention thus emerges in its implicit emphasis on the refugee's shared humanity, even as it registers the dominant security-oriented protocol of contemporary migration policy, where these doors are 'being discussed by world leaders as a major global crisis' (Hamid 2017a: 83). Borrowing from Abbas, the text thus negotiates the desired 'universalism to which claims to the category of the human worthy of protection [should] be forged' (2019: 2457), even while acknowledging how in practice this desire confronts exclusionary realities: for example, a highly restricted access to doors to 'richer destinations,' while those to 'poorer places' remain 'too many [...] to guard them all' (Hamid 2017a: 101).

The novel's protagonists, Nadia and Saeed, confront this security-oriented panorama following the outbreak of civil war in their unnamed home country, an event that drives them to leave friends and family to pass through one of the doors. Within this conflict-laden context, both characters negotiate identity-markers overtly linking them to Islamic culture, in this way signalling a contemporary post-Syria landscape in which the 'categories of "asylum seeker" and "terrorist"' are increasingly 'collapsing' (Abbas 2019: 2455). For Nadia, this identification involves a 'flowing black robe' reaching from 'the tips of her toes to the bottom of her jugular notch', while for Saeed, it is a beard in the form of 'studiously maintained stubble' (1). As Kundnani again explains, such markers act within the post-9/11 West as 'indicators of [...] potential for violence', 'parsed for signs of allegiance' to extremist ideologies (2015: 108), such that they situate these characters overtly as perceived enemies of the Western state: 'tomorrow's terrorists' as designated by a Prevent-oriented security policy (11). Hamid's response to this ideological alignment is to critically invert these associations: positioning Nadia's robe, for example, as self-conscious 'signal' to ward off men, while Saeed's 'stubble' offers little indication of his increasingly devout religious viewpoint, instead merely falling in line with 'the rules on beards' in his home country (110, 1, 83). Indeed, even the category of 'refugee' itself is here initially applied in direct contrast to Nadia and Saeed's situation, as before departing, they partake of the privileges of natural citizens.

The strategy of re-signification witnessed in these personal realignments thus emerges as one way in which *Exit West* confronts the contemporary War on Terror, as popular media and governmental prejudices regarding Muslims and refugees are overtly dismantled by the text, revealed as deceptive stereotypes irrelevant to these characters' intimate lives. Yet another means by which this reality becomes apparent is the text's ironic application of 'native' to white-British-born identities, this overtly reversing the conventional imperial application of this term to colonial subjects (131, 129). Responding again to gothic fears of 'reverse colonisation', wherein the nation becomes 'vulnerable to attack from more vigorous, "primitive" peoples' (Arata 1990: 623), whose counter-invasion supposedly justifies retaliatory attack, this understanding sees (white) British heritage as a marker of supposedly innate respectability, thus implicitly justifying a call to arms against the foreign 'other'. The seriousness with which the 'nativists' approach this narrative in the novel is mirrored in the militarized, dystopian portrayal of contemporary London, wherein 'the talk on the television was of a major operation, one city at a time, starting in London, to reclaim Britain for Britain, and it was reported that the army was being deployed, and the police as well' (132). In this militarized depiction, nativist forces institute a national 'state of exception', eventually confining migrants to designated labour camps, and exposing 'the systematic violence through which sovereign power is performed at the expense of civil populations' (Popescu and Jahamah 2020: 124). Put differently, biopolitical government is here employed as a means of monitoring and controlling incoming migrant communities, seeing these as in need of policing against the threat of violence.

As Lava Asaad reflects, such structures are in fact increasingly typical of the contemporary post-Syria Western state, where 'the right of movement has become hierarchical and border screening processes have become more rigorous and exclusive,' reaffirming 'hegemonic structures that produce and maintain the crisis in the first place' (2020: 10). On a similar note, Lindsey N. Kingston notes how contemporary biometric technologies, supposedly set in place to help migrants and refugees in their travels, may ultimately 'upend survival strategies that displaced families rely upon', requiring forms of identification often unavailable upon request, or in other cases, capable of being used to support invasive surveillance purposes (2018: 41–42). Against this discriminatory landscape, the novel emphasizes the terroristic violence enacted by this 'nativist' cohort, which Nadia sees as 'familiar, so much like the fury of the militants in her own city' (156). Thus, drawing connections between East and West, terrorism and counterterrorism, the text underscores what Elleke Boehmer and Stephen Morton identify as 'the category and experience of terror from the standpoint of the colonized and abject of history', connecting this implicitly to Brexit-era Britain and the defence of nationalist myths of origin (2009: 12). Indeed, as Shazia Sadaf notes, 'the word "Exit" in Hamid's title is clearly a direct nod to the exit of Britain from the European Union', reinforcing not only post-Syrian westward movements across the globe, but also, equally centrally, the shifting, increasingly right-wing geopolitical landscape *within* the West across the 2010s (2020: 640).

As Nadia and Saeed move to Marin, California, to restore their unravelling relationship, the novel also links this Brexiteer aggression to the Trump administration in the United States and its comparable 'nativist' violence in response to migrant and refugee populations. In this much-changed, futuristic city, British colonialism has 'long ago' 'exterminated' all actual natives (i.e. Native Americans), the text informs us, thus reminding the reader of a longer imperial project underpinning American history. Even so, the narrator explains:

> it was not quite true to say there were no natives, nativeness being a relative matter, and many others considered themselves native to this country, by which they meant that they or their parents or their grandparents or the grandparents of their grandparents had been born on the strip of land that stretched from the

mid-northern Pacific to the mid-northern Atlantic, that their existence here did not owe anything to a physical migration that had occurred during their lifetimes.

Hamid 2017a: 196

As with the British nativists above, this population's embrace of white nationalist sentiment – where 'the people who advocated this position most forcefully, tended to be drawn from the ranks of those with light skin who looked most like the natives of Britain' (196) – informs the novel's reading of American racism in no uncertain terms. Here again, as John Harris writes, 'a new breed of populist "strongmen"' becomes visible, 'defined by their hostility to the conventions of democracy and gleeful embrace of prejudice and bigotry', a new anti-migrant outlook, visible across the world in the 2010s (Harris 2019: n.p.). Even so, the novel also significantly registers 'a third layer of nativeness [...] composed of those who others thought directly descended, [...] from the human beings who had been brought from Africa to this continent centuries ago as slaves' (Hamid 2017a: 197). The inclusion of this additional reflection on nativeness thus underlines the 'vast importance' of African American identity for contemporary politics, as '[US] society had been shaped in reaction to it, and unspeakable violence had occurred in relation to it, and yet it endured' (197). In short, this defence of minority African American identity as 'native' here stands as a defensible counterpart to white nationalist sentiment, where despite a history of forced migration and ongoing systematic oppression, this population is seen to continue to demonstrate strength and resistance in the face of persistent racist oppression.

This critique thus explicitly recognizes the presence of persecuted minority 'native' communities across the West in opposition to a populist understanding of Western identity as inherently white. In Valluvan's terms, it counters 'the disproportionate importance of race' within contemporary politics in favour of prioritizing 'economic struggle, uncertainty and inequality', especially as experienced by disenfranchised migrant populations (2019: 8–9). Even so, the novel *does* show a certain degree of sympathy towards Western communities undergoing shock at the rapid pace of cultural change, as Nadia reflects on how 'I can understand it. [...] Imagine if you lived here. And millions of people from all over the world suddenly arrived' (162). Despite her position of difference, Nadia shows a willingness to contextualize cultural fears surrounding her arrival, embracing a shared humanity with her persecutors, rather than simply dismissing them. On a similar note, the novel also directly recognizes the strong affective pull of nostalgic sentiment, both in West and East, as in fact, this stands at the heart of Saeed's own often melancholic experience of refugeehood. As Nadia explains, it is as though 'the further they moved from the city of their birth, through space and through time, the more he sought to strengthen his connection to it, tying ropes to the air of an era that was unambiguously gone' (187). Rather than condemn this view to the past, the novel urges empathy, if also critique, registering Saeed's strong family ties and how these necessarily shape his identity and belonging across his travels, even while the need to resettle is also implicit. As Rask Knudsen and Rahbek (2021: 449) note, it is here where prayer becomes central to Hamid's narrative, as this offers Saeed a sense of connection to his past, even at a distance, and as it provides him a new community of fellow believers in his host country, allowing him to 'feel part of something, not just something spiritual, but something human' (Hamid 2017a: 148). The text's engagement with faith and spirituality in this way offers one strategy for coping with migratory loss, wherein, despite inevitable 'sorrow', it becomes possible to 'believe in humanity's potential for building a better world' (202), thus asserting a diasporic 'religious transnationalism' of a distinctly transgressive character (Tam 2017: 3).

By contrast to this faith-oriented perspective, Nadia's own viewpoint offers another approach to migratory politics, wherein she comes to embrace a secular nomadism and a love of diversity, realizing that 'she had been stifled in the place of her birth for virtually her entire life' (156). More specifically, Nadia savours the London-based multicultural panorama of 'all these people of all these different colours in all these different attires', seeing this cultural heterogeneity as a welcome alternative to her home country's ethnic and religious uniformity. The fact that this vibrant community has come under threat as a result of nativism thus becomes especially relevant to her character's outlook, most explicitly in connection with a radicalized right-wing, anti-migrant reassertion of white homogeneity. As the novel puts it, 'The fury of those nativists advocating wholesale slaughter was what struck Nadia most [...]. She wondered whether she and Saeed had done anything by moving, whether the faces and buildings had changed but the basic reality of their predicament had not' (156). In this way, Hamid foregrounds the geopolitical turmoil produced by the refugee 'crisis', but more principally by the Western state's persistent denial and denouncement of difference via recourse to militarized and exclusionary anti-migrant policies.

Nevertheless, by contrast to *Home Fire*'s tragic ending, *Exit West* retains hope of resolution produced by an eventual social acceptance of ongoing migration, seeing this as a necessary, if much-resisted response to globalization's reality. Thus, despite the possibility of 'a great massacre' (159) brought about by widespread nativism in the novel, including rumoured 'blood bath[s] in Hyde Park, or in Earls Court, or near Shepherd's Bush roundabout' (161), the novel registers the possibility of 'a pause' (161) in which 'the natives and their forces stepped back from the brink' (164), seemingly appreciating the potential for retraction and societal growth. As the text puts it, 'Perhaps they had grasped that the doors could not be closed, and new doors would continue to open [...]. Or perhaps the sheer number of places where there were now doors had made it useless to fight in any one' (164). In either case, the novel celebrates an apparent end to present conflicts based in a final realization of a global world and of the promising opportunities that come through an embrace of difference and diversity. As Hamid himself puts it, 'if we can recognize the universality of the migration experience and the universality of the refugee experience – that those of us who have never moved are also migrants and refugees – then the space for empathy opens up' (Chandler 2017, n.p.). In the novel's persistent emphasis on migrant courage and valour, and on the common human reality of moving and displacement, this critical lesson becomes paramount, reinforcing an elegy to the migrant as the central figure of our age.

Realism, violence, and second-generation resilience in *In Our Mad and Furious City*

Guy Gunaratne's *In Our Mad and Furious City* (2018) offers yet another take on this fraught contemporary context, again confronting anti-migrant animosity and migrant resilience, but here through the lens of a realism focused specifically on place and locality. Set on a council estate in the North London suburb of Neasden, home to second-generation migrants Ardan, Selvon, and Yusuf, the novel stages this group's renewed precarity in the wake of the 2013 murder of Lee Rigby: here fictionalized in the similar killing of a white off-duty soldier by a local black British Muslim: 'a homegrown bredda' (4), as Yusuf describes him. Told through the first-person narratives of each of the young men and two of their parents (Selvon's father, Nelson; and Ardan's mother, Caroline), with a detailed attention to particulars of idiom, appearance, and background, the novel underscores the shared, if varying, discrimination confronted by each generation, in this way registering a continuity between post-war and post-millennial contexts. In John McLeod's words, the text 'situat[es] contemporary riotous protest in a longer history of anti-racist righteous resistance' (2019: 19), locating this *ongoing* racist experience specifically in the 'mad and furious' context of urban London.

As with Shamsie and Hamid's novels, Gunaratne also registers important shifts shaping 2010s Britain, in this way distancing the protagonists in crucial ways from their parents' generation. Thus, while violence and racism are unmistakably central to their parents' uneasy, first-generation memories, turning principally around the 1980s Notting Hill race riots and the Troubles in Northern Ireland, nevertheless the critical primacy the narrative grants to Islamophobic sentiment post-7/7, and conversely, to Islamic radicalization in the context of 'War on Terror' politics, is something expressly new to this generation, affecting both the form and articulation of racist aggression and its material fall out in the novel. Insofar as the text expressly prioritizes Lee Rigby's murder as a real-life historical focus for investigation, registering this event's particular mixture of terroristic brutality and similarly violent white nationalist backlash, the novel indexes the decade's specifically security-driven framework for understanding identity and belonging, emphasizing, in Peter Morey's words, the centrality of the so-called 'Muslim problem', 'as the focal point of anxieties about citizenship, loyalty, and liberal values' (2018: 2). The endeavour to critically navigate this fraught context is what connects this novel to those discussed above, tying it to the anti-migrant and anti-Muslim discourses therein explored.

In accordance with a realist emphasis on geographical and linguistic markers, where, in Sue-Im Lee's words, realism 'must adequately invoke an empirical sense of place' (2002: 230), the feeling of security and belonging the young characters experience in this urban environment, despite their unmistakable disadvantage in terms of wealth and opportunity, is witnessed in their identification with the Estate they proudly inhabit. In Yusuf's words, 'Place was our own. This place. Whether we heard the whispers of our older roots never mattered. [...] This is where we found our young madnesses after all' (Gunaratne 2018: 4). Thus, while their parents find their subjectivities absorbed by memories pulling them back to their places of birth or to episodes of violence and resistance previously experienced upon arrival, for the boys, 'what mattered to us was the present, terse and cold, where we would make our own coarse music' (4). The form of the novel, with its mimetic register, echoes this presentism expressly, conjuring the particular, cross-ethnic slang and 'glocal' outlook this second-generation negotiates, while also affirming each characters' personalized, if communal experience of urban belonging.

For the young characters specifically, this comes through in a globally inflected medley of linguistic references, understood as a poetic weaponry against everyday violence. As Yusuf reflects, 'Our tongues were so soaked in our defences, we hoped only to outlast the day. Just look at how we spoke to one another: ennet-tho, myman and pussyo. Our friendships we called bloods and our homes we called our Ends' (3). Looking beyond particular ethnic backgrounds, the young men at once construct and perform their local inhabitancy, situating themselves in relation to a London-Caribbean patois they commonly recognize. The repetition of 'our' as a determiner in this passage also registers the shared possession the 'youngers' feel over the Estate, reaffirming a sense of communal belonging as a central aspect of their urban experience, an idea of common ownership over the space and terms of their upbringing. As Roger Bromley puts it, 'they convert their place into a space of possibility, empowered, entitled and not in thrall to the dominant discourse of power' (2021: 135–136). In other words, they claim this fraught, but diverse and animated environment as their own, affirming the terms of contemporary British identity as distinctly defiant.

The young men negotiate this project in different ways, in accordance with each of their interests and talents: Ardan through music, Selvon through sport, and Yusuf through faith. In each case they instance how, in Nira Yuval-Davis's words, 'belonging is always a dynamic process, not a reified fixity,' constructed in relation to 'social locations', 'emotional attachments', and 'ethical and political value systems' (2011: 12), in particular, those connected to a working-class and diasporic community of North-West London. For Ardan, this emerges most visibly in his love of local 'bars', or musical recordings specific to North London artists such as Wiley, Akala, Jammer, Skepta, and Kano, a culture which, he claims, has the ability to rival the 'romance' of the New York rap scene (Gunaratne 2018: 20). 'Why be on that gas', he reflects, 'when London's got our own good moves? [...] Even if it sounds ugly, cold and sparse. Even if the beats are angry, under scuddy verses, it's the same noise as the road. [...] Why would any man keep listening to Americans with their foreign chemistries after that?' (58–59). The possibilities offered by local 'youth' music are thus seen in terms of its unique insight on North London experience, capturing this urban space's hidden beauty and potential, and providing a sense of informed, creative promise. As John McLeod writes of the Calypso music enjoyed by post-war first-generation London migrants, so much is true here of Grime, Drill, and Eskibeat, namely that they offer second-generation migrants 'a short-term means of survival that comes from within the community [...], while its story of individual hardship and international affairs bears witness to the boys' experience of London *on their own terms*' (2004: 33). Ashley L. Lewis also reflects on how Grime culture creates 'a space for Black youth [and we might add, migrant youth more broadly] growing up in these environments to tell about themselves, their daily social and economic struggles, and ways of coping with perpetual desolation and despair'

(2019: 7). In short, this locally based artistry proffers a mechanism for creative 'rebellion' and 'rage' against the dominant white, middle-class culture and the barriers it establishes for working-class migrants (1, 10).

By contrast, Selvon (named after the post-war Caribbean author), looks to education and athletics to find his own way out of this environment, pursuing acceptance on a course at Brunel University as a means to achieving his academic and Olympic dreams. Driven by the refrains of the motivation tapes he listens to as he runs the Estate – '*If your mind can conceive it, you can achieve it*' (11), '*Boss your day or your day will end up bossing you*' (Gunaratne 2018: 47) – he sees ambition, rather than artistry, as the necessary tool for accessing social mobility, contrasting himself to the fixed and non-aspirational outlooks he ascribes to many Estate residents. He reflects, 'These Ends is full of pigeons. [...] They just wastemen who don't even try. [...] As if this place is a place for proper people' (48). Even so, while demonstrating a certain arrogance in his view towards the Estate, across the course of his narrative Selvon also comes to recognize the self-affirming support his local community provides him, his runs encircling the Estate and claiming this space as his own. As he puts it, 'In my mind this place owns a part of me too-tho, with its silence and grey. [...] This is where I run and where I'm known. For now' (10–11). Despite his desire to leave the area, then, Selvon betrays a positive outlook on this urban environment, this contrasting his father's memorially focused melancholia, driven by a desire to look 'Back, back' and to remind others that 'all of this is nothing new' (35).

For Yusuf, for whom faith, rather than sport or music, offers the desired sense of promise and reassurance his peers and he seek, yet another take on this North London habitat becomes visible, bringing to attention the heightened anxieties and fears surrounding Muslim identity post-7/7. Here, both radicalization and securitization play a central part in this narrative conjecture, Yusuf's understanding of belonging shaped by 'War on Terror' politics, but also by the increasingly isolationist and hostile attitude of his local Muslim community. On the one hand, this comes through via the new Imam at the local mosque, who brings with him what Peter Cherry describes as a 'pugnacious and reactionary form of Islam' (2022: 182), a harsher, more divisive perspective on the religion than that of Yusuf's father, antagonizing both Muslims and non-Muslims alike with his anti-Western outlook. As Yusuf relates to his distressed brother, 'This imam, the Mosque. It's got nuttan to do with us bruv. [...] It weren't the West bruv. We are the fuckin West' (179). The event of the local soldier's murder, like that of Rigby, is here implicitly connected to this radicalized outlook, but also to subsequent acts of anti-Muslim violence in the area: what Nelson calls the 'low tide,' bringing with it a new wave of right-wing hatred (35). As Mike Cole reports, Rigby's death itself was also similarly followed by widespread Islamophobic brutality: having occurred on the 23 May 2013, by the end of the day there were various incidents of anti-Muslim aggression reported in Gillingham, Essex, and Grimsby, and by the end of the month, 'about 200 incidents had been recorded by Tell MAMA [Measuring Anti-Muslim Attacks]' (2014: 83). This experience is mirrored in the novel by racist protest happening directly outside the grounds of the Estate, police tape marking the route of the protestors, while refusing to establish any further obstacles. As Ardan reflects:

> The police are letting the goons protest through here. [...] Skinheads. Bad-mind faces standing in small crowds, waiting. Men mostly, with banners, some in shirts and ties, others looking lairy, fixed and blood-ready. They holding signs giving the name of that soldier-boy and saying *Britain First*. One man with the Union Jack around his neck is laughing.
>
> Gunaratne 2018: 254

These nationalist symbols, then, – the banners, signs and flag: the means by which, as Homi Bhabha famously puts it, the nation emerges as a form of 'narration' (1990) – function here to parade an understanding of national identity implicitly delimited to a white ethnic background, threatening this majority migrant community as unwanted trespassers. As Anshuman Mondal also reflects, such iconography, while regularly defended as a form of 'free speech', in fact self-consciously '*enacts*' racist hatred, 'establish[ing] and maintain[ing] hierarchies of domination and subordination' as a performative means of inscribing Muslim inferiority, positioning the muted and demeaned Muslim subject as a powerless 'other' (2014: 23–24).

This opposition between radicalized Islam and an equally radicalized Islamophobia thus situates the novel's realist depiction of contemporary London, underpinning its tense and divided picture of post-7/7 urban life. Yet while the Rigby murder and subsequent anti-Muslim violence constitute perhaps the most direct historical markers of this era, registering the migrant communities' precarious experience of *both* terror and securitization, the framing of these events in the novel also brings into consideration other recent historical traumas, expanding the text's socio-political critique to encompass the wider decade. Most notably, Gunaratne's attention to Windrush history, considered especially in relation to recurrent political discourses of migrant repatriation (2018: 126), brings to mind the recent Windrush scandal of 2018, where, as referenced in my introduction to this chapter, 'popular outrage' emerged specifically in connection with the 'hostile environment' directed at Black migrant populations and with 'the deportation to the Caribbean of hundreds of people of Afro-Caribbean heritage who had lived much of their life in Britain' (Selwyn 2019: 125). While Selvon's family fortunately does not face such a radical threat, despite confronting considerable poverty and health issues, nevertheless, Nelson's memories of Oswald Mosley's promise to 'send we darkies back home' (Gunaratne 2018: 126), combined with his daily struggles with loss and violence in the context of North London's racial tensions, reinforce the systemic oppression still present within the country, as social, economic and political forces appear to join together against this minority community.

In a similar way, the novel's focus on a North London housing Estate, in explicit connection with a local fire that destroys the community, also indirectly references the Grenfell Tower tragedy of 2017, where 72 people (many of them immigrants) were burnt to death in their own flats, largely on account of mismanagement issues tied to a 2016 refurbishment (see Watkin 2021: x–xi). As William Watkin reflects, 'Around the country many spoke out about the belief that the victims of Grenfell were victims not of fire, but of neglect, exclusion and poverty. Addressing the perceived greed and dismissiveness of the planners and council members alike, it was not uncommon to hear the accusation "Murderers!"', both from activists and politicians, and from the local Grime culture that Ardan celebrates (xiii). Watkin continues, 'grime artist Stormzy used his performance [at the 2018 Brits music awards] to ask the question on the minds of so many of us. "Theresa May, where's the money for Grenfell?"' (xii). Both events, the Windrush scandal and the Grenfell fire, as Tom Selwyn comments, can be situated under a larger banner of austerity and anti-immigrant politics, wherein privatization, deregulation, and social funding cuts, justified on the back of fiscal responsibility, have taken a particularly cruel toll on working-class and migrant communities, a demographic being targeted as supposedly undeserving, 'feckless' recipients of social housing and other support mechanisms (2019: 151). As he puts it,

> we can see the Britain of Brexit, Grenfell, and Windrush being led, Pied Piper-like, towards a political and cultural space in which the realities of austerity and de-regulation on the ground have simultaneously been both orchestrated and shrouded from view by economic interests articulated by a political class making sizeable financial gains at the same time as wielding technologically-charged mythologies that have been lying dormant since the 1930s.
>
> Selwyn 2019: 126

Within this radically unequal context, *In Our Mad and Furious City* illustrates how the migrant poor are increasingly debilitated by Conservative Party policy:

scapegoated and neglected as 'scroungers' and 'parasites', their claims to basic rights to home and country thrown into question.

This then stands at the heart of this socially attentive novel: an attention to violence both physical and structural, underpinning contemporary neoliberal Britain, especially as this politics impacts on disenfranchised migrant communities. As Cole also reflects, 'We now live in a country in which immigration is something to be "controlled", "brought down", "mitigated". Immigration, and by extension immigrants, are a problem' (2014: 146). This comes through especially forcefully in the novel's repeated engagements with immigrant poverty, and with the vindictiveness expressed by local white nationalists towards this community. Even so, with an eye to postmillennial changes, Gunaratne also indexes a resilient response to this poverty and violence on the part of the younger generation, as their parents' painful memories of the race riots and the Troubles contrast the teenagers' emboldened, post-multicultural embrace of difference and diversity. In Bromley's words, the novel works with a concept of 'postmigration', interested in emphasizing 'conviviality'[2] over exclusion and difference, 'de-essentializing so-called migrant coherences and homogeneities [...], bearing in mind the ways in which dichotomised cultural differences can be overstated in ethnic discourse' (2021: 134, 133). While this second-generation cohort thus still understands itself as shaped by a history of otherness – 'a young nation of mongrels [...] measuring ourselves against what we were supposed to be' (3) – here this status is normalized, such that there is 'nothing more foreign' to the group than sameness: 'to have been moulded out of one thing and not of many' (4). The teenagers see themselves, by contrast to their parents, as 'held together [...] in this single, mad, monstrous and lunatic city', able to depend on one another, despite their 'own small furies' (5).

With an eye to this emboldened, collectivist perspective, the novel's ending is perhaps leavened by an awareness of Ardan and Selvon's fighting spirits, and by an attention to the community-based resources they call on to help them in their grieving following Yusuf's death. As the final chapter (told by a spectral Yusuf) reflects, a more optimistic perspective on urban survival is here made possible through overlapping, present-centred narratives, contrasting a London of 'hard knocks', 'madness' and 'fury' with 'the joy' still visible in those 'willing to run, run on and run forever just to prove it possible' (288). While this does not alter the reality of deprivation confronted by these characters on a mundane basis, it does give credit to the possibility of change and hope, praising these young 'heroes', who emerge as 'the only ones that can save us' (288).

Conclusion

In conclusion, the varying perspectives these three novels provide on contemporary Britain, and more largely on the oppressed situation of diasporic communities within this context, offer a much-needed insight on 9/11's ongoing relevance to society and politics, as well as on the complications introduced to this framework by subsequent transnational happenings. These concerns are registered here specifically in connection with recent historical events and debates defining the decade, such as the Shamima Begum case, the refugee 'crisis', and the Lee Rigby murder, but also and more generally, the discourses of populism, nativism, radicalization, and securitization which index a polarized 2010s experience. These texts' distinct generic approaches to this panorama, encompassing tragedy, speculative fiction, and realism, demonstrate the impressive range of creative modalities available within this literature, while also reflecting agreements and overlapping agendas between these texts. In short, these novels chronicle the changing contours *both* of British society and politics *and* British literature, making evident the strong, if varied viewpoints diasporic British South Asian writing brings to this.

Notes

1 For a fuller discussion of 'grievability', see Butler (2009: 14–15). Butler also wrote on the topical dilemmas raised by Sophocles' *Antigone* in her book *Antigone's Claim: Kinship Between Life and Death* (2000). The pre-9/11 publication of this text perhaps explains its relative obscurity alongside subsequent works, such as *Precarious Lives* (2004) and *Frames of War* (2009), where her application of similar questions to a post-9/11 context made them topical. Nevertheless, it is worth noting how Butler defended *Antigone* explicitly as a seminal text for contemporary culture, just as Shamsie does in *Home Fire*.
2 I would note that here Bromley is drawing on Paul Gilroy's terminology, from *After Empire: Melancholia or Convivial Culture?* In this latter text, Gilroy defines 'conviviality' as a space 'in which cultures, histories, and structures of feeling, previously separated by enormous distances, could be found in the same place, the same time: school, bus, café, cell, waiting room, or traffic jam' (2004: 70).

Works cited

Abbas, Madeline-Sophie. 'Conflating the Muslim Refugee and the Terror Suspect: Responses to the Syrian Refugee "Crisis" in Brexit Britain'. *Ethnic and Racial Studies* 42(14), 2019: 2450–2469.

Abbas, Sadia. *At Freedom's Limit: Islam and the Postcolonial Predicament*. New York: Fordham University Press, 2014.

Ahmed, Rehana. *Writing British Muslims*. Manchester: Manchester University Press, 2015.

Aistrope, Tim. 'The Muslim Paranoia Narrative in Counter-radicalisation Policy'. *Critical Studies on Terrorism* 9(2), 2016: 182–204.

Arata, Stephen D. 'The Occidental Tourist: "Dracula" and the Anxiety of Reverse Colonization'. *Victorian Studies* 33(4), 1990: 621–645.

Asaad, Lava. *Literature with a White Helmet: The Textual-Corporeality of Being, Becoming, and Representing Refugees*. London: Routledge, 2020.

Banerjee, Debjani. 'From Cheap Labor to Overlooked Citizens: Looking for British Muslim Identities in Kamila Shamsie's *Home Fire*'. *South Asian Review* 41(3–4), 2020: 288–302.

Bhabha, Homi. *Nation and Narration*. London: Routledge, 1990.

Boehmer, Elleke and Stephen Morton. *Terror and the Postcolonial*. Oxford: Wiley Blackwell, 2009.

Braidotti, Rosi. *Nomadic Subjects: Embodiment and Sexual Difference in Contemporary Feminist Theory*. New York: Columbia University Press, 1994.

Brice, Anne. '"Exit West" author Mohsin Hamid: "Migration is what our species does"'. *Berkeley News*, 1 September 2020: https://news.berkeley.edu/2020/09/01/on-the-same-page-exit-west-mohsin-hamid/ (accessed 4 July 2023).

Bromley, Roger. 'Class, Knowledge and Belonging: Narrating Postmigrant Possibilities'. In *Postmigration: Art, Culture, and Politics in Contemporary Europe*. Anna Meera Gaonkar, Astrid Sophie Øst Hansen, Hans Christian Post and Moritz Schramm (eds). Bielefeld: transcript, 2021: 133–143.

Butler, Judith. *Antigone's Claim: Kinship Between Life and Death*. New York: Columbia University Press, 2000.

Butler, Judith. *Precarious Life: The Powers of Mourning and Violence*. London: Verso, 2004.

Butler, Judith. *Frames of War: When Is Life Grievable?* London: Verso, 2009.

Chambers, Claire. *Making Sense of Contemporary British Muslim Novels*. London: Palgrave Macmillan, 2019.

Chandler, Caitlin L. 'We are all refugees: A conversation with Mohsin Hamid'. *The Nation*, 30 October 2017: https://www.thenation.com/article/archive/we-are-all-refugees-a-conversation-with-mohsin-hamid/ (accessed 7 April 2022).

Cherry, Peter. *Muslim Masculinities in Literature and Film: Transcultural Identity and Migration in Britain*. London: I.B. Tauris, Bloomsbury, 2022.

Choudhury, Tufyal. 'The Radicalisation of Citizenship Deprivation'. *Critical Social Policy* 37(2), 2017: 225–244.

Cole, Mike. 'Austerity / Immiseration Capitalism and Islamophobia – or Twenty-first-century Multicultural Socialism?'. *Policy Futures in Education* 12(1), 2014: 79–92.

Duman, Özgün S. 'The Rise and Consolidation of Neoliberalism in the European Union: A Comparative Analysis of Social and Employment Policies in Greece and Turkey'. *European Journal of Industrial Relations* 20(4), 2014: 367–382.

El-Enany, Nadine *(B)ordering Britain: Law, Race and Empire*. Manchester: Manchester University Press, 2020.

Gentleman, Amelia. *The Windrush Betrayal: Exposing the Hostile Environment*. London: Guardian Faber, 2019.

Gilroy, Paul. *After Empire: Melancholia or Convivial Culture?*. London: Routledge, 2004.

Githens-Mazer, Jonathan and Robert Lambert. 'Why Conventional Wisdom on Radicalization Fails: The Persistence of a Failed Discourse'. *International Affairs* 86(4, July), 2010: 889–901.

Gunaratne, Guy. *In Our Mad and Furious City*. London: Tinder Press, 2018.

Hamid, Mohsin. 'In the 21st Century, we are all migrants'. *National Geographic*, August 2019: https://www.nationalgeographic.com/magazine/article/we-all-are-migrants-in-the-21st-century (accessed 7 April 2022).

Hamid, Mohsin. *Exit West*. London: Penguin, 2017a.

Hamid, Mohsin. 'Mohsin Hamid on the dangers of nostalgia: We need to imagine a brighter future'. *The Guardian*, 25 February 2017b: https://www.theguardian.com/books/2017/feb/25/mohsin-hamid-danger-nostalgia-brighter-future (accessed 7 April 2022).

Harris, John. 'A politics of nostalgia and score-settling': How populism dominated the 2010s'. *The Guardian*, 26 November 2019: https://www.theguardian.com/culture/2019/nov/26/politics-of-nostalgia-score-settling-populism-dominated-2010s-john-harris (accessed 25 March 2022).

Heath-Kelly, Charlotte. 'Counter-Terrorism and the Counterfactual: Producing the 'Radicalisation' Discourse and the UK PREVENT Strategy'. *The British Journal of Politics and International Relations* 15, 2013: 394–415.

Hermann, Cristoff. 'Neoliberalism and the European Union'. *Studies in Political Economy* 79(1), 2007: 61–90.

Kingston, Lindsey N. 'Information Sharing and Multi-Level Governance in Refugee Services'. In *Digital Lifeline?: ICTs for Refugees and Displaced Persons*. Carleen F. Maitland (ed.). Cambridge, MA: The MIT Press, 2018: 35–53.

Kumar, Deepa. *Islamophobia and the Politics of Empire*. Chicago, IL: Haymarket Books, 2012.

Kundnani, Arun. *The Muslims are Coming! Islamophobia, Extremism, and the Domestic War on Terror*. London: Verso, 2015.

Kundnani, Arun. 'Multiculturalism and Its Discontents: Left, Right and Liberal', *European Journal of Cultural Studies* 15(2), 2012: 155–166.

Lee, Sue-Im. 'Suspicious Characters: Realism, Asian American Identity, and Theresa Hak Kyung Cha's *Dictee*'. *Journal of Narrative Theory* 32(2), 2002: 227–258.

Lewis, Ashley L. *Rebel Trends: A Study of Grime Culture in London, England*. Dissertation, Howard University, Washington, DC, July 2019.

Liao, Pei-chen. *'Post'-9/11 South Asian Diasporic Fiction: Uncanny Terror*. London: Palgrave Macmillan, 2013.

Masters, Mercedes and Salvador Santino F. Regilme, Jr. 'Citizenship Revocation as a Human Rights Violation: The Case of Shamima Begum'. *E-International Relations*, 28 November 2020: https://www.e-ir.info/2020/11/28/citizenship-revocation-as-a-human-rights-violation-the-case-of-shamima-begum/ (accessed 5 April 2020).

McLeod, John. 'When Memories Fade: Remembering Anti-racism in Contemporary Black British Writing'. *Wasafiri* 34(4), 2019: 18–23.

McLeod, John. *Postcolonial London: Rewriting the Metropolis*. London: Routledge, 2004.

Mondal, Anshuman A. *Islam and Controversy: The Politics of Free Speech after Rushdie*. London: Palgrave Macmillan, 2014.

Morey, Peter. *Islamophobia and the Novel*. New York: Columbia University Press, 2018.

Morrison, Jago. 'Jihadi Fiction: Radicalisation Narratives in the Contemporary Novel'. *Textual Practice* 31(3), 2017: 567–584.

Mukherjee, Ankhi. 'Migrant Britain'. In *Brexit and Literature: Critical and Cultural Responses*. Robert Eaglestone (ed.). London: Routledge, 2018: 73–81.

O'Gorman, Daniel. *Fictions of the War on Terror: Difference and the Transnational 9/11 Novel*. London: Palgrave Macmillan, 2015.

O'Toole, Therese, Nasar Meer, Daniel Nilsson DeHanas, Stephen H. Jones, and Tariq Modood. 'Governing through Prevent? Regulation and Contested Practice in State–Muslim Engagement'. *Sociology* 50(1), 2016: 160–177.

Popescu, Maria-Irina and Asma Jahamah. '"London Is a City Built on the Wreckage of Itself": State Terrorism and Resistance in Chris Cleave's *Incendiary* and Mohsin Hamid's *Exit West*'. *The London Journal* 45(1), 2020: 123–145.

Rask Knudsen, Eva, and Ulla Rahbek. 'Radical Hopefulness in Mohsin Hamid's Map of the World: A Reading of *Exit West* (2017)'. *Journal of Postcolonial Writing* 57(4), 2021: 442–454.

Rutkowska, Urszula. 'The Political Novel in Our Still-evolving Reality: Kamila Shamsie's *Home Fire* and the Shamima Begum Case'. *Textual Practice* 36(6), 2022: 871–888.

Sadaf, Shazia. '"We are all migrants through time": History and Geography in Mohsin Hamid's *Exit West*'. *Journal of Postcolonial Writing* 56(5), 2020: 636–647.

Selwyn, Tom. 'Post-Home: Dwelling on Loss, Belonging and Movement'. *Ethnoscripts* 21(1), 2019: 125–156.

Shamsie, Kamila. *Home Fire*. London: Bloomsbury, 2017.

Socialist Worker. 'The Brexit that we want'. 3 January 2017. Issue 2535: https://socialistworker.co.uk/news/the-brexit-that-we-want/ (accessed 3 October 2022).

Speckhard, Anne and Molly Ellenberg. 'Perspective: Can We Repatriate the ISIS Children?'. *Horizon Insights* 3(3), 2020: 17–35: https://behorizon.org/wp-content/uploads/2020/10/Horizon-Insights-2020-3.pdf#page=21 (accessed 5 April 2022).

Tam, Jonathan. 'Renegotiating Religious Transnationalism: Fractures in Transnational Chinese Protestantism'. IMI Working Series Papers, No. 138 (August). Oxford: International Migration Institute, University of Oxford, 2017: 1–20.

UNHCR. 'Figures at a Glance'. *UNHCR: The UN Refugee Agency*, 2021: https://www.unhcr.org/uk/figures-at-a-glance.html (accessed 7 April 2022).

Upstone, Sara. *British Asian Fiction: Twenty-First-Century Voices*. Manchester: Manchester University Press, 2010.

Valluvan, Sivamohan. *The Clamour of Nationalism: Race and Nation in Twenty-First Century Britain*. Manchester: Manchester University Press, 2019.

Watkin, William. *Bioviolence: How the Powers That Be Make Us Do What They Want*. London: Routledge, 2021.

Yeo, Colin. *Welcome to Britain: Fixing our Broken Immigration System*. London: Biteback Publishing, 2020.

Yuval-Davis, Nira. *The Politics of Belonging: Intersectional Contestations*. London: Sage, 2011.

4

'Defining it is a Struggle': Working-Class Fiction in the 2010s

Matti Ron

It is not merely for the academic conceit of beginning with a bold opening gambit that one can claim the 2010s to have been arguably the best decade in history for working-class writing. Such quality can be discerned not just in the commercial and critical success of writers like Zadie Smith, Bernadine Evaristo and Kit de Waal, but also in the heterogeneity among working-class writers in their approaches to fusing both aesthetic and social concerns. The all-too-frequent equation of working-class writing with realist aesthetics, though always an overgeneralization, is now surely untenable.

The flourishing of working-class writers in the 2010s is doubtless due in part to the gradual expansion of access to higher education and arts funding in the preceding decades (though these have both come under attack in recent years due to public spending cuts, the effects of which on future working-class writing are yet to be seen). However, working-class writing in the 2010s was also helped by a social context in which class as a lens for understanding the world had come out of the forced retirement imposed upon it by the defeat of the trade unions, the fall of the Soviet Union and the triumphant declaration in 1992 that history had ended. The 2008 crash shattered such capitalist hubris and returned a form of class analysis (and, to an extent, politics) back into public lexicon. Furthermore, the 2016 EU Referendum also brought class to the forefront of British political discourse (albeit in ways more problematic and, as will be discussed, less straightforward than immediately after 2008) as the rejection of the EU came to be viewed by many as a working-class protest against any number of issues relating to the EU as a vehicle for immigration, neoliberalism, undermining national sovereignty, or some combination of the above.[1]

2008 and 2016 throw up the varied ways in which class came to be deployed in the 2010s. However, this is in no small part due to difficulties internal to the term class itself. Raymond Williams points out a number of these difficulties in *Keywords*, noting a distinction between class as a distinctive grouping and as an economic relationship (2015: 32). Moreover, even within the conception of class as an economic relationship, Williams notes that class can sometimes be seen as 'an economic category, including all who are objectively in that economic situation' or as 'a formation in which [...] consciousness of this situation and the organization to deal with it have developed' (33). There is an ambiguity for Williams around the idea of working-class culture as either the 'meanings and values and institutions of the formation' or the 'tastes and lifestyles of the category' (33). Drawing on Williams, then, it becomes useful to think about class as being used in broadly three different ways, which are simultaneously related and overlapping, yet distinct and contradictory: first, class as identity, an affinity for the class culture of the category related to one's upbringing, geographical community, cultural tastes, even accent. Second, class as an economic grouping, useful for sociological categorization. The BBC's 2011–2013 "Great British Class Survey" is an illustrative example here: the largest ever survey on social class, its findings were subsequently published in a 2013 issue of *Sociology* (Savage et al.) and sorted respondents into seven discrete categories according to questions around social, cultural and economic capital.[2] Finally, class can be understood as a formation in response to the irreducibly antagonistic social relationship which defines the capitalist mode of production between those who subsist on waged work and those who profit from the waged work of others; that is, the conflict between labour and capital.

All of these approaches to class are valid in their own ways, variously emphasizing aspects of lived experience, the specificity of particular social problems or the framework through which the antagonisms underpinning class society can be understood. Moreover, there are productive ways in which each of these approaches to class may be run simultaneously, each potentially sustaining the other. However, issues begin when these approaches to class are run simultaneously – or even substituted for one another – without reference to their analytical distinctiveness. One such example can be seen in Channel 4's 2018 mini-series, *Working-Class White Men*, presented by the Hackney-born rapper Professor Green. In his interviews with numerous white working-class men, Professor Green covers an array of social issues from deindustrialization and the diffusion of precarious work to imprisonment and limited educational opportunities.[3] However, in episode two, he speaks to 17-year-old Jake, who works with his father in construction and, owing to the presence of a father with a strong work ethic, is able to be more ambitious than most of Professor Green's other interviewees. However, it should be noted how 'class' is deployed here: Jake's father is not simply a labourer or even a skilled tradesman, but rather owns a construction company, working alongside his sons and other employees. As such, while Jake and his father could be understood as working class in terms of their identification with a class culture related to the economic category – and even some aspects of the category itself – it also seems not insignificant to understand the family's class position in relation to the father being a relatively prosperous small businessman and employer. Again, this does not mean that the latter is the *only* valid approach to class; Jake's lived experience of class identity and relative cultural capital would certainly be deeply significant in understanding his engagement with, for example, the publishing industry or an English Literature department at a prestigious university. However, what this example illustrates is the predicament which can arise when different approaches to class are run simultaneously without accounting for how they may function differently.

The terminological slippage in *Working-Class White Men* is emblematic of how class came to be deployed in the 2010s: where the decade may have begun with an approach closer to the slogan of 'We Are the 99%' (which itself runs together approaches to class as both categorization and formation), by the time of the EU Referendum this was supplanted by one with an increasing emphasis on identity (and an often unstated white and nativist identity, at that). One event which serves as a precursor for these various forms of class politics – and the struggle between them – is the 2009 Lindsey Oil Refinery strikes. In opposition to redundancies by a subcontractor flouting the terms of the National Agreement for the Engineering Construction Industry, workers at the Lindsey Oil Refinery in Lincolnshire walked out on wildcat strike twice in one year and were joined both times by thousands of workers at multiple sites across the country, all similarly defying trade union legislation around unofficial and secondary strike action. Yet, despite the clear class basis for their grievances and workers' responses to them, strikers frequently expressed those grievances in fundamentally national terms: strikers held signs with the slogan 'British Jobs for British Workers' and, as photographed in one article, 'Put Brits first for once' ('Oil plant sackings spark walkouts', 2009). Certainly, there were profoundly material reasons for this (the workers had been employed by French oil company, Total, and the workers slated to replace them were largely Italian and Portuguese) and there were also instances of more internationalist forms of class politics during the dispute; however, in the main, class grievances during the Lindsey dispute tended to be expressed in the language of the nation, with occasional instances (such as the aforementioned 'Put Brits first for once' sign) framing those class grievances overtly as nativist resentment. The Lindsey strikes, then, were an ominous signpost for the way that the politics of class would develop in the following decade, albeit increasingly emptied of its antagonistic content as class formation, and replaced by that of class as an identity and culture rooted in a sense of place.

This is the fundamental impasse of 2010s working-class politics: despite the return of class to public lexicon and renewed (though frequently ventriloquistic) interest from journalists and social scientists into who the working class are and what they are concerned about, the continued lack of a class formation in this period (with its associated meanings, values and institutions), meant that the politics of class struggled to be expressed in its own terms. Indeed, this impasse often manifested in a sense of unease among 2010s working-class writers about how to approach the concept. Chris McCrudden, for instance, in his moving essay, 'Shy Bairns Get Nowt', from the *Common People* anthology (2019), discusses growing up in a working-class family from the North East. McCrudden draws on elements of class as culture related to an economic category, contrasting seemingly innocuous items like olives and sausage rolls as broader signifiers of middle and working-class cultural tastes (29), before bringing in elements of the economic category itself, writing that 'the class my grandparents inhabited looks very different today' so much so that 'even defining it is a struggle' due to the complicating factors of increased university education, home ownership and holidays abroad, among others (30). Meanwhile, Kerry Hudson, at the start of her memoir, *Lowborn* (2019), writes that 'being born poor is not simply a matter of economics or situation, it is a psychology and identity all its own that, in me, has endured well beyond my "escape"' (3). Yet this identity linked to her past exists simultaneously with a sense of ambivalence toward her present. As Hudson explains, she is 'unable to reconcile my "now" with my past [...] belonging nowhere and to no one, neither "back there" nor truly "here"' (3).

The sense of ambivalence or ambiguity vis-à-vis class in these passages relate again in large part to class as identity with their authors having to navigate between their working-class backgrounds and their adult lives in more middle-class dominated environments. However, these individual stories of ambivalence between past and present class experience, themselves map onto the broader narrative of the social change – and subsequent challenge of recognition – from the old working class to the new: in writing about class, working-class writers in the 2010s frequently return to the theme of working-class childhood, itself situated in earlier eras of class formation; the working-class present, then, is frequently engaged with as the loss or absence of working-class past. Undoubtedly symptomatic of a culture steeped in 'the End of History' and years of Blairite 'We're all middle class now' capitalist triumphalism, it nonetheless manifests in a palpable unease among writers (working-class ones included) attempting to apprehend what class means and how it operates in the present day. When Kerry Hudson asks 'What did working class even mean any more?' (2019: 3), she is not just pointing to her own detachment from contemporary working-class experience, but the broader lack of a shared understanding about it.

This emphasis on class as identity rooted in a sense of geographic space or community (and a related focus on working-class childhood), must also be understood in relation to the lack of emphasis in 2010s working-class fiction on contemporary waged work. In a talk on postwar British working-class writing, Raymond Williams mentions the 'striking irony' that texts from this period contain 'extraordinarily few descriptions of working-class work' (2020: 47). Williams describes the majority of these novelists as 'people who were born and grew up in working-class families' but their education (often from as young as eleven) had taken them away from 'working-class jobs but not working-class life and family connections' (49). As such, their novels typically involve 'an intense creation of the nature of working-class family life – the home, the meal, the outings and so on – but not this one central experience of the class which is work, which the child of such a family sees at that certain distance but do not themselves share' (49–50). This lack of focus on waged work, Williams argues, results in the relative exclusion of class as a social relationship, making such work 'not a class novel but a regional novel' in that their characters have 'their specific habits, they talk in their specific ways, their life is recreated in convincing detail' (50); however, because classes 'in any significant sense exist in their social relationships', this foregrounding of childhood memory and subsequent omission of waged work diminishes the exposition of those relations and serves to turn class culture into 'a kind of caste attribute' (50).

Williams's approach to class in this talk is arguably more rigid than in *Keywords*, where the 'the tastes and lifestyles of the category' are still included under a broader definition of class whereas here they are relegated to the position of caste attributes. Moreover, as Phil O'Brien and Nicola Wilson argue in their introduction to the 2020 issue of the *Key Words* journal, Williams's 'overriding concern with waged work as a defining feature of the working-class novel' is 'a masculinist blind spot that causes him to neglect other forms of working-class writing' (8–9). However, while O'Brien and Wilson are correct to point out the narrowness in Williams' conception of work, it nonetheless seems reasonable to highlight that the de-emphasis of waged work within working-class writing, while not diminishing their 'workingclassness', nonetheless places emphasis on particular conceptualizations of class over others; in particular, a move away from the idea of class as a formation in response to the irreducibly antagonistic social relationships of capitalism.

It is in the context set out above that it becomes interesting to look at the relative absence of waged work in the highly productive period of working-class writing that was the 2010s. As an illustrative contrast, in the 1930s, many working-class novels could be said to be fundamentally connected to specific industries – most significantly the mining novels of authors like Harold Heslop, B.L. Coombes, Lewis Jones, among others – while the journal *Left Review* ran a competition encouraging readers to 'contribute descriptions of "an hour or a shift at work"' (Hilliard 2006: 133). However, in the 2010s, waged work was markedly less prominent: for instance, returning to *Common People*, it seems not insignificant to note that in over thirty entries, not a single one involves a sustained engagement with the contemporary experience of waged work. Rather, working-class fiction in the 2010s is more rooted in a sense of place rather than the experience of waged work, evident even in many of the decade's titles: *NW* (2012), *Iron Towns* (2016), *The Cut* (2017), *Ironopolis* (2018). Even the subtitle of *Lowborn* mentions 'Britain's Poorest Towns' rather than, for instance, its lowest paid jobs. Indeed, where these titles do allude to work, it is often in relation to the old industries related to their locales: 'iron' as metonym for the heavy industry of a town or polis or 'the cut' as reference to the system of canal-ways that served industry in the Midlands.

The point of all this is not to argue that this fantastic body of work from arguably the most fruitful period of working-class writing in British history would somehow be improved if they included more workers; this is categorically *not* a call for the 'boy-meets-tractor literature' of which Adorno accused Socialist Realism (1980: 173). Rather, it is an attempt to understand why, precisely in such a productive period for working-class literature, the experience of working-class waged work is relatively absent.

In part this can be ascribed to the aforementioned issues of increased access to university (and, in some instances, even grammar school) taking working-class young people away from working-class adult life and, subsequently, waged work. However, this does not seem to be the only issue; after all, the Great British Class Survey notes that about one-fifth of those termed 'Emergent Service Workers' are graduates, predominantly from arts and humanities, usually working in 'relatively insecure' service sector occupations 'such as bar work, chefs, customer service occupations and call centre workers' (Savage et al.

2013: 241). So the issue is not just one of authors' relative detachment from working-class waged work; rather, it seems that waged work (and social relationships and formations around and within it) was, in the 2010s, of diminished importance in terms of how class was commonly understood and expressed. Class as an economic category and as an identity (that is, the culture related, but not reducible to, the category) increasingly took precedence over class as formation and relation of social antagonism. This understanding of class puts an increased emphasis on working-class belonging in space, up to and including the nation, whether as communities that are 'left behind' in contrast to the 'North London metropolitan elite', or the economic grievances expressed in a language of Britishness (or even whiteness) in opposition to encroachment on national borders either by migrant labour or supranational organizations like the EU. That the 2010s saw historic lows in terms of trade union activity seems relevant here (ONS 2019: 3): if, as Italian Marxist Mario Tronti argues, we cannot understand what the working class is 'without seeing how it struggles' (2019: 303), then it makes sense that in a period of diminished struggle what we are left with to understand class are largely its signifiers of culture and identity.

This struggle around how to define and express class, in a period where its discussion became increasingly ubiquitous as the cleavages between competing definitions became increasingly deep, is evident in the works of working-class novelists of the 2010s. As mentioned previously, one way this struggle manifests is in the recurring theme of working-class childhood, a motif that is skilfully deployed in Anthony Cartwright's *How I Killed Margaret Thatcher* (2012), in which Sean Bull recounts his childhood growing up in the Midlands following Margaret Thatcher's election. The novel's structure sustains an interplay between past and present, switching between Sean's childhood thoughts and his adult reflections on them, with chapters punctuated by quotes from Thatcher herself. This interplay thus draws together the aforementioned mapping of individual stories onto broader narratives of social change whereby Sean's personal tragedies (in particular, the death of his father) are inseparable from the processes of deindustrialization and neoliberalism enacted by Thatcher's Conservative government. Sean's dad, it soon transpires, had himself voted Conservative. Nine-year-old Sean rationalizes the situation thinking '*We're all Labour. Our MP's Labour: my dad's vote didn't really count; or my uncle Eric's. They made a mistake, I suppose*' about which his adult self reflects 'I supposed it then and I suppose it even more now' [emphasis in original] (4). Structurally, Cartwright's recycling of 'suppose' over these two temporal moments points the reader to his explicit drawing of them together over the course of the novel. In this instance, the 'mistake' that he supposes was made transforms from a largely innocent one whose implications Sean's childhood self cannot fully comprehend to, in adulthood, a more menacing one which his adult self now believes in 'even more'. Moreover, the shift in tense from present to past simple similarly draws together personal and political implications: Sean's childhood thoughts are transcribed in the present (as they would have been) while his adult self reflects on them using the past in a way that parallels a psychological working through of traumatic experience; yet this shift from present to past also seems to suggest a movement from a moment in which a (perhaps naive, certainly unfulfilled) possibility to act remains, to one which represents, if not an absolute finality, then at least one in which that chapter in Britain's political history has concluded. As Cartwright explains in his interview with Phil O'Brien, Sean 'is living in a time of political battle. By the nineties, the battle was over. We had lost' (2015: 413).

If, as Satnam Virdee contends, the postwar consensus represented 'the apex of an incremental but relentless process of working-class integration into the nation' (2014: 101), then Thatcher's election in 1979 represented the working class's extraction from it. Cartwright depicts that process by situating his narrative between the Thatcher years of Sean's childhood and the contemporary experience of neoliberalism in adulthood, producing the structure of a reverse *bildungsroman* where, instead of the socially dislocated child or adolescent growing up to achieve self-actualization and reconciliation with society, Sean goes from relative integration within the national community to become increasingly dislocated from and hostile towards the national body politic. Jed Esty, discussing colonialism and the novel, argues that imperialism 'unsettles the *bildungsroman* and its humanist ideals, producing jagged effects on both the politics and poetics of subject formation' (2012: 2). Neoliberalism can be read as performing a similar function, with Esty noting that the Thatcher/post-Thatcher era 'novels of youth often function as stories of alienation and of impossible social reconciliation' often due to 'unemployment and economic marginalization that produce arrested adolescence' (211). For instance, when Sean falls from a window ledge at the beginning of the novel, it symbolizes what he (and the British working class more generally) are about to lose, crashing through the shed roof to be saved by 'a big pile of dust sheets left by the council' (Cartwright 2013: 3). As he plummets, Sean is literally caught by the state's proverbial 'safety net'. However, as the novel progresses, this integration within the social compact of the national community begins to unravel as local industry shuts down, Sean's father loses his job and later dies in an accident related to stealing machines from disused factories while Sean himself embarks on an ultimately aborted attempt to assassinate Margaret Thatcher. The novel ends with an image of Dudley ravaged by Thatcherism, his uncle Johnny described as living the past thirty years in a state of chronic un(der)employment, standing 'on the pavement edge like it was a clifftop [...] equal parts timid and brave' (236), a marker of how public space has become a hostile environment for its working-class inhabitants. The welfare state that previously caught Sean as he fell, now plays an altogether more punitive role as an unspecified 'They [...] threaten to stop the little money [Johnny] gets' (236). In line with Esty's point regarding the 'arrested adolescence' produced by economic marginalization, Johnny has become one of the many 'lost boys, men' in the area, still 'watching the news and bickering with [Sean's] granddad' (236), much as he did thirty years previously. The novel then closes with the adult Sean admitting that there are days 'when I wish I'd just pulled the trigger' (238). Cartwright's reverse *bildungsroman* thus ends by resisting easy claims to reconciliation as Sean's coming-of-age story occurs against a backdrop in which the support systems of family, community and society are dismantled and replaced by dislocation and powerlessness. The individual-psychological merges with the social-political: Sean (and the broader British working class) ends the novel in the place where the traditional *bildungsroman* begins.

The importance of place is deeply significant in many of Cartwright's novels, and not least in *How I Killed Margaret Thatcher*. In his interview with Phil O'Brien, Cartwright argues that its centring on a specific locality is a particular feature of 'industrial age, working-class life [...] the typical few streets where your family lives, circumscribed by work, shops, pubs, sports clubs, and so on. There is a real contrast with middle-class culture here [...] and I think this difference remains in spite of the dismantling of much of working-class life, of the work in particular!' (2015: 404). Indeed, a concern with locality can be seen in Sean's contrast between his grandparents' community on Crow Street and the new house to which his family has moved (due to his father's skilled work and frequent overtime hours) in the better off area on Elm Drive:

> *I don't like Elm Drive. I don't like the way my room looks out on the trees and nothing else. At my nan and grandad's you can see for miles and there are all sorts of things going on: the factories and allotments and the little cars far away on the motorway and the trains creeping alongside the factory buildings and by the canal as they go into Dudley Port station.*
> *[...]*
> *Even the garden at our house isn't as good as it seems. We put a swing in it but you can't really see anything while you're swinging, only the fence. I prefer the swings at the park because as you swing you can watch the freight trains coming*

> *into the yard and if you go and stand at the wall you can see them shunting and look at all the different tracks as they criss-cross.*
>
> Cartwright 2012: 87–89, original italics

Sean's impulses here are fundamentally collective, decrying the anaemic privacy of the relatively better off Elm Drive in comparison with the '*all sorts*' that can be observed from Crow Street. Sean's attachment to Crow Street thus becomes an illustration of precisely that importance of locality in working-class life, which Cartwright discusses with O'Brien. Moreover, that sense of the communal within the local, is figured in large part through its circumscription by work: the trains creeping alongside factory buildings, the canal, the freight trains and Dudley Port station all allude to the area's industrial past, making Sean's identification with Crow Street in significant part an identification with that past; indeed, when towards the end of the novel, Sean comments that Crow Street is 'no place to live these days' (237), this can therefore be read as an allusion to the dismantling of that industrial identity.

Yet this passage and, indeed, the structuring effect of viewing narrative events through Sean's childhood perspective certainly seems (at least at first) to recreate Williams's issues which distinguish between class and regional novels. That is, the close representation of working-class family life, speech, and so on, but not that of waged work, which the child sees from a distance but does not share. Indeed, in the passage above Sean quite literally observes the world of waged work from a distance, in this case from a wall which acts as a border between the child's world of the playground and the adult world of employment. This absence of waged work, and therefore the social relationships on which it is predicated, certainly risks turning class into the kind of caste attribute Williams describes. However, Cartwright resists this tendency, not only by situating Sean's family closer to class culture as the 'meanings and values and institutions of the formation' than 'the tastes and lifestyles of the category', but also in how he depicts Thatcher's intrusion into – and disruption of – their lives and that of their community. As Williams argues, the absence of waged work in working-class fiction results in a situation whereby 'the relations with other classes are not present (2020: 50) and such initially seems to be the case in Cartwright's novel. However, as well as appearing on the family's television screens and newspapers (and, obviously, briefly when Sean almost assassinates her), Thatcher also appears in the novel via citations from her speeches between each chapter, which cast suggestive lights on the narrative: for instance, a quotation from Thatcher's infamous 'enemy within' speech (216) precedes the chapter in which Sean goes to assassinate her, while a quote on the economic approach she pursued in the 1980s being rooted deep in 'the nature of the British people' (235) is followed by the closing chapter depicting the daily struggles of Sean's community. This structuring device maintains Thatcher as a constant presence within the novel that is (almost) unassailably distant from its characters, yet nonetheless intimately involved with their fates. However, it is not so much Thatcher the individual that Cartwright integrates into the novel, but rather Thatcher the symbol of neoliberal triumph. Just as Marx describes the capitalist as merely 'capital personified' (1990: 342), Cartwright's Thatcher is Thatcherism personified; her presence serves as an embodiment of the processes of the neoliberal turn while her placement between chapters is a device for structuring the narrative at a level of detachment from the action of the narrative itself, just as the processes that come to structure the lives of the novel's characters operate at a similar level of detachment. The response of characters, particularly Sean's grandad, to the personification of Thatcherism by turning off the television or leaving the room only highlights their powerlessness in resisting the processes she personifies. As Sean himself acknowledges in adulthood, 'I think I might have realised then [...] I could kill her, but it wouldn't change anything. Nothing would come back' (223). As such, while the novel may focus in large part on working-class life viewed through the perspective of the child themselves a step removed from the adult world of waged work, it resists the slide into Williams' idea of the regional novel by maintaining an abstracted sense of class as social relationship and class culture as the meanings, values and institutions of the formation in response to that relationship.

However, this form of class culture remains almost entirely in Sean's memories of childhood when working-class life remained 'circumscribed by work'. In the sections of the novel dealing with Sean's adulthood, the dismantling of the older forms of waged work sees a significant shift in understanding working-class life into one of pure locality. This is evident in the fact that a major locus in these contemporary sections becomes the pub that Sean takes on as landlord. The pub, as an institution within working-class communities, is rooted entirely in the local (forming, as it does, its demotic alias) and this in itself is highly indicative of a contemporary understanding of class that foregrounds place over waged work. It is also significant that when Sean takes on the pub, he 'go[es] back to the original name: the Crow Cawing' (35) and relates the location to its history of struggle via the Roundheads who drank there during the Civil War, its public readings of Chartist newspapers and makeshift weapons which were made next door during the 1842 rebellion. However, the Crow Cawing also calls back to

Sean's own personal history on Crow Street, placing his grandparents' former community (and the class formation contained around it) into the area's longer rebellious tradition and making the pub itself a repository for these resistant traditions. The absence of the contemporary experience of waged work (and class culture based around it), means class as a formation with its meanings, values and institutions is more easily situated in the past; indeed, to do so in the present would border on speculative fiction. Contemporary working-class space in Cartwright's novel, in the form of the pub as a repository for earlier resistant traditions, becomes an expression for a class culture still struggling to be expressed. As Cartwright explains, he is 'much more interested in endurance than escape. [...] My characters are waiting it out for better days, even if they might not see them' (O'Brien and Cartwright 2015: 404–405). To this end, Cartwright describes the 'drops of water held in a spider's web woven in the old brickwork in the corner of the yard. The web trembles with the weight of the water but doesn't break' (Cartwright 2012: 237–238). 'Web', here, lends itself to multiple layers of meaning: as a home, again reinforcing the importance of place (Crow Street, the pub); but also 'web' as a network (formation) or net akin to the safety net that caught Sean as he fell at the start of the novel. These images are all linked by their fragility in an era of neoliberal triumph, trembling under the weight of neoliberal attack; yet, in not breaking, Cartwright suggests their ability to weather the storm.

Another structural aspect of the working-class childhood motif is the sense of social-historical impasse as chronology ends Fukuyamically in the present. Two 2012 novels which deal with this sense of impasse are Zadie Smith's *NW* and James Kelman's *Mo Said She Was Quirky*. Furthermore, it seems important to note the significance of these novels being set in London, a city often written out of (or otherwise figured more straightforwardly as an antagonist within) contemporary narratives around class, particularly via the 'North London metropolitan elites' rhetorical device. Smith's and Kelman's novels thus, in different ways, abjure common assumptions about working-class place and space whether in terms of its location (*NW* being quite literally an area of the so-called 'North London metropolitan elite') or in terms of belonging within it (as a migrant from Scotland, *Mo Said She Was Quirky*'s Helen is outside 'her place' while her partner Mo, as a British Muslim of Pakistani descent, is racialized out of a sense of British class belonging).

With this emphasis on stasis and problematizing notions of belonging, it is of little surprise that both these novels draw heavily from the locker of modernist technical innovation. Indeed, Smith intimated the necessity of moving towards such an aesthetic in her essay 'Two Paths for the Novel' (2008; later renamed 'Two Directions for the Novel' and included in the 2009 anthology *Changing My Mind*). Originally published when the financial crisis was only a year old, Smith makes an analogy between two aesthetic 'paths' and the present epoch of late capitalism. In this analogy, Smith contrasts what she calls the 'lyrical realism' (2011 [2009]: 73) of Joseph O'Neill's *Netherland* (2008), on the one hand, with the 'constructive deconstruction' (93) of a novel like Tom McCarthy's *Remainder* (2005) on the other. Smith places McCarthy's constructive deconstruction in the tradition of postmodern innovators such as Thomas Pynchon and David Foster Wallace, writers relegated to the position of 'misguided ideologists, the novelist equivalent of socialists in Francis Fukuyama's *The End of History and the Last Man*' (Smith 2011: 73); that is, as noble, but ultimately failed, experiments in surpassing older forms. By contrast, lyrical realists are more in the mould of Balzac and Flaubert, a model that remains, like liberal capitalism, 'the last man standing [...] on the evidence of its extraordinary persistence' (73). But, as Smith points out, 'the critiques persist, too' (73).

The persistent critiques of liberal capitalism are manifested in part in the aforementioned return of the term and concept of class to the public lexicon. However, this redeployment of class into public debate has often been done in a way that presupposes its distinction from London and its frequent invocation as a synecdoche for 'out of touch' 'metropolitan elites'. Not only does this elide the experiences of working-class Londoners but, somewhat more sinisterly, it hints at an implicit racialization of poverty in the capital, and its related social problems, as pertaining to subjects distinct from the (implicitly white and British) working class outside it.

In this context, then, Smith's *NW* and James Kelman's *Mo Said She Was Quirky* become vital counter-narratives to such nativist instrumentalizations of class identity and politics, variously drawing upon and subverting conventions of realism, modernism and postmodernism to apprehend class formation and decomposition. Thus, the analogy Smith makes in her 2008 essay between 'lyrical realism' and The End of History is one of the central motifs around which their textual strategies revolve: producing 'constructive deconstructions' within which their characters navigate the impasse of a class subject in a period when class as a formation (and its concomitant culture of meanings, values and institutions) is in retreat. Like Cartwright's novel, these novels also offer a critique, which – in spite of that literary and economic 'last man standing' – stubbornly continues to persist.

The decomposition of the British working class during and after Thatcher saw the key industries it was organized around dismantled and its organizations defeated. Though arguably felt most in those industrial heartlands similar to that depicted in *How I Killed Margaret Thatcher*, it was also significantly felt in London: the redevelopment of London's Docklands into a financial hub around Canary Wharf being an obvious example as well as the shift towards a service economy predicated on low paying retail and hospitality jobs. As such, London is the most unequal region in Britain with issues of economic disadvantage also being stratified along lines of ethnicity.

These issues form much of the subtext to the aesthetic and political concerns of *NW*, which follows the intersecting lives of Leah, Felix, Nathan and Keisha (who changes her name to the more ethnically ambiguous Natalie) as they navigate contemporary North-West London. Smith depicts class decomposition as a result of deindustrialization and its subsequent restructuring around a service-dominated labour market, illustrating what Nick Hubble, in their own discussion of *NW*, calls 'the collapse in skilled manual jobs that sustained the social working-class culture of the postwar period' (2016: 206). This lost culture haunts *NW*'s characters in the form of the older generation's lost radicalism: Felix, for instance, was born on the Garvey House black power commune, but is only able to access those experiences via a photography book which he subsequently fears is 'creating the memory for him' (Smith 2013 [2012]: 106). Meanwhile, there also exists a palpable disappointment with the adult world, in which he had expected men like his neighbour Phil Barnes, a radical postal worker, to be 'as common as [...] wildflowers' (107). Significantly, Felix is of a similar age to Cartwright's Sean Bull and so similarly saw the dissolution of that older class formation that their fathers (and Phil Barnes) were all part of; like Sean, Felix is similarly detached from that formation, not quite able to connect with it, as can be seen not only in the aforementioned mediation of his memories via the Garvey House book, but also the discrepancy in outlook between Phil Barnes and himself: 'I'm more about the day-to-day' Felix says when implored to be more politically engaged, before jokingly calling Phil 'a proper old leftie [...] proper commie' (115). At this point, Phil bends with laughter, but when he 'reared back up Felix saw tears in his eyes' (115). The passage rests on an ambiguity between amusement, but also a sadness at the kernel of truth underpinning the joke: that the class culture of which Phil is a part, with its meanings, values and institutions, no longer retains the currency it once did.

This lost class formation also manifests in the novel's depiction of waged work: Felix, for instance, reels off a lengthy curriculum vitae – itself indicative of the precarious post-industrial job market – of employment in restaurant kitchens, security, the postal service, logistics, painting and decorating, and retail

(126). Leah, meanwhile, is a university graduate with an 'unpaid, growing debt' (33) for a degree which is appreciated 'not [by] the institution that conferred it, not her peers, not the job market itself' (32). Indeed, as a social housing tenant in a low-level admin job, Leah (like Felix) can be thought to occupy the position of what the Great British Class Survey describes as an "Emergent Service Worker", with high levels of cultural capital, but low levels of economic capital. However, Smith's (admittedly very brief) depiction of working life provides a look not only at the experience of particular class categories, but also the fundamental impasse of contemporary class politics more generally: Felix's CV highlights the decline in waged work as a site of working-class identity construction while Leah experiences her work as aimless alienation, looking at the clock: 'Four forty-five. Zig, zag. Tick, tock [...] a minute seems to stretch itself into an hour' (33). This impasse also manifests in the anxieties expressed around consumer habits, shopping at 'the chain supermarket [that] closed down the local grocer and pays slave wages [...] leaving with broccoli from Kenya and tomatoes from Chile and unfair coffee' concluding that their consumer habits mean that she and her partner, Michel, are 'not good people' (80). Leah is a character deeply concerned about social injustices, both locally (in the supermarket's 'slave wages') and globally (with her awareness of 'unfair coffee' and global supply chains). In the contemporary neoliberal moment, however, the absence of the class formation of characters like Phil and Lloyd means Leah's grievances are experienced as individual failings, whether for having done the wrong degree (and so failing in the job market) or making the wrong consumer choices (as the only conceivable way of expressing grievances in an era of hyperindividualistic neoliberal capitalism), heightening her sense of existential angst. But rather than read this as Smith's pessimistic statement on some transhistorical human condition, it necessitates a reading as specifically historically located: if, as Adorno argues, 'loneliness is a social product' which 'transcends itself as soon as it reflects on itself as such' (1980: 165) then Smith's depiction of Leah's alienation reflects upon the broader social condition: the inability to externalize (and act upon) grievances following the collapse of older class formations. The alienation Leah experiences is embodied in this section of the novel's use of stream-of-consciousness narrative prose. As Knepper explains, this 'immerse[s] the reader in Leah's consciousness [...] disclosing the workings of the mediated self' (2013: 119) and is the formal expression of Leah's political paralysis: unable to act as either part of a collective class subject or neoliberal individualist consumer, Leah's grievances with society find no means for outward expression and so are internalized as personal failing and existential crisis.

By contrast, the Keisha/Natalie plot contains the novel's 'success story' of working-class ascent to precisely that position of individualist neoliberal consumer. As part of her escape from her working-class background, Keisha gets 'crazy busy with selfinvention' (Smith 2013: 209). Made up of 185 separate vignettes, the Keisha/Natalie plot can be read as Smith's deployment of fragmentation and pastiche typically associated with postmodernism as Natalie pieces together her identity from these diverse fragments to create a new image of her 'self', her name change being one example in this process. These fragments, however, never coalesce easily: one vignette, parodying the style of lonely hearts columns, states 'Low-status person with intellectual capital but no surplus wealth seeks high-status person of substantial surplus wealth for [...] longer life expectancy, better nutrition, fewer working hours and earlier retirement' (227), framing her marriage to upper-class Frank as a calculated drive at social mobility. It comes as little surprise, then, when later she realizes 'that she was not very happily married' (250) and her drive to escape working-class life, once achieved, only brings about its own existential crisis.

NW was Smith's first novel after 'Two Paths for the Novel' was published, and it can clearly be read as an attempt by Smith to produce a work of 'constructive deconstruction'. Indeed, as Knepper explains, '*NW* eschews chronology in favour of a spatially configured story concerning various "visitations" or encounters in the space of NW' (2013: 112). As such, there is movement around the space of North West London, but little in the way of progress: the text both begins and ends with Leah in a hammock in her garden. Furthermore, the fragmentation of Keisha's vignettes and parodic irony of the lonely hearts-style column show a clear nod to postmodern literature (though Keisha's unsatisfactory ending seems to problematize the promises of postmodernism's fragmentation and playfulness). Leah's aforementioned stream of consciousness symbolizes an inability to act upon the social world and is clearly indebted to modernist aesthetics while Felix's section, the one most closely resembling a form of 'lyrical realism', is the only story that suggests an arc towards redemption and resolution before his tragic murder forecloses any such possibilities. Smith's collage of forms, then, serves to depict a twenty-first-century working class in the aftermath of its destruction as a collective formation: in the absence of such a formation, Smith's characters pursue (unsuccessfully) individual methods for progress. Locating narrative movement in significant part in the movement around/within space, working-class experience is similarly located primarily in its existence in space, not necessarily just as an aspect of class as identity or economic category (though that exists in *NW*, too), but also as an exposition of the impasse facing the contemporary experience of class as formation.

James Kelman's *Mo Said She Was Quirky* similarly emphasizes a sense of stasis in depicting the class-based anxieties of its protagonist, Helen, as she spends the day at home in South London before going to her job in a casino. Despite the majority of the novel taking place in Helen's home (and, via its use of stream of consciousness, inside her head), it still deals obliquely with issues surrounding contemporary waged work, in that waged work takes up a significant amount of her thoughts (and, by extension, the narrative prose) even when she is not actually at work. To this end, Helen's job, and that of her partner, Mo, are highly illustrative of London's post-industrial economy: both work in the low-wage hospitality sector with Mo embodying the issue of low pay amongst restaurant workers and workers of Pakistani origin, 'working six nights a week [...] and even that isnt enough' (Kelman 2013 [2012]: 59). Furthermore, as a household, they are emblematic of poverty among London's working families, solving their overcrowding by turning a walk-in cupboard into a bedroom for Helen's daughter, Sophie (13). Helen's job and the cupboard-cum-bedroom are also both filled with symbolism – Helen's casino alluding to working-class London's subservience to the 'financial gambling' of The City, not to mention the processes that redeveloped places like Canary Wharf. Meanwhile, the walk-in cupboard-cum-bedroom encapsulates the precarious nature of London's twenty-first-century working class with Alex Clark describing it in his review as feeling 'scarily provisional: both faintly transgressive [...] and potentially dangerous' (2012: n.p.). Indeed, as Helen herself says, this bedroom installation has to be hidden from the landlord while also feeling like it poses an imminent danger to her daughter: 'you looked up to the ceiling and saw the stuff piled high, then down below and it was Sophie's bed! My God!' (16). Yet the simultaneous transgressiveness and potential danger of this bedroom is also, like Cartwright's web that 'trembles [...] but doesn't break', a testament to an underpaid working class's capacity to survive under the immense strains of neoliberalism.

Kelman's portrayal of Helen's working life is also insightful not only for its symbolic value, but also for what it discloses about the contemporary experience of low-paid waged work and the relative absence of working-class formation. Helen is depicted as atomized and powerless in the workplace, watched panoptically by the casino's inspectors and lecherously by its customers. Regarding the latter, Helen muses upon her feeling of 'being controlled' (200): 'she was a woman and she was an employee [...] he was not only a man but a customer; he had bought the right to control' (200). Kelman's sentences here, nominalizing Helen's multiple identities (as both 'woman' and 'employee', rather than "female employee") places emphasis on the importance and simultaneity of both, underlining how capital and patriarchy mutually reinforce one another in her experience of waged work.

Similar processes are evident when Kelman depicts Helen's work activities:

> She dealt: [...]
>> A card a card a card, a card a card a card. Pause.
>> Card card stay, card bust, stay, card bust, stay, stay. [...]
>> Helen raked in the chips and onwards
>
> Kelman 2013 [2012]: 195–196

The task's alienating repetitiveness is clear; but this passage also illuminates Helen's isolation and powerlessness in her working life: in the work process, she is an island of value production, detached from colleagues by a role which only requires she carry out her individual duties and thus lacks either the sociability of more collaborative labour processes or the workplace power of a position within a chain of production. In this sense, Helen symbolizes the twenty-first-century atomized workforce with its loss of collective organization and identification. In this context, stream of consciousness functions similarly in Kelman's novel as in Smith's: to highlight the degree to which class grievances struggle to be externalized and, as such, are internalized as personal anxiety and frustration.

Kelman's intentional and deeply political narrative aesthetics are, as Scott Hames explains, all too frequently reduced by critics to a simple – even anti-literary – reproduction of working-class speech (2010: 86–87). However, rather than simply representing working-class oral culture, what Kelman is doing is centring a working-class interiority which allows readers insight into the working-class experience – and also, by extension, the mechanics – of post-industrial capitalism. Modernism, as critic John Fordham argues, is 'transformed by the working-class writer', making it able to focus on 'those qualities of working-class experience which afford a unique expression of the social totality' (2002: 100). Kelman's stream of consciousness thus allows us to perceive what Helen's experience feels like – as in the passages above regarding her observation by both inspectors and customers – but through her subjective experience we can also make connections between those experiences and the broader social conditions which heighten her feeling (and actuality) of being controlled by a patriarchal class system. That is, in centring Helen's working-class interiority, Kelman obliquely affords an expression of the totality.

Ultimately, stasis and the depiction of an atomized class subject is the unifying motif of Smith's and Kelman's novels. As with Leah in *NW*, the modernist stream of consciousness represents Helen's inability to actualize class grievances in the external world. This sense of atomization is linked to the dissolution of older class formations: looking from the train at 'an old factory and warehouse area' Helen thinks of the 'Russian man Lenin', both of which are 'from a bygone age' (Kelman 2013, 186). As with Hubble's point regarding *NW* and the collapse in manual roles that sustained a collective working-class culture, the decline of industry is here linked to the decline of radical class politics. There is also a similar scepticism about the future: as Phil Barnes laments that 'they just feel no hope, the young people, Felix, no hope' (Smith 2013: 111), Helen similarly concludes about her prospects for moving into more suitable accommodation: 'Probably never. They didn't do the lottery' (Kelman 2013: 13). Gone, then, is the 'FORWARD TO A SOVIET BRITAIN' attitude of John Sommerfield's *May Day* (2010: 178) or the progressive historical movement of Lewis Grassic Gibbon's *A Scots Quair* (1932–34), both similarly indebted to modernist technical innovation, including a sustained use of stream of consciousness. By contrast, Kelman's novel, like Smith's, makes use of such innovation to depict a class adrift from the culture of its past formation and as yet unable to construct a new one.

One 2010s working-class novel, which attempts to do something along the lines of interwar working-class writing, is D.D. Johnston's *Peace, Love & Petrol Bombs* (2011). Unlike other novels from the 2010s, where contemporary waged work plays a relatively minor aspect in the narrative (if any at all), such work forms a central plank of Johnston's text. The novel follows Wayne Foster's exploits as a worker at Benny's Burgers in the fictional Scottish town of Dundule, organizing an informal workplace union ('Benny's Resistance Army') and eventually getting involved in the anti-globalization movement of the early 2000s. It can therefore be read in the traditions of interwar working-class novels that were similarly rooted in specific industries. For instance, in one passage, Johnston lays out the division of labour at Benny's, asking us to

> consider the life of a bun man. A beeper decrees when toasting should start, a buzzer stipulates when it should end. There are two toasters on overlapping cycles [...] And yet, at Benny's, bun toaster is as good as it gets. Take the poor dressings guy: he's got eighteen seconds to apply condiments to nine buns – a wet slice of pickle, squirts of ketchup and mustard, and a pinch of the onions that come dry in a packet. And the dressings guy is a labour aristocrat next to the grill man.
>
> Johnston 2011: 43

This passage is therefore very much in the tradition of earlier forms of proletarian fiction, which would frequently expend space within the text to elaborate on the mechanics of the production process; in Johnston's novel, however, such 'mechanics' are updated for the post-industrial economy.

Moreover, themes of resistance also suggest a degree of continuity between Johnston's novel and older proletarian texts. However, Johnston's text is no Socialist Realist treatise; rather, the resistance that takes place is frequently either poorly thought-out – such as when Wayne's workmate, Gordon, impulsively smashes a recently-installed CCTV camera with a broomhandle (100) – or comic, such as when a staff notice is defaced with a crude doodle of male genitalia, which Johnston integrates into the novel in the form of a Vonnegutesque illustration (59). There are also other, more collective, moments of resistance, such as when Wayne and his colleagues disguise themselves as Santas – and one Dalek as the shop had run out of Santa costumes – and hurl snowballs at their manager (63) and even the name 'Benny's Resistance Army' itself suggests an ironic use of hyperbole, which draws attention to its own distance from reality. Such moments of resistance all humorously underline the continuing existence of class antagonism, but it is a bittersweet humour in a moment understood as one of generalized retreat (evident not least in Wayne's descent into depression). This ironic self-awareness underlines the unhistoric nature of these times and actions, yet it still allows the reader to glimpse the possibilities for potential future class formations in the post-industrial context.

This continuity with older forms of working-class writing is something the novel seeks to unsettle, particularly through its use of intertextual references: for instance, Wayne's workmate, Owen Noonan (commonly known as Spocky), is a direct reference to classic socialist novel, *The Ragged-Trousered Philanthropists*, combining the names of its socialist hero, Frank Owen, with its author, Robert Tressell (real name: Robert Noonan). Indeed, at one point, Spocky even performs a version of Frank Owen's 'Great Money Trick', updated for a twenty-first-century capitalism of credit cards and widespread personal debt (97). Meanwhile, another of Wayne's colleagues is Lucy Guthrie from Kinraddie, an allusion to the character Chris Guthrie and the fictional hamlet from *Sunset Song* (1932), the first novel of Lewis Grassic Gibbon's *A Scots Quair* trilogy. Yet, Johnston's intertextuality serves more to highlight the distinctness, even discontinuity, between his novel's characters and those he alludes to (and, thereby, also those class formations). Both Lucy and Spocky remain unsatisfactory reconfigurations of their namesakes: at a Benny's Resistance Army reunion towards the end of the novel, Spocky's behaviour and political discussion is so disjointed as to seem as if he 'had gone completely mad' (230). Lucy, meanwhile, leaves her PhD scholarship for a relationship with an upper-class student who frequently disparages working-class people as only good for buying tinned spaghetti and Sunny Delight (217). Lucy also writes a column under the nom de plume 'Lucy Lesjoue' as 'Guthrie has the wrong sound' (217–218), the significance of this name change heightened by its relationship to the French word *jouer* meaning 'to play' or 'to act'. Like Keisha/Natalie, Lucy's name change seems part of a problematic attempt to assimilate into the middle classes by jettisoning her working-class background. Johnston's construction of these unsatisfactory arcs for these characters explicitly tied to older forms of working-class writing highlights the inapplicability of previous forms of class representation (both literary and political) to the present day. As such, intertextuality in Johnston's novel functions not so much to construct links back to previous formations, but rather to indicate our inability to simplistically reach back to them in order to deal with the working-class present.

As with previous novels discussed in this chapter, there is a sense in *Peace, Love & Petrol Bombs* of resistance towards the easy imagination of forward historical motion. Indeed, despite being a political coming-of-age story (an *aktivistroman*, perhaps?), the novel is broken up via its use of a non-linear narrative structure in a way that resists ideas of straightforward linear progress. As Wayne explains in a moment of meta-narrative:

> Lives are shaped like asterisks. At any point, lines intersect in a multitude of directions. You can be diverted, driven down tangents, and then made to reverse. It's the same when telling a story. You start off talking about one thing, then you have to describe another thing, and if you follow that track then you'll forget about the thing you were talking about in the first place. [...] I was telling you about 1999, when Lucy and I were in the Students' Union. [...] Her lips were red from the blackcurrant cordial in her snakebite. This is somewhere we have been before, right?
>
> Johnston 2011: 75

When Wayne asks if this is 'somewhere we have been before', it highlights that this passage is picking up the narrative from the last time he commented on Lucy's lips being 'red from the blackcurrant cordial in her snakebite' (25). In the context of this passage, then, the intervening fifty pages are therefore framed as a lengthy digression, an example of a story which starts 'about one thing', having to 'describe another' and eventually forgetting 'the thing you were talking about in the first place'. Significantly, this idea of how stories can move in multiple directions is conceived entirely in the passive: individuals are 'diverted', 'driven down tangents' and 'made to reverse'. Understood in this fashion, the novel's non-linear structure becomes another expression in 2010s working-class fiction of the difficulty in imagining historical progress. Wayne's inability to recount a story in a linear fashion is thus an expression of his sense of impotence within the wider movement of history. Indeed, for Wayne, history does not feel like something he makes (even if under conditions not of his own choosing), but rather as something in which he struggles to chart a course forwards, instead being variously 'diverted', 'driven down' or 'made to reverse'.

Despite all this, the novel nonetheless ends with a distinctly Gramscian 'optimism of the will'. Wayne's French anarchist girlfriend, Manette, calls him 'le Petit Fantôme', referencing the French title for Casper the Friendly Ghost. Ostensibly due to Wayne's pale complexion, the reference also functions as an analogy for Wayne's alienation: Manette recounts one of le Petit Fantôme's stories in which he begins to disappear after making a wish to stop daydreaming at school. As Manette explains, ghosts are 'only their memories and dreams and without them they do not exist' and so Petit Fantôme's friends save him by telling him 'all the adventures he has forgotten, and all the dreams he used to believe in' (196–197). As Manette and Wayne argue during the collapse of their relationship, Wayne declares that he does not see the point of their activism, to which Manette replies that it is to 'keep the ideas alive' (207). Wayne's alienation and increasing depression ought therefore to be read as akin to Petit Fantôme's disappearing when he stops himself from dreaming while Manette's attempts to keep the ideas alive parallel the adventures and dreams of which Petit Fantôme's friends remind him. When Wayne returns to Dundule at the end of the novel, he passes the Benny's Burgers in which he once worked. Seeing two young employees, he notices how they 'paused and spoke, their voices lost behind glass, the peaks of their caps just low enough to hide their eyes' (244). The novel finally closes with a monologue, containing strong undertones of Calvino's opening to *If on a Winter's Night a Traveller*, in which Wayne speaks directly to the reader, advancing possibilities about his future ranging from petit-bourgeois respectability to middle-aged suicide before saying 'I'd like to think that you and I will meet during some as yet unimagined social struggle' (246). The novel thus concludes simultaneously in resistance to and hemmed in by the popular adage of capitalist realism (that is, that it is easier to imagine the end of the world than the end of capitalism) with Wayne unable to imagine the struggle in which he hopes to meet the reader. Yet there is also a degree of hope (or, at least, 'willed optimism') in the idea there may one day be such a future struggle; though its actuality may be beyond current imagination, the conditions for such a movement's emergence are now in existence, even if only discernible at the edges of our perception: in this sense, the Benny's Burgers employees, with their unheard conversation and eyes hidden by caps, indicate the possibility for the recomposition of a working-class culture around the meanings, values and institutions of its formation in the post-industrial era. Despite Wayne's physical separation from them, they exist to keep his (and the reader's) dreams alive.

Published at the start of the 2010s, *Peace, Love & Petrol Bombs* embodies an aspect of class politics at the start of the decade. Before concluding this chapter, however, it seems necessary to briefly discuss a novel which encapsulates how the politics of class came to be expressed towards the end of the decade. Returning to Anthony Cartwright, his novella, *The Cut* (2017), was commissioned by Peirene Press in response to the result of the EU Referendum. In her brief introduction to the text, Peirene Press founder, Meike Ziervogel, writes that she was 'shocked' by the referendum result, realizing that she 'had been living in one part of a divided country' (Cartwright 2017: 3). The divide that Ziervogel is talking about is certainly (given the choice of author she commissioned) one around a culturally/geographically conceived class identity; however, Cartwright's novella contains an approach to class that is more multifaceted than many critics have noted.

The text follows Cairo Jukes, a precarious labourer and former boxer from Dudley, and Grace Trevithick, a documentary filmmaker from London, as they embark on a fragile (and, ultimately, tragic) romance around the time of the EU Referendum. That the two of them stand in as ciphers for the geographical/class-cultural divide that has come to define the referendum (however inexactly) is obvious: as Kristian Shaw explains, 'Cartwright dramatises the divide between nationalist and cosmopolitan forms of identification [...] demonstrating how class inequality continues to run deep and informs the public mood towards European integration' while also showing 'how geography emerged as a crucial factor in the referendum result' (2018: 23). As such, Grace, whose first named appearance in the text is swimming in Hampstead Heath's ladies' pond, is clearly intended to represent the 'North London metropolitan elite' while Cairo represents the 'left behind' Leave voter from England's deindustrialized heartlands. In this sense, his work – both past and present – is itself deeply symbolic. In his present job, Cairo cleans up industrial sites, obliterating the evidence of Dudley's industrial past. Meanwhile, his previous work as a boxer is itself symbolic of that past: as a boxer, Cairo was quite literally a manual worker with Cartwright using it to invoke the loss of such forms of employment. Discussing the possibility of a return to boxing, Cairo thinks to himself 'There is a whole history of men who got beaten up, knocked senseless, in order to pay the rent, put food on the table

[...] he is part of a proud Dudley tradition' (12), while later he talks about his pride when people spoke to him after fights: 'it felt good, to be somebody' (68). While outwardly a reference to boxing, it also functions as a reference to the sense of working-class identity and belonging to a locality circumscribed by work engendered by the proliferation of industrial labour. Yet Cartwright does not simply indulge in nostalgia, rather he shows how such industrial labour was simultaneously a source of both pride and pain, knocking its workers senseless as they struggled to survive financially. Cairo's boxing, then, represents both the sense of identity which the older patterns of working-class industrial life produced without erasing the strains on the people who participated in it. As Cairo's father tells Grace, 'you shouldn't wish it back, but we never wished for the way things am today either' (56).

However, while Cairo and Grace clearly represent this kind of geographical and class-cultural divide, an under-discussed aspect of Cartwright's novella is how he depicts class not only in terms of identity or economic disadvantage, but also in terms of a formation (or lack thereof) active within antagonistic social relations. However, in keeping with the prevailing trajectory of class politics in the 2010s (and particularly around how the politics of class were mobilized around the referendum), Cartwright's text submerges such politics within the arc of the broader narrative. As such, the primary way in which class animates the action of Cartwright's narrative is certainly in the sense of an identity linked to an economic category and geographic space. When the North London metropolitan elite and deindustrialized regional working class meet, their interactions are fraught with an awkward tension and misunderstandings. Class and geographic space are also linked when Grace's recording of Cairo is broadcast on national television sometimes with 'subtitles under his words, translated into his own language' (21). As Chloe Ashbridge explains, 'Cairo's words are appropriated and effectively given back to him by a middle-class narrator in order that they may be broadcast to the nation' (2020: 13), his dialect underlining his otherness from a national mainstream defined in terms of a proximity to the culture of the South-East England middle classes.

Yet Cartwright also works to ensure that the novel does not lapse into a conception of class that deploys it interchangeably with geographic space. In one passage at dinner, Cairo tells Grace that '"It ay like London, you know" [but] wasn't really sure what he meant by this and was glad she didn't press him on it. When he'd had those fights in London, the people had been much the same as at home' (72). In this passage, then, there is an awareness on Cairo's part of the inability to substitute geographic space for class and yet it nonetheless animates his thinking as 'London' comes to function metonymically for a specific (middle-)

class culture despite not even aligning with his own experience. This is evident in Cartwright's move from Cairo's reported speech to free indirect discourse, the latter of which, as Jeri Johnson explains in her excellent introduction to *Ulysses*, 'shares a preoccupation with representing character through pre-verbal or unspoken "thoughts"' (1993: xxi). Drawing on Johnson thus allows a reading of Cairo's London memories as preverbal 'thoughts' which remain unspoken, even to himself, but which nonetheless exist on the edge of an awareness of his statement's incompleteness. The awareness of that incompleteness means he is glad not to be pressed on the topic and, indeed, the fact that Grace does not is itself proof of the extent to which the notion of class as understood in cultural/geographic terms has reached a broad, cross-class, 'common sense' consensus.

The submerging into Cairo's unconscious of this problematization of how class politics is frequently deployed is matched by Cartwright's similar submerging of class as the culture of the formation. As mentioned already, the primary axis around which class tension revolves is that of the geographically inscribed economic category (that is, Grace and Cairo). However, there are also frequent allusions to an older (and lost) class culture around the meanings, values and institutions of the formation, whether in Cairo's statement that Dudley is 'a fighting town' (28) or his father's comment about the 'culture that went alongside the work' (55). However, perhaps most significant is Cairo's relationship to Tony Clancey, his employer and current partner of Cairo's ex-wife. Tony would undoubtedly be coded by many as culturally working class in much the same way as Jake and his father in Professor Green's Channel 4 documentary, having grown up with Cairo before moving to a nicer part of Dudley. Indeed, Cairo resentfully comments about Tony behaving 'like no one knows where he comes from, like he isn't who he is, has become something else' (37). The contradiction here between Tony's simultaneously being 'who he is' and becoming 'something else' itself speaks to precisely the differing definitions of class discussed in this chapter, from Kerry Hudson's 'then' versus 'now' to identity versus antagonistic social relationship. The 'something else' which Tony has become is part of the employing class that exploits workers like Cairo (and, significantly, his migrant workmates). Yet despite the multiple antagonisms which constitute their relationship, the conflict between Cairo and Tony never develops and does not animate narrative progress to the extent that Cairo and Grace's does. This is categorically *not* a criticism of the text; on the contrary, by constructing his work in this manner, Cartwright has captured how the politics of class around the referendum (and in the 2010s more broadly) was mobilized in such a way that the politics of class as an identity came to engulf and efface the politics of class as a formation (indeed, it is not insignificant in this regard that, despite their antagonisms, both Cairo and Tony support the Leave campaign). Similarly to Cairo's awareness of the incompleteness of his comment about London, the inability of the tension between Cairo and Tony to drive Cartwright's narrative, despite Cairo's acute awareness of that tension, is the literary embodiment of how the politics of class as a formation was ultimately unable to drive the political narrative of the 2010s.

Ultimately, the 2010s was an extremely rich decade in working-class literature that drew on a wide range of aesthetic practices to engage in ongoing debates about class after at least twenty years when the discussion of class was, if not taboo, then certainly passé. The paradox of this period's working-class fiction was that it came about when class as a subject had returned discursively, but the class-subject remained largely absent politically. As such, the relative absence of waged work in 2010s working-class writing speaks not only to its diminished significance in class identity, but is in fact a literary manifestation of that paradox, where class and its multiple definitions are increasingly talked about and contested with one another, but in a period where working-class self-activity remains at an historically low ebb. Thus, to engage with the contemporary meaning of class, rather than awkwardly insert workers into their novels, writers employed other motifs, frequently that of a lost and inaccessible past class formation (such as Sean Bull's family) and of the sense of a broader societal impasse, expressed in the frequent eschewal of linear narrative or plot (as in *NW* or *Mo Said She Was Quirky*). Yet, as this chapter is being written, rocketing inflation and a cost-of-living crisis has led to strike action by workers in a number of sectors. Industrial disputes in the UK have hit a five-year high (Wall 2022) and the rail union leader, Mick Lynch, has declared that 'the working class is back' (Sleigh 2022). What this may mean both in literary and political terms is still impossible to say, but it is certainly not beyond the bounds of possibility to imagine that should the workplace once again become a site for the actualization of class politics, then so too might it again become a site for imagining the drama of everyday life, its social implications, and even how the emotion, tension, and relationships contained within the workplace may point towards a reimagining of the social itself.

Notes

1   See, for example, Goodwin and Heath's 2016 research for the Joseph Rowntree Foundation, which found that poverty and lack of formal education were major

drivers for the leave vote, or Conservative minister Alan Duncan's comment that Brexit was a working-class 'tantrum' over immigration (*The Guardian* 2017). As this chapter will argue, how one defines 'working-class' is obviously extremely fraught and drastically alters the extent to which Brexit can be considered a class response. Phil O'Brien is correct when he writes that the post-referendum desire to blame 'an imagined working class' glosses over the fact that Leave mobilized 'a broad-based coalition of voters which is much more wide-ranging than the "left behind"' (O'Brien, 2020: 15). Despite this, however, a form of class politics was nonetheless 'at play' in the referendum, regardless of the reactionary coalitions it was ultimately martialled within.

2   Interestingly, in *Keywords*, Williams notes that those using class in this descriptive sense will 'have to break these divisions [between classes] into smaller and smaller categories' (2015: 32).
3   Issues which, it must be noted, are not limited to the white and male working class; indeed, with the exception of education, other sections of the working class consistently fare worse by most metrics than white working-class males. Though Professor Green himself has no investment in the politics of white, male resentment, it is unfortunate that his series, in detaching the very real social issues faced by white working-class men from those faced by the working class in general, accepts the framework of such resentment.

Works cited

Adorno, Theodor. 'Reconciliation Under Duress'. In Theodor Adorno et al., *Aesthetics and Politics*. London: Verso, 1980: 151–176.
Ashbridge, Chloe. '"It aye like London, you know": The Brexit Novel and the Cultural Politics of Devolution'. *Open Library of Humanities* (1)15, 2020: 1–29.
Cartwright, Anthony. *How I Killed Margaret Thatcher*. London: Tindal Street Press, 2012.
Cartwright, Anthony. *The Cut*. London: Peirene Press, 2017.
Clark, Alex. 'Mo Said She Was Quirky by James Kelman – review', *The Guardian*, 1 August 2012: https://www.theguardian.com/books/2012/aug/01/mo-said-quirky-james-kelman-review (accessed 18 May 2022).
Esty, Jed. *Unseasonable Youth: Modernism, Colonialism, and the Fiction of Development*. New York: Oxford University Press, 2012.
Fordham, John. *James Hanley: Modernism and the Working Class*. Cardiff: University of Wales Press, 2002.
Goodwin, Matthew J. and Oliver Heath. *Brexit Vote Explained: Poverty, Low Skills and Lack of Opportunities*. York: Joseph Rowntree Foundation, 2016: https://www.jrf.org.uk/report/brexit-vote-explained-poverty-low-skills-and-lack-opportunities (accessed 23 June 2023).

Guardian. 'Brexit vote was "tantrum" by British working class, says Alan Duncan'. 3 October 2017: https://www.theguardian.com/politics/2017/oct/03/brexit-vote-was-tantrum-by-british-working-class-says-alan-duncan (accessed 23 June 2023).

Hames, Scott. 'Kelman's Art-Speech'. In *The Edinburgh Companion to James Kelman*. Scott Hames (ed.). Edinburgh: Edinburgh University Press, 2010: 86–98.

Hilliard, Christopher. *To Exercise Our Talents: The Democratisation of Writing in Britain*. Cambridge, MA: Harvard University Press, 2006.

Hubble, Nick. 'Common People: Class, Gender and Social Change in the London Fiction of Virginia Woolf, John Sommerfield and Zadie Smith'. In *London in Contemporary British Fiction: the City Beyond the City*. Nick Hubble and Philip Tew (eds). London: Bloomsbury, 2016: 195–210.

Hudson, Kerry. *Lowborn: Growing Up, Getting Away and Returning to Britain's Poorest Towns*. London: Chatto & Windus, 2019.

Johnson, Jeri. 'Introduction' in *Ulysses* by James Joyce. Oxford: Oxford University Press, 1993.

Johnston, D.D. *Peace, Love & Petrol Bombs*. Edinburgh: AK Press, 2011.

Kelman, James. *Mo Said She Was Quirky*. London: Penguin, 2013 [2012].

Knepper, Wendy. 'Revisionary Modernism and Postmillennial Experimentation in Zadie Smith's *NW*'. In *Reading Zadie Smith: The First Decade and Beyond*. Philip Tew (ed.). London: Bloomsbury, 2013: 111–126.

Marx, Karl. *Capital: A Critique of Political Economy, Volume One*. London: Penguin Classics, 1990.

McCrudden, Chris. *Common People: An Anthology of Working-Class Writers*. London: Unbound, 2019.

O'Brien, Phil. *The Working Class and Twenty-First-Century British Fiction: Deindustrialisation, Demonisation, Resistance*. New York: Routledge, 2020.

O'Brien, Phil and Cartwright, Anthony. 'An Interview with Anthony Cartwright.' *Contemporary Literature* 56(3, Fall), 2015: 397–420.

O'Brien, Phil and Nicola Wilson. 'Introduction: Raymond Williams and Working-Class Writing.' *Key Words* 18, 2020: 5–21.

'Oil plant sackings spark walkouts'. *BBC News Channel*, 19 June 2009: http://news.bbc.co.uk/1/hi/uk/8108941.stm (accessed 18 February 2022).

ONS [Office for National Statistics]. (2019). *Labour Disputes in the UK: 2018*: https://www.ons.gov.uk/employmentandlabourmarket/peopleinwork/workplacedisputesandworkingconditions/articles/labourdisputes/2018 (accessed 25 April 2022).

Savage, Mike et al. 'A New Model of Social Class: Findings from the BBC's Great British Class Survey Experiment', *Sociology* 47(2), 2013: 219–250.

Shaw, Kristian. 'BrexLit'. In *Brexit and Literature: Critical and Cultural Responses*. Robert Eaglestone (ed.). Oxford: Routledge, 2018: 15–30.

Sleigh, Sophia. '"The working class is back and we refuse to be poor anymore" – Mick Lynch tells crowd'. *The Huffington Post*, 18 August 2022: https://www.huffingtonpost.

co.uk/entry/mick-lynch-tells-enough-is-enough-campaign-working-class-is-back_uk_62fdf347e4b071ea958cdee7 (accessed 2 September 2022).

Smith, Zadie. *NW*. London: Penguin Books, 2013 [2012].

Smith, Zadie. 'Two Directions for the Novel'. In *Changing My Mind: Occasional Essays*. London: Penguin Books, 2011 [2009]: 71–96.

Tronti, Mario. *Workers and Capital*. London: Verso, 2019.

Virdee, Satnam. *Racism, Class and the Racialised Outsider*. Basingstoke: Palgrave Macmillan, 2014.

Wall, Tom. 'Industrial disputes in UK at highest in five years as inflation hits pay'. *The Guardian*, 2 April 2022: https://www.theguardian.com/uk-news/2022/apr/02/strikes-in-uk-at-highest-in-five-years-as-pay-is-hit-by-inflation (accessed 25 April 2022).

Williams, Raymond. *Keywords: A Vocabulary of Culture and Society*. New York: Oxford University Press, 2015.

Williams, Raymond. 'British Working-Class Literature After 1945'. *Key Words: A Journal of Cultural Materialism* 18, 2020: 45–55.

Working-Class White Men. Channel 4, 16 January 2018, 22:00.

5

What's To-day? Politics and Typography in Ali Smith's Decade

Tory Young

Introduction: A Political writer?

Summer, the final novel in what is known as Ali Smith's seasonal quartet, won the Orwell Political Fiction Book Prize for 2021. In a subsequent celebration on Radio 4's *Start the Week*, Andrew Marr began his interview by sharing a commonly expressed view that having read all Smith's novels, it was not until the seasonal quartet that he thought of her as a political writer. Smith responded, as she always has, that she thinks 'all novels are political [...] all the arts are political' because they speak of the time and context in which they are produced (*Start the Week* 2021). When I interviewed Smith in 2013, I also suggested that in the first decade of reception, the politics of Smith's writing had been somewhat overlooked, and again she both resisted the label ('I don't feel that I am an "anything" writer') and denied writing with what might be called an agenda ('If I sit down thinking I've got a political axe, then I will write grinding rubbish') even though she is 'very politically informed, and formed' (Young 2015a: 142). I think there is a slippage here, hers or mine, between 'Political' and 'political': 'all the arts are political' but a 'Political' axe is only destructive, not creative. There may be a subtext here that 'Political' writing is so time-bound that it cannot generate enduring 'Art'; it serves my argument in this essay very well that typography conveys – in this case obfuscates – meaning. Certainly, the seasonal quartet, each volume published in the season of its title, produced urgently in what 'she has described as a "time-sensitive experiment"' (Kellaway 2021: n.p.), has been recognized as 'an experiment in writing about how we live now, and especially about how we register the language of politics in our everyday lives' (Wills 2020: n.p.). It has brought Politics to the fore.

In the same year as the award of the Orwell Prize, Patricia Waugh and Marc Botha published an edited collection of essays, *Future Theory: A Handbook to*

Critical Concepts (2021), as a redress to the horrifying emergence of the society that Orwell wrote of in *Nineteen Eighty-Four* (1949), one in which 'the corporate, the consumer-driven and the totalitarian have narrowed and even shut down independent and creative thinking' (Waugh and Botha 2021: 1). According to Waugh and Botha, 'Orwell's major theme [...] was that the ability to imagine and work towards alternative futures depends on keeping alive the experience of an historical moment through language that is conceptually rich enough to grasp and convey its true complexity' (1). Smith's award of the Orwell Prize is not in itself a sign that she is a 'Political' writer but an acknowledgement that her writing defies what Orwell termed 'Newspeak' by broadening not 'narrow[ing] the range of thought' (1); the broadness and complexity of her language, including its typography, enables the possibility of alternative futures as well as 'keeping alive the experience of an historical moment' (1). Each chapter of *Future Theory* is a reading of the multiplicity of a word; the final one being 'Hope' for obvious reasons. In this essay, I shall explain why Smith's writing of the 2010s is widely read as hopeful in spite and because of its increasingly overt Political consideration of issues such as the imprisonment of asylum seekers in inhumane detention centres.

Smith is prolific. Since her first collection of short stories, *Free Love and Other Stories* in 1995, she has published almost exactly one book a year, in addition to journalism, short stories in magazines, journals, anthologies, and introductions to the collected and republished works of other authors, and her Patronage of the charity *Refugee Tales*. She was first nominated for The Man Booker Prize for *The Accidental* (2005) and although this prize has escaped her thus far, critical acclaim and scholarly interest have continued to grow, peaking with attention to the seasonal quartet published between 2016 and 2020 (a quintet extending to 2022, if *Companion Piece* is included). Scholarship on Smith's work prior to 2011 often focused on gender fluidity and metamorphosis (see Young 2015b, 2018), or narrative time (Currie 2007) but since then has expanded into topics like hospitality in an age of surveillance (Bennett 2018; Popa 2021), trauma (Horton 2012), borders (Conway 2021). Smith's corpus is recursive; many themes, motifs and concepts have a germ (perhaps 'supplement') in an earlier work. The continuity is rich, overwhelming, sometimes elusive, but very marked. So, for example, whilst 2011's *There But For The* inaugurated discussion of refuge, when Miles, an uninvited dinner guest, locks himself into the spare room of Genevieve and Eric Lee, we can see that he is prefigured by Amber in *The Accidental* (2005), who also turns up in a family home unexpectedly. Whilst Miles and Amber may be perceived as puzzling irritants, fear of invasion is explored in 2022's

Companion Piece when a whole family of Covid-deniers take over the protagonist's house, after they have also been visited by a historical plague figure. All of Smith's writing is driven by concerns about the plight of refugees; the hostile environment; surveillance; screens, walls, fences and boundaries; the increase of privately owned public spaces (POPS); the marketization of health services and care homes; the closures of public libraries; the internet; climate change. It is often underpinned by a frightening sense of a historical precedent in the Nazi Holocaust and Second World War. But depictions of creeping totalitarianism are countered by thematic celebrations of the energetic and life-affirming provocations of literature, film and song and a material lightness on the page, a typographical layout which allows for lots of blank space, and formal aspects of ludic non-linearity, puns on homonyms and homophones, which demand that the reader 'hears' the texts. Through a particular focus on the typographical mark of the hyphen, I want to add to readings which explore graphic, textual and paratextual features – the book as an object, spatial dimensions, running motifs and metaphors, words as graphic objects, punctuation in general and hyphens in particular – as the ground on which her politics develops, and where her Politics come into view. The perceived split between content and form that Modernist literary experimentation refuted is here challenged when the reader attends to typography and the page. Reading the words as independent from their visual representation, I argue, strengthens the sense of those like David Grylls in his review of *Winter* for *The Times* that the 'aesthetic' or literary (Barthes's 'scriptible') qualities are 'self-conscious', perhaps even detrimental showing off: 'Artiness and preachiness can be an awkward mixture' (Grylls 2017: n.p.). But it is this playfulness with language, which allows her to be at once political and Political; the ludic approach to her craft and to literary aesthetics more generally grants her access to a topic which might otherwise be out of reach.

The politics of words: Sticky signs

Smith's approach to the politics of words resembles Sara Ahmed's thesis about 'affective economies' in *The Cultural Politics of Emotion* (2014). Ahmed asks 'Why is social transformation so difficult to achieve? Why are relations of power so intractable and enduring, even in the face of collective forms of resistance?' (11–12). Her answer lies partly in the operation of 'sticky signs' in affective economies. The approach is distinctly textual, and her texts are clearly Political. Ahmed reads the polemics of the British National Front and the speeches of Government ministers in search of 'metonymic slide' – a form of associative bond that forms not, as Saussure would have it, between signifiers and signifieds, but sideways between signifiers and adjacent, contiguous concepts. Signs, in other words, join to other signs in a process of adhesion, rather than cohesion, and form associations that are not rooted in reason but in affective association. The result is that political feelings are not 'resident' in subjects but distributed across associative or sticky relations forged in discourse in a way that is comparable to economic circulation. An example is the way that the threat of loss might cause very different issues to adhere to each other in a way that is never reasoned:

> hate is *distributed* across various figures [who] come to embody the threat of loss: lost jobs, lost money, lost land [...]. They threaten to violate the pure bodies [...] an invasion of the body of the nation [...]. The slide between figures construct a relation of resemblance between the figures. What makes them 'alike' may be their 'unlikeness' from 'us'. [...] Importantly, then, hate does not *reside* in a given subject or object. Hate is economic; it circulates between signifiers in relationships of difference and displacement.
>
> Ahmed 2014: 44

There is a kind of non-intentional abuse of argument at work in these relationships, rooted in some unargued resemblance. The formation of 'us', for example, entails the interpellation of 'you' into a position of generalized or national threat, and it is easy to see the importance of both ideas, resemblance and the work performed by the 'you-address', for an understanding of Smith's thematic interest in words, from the persistent interest in the category of resemblance ('like') and in 'you', which Smith herself presents in the sinister chorus of social media or global corporation in *Spring*. It begins with the promise 'We want the best for you' (Smith 2019: 119) and progresses through a series of declarations which spy on you 'We want to be able to see you through that screen while you're looking at something entirely other than us' (121) and finally interpolates 'you' into acts of racial exclusion and abuse 'We want the black and Latino people who work for us to feel a little less important and protected and able to rise in the company hierarchy than the white people' (121) all under the guise of 'keeping you safe' (122). As Ahmed points out, not every citizen is embraced into 'you'. For Smith, everything is meant, and metonymic slide is far from being a non-intentional abuse of argument. It is a kind of play that exposes adherences and associations as a form of enquiry into the affective political resonances of written and spoken words.

Surveillance was a prominent example of this kind of intentional metonymic slide in Smith's work in the 2010s. The political context for this is a set of widespread assumptions about criminality and nationhood: first, that you have no reason to fear surveillance if you have not done anything wrong, and second, that if you have 'done something wrong' then you deserve to be seen. The 'innocent', according to this metonymy, may be protected from crimes such as attack and theft by CCTV cameras in public places. Theresa May's hostile environment policy relied on both myths and expanded the metonymy into a criminalization of migrants in general, who deserve to be found if they are 'illegal' and then in being 'illegal' are associated with further crimes such as stealing resources of housing and the NHS from citizens, those interpellated as Ahmed describes, as legitimate owners. Increasing surveillance increases suspicion: why place a CCTV camera in a location where crime has not occurred or is not likely to occur? Why send a 'Go Home' van into an area without irregular migrants? Although May's original formulation, as reported by Amelia Hill in *The Guardian* amongst others, sought to establish 'a really hostile environment for illegal migration' (Hill 2017: n.p.), this hostile environment can only exist if its hostility extends outward in this way, into what Ahmed describes as an evocation of '*a history that is not declared*' (2014: 47); it must unsettle all those who are vulnerable by being poor, not white, female, or old, and does so by not being attached to a particular body. At the same time, hostility, as Ahmed argues, is dependent upon a notion of hospitality; in 'differentiating between genuine and bogus asylum seekers. [...] The nation is hospitable as it allows those genuine ones to stay' (46). The answer to Ahmed's opening question, 'Why is social transformation so difficult to achieve?', is found in this sense of hospitality and positive emotion; the National Front and the Conservative party do not build their ideologies around openly voiced hatred but expressions of love; in order to become the 'you' who is addressed in polemical material, you are worked on 'to feel love for the nation, whereby love is an investment that should be returned (you are "the taxpayer")' (1). In other words, the stickiness of the signs works in all directions, 'you' are valued and will be rewarded, 'they' will be punished for their theft of what is rightfully yours.

In what follows, I would like to explore Smith's engagement with these structures of feeling, through topics related to questions of surveillance, community and nation, but mainly as those topics are represented at a graphic level, in words and in books. My thesis is that the politics of Smith's writing can be read in the relationship between inherent political content and its representation in written words. At a fundamental level, the continual focus on puns and idioms invites the reader to consider not just meaning but how meanings change, using novelty to draw attention to the fact that words are a record of a historical moment, one that will change as language itself does. Like Joseph Conrad, her 'task is [...] by the power of the written word [...] before all, to make you see!' (1984: xlii) recognizing 'that the light of magic suggestiveness may be brought to play for an evanescent instant over the commonplace surface of words: of the old, old words, worn thin, defaced by ages of careless usage' (xli) precisely by shining this light on and drawing attention to their own presence. I will suggest that this is where her hope can be found: signs are sticky but metaphors can be changed to alter the public discourse and mood, associated meanings can be and will be unstuck. Almost compulsively, Smith draws attention to the changing meanings of words, visibly highlighting their changed spellings and presentation such as the disappearing hyphen, as I shall go on to discuss.

Metaphors change the direction of travel

Ahmed's thesis about the insidious power of *sticky words* chimes with recent philosophical thinking about metaphors and Smith's frequent literalization of metaphors firstly to expose their use, to bring them into sight. In 2015, Smith published her only single-authored collection of short stories of this decade: *Public Library and Other Stories*. The first story in *Public Library*, which immediately raises a smile in being titled 'Last', illustrates her method. A depressed first-person narrator begins:

> I had come to the conclusion. I had nothing more to say. I had looked in the cupboard and found it was bare. I had known in my bones it was over. I had reached the end of my tether. I had dug until I'd hit rock bottom. I had gone past the point of no return. I had come to the end of the line.
>
> Smith 2015: 5

The narrator employs a series of familiar metaphors, *clichés*, seemingly to reflect upon the end of a relationship; 'it was over' (5). But no relationship is referred to and as the story progresses, it seems as though the relationship that is over is the one with *clichés*, a narrow singular use of words. After all, how can a storyteller begin their story with a conclusion, the phrase 'I had nothing more to say'? It is typical of Smith to do so, to start her collection of stories with one called 'Last'. (In 2003's *The Whole Story and Other Stories*, the final story in a collection of twelve is called 'the start of things' and seems to refer to January, the beginning of the calendar year). But when the narrator explains that a 'last' is 'the piece of metal shaped like a foot which a cobbler uses to make shoes' (2015: 17), we not only realize that it can be a foundation, a starting point too, but also consider the fact that meanings of words change and are forgotten. Smith and the narrator are keen to remind us that there is a beginning, a starting point, in every ending, every 'last'. And what follows the final assertion above – 'I had come to the end of the line' – is the literalization of the metaphor; the revelation that the narrator is on a train. They had come to the end of the line physically, as well, perhaps, as emotionally: 'But at the end of the line, when the train stopped, like everybody else I got off and walked back along the platform to the exit.' (17). For the reader, there is, first, comedic relief in the immediate change of linguistic tenor; the end of the line is now a railway station not a moment of despair. As the story unfolds, contemplation of language's evolution, 'travelling etymologies' (8), rouses the narrator out of their depression until metaphor and reality combine: 'I turned around' (8). There are several jokes, or at least puns, here. I.A. Richards (1936) defined a metaphor as having a tenor and a vehicle; the tenor being the subject and the vehicle that to which it is being compared. This is a story about trains, travel, and movement but one which uses language itself as the vehicle for change.

In using the phrase 'travelling etymologies', the narrator of 'Last' seems knowledgeable about linguistics, perhaps knows about Richards' tenor and vehicle. The widest concept of transport as 'mental exaltation' (*OED*) is evoked through mechanical modes of travel in *Public Library* (here the train; in 'The definite article' the Tube; in 'Grass' a car). It is the fanciful meditation upon train travel, and metaphors from its semantic field, which free the narrator from depression:

> There was something fine in it, just walking along a forbidden track, thinking pointlessly about words. Travelling etymologies, that was a good phrase. It would be a good name for a rock band. It would be a good social-anthropological name for a tribe of people who jumped rolling-stock and lived on it, sheltering under waterproofed tarpaulins when it rained, sitting when it was sunny on the footplate spaces, if that's what they were called, or lying stretched out on the tops of the cargoes of carriages; reprobates, meaningful dropouts, living a freer, more meaningful life than any of us others was able to choose. The Travelling Etymologies. It was a good idea, and now, background-murmuring through my head again, for the first time in ages, was a welcome sound, the sound of the long thin neverending-seeming rolling-stock of words, the sound of life and industry, word after word after word coupled to each other by tough little iron joists, travelling from the past to the future like rolling stones that gather moss after all.
>
> Smith 2015: 8–9

Smith is clearly alluding to the 'supergroup', *The Traveling Wilburys*. If you Google them, you will find that the video that rises to the top of the search is for a song called 'The End of the Line'. In the black and white video for this song ('track'), the band members perform in an open-sided train carriage in a scene that depicts a familiar idealization of free-spirited travellers, just as the narrator of 'Last' describes. According to *Wikipedia*, the band's name itself is an example of a 'travelling etymology': 'Referring to recording errors created by faulty equipment, Harrison jokingly remarked to Lynne, "*We'll bury* 'em in the mix." Thereafter, they used the term for any small error in performance. Harrison first suggested "the Trembling Wilburys" as the group's name; at Lynne's suggestion, they amended it to "Traveling Wilburys". This is a very Ali Smith kind of pun.

As the narrator of 'Last' walks along 'the forbidden track', they hear 'the welcome sound of the long thin neverending-seeming rolling-stock of words' (9); that is, they are able to envisage a future once more as words themselves transform and continue forever. Hope is a form of futurity appropriate for the first story in a book. For the reader, this hopeful, continuous future is performed across the page, through the hyphenated words resembling train carriages that travel in a long sentence. Since 2001's *Hotel World*, Smith's prose is unusual in not being justified. This makes it much easier to read, according to 'study after study' (Houston 2013: 143). Her words are thus never hyphenated to meet the demands of the page meaning that all hyphens are intentional and rare. So these train carriages of words – 'neverending-seeming rolling-stock' – are visible and prominent, travelling across the page. The hyphens are the 'tough little iron joists' (9); they look like the 'couplings' (the term for mechanisms that join carriages) that they represent. They show us that words are metaphors.

The hyphen

The hyphen has an additional affective value. As well as being two (or more) parts joined by a hyphen', the *OED* also defines 'hyphenated' as persons 'born in one country but naturalized citizens of another [...] a person whose patriotic allegiance is assumed to be divided'. Here the conjoining of, for example, *Anglo-American*, is a negative, a division, rather than a doubling or a strengthening by the tough little joists of the hyphen; in her reclamation of the hyphen, Pardis Mahdavi describes how '[b]etween 1890 and 1920, the epithet "hyphenated American" came into use to bolster the xenophobia that accompanied the second wave of immigration to the United States' (2021: 53). This is a sticky sign in action: to be hyphenated is a cause of suspicion, of split loyalties at a time when singular patriotism is demanded. The hyphen seems to be the sticking sign, even a weapon; Mahdavi reports that President Woodrow 'Wilson famously said "Any man who carries a hyphen about with him carries a dagger that he is ready to plunge into the vitals of this Republic whenever he gets ready"' (56). John Wayne even sang a song 'The Hyphen' about 'the harm a line has done – /A simple little line, and yet/ As divisive as a line can get' (56) proclaiming that a hyphenated American could not be an American at all. Mahdavi reports that 'because of the weight of the associations with hyphenated Americanism, grammar sources such as the *Chicago Manual of Style* encouraged writers to drop the hyphen when referring to any immigrants' (56). The apparently neutral typographical mark is here a visual depiction of the ways that language and identity intersect. Mahdavi's book is an attempt to revivify 'the hyphen's connective force [...] showing us that to embrace the hyphen is to choose wholeness' in a way that seems closer to Smith's celebration of these possibilities of the mark; Mahdavi attempts to unstick the sign from the destructive associations that have devastated communities and lives. The damaging associative bond of the hyphenated American concerns nation but the hyphen's negativity has stuck to other forms of identity.

In his introduction to the poetry of Louise Glück, Daniel Morris celebrates its repudiation of 'critical assessments that affirm identity politics as criteria for literary evaluation. She resists canonization as a hyphenated poet (that is, as a "Jewish American" poet, or a "feminist" poet, or a "nature" poet), preferring instead to retain an aura of iconoclasm, or in-betweenness.' (Morris 2006: 31). This desire for an artist to remain unaffiliated returns us to Smith's own refusal to be 'an "anything" writer' (Young 2015a: 142). In Smith's and Morris's readings, being labelled at all is dangerous; it is a form of threatening surveillance and limitation rather than proud visibility and freedom. Mahdavi wants the hyphen to become an affirmation of wholeness achieved *through* multiplicity – bothness – hyphens as Smith's 'tough little [...] joists' (Mahdavi 2021: 9). Smith's boldest experiment with the materiality of a text *How To Be Both* (2014) – the book is printed in two formats with either section 'Eyes' or 'Camera' first – co-opts every visual aspect to suggest that being more than one thing, being both (male and female? Past and present?) is a possibility, perhaps even an inevitability. About *How To Be Both*, I have argued that '[a]t every state, the linguistic surface, both its visual surface and its grammatical conventions, co-operate in this way with the enquiry into what can be seen and what is unmarked' (Young 2018: 999) to remind us that no one has a single identity.

Hope

Caroline Edwards's final chapter on 'Hope' in *Future Theory*, begins with reference to the 2011 Occupy protests, their lasting symbolic achievement, and the work of Lynne Segal, by outlining the life-affirming joy experienced by those involved in 'Grassroots community organizing' (Edwards 2021: 434). The *Refugee Tales* project, of which Smith is a patron, and that I'll go on to discuss, is one such campaign but it is Edwards's elucidation of 'hope as an ontology' (435) which illuminates my enquiry into Smith's seasonal quartet as hopeful in spite of subject matter, such as the inhumane treatment of asylum seekers in detention centres, that is likely to cause profound despair. Following Terry Eagleton and other thinkers on the left who perceive optimism as faith in capitalist tenets of progress, Edwards examines hope through reading German utopian philosopher Ernst Bloch, to explain its temporality: 'hoped-for futurity is an ontological component of our experience in the present, which contains residual strands of past hopes, still waiting to be redeemed, as well as future-glancing anticipatory consciousness' (435). The temporal complexity of the moment here, as she describes it, recalls the modernist narratives, replete with analepsis and prolepsis, whose style Smith is commonly thought to be continuing, even sometimes extending, as for example in the radical experiments with the physicality of the book in *How To Be Both*, described above. Bloch was writing of and in the early twentieth century, their dangerous time; Edwards likens his 'understanding of the present as the darkness of the lived moment' (437) to 'Walter Benjamin and Theodor Adorno's model of historical images' (437). For Benjamin, political hope cannot emerge from a capitalist progression of time but instead is like a 'lightning flash of a future knowledge striking unerringly into our darkness' (Edwards 2021: 438). Edwards's reading of Bloch's 'unactualized Novum, in which the careful historian may discern the "still undischarged future in the past"' (442), alludes to Benjamin's reading of Paul Klee's *Angelus Novus* in which the Angel of History trembles 'between backward and forward motion' (Farago 2016), before being propelled 'irresistibly [...] into the future to which his back is turned' (Benjamin 1999: 249). Smith's project in the seasonal quartet echoes Benjamin's imperative to 'seize hold of a memory as it flashes up at a moment of danger' (247) in order to rescue the defeated from the historians of the victorious. She does so through temporal complexities of Benjamin and the linguistic complexities of Orwell with the addition, as I have argued, of her own spatial and typographical distinctions. But these material and linguistic ('scriptible') qualities are not at the expense of story, characters and images who embody the themes (the 'lisible') as I will now go on to show.

Autumn (2016), *Winter* (2017), *Spring* (2019) and *Summer* (2020) can be read as stand-alone novels but in addition to their seasonal progression (echoed in the paintings by David Hockney of the same lane through the corresponding seasons which adorn the covers) they are united by shared motifs; each has a presiding Shakespeare play, a Charles Dickens novel, a visual artist (whose work is featured in the endpapers), returning characters, primarily Daniel Gluck, and an image which appears on a postcard that recurs in each volume: Edouard Boubat's *La Petite Fille aux Feuilles Mortes, Paris* (1947). Boubat's black-and-white photograph is of a small child in a park strangely covered with dead leaves, whose back is turned to the camera. The leaves are worn like a dinosaur's spines and tail, as though the child is in fancy dress, but the child's posture is dejected rather than joyous or playful, and she seems to be alone. The image resonates through Daniel's mind in the opening of *Autumn* when we first encounter him through his own interior monologue. He thinks that he has died, is in heaven, naked and youthful on a beach. He covers himself with leaves to keep warm and 'Decent' (8), hiding his body from a girl he has seen in the distance. Layering the leaves reminds him of the Boubat image:

> Remember that postcard he bought off a rack in the middle of Paris in the 1980s, of the little girl in one of the parks? She looked like she was dressed in dead leaves, black and white photo dated not long after the war ended, the child from behind, dressed in the leaves, standing in the park looking at scattered leaves and trees ahead of her. But it was a tragic as well as a fetching picture. Something about the child plus the dead leaves, terrible anomaly, a bit like she was wearing rags. Then again, the rags weren't rags. They were leaves, so it was a picture about magic and transformation too. But then again *again*, a picture taken not long after, in a time when a child just playing in leaves could look, for the first time to the casual eye, like a rounded-up and offed child (it hurts to think it) or maybe also a nuclear after-child, the leaves hanging off her looked like skin become rags, hanging to one side as if skin *is* nothing but leaves.
>
> Smith 2016: 9

The postcard depicts a dangerous historical moment, shortly after the second world war, recalling for Daniel the painful story of his own sister, Hannah, who we later learn (in *Summer*) was 'offed' (9). But like Benjamin's reading of the *Angelus Novus*, in trembling between the past and the future, the photograph also incorporates a future horror of 'a nuclear after-child' (9). Daniel Gluck (a name, minus the umlaut, shared with Louise Glück's father, which does not feel like a coincidence as little does in Smith's writing) and the postcard are the key to hope in the quartet, in spite of the horrors of twentieth-century history that he has experienced and that the image suggests. It is through them, and piecing together Daniel's story, that readers find the connections of humanity that can feel like the only method of hope, of avoiding despair. In *Autumn*, Daniel regrets sending the postcard to: 'yet another woman he wanted to love him but she didn't [...] her name was Sophie something [...] He wrote on the back of it, *with love from an old child*. He is always looking out for that picture. He has never found it again.' (10). Daniel may not have found romantic love again either but in *Spring* his relationship with his neighbour's daughter, Elisabeth Demand, is mutual, deep and caring. Daniel introduces Elisabeth to the visual arts which become her career and she uses imagination and cunning to secure funds for his care home. The story is reassuring; in *Winter* the reader discovers that Daniel was actually the love of Sophia (not Sophie)'s life and that she gave birth to his son, Arthur (Art) who he meets in *Summer*. But the connections are made through the text rather than in the storyworld; the comforts and reassurance of art are for the recipient, the reader, whilst Daniel remains unaware. There is another father–child relationship that is not 'spelt out', to use the idiom, but is indeed spelled out; the careful reader, attending to the spelling of Elisabeth Demand's name with an 's' not the more common 'z', later realizes that she is the child of *Spring*'s Richard Lease. (Possibly a wry allusion to Barthes's *S/Z* in which the pleasures of the writerly, 'scriptible', text are outlined?). Likewise, rather than being stated, Daniel and Art's relationship is signalled through the symbolism of another presiding artwork of the quartet: Barbara Hepworth's *Mother and Child*. Hepworth made several sculptures with this title, each composed of two abstract stone figures of mother and child, and which Smith has described as embodying 'the intimate pull of love between two living beings' (Smith 2021: 6). In *Summer*, Charlotte (Art's ex-girlfriend) and Art return one part of the Hepworth maquette, the child, to Daniel to whom it belongs, having found it in Sophia's cupboard. The stone parent and child are reunited, paralleling the unwitting coming together of father and child. The parent and child do not know each other in the storyworld; it is only known to the reader. Here is the consolation of art; the pleasure of the 'scriptible' text.

Refugee Tales: Travelling signs, physical punctuation

Since 2015, Smith has been Patron of the *Refugee Tales* project sharing the stories of refugees, and which is a collaboration between writers, asylum seekers, former immigration detainees and the lawyers and interpreters who work with them. It is an example of storytelling and friendship as activism, the agency described by Segal which 'reinvigorates a sense of joy' (Edwards 2021: 434). In his Afterword to the first collection, David Herd describes how the stories were first told as punctuations on a walk along the Pilgrim's Way in June 2015; an image that recalls Smith's hyphens, and chains of like-minded and compassionate demonstrators such as the women at Greenham common referred to in *Winter*. The walk's visibility is crucial to the project, as a means of promoting awareness of the group of people who are hidden out of sight in Immigration Removal Centres. Herd reports that the government's removal of the detainees from view is replicated in their symbolic removal from systems of currency and language. Visitors are not allowed to take pen or paper into the buildings; no record is made during immigration bail hearings; everything is 'off record. It is this fact, the holding of people outside the skin of the language, that principally motivated *Refugee Tales*' (Herd and Pincus 2016: 140). The detainees want their stories to be told and find great relief in sharing them but have much to fear from identification so the anonymity granted by having writers tell their tales is paramount. The process of the tales being gathered involved careful listening: 'This is what the writers reported; that having collaborated in the way they did their relation to the language was significantly changed' (141–142). Furthermore, the collaboration in telling and receiving the tales constructs a collective responsibility: 'These are tales [...] that call for and generate a collective; tales that need to be told and re-told so that the situation they emerge from might be collectively addressed' (142). These are the politicized acts of friendship which give us hope through examination of language and the power of storytelling that Smith has always enacted through her own pages. It might be a statement of the obvious to claim that hope is a future-orientation, but in Ali Smith's work, it is the metaphoricity of future orientation itself, its linguistic and narrative manifestations, that is the object of enquiry and the character of its political affect.

What's to-day?

There is an episode towards the end of *Winter* which emblematizes this optimism; its theme is conventional but the formal analysis is punning and playful. It is an unspecified future and Art is reading *A Christmas Carol* to a child, presumably his child, on his knee. The child asks 'What's to-day?' (2017: 223). We hear the words spoken in our heads as Art hears them, as a question echoing Scrooge's famous enquiry about which day of the week it is. But the child, nameless and as such symbolic, is asking about the words on the page which are hyphenated, as they appeared in the 1843 text, reading 'to day' as a verb in its infinitive. This leads to a characteristic enquiry about time, for the child understands this to mean that 'to day' is to seize the day, to live, but Art explains how the 'today' in *A Christmas Carol* 'is in the past now [...] that's one of the things stories and books can do, they can make more than one time possible at once' (224). The seasonal quartet is replete with such temporal complexity, which echoes Benjamin's reading of the *Angelus Novum*, outlined above; one example is Daniel's recall of a future heaven, reunited with the girl, his sister, which opens *Autumn*. In *Winter*, an unnamed narrator asks the familiar and rhetorical question, 'why underestimate, ever, the mind of a child?' (225), but the child, in drawing attention to the hyphen, 'the little line between its parts' (224), sees the surface of the page anew pointing out the sign that indicates combination and connection, or conversely distinction and difference.

As discussed, the hyphen joins (at least) two words and thus represents a relationship between (at least) two things. But as Houston points out, even before the political intervention of the style guides, the history of the hyphen shows that it is 'an unstable punctuation that tend[s] to disappear' (2013: 126). It is a form of punctuation that writers can be uncertain about or forget to insert. In *Winter*, Smith draws our attention to a disappearing hyphen in a way that points towards Ahmed's thesis that 'sticky words' can become unstuck, what was once seen as distinct and complex, can become singular and ordinary, or invisible – differences can be erased. As Art tells the child, art can erase linear sequence: in 'today' the hyphen has disappeared. In art connections are revealed that life obscures; in *Winter* the hyphen reappears to remind the reader this. That discussion of the hyphen arises from *A Christmas Carol* suggests the concept of the 'old child', the sad girl in Boubat's photograph, or conversely the ageing adult animated by a childlike spirit, Daniel, whose ability to see things afresh is an imperative of the quartet. 'To-day' has lost its hyphen today, that is, in contemporary usage; losing 'the little line between its parts' which both join and separate them, to become closer instead, one word, one unit. Separation, in time, is seemingly erased.

Works cited

Ahmed, Sara. *The Cultural Politics of Emotion*. 2nd edn. Edinburgh: Edinburgh University Press, 2014.

Barthes, Roland. *S/Z*. Oxford: Blackwell, 1990.

Benjamin, Walter. 'Theses on the Philosophy of History'. In *Illuminations*. Hannah Arendt (ed.). Harry Zohn (trans.). London: Pimlico, 1999: 245–255.

Bennett, Alice. '"This Ridiculous Thing That Passes for a Passport": Seeking Asylum in Ali Smith's Fiction'. *Contemporary Women's Writing* 12(3, November), 2018: 322–337.

Conrad, Joseph. 'Preface'. *The N— of the Narcissus*. Oxford: Oxford University Press, 1984: xxxix–xliv.

Conway, Tove. 'Feminist Forms and Borderless Landscapes in Ali Smith's Seasonal Quartet'. *Iowa Journal of Cultural Studies* 21(1), 2021: 105–114.

Currie, Mark. *About Time: Narrative, Fiction and the Philosophy of Time*. Edinburgh: Edinburgh University Press, 2007.

Dickens, Charles. *A Christmas Carol*. London: Penguin, 2003 [1843].

Edwards, Caroline. 'Hope'. In *Future Theory: A Handbook of Critical Concepts*. Patricia Waugh and Marc Botha (eds). London: Bloomsbury, 2021: 433–448.

Farago, Jason. 'How Klee's "angel of history" took flight', 6 April 2016: https://www.bbc.com/culture/article/20160401-how-klees-angel-of-history-took-flight (accessed 21 March 2023).

Grylls, David. 'In the bleak midwinter'. *The Times*, 28 October 2017.

Herd, David and Anna Pincus (eds). *Refugee Tales*. Manchester: Comma Press, 2016.

Hill, Amelia. '"Hostile Environment": The hardline Home Office policy tearing families apart'. *The Guardian*, 28 November 2017: https://www.theguardian.com/uk-news/2017/nov/28/hostile-environment-the-hardline-home-office-policy-tearing-families-apart (accessed 21 March 2023).

Horton, Emily. '"Everything You Ever Dreamed": Post-9/11 Trauma and Fantasy in Ali Smith's *The Accidental*'. *Modern Fiction Studies* 58(3, Fall), 2012: 638–654.

Houston, Keith. *Shady Characters: The Secret Life of Punctuation, Symbols and Other Typographical Marks*. New York: W.W. Norton, 2013.

Kellaway, Kate. 'Interview: Ali Smith: "Hope is a tightrope across a ravine"'. *The Guardian*, 1 May 2021: https://www.theguardian.com/books/2021/may/01/ali-smith-hope-is-a-tightrope-across-a-ravine (accessed 22 March 2023).

Mahdavi, Pardis. *Hyphen*. London: Bloomsbury, 2021.

Morris, Daniel. *The Poetry of Louise Glück: A Thematic Introduction*. Columbia: University of Missouri Press, 2006.

Popa, Andrei Bogan. 'The Future as a Scenario of Hospitality in Ali Smith's *There But For The*'. *American, British and Canadian Studies* 37(1), 2021: 29–47.

Refugee Tales. Available online: https://www.refugeetales.org/about (accessed 14 June 2022).

Richards, I.A. *The Philosophy of Rhetoric*. Oxford: Oxford University Press, 1936.

Smith, Ali. *Autumn*. London: Hamish Hamilton, 2016.

Smith, Ali. *Companion Piece*. London: Hamish Hamilton, 2022.

Smith, Ali. 'Foreword'. In *Barbara Hepworth: Work and Life*. Eleanor Clayton (ed.). London: Thames & Hudson, 2021: iii–v.

Smith, Ali. *Free Love and Other Stories*. London: Virago, 1995.

Smith, Ali. *Hotel World*. London: Hamish Hamilton, 2001.
Smith, Ali. *How To Be Both*. London: Hamish Hamilton, 2014.
Smith, Ali. *Public Library and Other Stories*. London: Hamish Hamilton, 2015.
Smith, Ali. *Spring*. London: Hamish Hamilton, 2019.
Smith, Ali. *Summer*. London: Hamish Hamilton, 2020.
Smith, Ali. *The Accidental*. London: Penguin, 2005.
Smith, Ali. *There But For The*. London: Hamish: Hamilton, 2011.
Smith, Ali. *The Whole Story and Other Stories*. London: Hamish Hamilton, 2003.
Smith, Ali. *Winter*. London: Hamish Hamilton, 2017.
Start the Week. *BBC*, 28 June 2021: https://www.bbc.co.uk/programmes/m000xdx4 (accessed 17 December 2021).
'Travelling Wilburys'. Wikipedia: https://en.wikipedia.org/wiki/Traveling_Wilburys (accessed 25 November 2021).
Travelling Wilburys. 'End of the Line': https://www.youtube.com/watch?v=UMVjToYOjbM (accessed 25 November 2021).
Waugh, Patricia and Marc Botha. 'Introduction'. In *Future Theory: A Handbook of Critical Concepts*. Patricia Waugh and Marc Botha (eds). London: Bloomsbury, 2021: 1–38.
Wills, Clair. 'Caricature Time'. *London Review of Books* 42(19), 2020: https://www.lrb.co.uk/the-paper/v42/n19/clair-wills/caricature-time (accessed 23 March 2023).
Young, Tory. 'Invisibility and Power in the Digital Age: Some Issues for Feminist and Queer Narratology'. *Textual Practice* 32(6), 2018: 991–1006.
Young, Tory. '"Love and the Imagination Are Not Gendered Things": An Interview with Ali Smith'. *Contemporary Women's Writing* 9(1), 2015a: 131–148.
Young, Tory. 'You-niversal Love: Desire, Intimacy and the Second Person in Ali Smith's Short Fiction'. In *Twenty-First-Century British Fiction*. Bianca Leggett and Tony Venezia (eds). Canterbury: Gylphi, 2015b: 293–312.

6

The 'Teenie' Novels of Jonathan Coe: Intertextuality, Satire, Parody, Farce and Irony

Philip Tew

Introduction: Coe's 2010s fiction, parody, intertextuality, and *What a Carve Up!*

In the 2010s Jonathan Coe published four novels: *The Terrible Privacy of Maxwell Sim* (2010); *Expo 58* (2013); *Number 11* (2015); and *Middle England* (2018). The first two are shaped by dynamics drawn from employment undertaken by their central characters, the eponymous Maxwell Sim and Thomas Foley; the first decidedly humdrum (a complaints officer in a department store) and the second seemingly more unusual and potentially thrilling (an ad hoc spy of sorts). The third and fourth chart the lives of the lower middle classes set against in each case a political and an economic crisis, Blair's dodgy Iraq dossier and its fallout in *Number 11*, as well as the so-called Great Recession from 2007 to 2009. In *Middle England* the social divisions caused by the Brexit campaign overshadow all other plotlines, which offer a sense of further fracturing. As Vanessa Guignery indicates, in these subsequent novels, 'The author [...] plays with intra-textual references' (2018: 170) to his own earlier work, and as Merritt Moseley comments '*What a Carve Up!* remains still the novel for which he is best known despite the seven subsequent novels' (2018: 21). So given these two coordinates I will situate and assess the merits of Coe's 2010s fiction through the prism of his most celebrated novel and his favoured technique of interspersing postmodern decentring and pastiche with parody, a technique Linda Hutcheon reminds us 'is one of the major forms of modern self-reflexivity; it is a form of inter-art discourse' (2000: 3) that is capable of traversing genres. As Violetta Kostka summarizes 'It [parody] is composed of two structural levels, of which the first one is an authority; the second – a transgression of authority. Its entire act of enunciation includes also a pragmatic frame, i.e. the intent of parody which spreads from comedy through neutrality to seriousness' (2016: 67). The neutrality is essential in that it provides at least an illusion of a balance or equilibrium. Such a central albeit often fluctuating coordinate of non-partisanship is both critical to the process of parody and represents an element that Coe both toys with and subverts in his satirical structures, as we shall see below.

At the start of the decade, twenty-three years after the publication of Coe's first novel, *The Accidental Woman* (1987), this well-established writer was in his fiftieth year. Already awarded six literary prizes for fiction and biography, two rewarding his most celebrated work, *What a Carve Up!* (1994), his work was feted most especially in Europe (see Laity 2010). According to Helena Chadderton it was this book 'which made his name [...] and began his popular rise outside the United Kingdom' (2017: 270). Huw Marsh concurs, concluding that it 'is widely read as one of the defining satires of Thatcherism and still probably Coe's best-known work' (2020: 22). Coe emerges not simply as a satirist, but primarily as an intertextual writer, drawing upon a postmodern propensity that María Jesús Martínez Alfaro describes thus: 'While all authors re-write the work of predecessors, many contemporary writers *consciously* imitate, quote, plagiarize, parody ... extensively' (1996: 271). Indeed, Coe's very title, major aspects of his plot and certain characters were all drawn intertextually from a 1960s spoof horror film of the same name that also features in Coe's narrative. As Michael Shallcross reports, this 'artistically negligible British horror-comedy film named *What a Carve Up!* (dir. Pat Jackson, 1961) was released to minimal fanfare' (Shallcross 2016: 124). It was thereafter not lauded or much remembered, apart from by Coe. As Coe's 'Author's Note' makes clear at the end of this fiction, the writer also draws upon Frank King's *The Ghoul* (1928), the novel on which Jackson's cinematic *What a Carve Up!* is loosely based' (500). And as Shallcross indicates, a key parallel with the originating film (which as stated ironically itself draws on a prior fictional source) is subtly subverted, allowing Coe to make Owen a 'more self-consciously highbrow novelist' (126), and thus

> This premise enables Coe to merge a formal parody of the 'golden age' detection genre with a thematic satire of free-market capitalism (a conflation suggested by the pun operative in the original film title), in order to fashion a complex exploration of the ethical dilemmas facing the professional writer in the free-market free-for-all of 1980s Britain.
>
> Shallcross 2016: 126

At least by implication, Coe turns his parodic tendency upon his own role as a writer, thus facilitating an ironic gap between a character with writerly affinities to

Coe and the author himself over which the reader appears to exercise a degree of interpretative control. Coe's borrowings become part of a technique Linda Hutcheon in *The Politics of Postmodernism* calls 'the assertion of external reference and the contradictory reminder that we only know that external world through other texts. This postmodern use of paratextuality as a formal mode of overt intertextuality both works within and subverts that apparatus of realism still typical of the novel genre [...]' (1989: 89). My primary thesis in the following analysis is that in Coe's fiction such bifurcating aesthetic reciprocity or repetition is central, involving a complex, multi-layered literary-cinematic-factual sets of correlations, equivalent to what Hutcheon tellingly terms 'literary borrowing' (1986: 231).

In this novel Coe exhibits a high degree of virtuosity in his elaborate set of borrowings. Craig Brown praises the novel as 'a satire on the greed of the Thatcher years, and, unlike so much satire, zesty, fun, inventive and largely free of sanctimony' (2018: 26). Shallcross describes Coe's engagement in terms of Leavis's once celebrated rejection of parody in which he regarded this specific intertextual set of gestures as being part of a playful and highly unoriginal 'cultural mass market in the mid-twentieth century' (124). Coe celebrates such Leavisite deficiencies according to Shallcross, who cites John Gross's argument that the parodist 'must create something absurd himself – something deliberately, enjoyably absurd' (2010: xii), adding that 'what started out as mimicry turns into independent fantasy' (xiii). This is precisely Coe's approach, part of what Shallcross describes as 'the requirement of an awareness on the parodist's part that he or she is fundamentally implicated in the world being critiqued and the laughter being generated' (126). The permeation of the narrative with so many parodic and satiric interconnections, allows Coe in essence to efface Kostka's neutrality through the energy and reach of the story.

A key question in unpacking the various dynamics of these novels will be whether Coe sustains the credibility, ingenuity and level of artistry many critics believed he did with regard to the overt intertextual parody that is so clearly central to his most celebrated novel (negating the need for balance or neutrality). I will first outline what might be involved in foregrounding explicitly key elements drawn from other texts and/or cultural products during a period that Alfaro (drawing on Bakhtin) says is marked by 'the author's ability to move freely within his/her field of representation (something unthinkable in the case of the epic), which makes possible the introduction of one of the novel's basic features: its literary self-consciousness' (1996: 275).

Hutcheon in her earlier essay ('Literary Borrowing...') summarizes how Julia Kristeva, the Bulgarian-French philosopher, in coining the term *intertextuality* 'noted that there were three elements involved besides the text under consideration: the author, the reader and the other exterior texts. These elements she arranged along two axes: a horizontal one of the dialogue of the author with his/her potential reader, and a vertical one between the text itself and other texts' (1986: 231). Hutcheon perceives the reader as central to this process, but I would suggest the key (but not only) dynamics of such influences in Coe's writing are fundamentally self-referential and authorial, his adaptations and incorporations being decidedly deliberate rather than latent, and often the sources prove so obscure that various literary and cultural sources must be identified explicitly within the text itself, or its supplementary two-page, yet crucial 'Author's Note' (500–501), in full explicatory fashion, otherwise such points of reference are left obscured or are even missed. For Mary Orr, Kristeva's key aspects are revealed by recognizing that 'Strangeness, alienation and foreignness are not the Other, or other, but (an)other of the self [...]' (2003: 31), a dimension inherent in Coe's intertextuality. Below I will examine critically a crucial structural paradigm created by the overlapping layers of intertextuality and reference (in their various manifestations) in the four selected novels. These texts might seem very disparate, but I will argue for essential underlying thematic and other commonalities, including pathos, the role of the petit-bourgeois (mostly male) underdog, failure, unfulfilled longings and equally I will consider structural similarities, particularly stories within stories creating a *mise en abyme* effect, thereby achieving what Lucien Dällenbach describes in terms of pictorial examples: 'At the frontier between interior and exterior, they are a way of taking two dimensionality to its limits' (1989: 12), comparable to Coe's use of life-world figures and events both as coordinates but also ironically within the frame of the novel. As regards literature he identifies a reciprocity of the self (14) and a 'narcissistic doubling' (16), adding 'the imaginary reflexion that aims to restore the immediate and continuous relationship between self and self comes up in this scenario against the discontinuity and the shift caused by the very act of writing itself' (16). In *What a Carve Up!* one might regard such dissonant and ludic ambiguities as always potentially vertiginous, as Michael's final jaunt in a plane turns out to be. His naiveté and indifference during periods of being a virtual recluse create a space that appears to offer neutrality, but the revelation of his parentage demonstrate how illusory that to be. Nevertheless, at least until the final phase the ever watchful and at times diffident Michael appears to serve as that critical coordinate indicated by Kostka, balancing the other two. A consistent thread through all of the novels analysed below is that despite great differences in emphasis, as with much of Coe's preceding fiction, there exists an overarching perspective on larger issues to be gleaned from mundane people and scenarios, foregrounding the opinions and perspectives of those whose existences are defined by humdrum, often uneventful lives that unexpectedly face a rupture or disturbance. Coe's characters seem riven by a longing for change and passion on the one hand, and on the other a deep investment in acquiescence and continuity, even where the latter is extremely painful, a dichotomy that will be played out in the author's fiction of the 2010s in terms of personal sexual relationships and identity in *The Terrible Privacy of Maxwell Sim* and in *Expo 58*, and through social interactions in class and political terms in *Number 11* and *Middle England*, as explored below.

The Terrible Privacy of Maxwell Sim

Coe adopts as an implied framework a macro-view of socio-cultural trends and events – hence so many critics reference his 'state of the nation' fiction – that permeates the microcosmic experience of humdrum lives he deploys to evoke that larger picture, which is therefore seen through the more tightly focused prism of seemingly ordinary people, often emphasized by small parabolic details. As regards the protagonist of *The Terrible Privacy of Maxwell Sim*, Coe's reader knows from the very start that the outcome of events and interactions for Sim is likely to be negative. Ironically, and suggestive of a fundamental malaise, the novel is prefaced by a news item purportedly from the *Aberdeenshire Press and Journal* dated Monday, 9 March 2009, which indicates that Sim was a freelance salesman of toothbrushes 'found by 'Grampian Police patrolling the snowbound stretch of the A93 between Braemar and Spittal of Glenshee' (n.p.) almost naked, suffering from hypothermia, while 'On the passenger seat beside him were two empty whisky bottles' (n.p.) and it also reports that his 'company had gone into liquidation that morning' (n.p.). As Laurent Mellet reflects: 'Sim's life and narrative hover between humour and melancholy [...]' (2016: n.p.). As the novel begins, Sim reflects on dining alone on '14 February 2009. The second Saturday in February, Valentine's day, in case you hadn't noticed' (Coe 2011: 4). In a restaurant he finds himself fixating on the seamless intimacy between a Chinese woman diner and her daughter in a restaurant overlooking Sydney Harbour while playing cards. This reminds Sim of all that he has been denied during his life, with its gaping emptiness and constant marginality, a curious neutrality, that extends to his cautious preference for food from restaurant chains renowned for their blandness. Subsequently as a context to ground such feelings, he mentally outlines the minutiae of his personal life, his first date in a Spaghetti House with his wife, and while staring at the Chinese woman and her daughter, he notes without preamble 'Caroline had left home by then. Walked out, I mean. She had been gone six months and had taken our daughter, Lucy, with her. They had moved up north to Kendal in the Lake District. What was it, finally, that drove her away. Just a long-standing build-up of frustration, I suppose' (10). Such dull, disconnected and digressive generalizations typify Sim, confirming his essential banality and humdrum qualities. In the toilet, he realizes no one would really miss him if he died suddenly of a heart attack like former Labour leader, John Smith. Sim recollects the politician because the man had been a subject of a conversation during Sim's first encounter in a work canteen with Caroline, defined by her anger with dismissive colleagues joking tastelessly about the death. Sim ironically reflects 'I've never been very interested in politics' (9), very much a symbol of neutrality and non-commitment, displaced momentarily by his love affair, returned to on his departure for London and a seemingly loveless marriage. According to Marsh, 'Sim is [...] more of an innocent abroad, his naivety played off against the more knowing reader [...]' (2020: 32). In Sydney the two diners' closeness highlights how in contrast he seems at one remove from such conviviality. As Christopher Lasch observes in *The Culture of Narcissism*: 'Experiences of inner emptiness, loneliness, and inauthenticity are by no means unreal or for that matter, devoid of social content [...]. They arise from [...] the dangers and uncertainty that surround us, and from a loss of confidence in the future' (1979: 27). Revealingly, the aftermath of Sim's journey foregrounds his insignificance, evidenced when he checks his Facebook page: 'Not a single friend had sent me a message or posted anything on my wall in the last month' (72). Several other key elements underpin Sim's earlier mention of a family flat in Lichfield that his father (who lives in Sydney, hence Sim's presence in a restaurant overlooking the famous harbour) reveals that he still owns twenty years after his divorce from Sim's mother.

> I thought he meant he wanted me to start the process of putting it on the market, and I began telling him that it wasn't a good time to try selling property in the UK right now, the credit crunch was starting to bite, people were losing their jobs and their savings, everyone was in a state of financial uncertainty, and house prices were falling every month.
>
> Coe 2011: 16

First, Sim being so seemingly well-informed acts as a mild satire on Britain's obsession with property ownership rather than other more pertinent values.

Second, as in much else in his life, Sim seems disconnected from and unaware of any grounding facts or principles of even the utterly mundane concerning those supposedly closest to him. His presumptions turn out to be radically incorrect. Ironically, the father simply wants Sim to retrieve some poems and other writing composed during the years of his youth. The son's words also offer a parable for the economic hardships of these years and their underlying ideological coordinates. As Chadderton says 'Coe has expressed his personal anger towards the politics of Margaret Thatcher and the neo-liberal order which followed, as well as the more recent banking crisis and the subsequent politics of austerity' (2017: 271).

Throughout the narrative Sim's first-person account ironically evokes various failings that define this middle-aged former complaints assistant at a department store in Ealing and now freelance salesman of toothbrushes. He is positioned as an 'involuntary hermit' (13) after separating from his disgruntled wife, Caroline, and their daughter, Lucy. He is also limited in terms of emotional register. His account of Caroline's failed relationship with a fellow English graduate from Manchester with whom she moved to London – Sim admits 'There's a phrase, a cliché, for the state Caroline was in back then: on the rebound (10) – is reductively factual, barely admitting the visceral dimension of her betrayal and loss, indicating his lack of empathy. Very rapidly he emerges as a boring nonentity, so much so Alex Clark suggests the novel is 'deeply irritating' although 'Max is an immediately recognisable type, both literary and social, a Pooterish chronicler of daily life, entrapped by minutiae and unable to fathom their wider significance' (n.p.). Finally, in a belated postmodern gesture Coe has Sim confronted in his fictional narrative by 'the writer' (312) who is finishing off his book, revealing Sim as one of its characters:

> Suddenly I felt like the hero of a low-rent spy movie, just when he realises he's walked straight into a trap set for him by the villain.
> 'I see. So that's ... me, is it?' I said, playing for time as much as anything else. 'I'm just a by-product of your ideas, is that right? Well, I have to say that doesn't do wonders for my self-esteem.'
>
> Coe 2011: 312

Subsequently, to Sim's growing horror, this writer-as-chartacter outlines a series of events that Sim finds uncannily familiar, being essentially the coordinates of his recent life. Finally, he confronts Sim with the reality that as a character he can be eliminated at his creator's whim, the ultimate existential challenge:

> 'But the story's finished, Max,' he said.

> I looked into his eyes, and they no longer seemed kind. It was like looking into the eyes of a serial killer.
> 'It can't have finished,' I protested. 'I still don't know how it ends.'
> 'Well, that's easy,' said the writer. 'I can tell you exactly how it ends.' He gave me one last smile – a smile that was both apologetic and ruthless – and clicked his fingers. 'Like this.'
>
> Coe 2011: 314

Coe's stance mirrors that of B.S. Johnson in *Christie Malry's Own Double-Entry* (1973), explored in fuller detail below. Earlier, after the encounter with the Chinese woman Sim reviews his existence, particularly his recent history marked by a disintegrating relationship, and his feelings of both dislocation and an inability to be close to people, even family and friends; a radical disassociation heightened by modern technology:

> I seem to have lost a number of friends in the last few years. I don't mean that I've fallen out with them, in any dramatic way. We've just decided not to stay in touch. And that's what it's been: a decision, a conscious decision, because it's not difficult to stay in touch nowadays, there are so many different ways of doing it. But as you get older, I think some friendships start to feel increasingly redundant.
>
> Coe 2011: 3

As with much in Sim's life, his statement is haunted by a sense of melancholy, permeated perhaps by his apathy and indifference. Sim's wife accuses him of not liking himself, and he exists at times as if sucked into a vacuum, bemused by his clinical depression. Sim suppresses struggle, dialogue and self-awareness in favour of scenarios and contexts defined by the humdrum, insipid and unchallenging.

Prone to introspection of the most banal kind, Sim finds parallels between his fate and that of Donald Crowhurst, whose tale is introduced to Sim by fellow traveller Poppy, who loans him a file of a letter from her Uncle Clive about the real-life sailor that she has scanned onto her laptop. In 1968 Crowhurst faked logbooks, having entered his catamaran, *the Teignmouth Electron*, in the *Sunday Times* Golden Globe Race, a single-handed, round-the-world challenge. Despite haphazard preparations and a decision to only pretend to circumnavigate, ironically he seemed likely to win one of the prizes and Clive reflects 'as the horror of his predicament began to bear down on him more heavily, Crowhurst's logbook entries became still more peculiar. [. . .] [I]f he carried this hoax off, he was going to have to live an enormous lie for the rest of his life' (54). According to Yulia Anatolyevna Khramova (2020: 263–264), Crowhurst's despair and mad philosophical ruminations calculating the square root of minus one that lead to his suicide are akin to Sim's delving deeper into his own past during the isolating promotional voyage toward the Shetlands, where he sinks ever lower despite visiting friends and family as he progresses slowly. So complete is his delusional isolation that he falls in love with Emma, as he has christened the voice of the Satnav in his company car. Yet, despite this, Khramova perceives a sense of self-awareness, arguing that Sim recognizes the absurdity of his existence and identifies completely with the sailor who according to Sim in the novel is utterly lost (surely this is for a while quite unlike the Sim we first encounter after his apparent recovery when he revisits Sydney and starts looking forward positively, albeit only momentarily), which Sim explains thus:

> Donald Crowhurst started to contemplate the insoluble mystery of the square root of minus one and before long found himself 'entering a dark tunnel' from which he was never to emerge. [...] The one I was in ... well, it turned out to be longer and darker than I could ever have imagined. I realise now that I had been lost in it for most of my life. But the important thing is that I escaped in the end, and when I did finally step out into the sunlight, blinking and rubbing my eyes, it was to find myself at a place in Sydney called Fairlight Beach.
>
> Coe 2011: 295

I would argue that Sim's rather vacuous optimism here starkly contrasts the real-life, tragi-comic end of Crowhurst, and rather indicates the possibility of a potential (if unlikely) epiphany, which is why the ending (quoted above) is so emphatically shocking and inculcates in the reader on first reading feelings of angst, discomfort and even displeasure, despite a small trail of often unnoticed breadcrumbs trailing Sim's status as merely a fictional creation. Coe's strategy in confronting and killing off his protagonist is drawn directly from B.S. Johnson's *Christie Malry's Own Double-Entry* (1973) as an intertextual borrowing, used presumably as an homage to this earlier comic narrative on violence and terrorism that is itself a laconic parody of the angry young man novel of the period. As Brian Crews points out, describing a key element of the illusion of 'independent autonomous characters' that attracts Coe:

> Johnson draws attention to the relation between fiction and reality at a number of levels. One of these is to consider the nature of character as a fictional construct, which also involves an exploration of the relation between author and character. This involves playing with the logic of realism and draws attention to the basic absurdity behind the realistic fallacy.
>
> Crews 1994: 59

Absurdity might be overstating his point, since realism acts as a framing device, and Johnson's intention appears to be to disturb his readership, make individual readers think about accepting stock truths that do not relate to the underlying realities in the world, especially in an outmoded genre. As Johnson's eponymous protagonist observes within the narrative:

> 'Christie,' I warned him, 'it does not seem to me possible to take this novel much further. I'm sorry.'
>
> 'Don't be sorry,' said Christie, in a kindly manner, 'don't be sorry. We don't equate length with importance, do we? [...] The writing of a long novel is in itself an anachronistic act: it was relevant only to a society and a set of social conditions which no longer exist.'
>
> 'I'm glad you understand so readily.'
>
> 'The novel should now try simply to be Funny, Brutalist, and Short,' Christie epigrammatised.
>
> 'I could hardly have expressed it better myself [...].'
>
> Johnson 1984 [1973]: 165

The final irony emphasizes the reality that through Christie, Johnson speaks again, to himself as well as to his readers, in performative fashion. The interchange above is one of many examples of Johnson's authorial reflexivity, in which as a narrator he reflects upon the form of narrative fiction. That Christie does so in parallel with his creator – whom he chastises – initiates a different set of relations to those between Coe and Sim. So, if on one level Coe does engage similarly (through ironic reflexivity and control), there are radical differences, since he engages with his task with such subtlety that the parallels are missed. The residual affinities only emerge in any truly apprehensible fashion toward the end, with Coe undermining not only the character but also his readers (whereas Johnson has drawn us into complicity with himself as creator-author). Clearly, there is however, a fundamental difference between the two writers and their texts. Johnson (as writer and narrator) intrudes into this darkly comic narrative throughout, revealing his presence multiply, often as if bored with his task. Christie dies from an accelerated form of cancer, although for Crews 'Christie's, like all deaths, is meaningless' (1994: 60); in contrast, Sim simply disappears, as if effaced or subject to a magic trick, taken beyond neutrality to nothingness, appropriately perhaps for someone who hardly seems to want to exist, therefore reduced to nullity, the ultimate nobody. However, while Laity finds this to be 'an audacious conclusion' (2010: n.p.), for John Hieff the ending deviates from what precedes as he concludes 'a metafictional twist near the end feels tacked on' (2011: n.p.). Perhaps, though, Coe does thereby confirm a central quality, Lasch identifies in contemporary existence: 'When art, religion and finally even sex lose their power to provide an imaginative release from everyday reality, the banality of pseudo-self-awareness becomes so overwhelming that men finally lose the capacity to envision any release at all except in total nothingness, blankness' (1979: 98). Sim becomes, in his curious disappearance, a paradigm of such an existence.

Expo 58

Expo 58 details events in the late 1950s – at a point in that decade when initial austerity had given way to consumerist culture – as encountered by Thomas Foley, a minor, albeit handsome bureaucrat. He is drawn tangentially from his post 'at the Central Office of Information at Baker Street' (2014: 2) into a world of espionage, when sent to an international trades fair (that of the book's title) in Brussels, literally a world away from his usual ultra-modest and circumscribed existence in suburbia. Coe stated in an interview with Clifford Armion undertaken in February 2014: 'the world of Expo 58 which Thomas lands in – finds himself shipwrecked in – is like something out of a fairy tale. Nothing there is real' (Armion and Coe 2014: n.p.). Despite this fantasy environment and Thomas's unworldliness and naiveté, back at home he has tried to keep up with scientific developments such as nuclear technology in an attempt to make himself relevant: 'A potentially infinite source of clean, cheap energy, for one thing. Thomas still didn't know where he stood in this particular debate [...]. He had to believe that somewhere out there, beyond the silent confines of suburban Tooting, was a world of ideas, movements, discoveries and momentous changes [...]' (2014: 16–17). In the interview cited above, Coe outlines his time at a writer's retreat in Belgium, through which he developed a keen interest in the Atomium monument as a symbol of futurity, representing scientific progress of a sort that many believed in during the 1950s (including Thomas in his own vague, neutral fashion, as seen above). Coe explains 'The book is a kind of satire on naivety or a comic celebration of idealism, whichever way you want to look at it, specifically in relation to science and technology because this is what the Atomium, which was at the centre of the expo site, represents for me' (2014: n.p.).

In situating this novel culturally as an intertextual coordinate, Marsh notes that it is characterized by:

> [...] its allusiveness to other works of literature and film, including an array of characters taken from British cinema of the 1930s, the 1940s and the 1950s, and

a series of in-jokes based on these films, as well as Ian Fleming's James Bond novels and other playfully invoked intertexts. [...] In fact, whether consciously or not, it is part of a lineage of 'innocent abroad' comic *farces* that can be traced through novels such as Evelyn Waugh's *Scoop* [...].

Marsh 2020: 35

A recurrent intensity of farcical exchanges marks out this novel among Coe's fiction, as it blends satire with slapstick, verbally expressed by the routines of Mr Radford and Mr Wayne – named after the actors Basil Radford and Naunton Wayne, who appeared as cricket-mad Charters and Caldicott in Alfred Hitchcock's *The Lady Vanishes* (1938) – who appear after the meeting where Thomas is asked to volunteer to work in Brussels at Expo 58 for six months. The pair turn espionage into a knowing comic double act, appearing on the train back to London after Thomas has accepted a new post in the midlands: 'Really, Birmingham was not half as grim as he had imagined' (236). Coe's narrative reveals that Mr Radford and Mr Wayne have set up this job for Thomas so he might continue covert tasks for them in the Soviet bloc. When Thomas tries to refuse, while stressing their reluctance, they use explicit photographs of Thomas and Anneke to persuade him to carry on spying:

> 'You had a rendezvous with Miss Hoskens, I believe ...'
> 'And took her back to the Motel Expo ...'
> 'Where, by an extraordinary coincidence, our colleague Mr Wilkins ...'
> 'You remember Wilkins?'
> '... was roaming around with his camera.'
> 'Bit of a loose cannon, old Wilkins ...'
> 'Bit of a lone wolf ...'
> 'Takes a good photograph, mind you.'
> 'My word, Radford, have a look at that one.'
> 'Good lord. Doesn't leave much to the imagination.'
> 'Nor this.'
> They both chuckled.
> 'I must say, Foley, you've certainly got an inventive approach in these matters.'
> 'And a highly versatile partner, I might add.'

Coe 2013: 248–249

This is entirely appropriate since as Jessica Milner Davis indicates, farce often uses underlying (threatened), if not actual violence (2017 [2003]: 3), as well as 'pairs and triangles' (4). Davis explains that slapstick (x) and burlesque (3) are important components of farce which is peopled 'by simplified comic types' (2), while satire has long deployed 'farcical techniques' (x). Their comedic blackmail incorporates all of these characteristics, but the underlying threat is deadly serious in its own way, since one of the Russians, Mr Chertsky, is killed by a female American counterpart to keep him quiet. However, despite the poignancy toward the novel's end, where we encounter Thomas's regret at conforming to the desires of the establishment, for Hannah McGill any comedic bathos undermines the characters, who therefore fail in terms of engagement on the part of readers:

> After all, if characters are written as daffy caricatures, it's hard to care about any darkness that might befall them. Throw in Coe's weakness for sitcommy gags, and you can end up with… well, something like this: a sporadically engaging but distinctly flat-footed romp in which the characters and their situation feel insubstantial, and the jokes land with a heavy thud.
>
> McGill 2013: n.p.

I would argue the farcical elements mediate this tendency, that the obvious quality of some of the jokes functions as a novelistic pratfall, part of its comedic quotidian mundanity.

On a more satirical level, Coe delineates Britain through the class differences of the 1950s, for as Cressida Connolly comments 'Coe's real satirical butt – as ever – is England […]. There are jokes at the expense of our rigid opposition to new ideas, our racism, our inability to say what we mean, our food' (Connolly 2013: n.p.). As a grammar schoolboy, Thomas feels instinctively inferior among his upper-class colleagues and as Chadderton observes he is 'intimidated at work' (2017: 273) by their plummy voices.

Thomas is chosen for the trip because of his experience of the trade of his father, a publican, and on that basis Thomas is co-opted to maintain the efficient running of the focus of the British exhibition, a replica pub called Britannia (based on an actual hostelry that featured at Expo 58), used in part to parody the stolid quality of post-war Britain. On one level, as Paul French indicates, Thomas's amateur engagement with a world of espionage fits with a pre-James Bond tradition of the accidental spy:

> Before Ian Fleming gave us Bond, espionage writers mostly wrote about ordinary people, everyday folk who somehow slipped into the spy business. Their heroes/antiheroes invariably found themselves in the right, or rather the wrong, place at the right, or the wrong, time. From the start, spy fiction often relied on happenstance as a route into the trade.
>
> French 2014: n.p.

Nevertheless, this is not simply a matter of literary and filmic genres, for as Marsh suggests wider ideological and political choices are played out in the protagonist's experiences: 'Foley becomes the unwitting dupe in a plan to smuggle information […] [and] as the story develops, Foley's life becomes emblematic of a broader series of choices and conflicts: Britain or continental Europe; isolation or integration; futurity or nostalgia' (2020: 36). Hence, this comic narrative is an exemplary account of the interplay and interaction of the major participants in the Cold War, with nuclear secrets at the heart of the underlying attempt by members of the Russian delegation, principally Mr Andrey Chersky, to obtain the plans to the ZETA machine which appears to offer nuclear cold fusion and the promise of limitless energy. The final joke is that the machine is a fake and the original does not work. The pub, the Britannia, is a pastiche of tradition and contemporary styles, still uncomplete on Thomas's first scoping visit. However, 'A number of naval prints already hung on the walls; there were also model ships in glass cases, and a larger model of a Britannia airliner, suspended as if in flight' (49). That the country's grandiose ambitions are nullified seems appropriate to a Britain in decline as its empire dissipates.

Throughout this elaborate skulduggery that combines the world of Bond with that of musical farce (as yet another level of parody), Thomas remains largely a naïf until the revelation of the subterranean struggle of the two socio-cultural camps. He is immersed from his arrival in Brussels in the ludic interaction of the participants, potentially a deadly and serious evocation of a carnival spirit. In the Britannia and elsewhere this ideological contest – in the bar of the Monnaie Theatre, '"My goal," said Andrey, "is to make Communists of you all. My weapons are ballet and vodka"' (117) – is made more emphatic by the interfusion of erotic desires, perhaps the most elaborate of human games. Finally, even Thomas perceives the vacillating duality of such interplay, stitching between its surface and depth: 'He was beginning to feel that the others were somewhat too ready to accept Andrey's relentless outpourings of pro-Soviet sentiment as little more than a charming foible; whereas it was all intended, as far as he could see, in deadly earnest' (117–118).

Thomas returns home after this adventure that included his elaborate flirtation and brief affair with gorgeous Anneke, an Expo hostess, only to find his wife appears to have been unfaithful with a neighbour. Despite the wife's pregnancy and his doubts, he continues their marriage and relocates, as we have seen, to Birmingham to be near her parents, having found a new job in the vicinity. The failed marriage, and even the lost romance, together become part of a pattern of existence many believed typified the post-war era even into the early 1960s. The peak of Thomas's existence is past, his blossoming youth lost and faded. With Expo 58 long gone, the couple's empty lives become paradigmatic, the relationship mirroring the underlying antipathy of the age as described by Lasch that is about to burst forth: 'Women's rage against men originates not only in erotic disappointments or the consciousness of oppression but in a perception of marriage as the ultimate trap, the ultimate routine in a routinized society, the ultimate expression of the banality that pervades and suffocates modern life.' (1979: 198). In 2009 as a widowed old man of eighty-four, Thomas returns to see Clara, Anneke's plain friend who was also an Expo hostess. Thomas hears of Anekke's death and her marriage to Frederico:

> Anneke worked for a long time in a shop, I believe. She worked very hard. Frederico was a good man, but lazy. He was always complaining about feeling ill, always taking time off work. He stopped working altogether, when he was still quite young. He became very fond of this game, this Italian game – what is it called? *Bocce*. [...] He used to enter competitions, travel round the country. And Anneke would stay in Bologna, with the shop, with the children. A hard life for her, I think.
>
> Coe 2013: 260

Later, Clara reveals that at an Expo 58 reunion, Frederico had confessed his doubts about his daughter, Delfina, being his own child, a revelation Thomas seems unmoved by, despite Clara's implication of his own parentage being obvious. Perhaps wisely so, for as James Lasdun insists 'the farcical spy story that occupies so much of the book has turned Thomas into too much of a cartoon character for him to carry this kind of elegiac weight' (2013: 11), although as such he offers Coe the neutrality upon which his farcical satire might reassert itself. The other central issue is surely whether Coe's parodic approach sustains its credibility with the abutment of two such opposing modes of feeling, and I would suggest Thomas's silence over his possible fathering of Anneke's child suspends that tension, creating an equivocal economy of meaning that is purposely unresolved.

Number 11

Such irresolution is largely absent in *Number 11* (2015), which opens with events that occurred in the life-world in 2003, including the controversial death (supposedly by suicide, but subject to great doubt by many) of government scientist, Dr David Kelly (formerly one of the United Nations Special Commission chief weapons inspectors in Iraq). His off-the-record briefings to BBC journalist,

Andrew Gilligan, served to question the case for invading Iraq set out in the so-called 'dodgy dossier' compiled in 2002 for Blair's government to persuade both parliament and the public to support this military action. Coe's novel emerges as highly politicized (at least its subtexts and occasional vignettes concerning political issues), but at another level it remains a quasi-Gothic tale set in the early years of the twenty-first century. Its narrative centres on two young women, initially children, Rachel and Alison, and their families' struggles to maintain bourgeois respectability in the provinces during a period of austerity after a severe financial crisis, whilst the mega-rich in Kensington thrive. In the novel's first section, 'The Black Tower', initial events occur in the shadow of the invasion of Iraq and the death of Kelly, whose fate haunts ten-year-old Rachel since 'It was the first time the reality of death had been brought home to me. It was, if you like, the first death in our family' (2015: 22). Despite such external points of reference, Coe works hard with his incorporations to still achieve two aspects of a reflexive aesthetic that Dällenbach describes: first 'the reflexive work of art is a *representation*, and one with great internal cohesion' (71), and second is its 'polysemic richness' (71). As with much Gothic fiction, Coe's novel foregrounds fantasy and a fearful sublime: a strand of the novel's narrative centres on Rachel's sense of a persistent, radical if understated threat from the imaginary, that at the end actually emerges in the form of monstrous spiders drawn to the wealthy and privileged. In the opening section, initially Rachel and her elder brother encounter a figure who they presume is a man wheeling an old lady in a wheelchair and swinging the lure of a kestrel in training. The siblings intrude and anger the figure who turns out to be a woman with a crewcut:

> Her ears and nose were pierced and decorated with multiple silver rings and studs. A livid, dark blue-green tattoo of some indeterminate shape seemed to cover most of her neck and throat. She was the most terrifying woman, without a doubt, that Rachel had ever seen. Even Nicholas seemed taken aback.
>
> Coe 2015: 6

In her mind Rachel christens her 'the Mad Bird Woman' (7). In teasing fashion, Nicholas evokes the spectral and Rachel's fears of the ghostly during this visit to the abbey near Beverly in rural Yorkshire, where the narrator reflects 'Rachel did not like the look of the Minster at all' (7). Nevertheless in a visceral sense for Rachel, these dynamics both disturb and yet curiously underpin the apparent normality of the world she and her one-legged friend Alison (who wears a prosthetic) are immersed in, during their stay four years later in the town where Rachel's grandparents live, where they encounter the Mad Bird Woman, who they're told has been left a large house 'by the wheelchair-bound old lady when she died' (27). The girls suspect foul play and naively set out to investigate. After an argument in the woods the girls separate and, on her return, Alison claims to have seen a dead body, which they seek. They encounter the Mad Bird Woman seeking grotesque and strange cards for playing the 'game of Pelmanism' (58). These startling images are used by a Chinese worker, Lu, their supposed dead body, whom Rachel (the Mad Bird Woman, who in later befriending Alison, inspires her to become a visual artist) suspects is a modern slave manipulated by people smugglers and gangers. Such shifting perceptions and roles and intersecting narrative elaborations evoke the provisional, where knowledge and meaning are not only complex but must be worked upon much as Phoebe does in her assessment of possibilities concerning Lu. She replies to Rachel's conjecture with evidence of forced labour, including his negative response to the mention of chickens, in her mind probably an aversion to the factory farm that she supposes employed him before he absconded. The episode is left unresolved, apart from Lu going off without further trace, unable to communicate with Phoebe in his presumed search for a companion or friend called Xiang. In *Number 11*, there is no resolution concerning the fate of either of the Chinese characters, apart from Rachel's later oblique, unsubstantiated account:

> The men who drowned in Morecambe Bay the next year, picking cockles for their gangmaster as the treacherous tide rushed inwards ... they were Chinese, most of them. Just the other day, I read once again about their terrible deaths on the internet and my stomach tightened when I saw one of them was called Xiang. But I expect it's a very common name in China.
>
> Coe 2015: 67

Those effaced from the records, and therefore the historical moment, lose their identity and presence, going unrecorded. Hutcheon refers to such incompletion as 'radical uncertainty' (1989: 97) and Coe incorporates such moments into his pantheon of literary techniques to highlight the inequalities of contemporary culture.

As Jean-Michel Ganteau observes – after first indicating comparatively via *What a Carve Up!* the presence and importance of vulnerability as a theme in that novel and *Number 11* – 'as in a fair part of contemporary British fiction, ordinariness seems to have morphed into precariousness, and invisibility has come to affect larger shares of the population' (2017: 443). In Coe's later novel the two worlds of the privileged and the marginal are again starkly contrasted. As part of a highly affluent and well-connected elite, certain members of the

Winshaw family reappear. These dynamics offer a strong sense that the nation's morality is hollowed out by such privileges, much as one super-affluent family's basement project finally releases monstrous spiders that devour those marked out by such greed, demarcated as socially guilty and culpable. Typically, as in Coe's other fiction, the political becomes intensely personal, as Rachel realizes how angry adults like her grandfather are about certain key political issues such as Kelly's death (16, 22), immigration (29) and vagrancy (35), although awaiting tests for a potential diagnosis of cancer, Rachel's grandmother responds to Rachel's interrogation of such matters: 'She let out a heavy sigh. "Frankly, Rachel, right now I think I'm one of those people who's starting to believe that none of it matters in the slightest"' (37). Certainly, Coe works hard to make his narrative reflect contemporaneous culture and events, as seen from the position of those without either authority or power, for whom as Ganteau indicates 'precariousness and the attendant consequences of invisibility and inaudibility are a permanent risk' (2017: 444). Among the marginal, as Mellet observes, 'Coe imagines artistic productions (Alison's portraits) and academic work (Jamie's thesis)' (2018: n.p.) as well as Alison's mother, Val, a librarian whose post has been casualized; she suffers from the governmental cuts of funding to local authorities when she loses most of her income, a symbol and victim of the recession who offers an understanding of austerity though her own reflections upon the banking collapse. Rather than freeze at home (unable to afford heating) as Richard Bromhall details:

> Val rides the No. 11 bus, which orbits Birmingham's outer-circle route. On one of her journeys, Val reflects on economic developments and political changes since the financial crisis began and, via Val, Coe provides an overview of what has occurred since the early days of austerity as an emergent term [...]
>
> The consequences of these [governmental, economic] actions are, in turn, mapped onto Val's experience and reduction of the standard of living she enjoys. Val is a character-driven case study for what effects austerity has on individuals who are, or who become, reliant on provision provided by the state.
>
> Bromhall 2019: 277–278

She is also diminished later at the hands of a reality television producer (chosen to appear because in her youth she had been a singer with a single hit, so a one-hit wonder). There is an additional dimension that motivates Val: 'And it was boring, sitting at home by herself all afternoon, watching daytime TV. Boring and lonely' (89). According to Fay Bound Alberti, 'Loneliness thrives where there is a disconnect between the individual and the world, a disconnect that is so characteristic of neoliberalism, but not an inevitable part of the human condition' (2019, xii). Clearly, Val misses and craves company, and ironically as Alberti points out cuts to libraries are critical since they 'have long played a civic role in bringing people together across a wide social demographic, and in providing a shared space in which community can be enacted' (158). Such neoliberal isolation in a metropolitan centre among millions of fellow citizens would appear to be an underlying reason for Val's acceptance of a part in the reality show, a decision that initially and momentarily baffles her daughter.

In such abjection (amplified throughout the novel), according to Mellet's reading, Coe follows a Wellsian trajectory, 'from the utopian to the dystopian mode when commenting on the political and social evolutions of this world, or when theorising on the underworld' (2018: n.p.). The plight of the have-nots that Mellet sees as central is heightened by a reappearance of members of the Winshaw family, and from the new generation journalist, Josephine Winshaw-Eaves, who attends a literary prize (sponsored by and named after the Winshaws) in Birmingham seeking a story. Her appearance ties this novel to *What a Carve Up!* where Josephine appears doubly as a baby: first in a feature on her mother, Hilary, and working motherhood from *Hello* magazine where Hilary literally eulogizes her bond with her child, followed by the reality where Hilary complains to her nanny about her daughter's disruption of her working lunch. '"Well can't you take it outside for a while? It's showing us up in front of everyone"' (80). Earlier Josephine's editor and father, Sir Peter, remained unimpressed by her attempt to rework her mother's journalism, doubly ironic given her mother's indifference to her as an infant. It appears from the paternal conversation that Josephine thinks 'Hilary's "black one-legged lesbian on benefits" could still be held up as a paragon of modern entitlement' (195):

> He thought that the archetype Josephine had resurrected from her mother's columns was hopelessly out of date. 'You fucked up your argument in the last few paragraphs,' he told her. 'A black one-legged lesbian on benefits? Even our readers know there's no such thing. They're only worried about Muslims these days. Put your straw woman in a niqab and then you've got something to worry about.'
>
> Coe 2015: 195

Ironically, chance offers her an opportunity to prove her father wrong, by exploiting Alison, who is now a struggling artist on benefits producing portraits of homeless people and is estranged from her former friend, Rachel. Josephine encounters Alison's girlfriend, Selena, working as an occasional waitress, while both are smoking outside the venue in Birmingham. About to re-enter, a throwaway remark about the artist's one-leggedness attracts her attention, leading her to a structured and blunt interrogation:

> 'No – I mean, is she black as well?'
>   'Ah.' Christ, this woman is blunt, Selena thought. But she'd caught her interest, for some reason, and she was going to make the most of it. 'Yes, she is.'
> 'And does she have a job, your friend. Apart from the painting, I mean.'
> 'No. Neither of us have, since we finished our course.'
> [. . .]
> 'Your girlfriend,' Josephine said, 'sounds *absolutely amazing*.'
> 'Could you write something about her, do you think?'
> 'Yes, I think I could.'
>
> Coe 2015: 223

The calculating Josephine will turn this into a classic piece for the right-wing populist press. First, she organizes a showing at an art gallery for the artist so that Josephine can buy several of the displayed pictures. She writes about her mother's hate figure from a supposed real example, largely confected by Josephine, but abetted by Alison who fails to declare a relatively small sum for which she is paid for her art, all of it from Josephine. For this transgression Alison is imprisoned for benefit fraud, making her future life far more difficult and challenged. When Rachel encounters Val, after the latter's humiliation on television, she reveals her daughter's fate in an email, with a link to Josephine's article, which Coe includes as a supposedly online document, entitled:

THE ART OF DECEPTION
BLACK, DISABLED LESBIAN ON BENEFITS IS ACTUALLY BLACK,
DISABLED LESBIAN BENEFIT *CHEAT*

Coe 2015: 291

Josephine's extended and arch manipulations mirror that of her mother in Coe's earlier novel; moreover, both mother and daughter lack any ethical framework and share an intense self-centeredness, exhibiting a radical lack of empathy. As Hutcheon suggests, '[i]ronic meaning comes into being as a consequence of a relationship, a dynamic performative bringing together of different meaning-makers, but also of different meanings, first, in order to create something new and, then [. . .] to endow it with the critical edge of judgement' (1994: 58). The affinity of mother and daughter is offset by the involvement of the father's perspective, and that of Selena, Alison, Val and Rachel. In essence, in *Number 11* Coe incorporates a layered, multiple irony (and voicing and meaning) in this encounter and its aftermath, initiated by an entirely casual conversation as both women smoke outside the venue, Josephine initially bored by the exchange. The structure is both intriguing and suggestive. Coe indicates not only the role of chance in delivering this archetype to the journalist, but conveys just how easily it can be worked into a public narrative feeding the prejudices of those with supposedly naïve and easily manipulable viewpoints, which represents another multiple negation. First, Coe suggests that the ruling and intellectual elites understand and exploit such underlying tensions that subtend these propagandist dynamics. Second, one realizes the policy objections of the majority of the populace are subject to such manipulation and become otherwise irrelevant. Coe's implication is that the ruling elite believe the policy objections of the majority of the populace to be founded on ignorance and prejudice rather than being truly experiential, so most social concerns are inevitably disregarded. Given such perspectives recur in the majority of Coe's fiction where his parodic satire is foregrounded, including *Number 11*, this hints at Coe's critique of political life. Coe referred to the importance of an underlying veracity in an interview I conducted with him in Tufnell Park on 12 December 2006. He insisted 'Historical accuracy is very important to me. Actually, I find it impossible to work imaginatively unless the actual underpinnings of what I am writing are absolutely set in stone' (Tew 2008: 39).

Middle England

Coe published *Middle England* (2018) consciously as a narrative centred on the West Midlands, the region where Coe seems at ease, given he was raised and educated there prior to attending Cambridge University, where he was an unhappy undergraduate. Nevertheless, it deals with issues of national affairs, assessing the regional, provincial view of Brexit. The narrative opens as divorced Benjamin Trotter – previously a major character in both the *Rotters' Club* (2001) and *The Closed Circle* (2004) – sneaks away before the end of his mother's funeral at the insistence of Colin, his father. The 2010 General Election is imminent and 'Colin would vote Conservative, as he had done in every British election since 1950, and Benjamin, as usual, was undecided, except in the sense that he had decided not to vote' (2018: 4). At Benjamin's converted mill house in Shropshire, the presence of his sister Lois Potter (née Trotter), her daughter, Sophie, and Benjamin's old school-friend, Doug Anderton, confirms the intertextual linkages with the two precursory novels by Coe alluded to above. The next day, Doug, a financial journalist outlines the broad sense of anger about the effects on the economy and their lives caused by the 2007-08 financial crash, concerning which Benjamin later reflects 'on Gordon Brown's campaign trail, the sense of simmering injustice, the resentment towards a financial and political establishment which had ripped people off and got away with it, the quiet rage of a middle class which had grown used to comfort and prosperity and now saw those things slipping out of their reach [...]' (19-20). As Craig Brown indicates, this is a state-of-the nation narrative, again in the vein of *What a Carve Up!*, and he details references to political events that abound in *Middle England*, in which Coe 'tackles big, ambitious themes, in this case, the effect of politics on people's lives, and political opinions on personal relations' (2018: 26). Brown offers examples, including the Joanna Yeates murder in Bristol, yet he adds 'But it is the prospect of Brexit that hangs over all the proceedings, so much so that it could rightly be described as the novel's principal topic' (26). For Imad Zrari, Coe's novel is part of a sub-genre responding to a national crisis:

> *Middle England* illustrates how Brexit is concerned with emotion, staging the divorce of a British people for whom cohabitation has become increasingly difficult. This new genre, Brexlit, can be read as a means to depict a nation in crisis and to put to the test notions such as the interweaving of the emotional and the political, the definition of satire and engagement, as well as the representations of nostalgia and anger.
>
> Zrari 2020: n.p.

In a subsequent phase, Corbynite Sophie (Benjamin's niece and a lecturer in art history) after being caught speeding – 'doing thirty-seven miles per hour in a thirty-mile limit' (36) – attends a driving safety class. She meets an instructor or '"your facilitator"' (37) as he calls himself, Ian, with whom she will fall in love, polar opposites attracting. Another instructor, Naheed, an Asian woman, argues with another attendee on the course, Derek, about the suitability of a specific speed limit. This retail manager in sports equipment objects. Sophie senses an undercurrent of racism in his dismissal of Naheed's claim for her superior expert knowledge in this matter:

> 'Good. Then, when it comes to sports equipment, your opinion is more valuable than mine. But perhaps when it comes to road safety—'
> 'I've been driving for forty years,' he interrupted. 'And I've never had an accident. Why should I take lessons from someone like you?'
>
> Coe 2018: 40

This implied racial positioning later becomes acutely relevant since after their marriage Ian's hoped-for promotion is awarded to Naheed, and he and his mother clearly believe that the basis of this is preferential treatment in a wider campaign of affirmative action used to counter an entirely imagined set of racist biases. Later, Sophie is invited as an expert on art history to offer a lecture on the subject entitled '"Treasures of the Hermitage"' (161) on a cruise, to be joined in Stockholm by Ian. He befriends Mr Wilcox, who with his wife shares the same dinner table as Sophie. Wilcox is loquacious on political correctness and the failings of the BBC. With Sophie expecting an early night on the night of Ian's arrival, she is disappointed. 'She had not counted on the warmth of Ian's and Geoffrey Wilcox's liking for each other' (160). Reaching St Petersburg, in vicarious fashion Mr Wilcox tells her of Ian's failed bid for promotion, and her husband's preference that she goes ahead with the visit to the Hermitage without him. On their return she argues with Mr Wilcox as to whether a prevailing positive discrimination has undercut Ian's trajectory at work:

> 'Or maybe,' said Sophie, 'they just gave the job to the better candidate.'
>
> She regretted saying it immediately. Ian was still silent, but she could tell he was smarting; and Mr Wilcox had pounced on her misstep in no time.
>
> 'I think you'd better decide,' he said, 'which is more important to you: supporting your husband, or being politically correct.'
>
> Coe 2018: 166

Coe returns to this theme in a further set of encounters where this context recurs, Coe layering and balancing the issues to some degree. The first is her mother-in-law, Helena's speech to a Chinese visitor over lunch at the golf club carvery about '"this absurd political correctness"' (213) that blighted her son's career when she warns Sophie too will fall victim to this propensity. As Zrari suggests of the tensions the novel features: 'The divisions then were not just between Leavers and Remainers. The referendum brought to the surface, condensed and amplified deep-seated fissures – of class, of gender, of race, of age, and of place – as well as producing new antagonisms' (2020: n.p.). Ironically Helena's prediction is proved correct as regards a complex encounter at her university when accused by an undergraduate student, Doug's daughter, Coriander or Corrie, of undermining fellow student, Emily Shamma. Ian informs his estranged wife, Sophie, of a Twitter campaign against her. After she discovers her seminars are boycotted, her Head of Department outlines a formal accusation made by Corrie on Emily's behalf: 'Martin looked at his meeting notes. "You addressed a transgender student in such a way as to imply that her gender dysphoria was the result of a character weakness"' (246). He also refers to the specific complaint concerning Sophie:

'Well, that's what you were guilty of, in this student's opinion, a huge microaggression.'

Sophie frowned. 'How can you have a huge microaggression? That would just be ... an aggression.'

Martin smiled wanly, then rose to his feet and extended his hand.

'Let's just follow the proper procedure,' he said. 'If you do that, in my experience, you can't go wrong.'

Coe 2018: 249

Coe's irony is that procedural probity confers a status of validity upon such objections, illogical as they are, even before the salient matters are discussed. The weakness of Corrie's accusations is much as Sophie points it out to be, and Martin's smile reveals both his empathy for Sophie's position and simultaneously reveals his weakness.

Between some of the episodes concerned with such personal politics, Benjamin plans to meet an old school-friend, Philip, to discuss Benjamin's mammoth, unwieldy novel project of 'some one and a half million words' (107) that he has worked on since being an undergraduate at Oxford, with matching music. Philip suggests as a venue the Victoria pub in central Birmingham and promises to organize a committee (because of the scale of writing involved). On arrival Benjamin identifies Steve Richards, the only black boy in their year, plus an older man who reveals himself to be Mr Serkis, Benjamin's Sixth Form English teacher, almost unchanged since the nineteen-seventies. In this pivotal scene the others find most of Benjamin's creativity redundant, apart from the section on romance. '"Don't get me wrong," said Steve. "I mean, there was one section I really enjoyed. That one about you and Cicely"' (112). After general agreement, Philip offers to publish this as a novel, entitled '"A Rose Without a Thorn"' (113), leading eventually to a Booker nomination and the final episode of Coe's novel concerning a writing school in France.

Intensely and overtly political, as Brown indicates, the plot of *Middle England* has as its central spiral the often-vexatious debates that animated the Brexit campaign. As such, *Middle England* is part of what Zrari calls 'Brexlit' and he argues 'the portrait of Brexit according to Coe oscillates between the political and the emotional, two notions that turn out to be antagonistic' (2020: n.p.). For me this critique tends to wilfully diminish the many rational reasons underpinning the Leave campaigns, both political and economic, and radically downplays the bias against such positions adopted by much of the mainstream televisual media. It also serves to secrete into the frame of supposedly impartial analysis a definitional context whereby the limitations of Coe's own fictional response may be validated. Despite the importance of Brexit to the narrative, Brown insists, 'Coe's treatment of the Brexit debate strikes me as the novel's main weakness. His own bias is so resolutely and nakedly Remain that it infects his characters, and undermines the necessary illusion that they have thoughts independent of their creator' (2018: 26), which in turn negates the neutral element at the heart of the parody upon which Coe's satire depends. Zrari's claims for the novel are rather grandiose and I will suggest run contrary to the book's actual scope:

> [T]he author traces the fracturing of Britain from April 2010 to September 2018 [...]. In his novel, Brexit and the referendum of 2016 are portrayed as pivotal events in the history of British politics. By attempting to grasp the national mood of that period, Coe offers different perspectives on how the decision to leave the European Union has affected the country and its inhabitants and proves, once again, his ability to weave together national history – especially current affairs – and fiction.
>
> Zrari 2020: n.p.

In this novel, for me the warp and weft are misaligned, for first as Brown observes 'Coe's goodies are Remainers, and his baddies are Brexiteers' (2018: 27). And second, as David Martin Jones notes concerning the traumatic response of Lois (while immediately recollecting her boyfriend's murder by an IRA bomb) to

> [T]he news of Remainer MP Jo Cox's murder by a man shouting 'Britain First'.
> She has a fit, beats the wall with her fists and screams [...], 'You stupid people, letting this happen.' Curiously, the Islamic State-inspired murder of Lee Rigby, the attacks on Charlie Hebdo's office and the Bataclan theatre in Paris, and in Nice and Brussels, evoke no such traumatic response in Lois or disturb the progressive verities of Brexlit more generally.
>
> Jones 2020: n.p.

Clearly these other deaths preceded the referendum by a far longer period than Cox's murder, yet there is in this insistent and immediate focus an issue of partiality, and the dissipation of any residual neutral element. I cannot concede the balance Zrari imagines is present in Coe's narrative when claiming '*Middle England* is a social and political meditation that aims at voicing the emotional state of a whole country. Coe endeavours to understand what led people to vote remain or leave through his exploration of the imbrication of personal and collective narratives' (2020: n.p.). Toward the end of the novel, out for a meal in Birmingham, Sophie tells her father of her decision to quit her job; and after an encounter that confirms her mother-in-law's racism and Ian's rejection of his mother, finally Sophie reconciles with her husband. In the last episode after a school reunion, a semi-retired Benjamin capitalizes on his nomination for the Booker Prize longlist by opening a creative writing school in France, taking his sister with him. The usually self-deprecating and neutral Benjamin, now a published writer, finally reveals his partiality, when called on to make a speech at an informal opening dinner, he responds '"Fine," said Benjamin. "I can say what I want to say in two words." He paused and looked around the table at the circle of expectant faces. Then, in a tone of belligerent triumph, he said, "*Fuck Brexit!*", and sat down to a round of applause' (415). The mask of neutrality is dropped entirely, and Charlie, Benjamin's primary school friend – who has been imprisoned for attacking a fellow children's entertainer – identifies the British malaise with the election of Thatcher which initiated the unravelling of the Welfare State, implicitly eulogizing the 1970s that preceded her election. Claire disagrees, 'and [seeks] to point out that the decade he was seeking to idealize had also seen record inflation, economic instability and industrial unrest. The conversation among the four middle-aged English diners became heated [...]' (416). Having the characters adopt such polemical postures seems neither satirical nor parodic, and Coe does so only after Benjamin has expressed their unanimity about opposing Brexit. In effect Coe risks privileging his authorial voice through his fictional alter-ego, Benjamin, who ventriloquizes Coe's ideological discomfort concerning, and opposition to, Brexit. And what follows is a final revelation by Lois concerning her daughter's pregnancy: 'Sophie and Ian's tentative gesture of faith in their equivocal, unknowable future: their beautiful Brexit baby' (421), so finally even Brexit is appropriated by those opposing its overall trajectory through this act of procreation as if the future will be theirs, a curiously sentimental ending to such a fractured narrative, one which contrasts an implicit reality the reader of whichever persuasion (leave or remain) would surely be struck by, which is the unlikeliness of the Ian and Sophie relationship working out long term. In this respect, their procreative union seems more of a structural convenience than a milestone in personal and cultural relations.

Conclusion

In the case of *Middle England*, as the above analysis suggests, Coe has not managed to sustain the credibility, ingenuity and level of artistry displayed in *What a Carve Up!* In this case he neither managed to maintain neutrality nor successfully offset it with intertextual interplay. One might explain this as due to the particular divisiveness of Brexit but this would be to downplay the wider point that the primacy of postmodernism is historically waning and Coe's ongoing use of its central modes of understanding – what Hutcheon describes as 'Parody – often called ironic quotation, pastiche, appropriation, or intertextuality' (1989: 93) – has therefore become both increasingly challenging and subject to challenge. One possible judgement on the novels Coe has published in the 2010s would be that his persistence with parody appears to offer diminishing returns in a culture reacquainting itself with solid points of reference. Alternatively, *Middle England* in particular might be seen as sustaining at least a form of self-parody as reflected in Benjamin's (and Coe's) very inability to stay neutral. Whether this will prove as enduring as his earlier work remains to be seen but Coe remains an interesting case study for how the literary politics of the 1980s and 1990s continue to play out in the very different cultural climate of our post-Brexit times.

Works cited

Alberti, Fay Bound. *A Biography of Loneliness: The History of an Emotion*. Oxford: Oxford University Press, 2019.

Alfaro, María Jesús Martínez. 'Intertextuality: Origins and Development of the Concept'. *Atlantis: Revista de la Asociación Española de Estudios Anglo-Norteamericanos* 18(1/2, June–December), 1996: 268–285.

Armion, Clifford and Jonathan Coe. 'An interview with Jonathan Coe (*Expo 58*)'. *La Clé des Langues* [en ligne]. February 2014: https://cle.ens-lyon.fr/anglais/litterature/litterature-britannique/an-interview-with-jonathan-coe-expo-58-.

Bromhall, Richard. *Refiguring Class: The Precariat in Contemporary Writing About Britain* [doctoral thesis]. Nottingham: Nottingham Trent University, September 2019.

Brown, Craig. 'Coe set out to pen a state of the nation novel... and ended up writing a *Guardian* editorial'. *The Mail on Sunday: Review Section*, 27 October 2018: 26–27: https://www.dailymail.co.uk/home/event/article-6316659/CRAIG-BROWN-Jonathan-Coes-Middle-England-obvious-satire.html.

Chadderton, Helena. 'Translating class in Jonathan Coe'. *The Translator*, 23(3), 2017: 269–278.

Clark, Alex. '*The Terrible Privacy of Maxwell Sim* by Jonathan Coe'. *The Guardian*. 22 May 2010: n.p.; https://www.theguardian.com/books/2010/may/22/terrible-privacy-maxwell-sim-coe.

Coe, Jonathan. *What a Carve Up!* London: Penguin, 1995 [1994].

Coe, Jonathan. *The Terrible Privacy of Maxwell Sim*. New York: Alfred A. Knopf, 2011 [2010].

Coe, Jonathan. *Expo 58*. London: Penguin, 2014 [2013].
Coe, Jonathan. *Number 11*. London: Viking, 2015.
Coe, Jonathan. *Middle England*. London: Viking, 2018.
Connolly, Cressida. '*Expo 58*, by Jonathan Coe – review'. *The Spectator*, 21 September 2013: https://www.spectator.co.uk/article/expo-58-by-jonathan-coe---review.
Crews, Brian. 'Christie Malry's Own Double-Entry: B.S. Johnson's Oppositional Discourse of Unbelief'. *Revista Alicantina de Estudios Ingleses* 7 November 1994: 55–66.
Dällenbach, Lucien. *The Mirror in the Text*. Jeremy Whiteley with Emma Hughes (trans.). Chicago, IL: University of Chicago Press, 1989 [1977].
Davis, Jessica Milner. *Farce*. With new introduction. Abingdon: Routledge, 2017 [2003].
French, Paul. 'Fake Britannia'. *LARB: Los Angeles Review of Books*, 2 September, 2014: https://lareviewofbooks.org/article/fake-britannia/.
Ganteau, Jean-Michel. 'The Powers of Exposure: Risk and Vulnerability in Contemporary British Fiction'. *Textual Practice* 31(3), 2017: 443–455.
Gross, John. 'Introduction'. In *The Oxford Book of Parodies*. John Gross (ed.). Oxford: Oxford University Press, 2010: i–xviii.
Guignery, Vanessa. 'Gothic Horror and Haunting Processes in Jonathan Coe's *Number 11*'. In *Jonathan Coe: Contemporary British Satire*. Philip Tew (ed.). London: Bloomsbury, 2018: 169–183.
Hieff, John. '*The Terrible Privacy of Maxwell Sim*' [review of audio book]. *Library Journal* 136(11, 15 June), 2011: 46.
Hitchcock, Alfred (dir.). *The Lady Vanishes*. London: Gainsborough Pictures, 1938.
Hutcheon, Linda. *A Theory of Parody: The Teachings of Twentieth-Century Art Forms*. Urbana: University of Illinois Press, 2000 [1985].
Hutcheon, Linda. 'Literary Borrowing . . . and Stealing: Plagiarism, Sources, Influences, and Intertexts'. *English Studies in Canada* XII(2, June), 1986: 229–239.
Hutcheon, Linda. *The Politics of Postmodernism*. London: Routledge, 1989.
Hutcheon, Linda. *Irony's Edge: The Theory and Politics of Irony*. London: Routledge, 1994.
Johnson, B.S. *Christie Malry's Own Double-Entry*. Harmondsworth: Penguin, 1984 [1973].
Jones, David Martin. 'Brexlit and the decline of the English novel'. *The Critic*, January 2020. Available at: https://thecritic.co.uk/issues/january-2020/brexlit-and-the-decline-of-the-english-novel/ (accessed 23 June 2023).
Khramova, Yulia Anatolyevna. 'The Themes of Loss and Loneliness in Jonathan Coe's Novel *The Terrible Privacy of Maxwell Sim*'. *Philological Class* 25(2), 2020: 258–266.
Kostka, Violetta. 'Linda Hutcheon's Theory of Parody and Its Application to Postmodern Music'. *Avant* VII(1), 2016: 67–73.
Laity, Paul. 'A Life in Writing: Jonathan Coe. *The Guardian*, 29 May 2010: https://www.theguardian.com/books/2010/may/29/life-writing-jonathan-coe.
Lasch, Christopher. *The Culture of Narcissism: American Life in an Age of Diminishing Expectations*. New York: W.W. Norton, 1979.

Lasdun, James. 'An Englishman abroad: Parody or homage? James Lasdun is mystified by Coe's nostalgic trip: *Expo 58* by Jonathan Coe'. *The Guardian*, 21 September, 2013: https://www.theguardian.com/books/2013/sep/19/expo-58-jonathan-coe-review.

McGill, Hannah. 'Book review: *Expo 58* by Jonathan Coe'. *Scotsman*, 11 August 2013: https://www.scotsman.com/arts-and-culture/book-review-expo-58-jonathan-coe-1565079.

Marsh, Huw. *The Comic Turn in Contemporary English Fiction: Who's Laughing Now?* London: Bloomsbury, 2020.

Mellet, Laurent. '"[Laughter] was something that drew people together. It was something shared". ('The Paradox of Satire [I]'): from laughing along to mislaughing oneself away and coming out in Jonathan Coe's fiction'. *Études britanniques contemporaines* 51, 2016: https://journals.openedition.org/ebc/3360?lang=en.

Mellet, Laurent. 'London Doubts: Wellsian Undersides and Undertones in Jonathan Coe's *Number 11* (2015)'. *Études britanniques contemporaines* 55, 2018: https://journals.openedition.org/ebc/5145.

Moseley, Merritt. 'Jonathan Coe: The Early Novels'. In *Jonathan Coe: Contemporary British Satire*. Philip Tew (ed.). London: Bloomsbury, 2018: 21–34.

Orr, Mary. *Intertextuality: Debates and Contexts*. Cambridge: Polity, 2003.

Shallcross, Michael. '"The Parodist's Game": Scrutiny of Cultural Play in Jonathan Coe's *What a Carve Up!*' *Adaptation: the Journal of Literature on Screen Studies* 9(2), 2016: 123–141.

Tew, Philip. 'Jonathan Coe'. In *Writers Talk: Conversations with Contemporary Novelists*. Philip Tew, Fiona Tolan and Leigh Wilson (eds). London: Continuum, 2008: 35–55.

Zrari, Imad. '*Middle England* by Jonathan Coe: A Brexit Novel or the Politics of Emotions'. *Observatoire de la Société Britannique* 25, 2020: 213–235.

7

'The English Problem': Reading the Body Politic in Post-Brexit Fictions

Kristian Shaw

In the fallout of the 2016 EU referendum, the Brexit vote was immediately positioned as an English revolt, with commentators expounding on the ways in which Englishness and Euroscepticism were symptomatically entwined in securing Britain's exit from the EU. Outside of London, the English Leave vote was a substantial 55.4 per cent, drawing attention to a cultural disconnect between the capital and the traditional heartlands of England; a disconnect that had been evident for decades yet ignored by successive governments. Countless surveys and studies indicated that England was suffering from an identity crisis that had little to do with its tempestuous relationship with the EU. In 2012, an IPPR report, entitled 'The Dog That Finally Barked', identified a growing attachment to the 'Anglo' component of British identity amongst English voters (Wyn Jones et al. 2012: 3). The follow-up report, 'England and its Two Unions' – produced the same year David Cameron delivered his fateful Bloomberg speech – proved to be even more prophetic, stating 'It is English, rather than British, hackles that rise in response to Europe', and predicting 'overwhelming majorities of the exclusively and predominantly English would probably vote Leave' (2013: 22, 17). For Ben Wellings, Euroscepticism was 'in all but name English nationalism' as voters in England bought into media narratives which sought out convenient proxies and external threats as explanatory causes of cultural decline while political forces discovered a series of distinctly English underlying grievances could be mobilized for personal gain (2010: 503). For a confused and disillusioned English electorate, the allure of Brexit became a curative for a range of cultural and socioeconomic factors responsible for diminishing the nation's standing.

According to Matthew Levinger and Paula Franklin Lytle, nationalist rhetoric relies on this triadic structure: political figures juxtapose the 'golden age' of the past with the inferiorities of the 'degraded present' and allude to a 'utopian' dawn which will allow the nation to regain its autonomy and former glory (2001: 175). The deployment of Englishness and Britishness as interchangeable terms in media discourses during the referendum campaign contributed to this defensive assumption of Britain as 'Greater England' and reinforced a sense of English political exceptionalism.

A range of well-known literary voices immediately engaged with the unprecedented developments of 2016, their works becoming part of a 'Brexlit' movement (Shaw 2018). With the exception of a few outliers, such as Paul Kingsnorth or John King, the literary community formed a distinctly Europhilic chorus, expressing concerns that Britain would simply become poorer for its act of political withdrawal.[1] While several post-war Eurosceptic fictions directed their attention towards European 'otherness' and drew on dystopian logics to insinuate the threat of supranational structures on the sovereignty of the British people, this first wave of post-Brexit fiction looks inward to the internal ailments weakening the body politic, particularly the anxieties of England-outside-London, and gestures to the need for institutional change. In 'Fences: A Brexit Diary', Zadie Smith reacts to this 'London vs. the rest' explanation, appearing confused as to the motivations for the Leave vote, 'What was it really about? Immigration? Inequality? Historic xenophobia? Sovereignty? EU bureaucracy? Anti-neoliberal revolution? Class war?' (2016: n.p.). The problem, of course, as Smith's 'Fences' or Julian Barnes's 'People Will Hate Us Again' (2017) confirm, is that there was little appreciation of the scale of these issues prior to the vote, particularly in London-based academic circles.

Elsewhere (Shaw 2021), I have examined an entrenched Euroscepticism within British literature from 1945 to the present, charting the differentiated responses of English, Scottish, Welsh and Northern Irish fictions to the European project and the key catalysts that laid the groundwork for Britain's Leave vote, including the perceived dilution of national sovereignty, the maintenance of an ethnonationalist imperial fantasy, the politicization of EU migration, and fears surrounding the introduction of devolutionary dispensations. This chapter will assume a narrower approach in assessing the main catalysts underpinning the Leave vote, indicating the ways by which a resurgent English identity became a source of nostalgic protection for those citizens disillusioned with the state of the nation. The first section of the chapter will examine *Ghost Wall* (2018) by Sarah Moss and *All Among the Barley* (2018a) by Melissa Harrison, which dig into England's turbulent history to excavate the deep roots of the English cultural imaginary, demonstrating how a misplaced fetishization of the past can stimulate self-destructive nativist urges. The following section will turn to *Perfidious*

Albion (2018) by Sam Byers, which gives voice to the lingering resentment and restlessness of the English electorate following the referendum. Byers details the propensity for right-wing elements to exploit patriotic sentiments in their colonization of the political landscape, employing post-truth tactics to fuse racial logics and concerns surrounding cultural conservation in the minds of voters. The concluding section will draw on Anthony Cartwright's *The Cut* (2017) and Glen James Brown's *Ironopolis* (2018) to illustrate how the profound socioeconomic changes wrought by processes of deindustrialization produced lasting psychological and cultural traumas that continue to shape the political landscape in the post-Brexit moment. As Ian McEwan succinctly puts it, 'Brexit is the continuation of an old story' (2016: 36). The chapter will thus position England's forceful Leave vote not as a clear break from earlier political periods but as a pathological symptom of entrenched socioeconomic imbalances, cultural insecurities and internal structural anxieties which have lain dormant for decades.

The sound of the gone away

As Sarah Moss reminds us, 'Brexit is a symptom of wider changes of mood, or articulations of mood' with deep roots that pre-date the Eurosceptic discourses of the contemporary moment (Moss 2020: n.p.). Her novel *Ghost Wall* (2018) delves into the historical impulses which informed fascistic debates surrounding national tradition during the referendum campaign. By scrutinizing the venerated rituals and myths of past ages, Moss, in turn, excavates the roots of Brexit discourse. The novel documents the traumatic experiences of seventeen-year-old Silvie, forced by her domineering father Bill to participate in an experimental archaeology course investigating Iron Age practices in the rural Northumbrian landscape. Whereas Professor Slade, who leads the expedition, is more concerned with the research potential of his practice-based experiment, Bill, an amateur historian, longs to reconnect with an imagined community of Ancient Britons, united by their whiteness and unwavering loyalty to an instinctual perception of nationhood. Moss begins her narrative with an account of an Iron Age sacrifice, gesturing to the continued presence of tribal patriotism in the present, and foreshadows the ways by which violence so easily emerges from nationalist debates.

Appropriately, media discourses during the EU referendum galvanized this re-enactment of past nationalist debates and resurrected traumas of the destructive past to inform contemporary political debates. In this sense, the numerous cultural grievances nurtured by Bill – an arrogant dismissal of gender equality, a staunchly anti-immigration stance, a festering anger concerning the dissolution of English racial purity – are animated by what he perceives to be the gradual erosion of national tradition, the loss of dominant male expression, and the subsequent socio-cultural disorientation and victimization that follows. His interest in the Iron Age is energized by a more general recovery of the idealized past, and he is quick to inhabit its traumas and repackage its foundational stories whenever they fail to align with his nostalgic vision, revealing a profound insecurity and acute awareness of the hollowness at the heart of the national mythopoeia. Such dreaming, Zygmunt Bauman reminds us, is concerned not with the past 'wie es ist eigentlich gewesen' (how it really was) but an elusive imagined territory, which serves to correct current states of decline (2017: 10). Bill excavates the Northumbrian terrain in order to properly mourn the erosion of a once-great national identity, almost believing it can be rediscovered in an English bog, preserved like a Bronze Age relic. His fascination with 'dead things' is reflective of the wider English chthonic fascination with a morbid national heritage, and the tendency of political figures to retreat into ethnocentric cultural fantasies or champion outdated belief systems as a protective measure when faced with difficult social developments facing contemporary society (Moss 2018: 25). For Fintan O'Toole (2018), the fatal attraction of what he terms 'heroic failure' in the English cultural imagination, powers these fantasies of loss and cultural decline. Silvie comes to understand 'that was the whole point of the re-enactment, that we ourselves became the ghosts'; her father's obsession with the tenebrous past transmogrifies into a celebration of a dead Englishness untainted by the present (2018: 34).

Bill's consoling tribal nationalism, reliant on the belief that 'there's some original Britishness somewhere', ensures he is particularly averse to so-called experts, represented by the Professor, who are inclined to deconstruct or even denigrate the foundational fictions and collective memories on which such idealized nationhood is built (Moss 2018: 20). Affect-memory, as Robert Eaglestone accentuates, 'does not check evidence, has no rules, no form of argument, no need to be consistent, or to be engineered into a full, explanatory account', clashing uncomfortably with historical details that expose the simplification and manipulation of ethnonationalist forms of reminiscence (2018: 96). Indeed, though the Professor initially leads the experiment, Bill soon starts to dominate control of events and the narrative itself – being almost invigorated by this imaginary connection to the past and viewing himself, as an 'ordinary' everyman, as its true custodian – echoing the momentum of ethnonationalist rhetoric during the referendum campaign and substantiating Patrick Wright's assessment that 'a simplifying nostalgia can replace any principled democratic consideration' (1985: 244).

Bill's disillusionment with modern society is not simply powered by the oft-cited issues central to the Brexit vote but evokes a wider disdain for the destructive aspects of globalization and deindustrialization. Reflecting on an earlier trip to Newcastle, Silvie recalls her father grieving for the dilapidated docks, 'Used to send ships all over the world from here. Look at it now', the cranes haunting the landscape like 'ceremonial pillars of lost civilisations' (25). Rather tellingly, Bill's 'mood lifted' as they travelled north to Hadrian's Wall, 'a physical manifestation of Ancient British resistance still marked on the land', and he 'draw[s] strength from it' (26). As Wright states, the persistence of the 'styles and potentials of the past [...] as residue only testifies to the fact that they lack any leverage or active historicity in the present', yet the national imaginary still holds the potential 'to re-enchant a disenchanted everyday life' (1985: 243, 24). By 'Ancient British', of course, we can infer Bill's inchoate predilection for a sacred white *Englishness* and his assumption of a lingering hierarchy within the UK which privileges Anglocentric dominance; the Leave campaign, after all, clung to an invasion theme that not only attacked immigrants but dramatized 'devo-anxiety' as an immediate threat to English tradition. When the Professor corrects his misconception, pointing out that Hadrian's Wall was initially just a 'marker' for the edge of Europe, and his imaginary Britons were a mixture of Celtic tribes from France and Ireland, Silvie notices her father bristle, intuitively connecting his faith in English racial purity with his hostility to contemporary forms of immigration: 'Foreigners coming over here, telling us what to think. He wanted his own ancestry, wanted a lineage, a claim on something. Not people from Ireland or Rome or Germania or Syria but some tribe sprung from English soil like mushrooms in the night' (Moss 2018: 45). As Ailsa Henderson and Richard Wyn Jones argue, when it comes to the preservation of Englishness as a political force, 'the problem is not immigrants per se; it is immigrants who are not considered as "kith and kin" or fellow members of what used to be termed the Anglo-Saxon race' (2021: 94). This valorization of earlier historical periods protects the maintenance of historical inequalities in the cultural imaginary. Although Bill's nativist fetishization seemingly provides succour to his fragile psychological well-being, it is little more than a *vampiric* Englishness that feeds off the misconceptions of the past without providing any real nourishment and merely sustains his chthonic fascination with morbid mythopoeia.

Through his misogynistic manipulation of Silvie, Bill attempts to conserve his imagined racial purity, her lack of a passport being indicative of his desire to restrict European influence; we learn her full name is Sulevia, taken from Ancient British mythology, but even this 'proper native British name' is tainted by its Roman corruption, ridiculing the deluded ideology behind patriotic jingoism (2018: 19). There are, however, signs that Silvie is aware of her father's misguided understanding of British history and the limitations of his isolationist mindset. Ruminating on the Neolithic Doggerland, that connected Britain to continental Europe, she comes to understand that 'the edge of an island is infinite' with 'England's blurred margins' complicating such simplistic and stable conceptions of national identification (54). *Ghost Wall* resonates with the historical violence and island mentality that has characterized the English cultural imaginary, yet Moss is speaking to the bitter divides of the Brexit moment, where the drum beat of nativism once again drowned out reasoned debate. The dangers of resurrecting spectres of the past become evident in the closing stages of the novel as Bill gradually retreats into an ethnocentric cultural fantasy defined by its chthonic fascination with a morbid national heritage. Guided by the Professor, the group erect a 'ghost wall' – a defensive palisade consisting of ancestral skulls – that once functioned as a 'last-ditch defence against the Romans' and, in Bill's mind, now signifies a symbolic resistance to the effacement of the English sublime (108). The use of rabbit skulls for the aforementioned ancestral remains of tribal ancestors hints at the farcical limitations of resuscitating outdated historical dogma and its impotent efficacy as an inauthentic bulwark against the impositions of the present.

Events take a more sinister turn when Bill convinces the Professor to re-enact an Iron Age ritual sacrifice, using Silvie as the symbolic victim, indicating just how quickly a movement can progress from 'being a bit daft to feeling like something real. I didn't know people could decide to make that happen' (124–125). By ensuring Silvie's fate is foreshadowed by the Iron Age ritual sacrifice at the opening of the novel, Moss signals how political ideologies of the past assume new forms, with the younger generation suffering the mutilatory effects of – and becoming the sacrificial objects for – the nativist tribal inclinations and toxic psychological impulses of nationalist forces. As one of the students tells Silvie, 'people don't bother to hurt what they don't love. To sacrifice it', reinforcing the ceremonial reverence with which her father treats the English past; sacrifice becomes a means of resurrecting and reclaiming that which is denied to him in the present, operating as a 'talisman against the pain' (126, 71). Like the Iron Age bodies preserved in the bog, this morbid cultural nostalgia is therefore 'dead and still present' (103). Stripped, bound and cut with a hunting knife on the moor, Silvie's performative sacrifice is all too real, with some of the students actively participating in the re-enactment, caught up in the collective tribal fervour. Silvie is saved from further torment by one of the Professor's female students, who alerts the authorities and puts an end to her father's chthonic fantasy, yet this unexpected emancipation from his patriarchal control is only a temporary reprieve; we do not witness Bill being forced to recant either his ethnocentric worldview or his abusive, almost-tribal display of masculine authority, meaning his toxic ideology may continue unabated. For Moss, then, earlier periods of English history provide fertile ground to comment on the social and cultural insecurities and backward-looking political discourses stimulated by the Brexit vote.

This mournful longing for the 'sound of the gone away' also fuels Melissa Harrison's haunting *All Among the Barley* (2018a: 2). Set in the fictional village of Elmbourne, Harrison's novel paints a wistful portrait of 1930s English rural life as the threat of fascism begins to rear its ugly head, forging parallels with current political instabilities. As in so many Brexlit novels, the legacy and impact of the world wars emerges as the primary cultural touchpoint in alleviating fears regarding external European influence, with Harrison citing the EU referendum and rise in English far-right political support as reasons why the 1930s became 'highly resonant years' for a discussion of the contemporary moment (Harrison 2018b: n.p.).[2] The inhabitants of Wych Farm long to retreat 'back in time to the olden days [...] to be granted a temporary reprieve from all the anxieties of the modern age, the sense of things speeding up and going wrong', caught up in the allure of national nostalgia as a distraction from the destabilization of their community in the interwar years (Harrison 2018a: 61).

Harrison's adolescent narrator, Edie Mather, who has spent her entire life on the farm, 'a world of ancient and immovable rhythms and beliefs', finds her quiet life disrupted by the arrival of Constance FitzAllen, a forthright woman from London who seemingly desires to document rural traditions and farming practices (2018a: 96). FitzAllen initially hides her true intent behind a façade of sociological interest, producing short articles in a London journal, 'Sketches from English Rural Life', that valorize villages as 'the repository of our national pride' and draw on idyllic qualities of the English sublime in order to reconnect the local people with their 'ancient way of life [...] England is the country, and the country is England' (91, 162). FitzAllen's outspoken support for the Order of British Yeomanry in a public meeting, a group of patriotic farmers and landowners who perceive the encroachment of European and international financiers as an infection on 'the health and purity of our English soil', building on her earlier calls for 'proper import controls to protect our native English farmers', develops a clear parallel between the rhetoric of the interwar and Brexit years (299, 113). In a historical note following the novel, Harrison details how her microcosmic concentration on British yeomanry was inspired by the drive towards fascism in the 1930s, when disparate 'fragmented groups', often faced with difficult socioeconomic prospects, 'all drew from a murky broth of [...] nativism, protectionism, anti-immigration sentiment, economic autarky, secessionism, militarism, [and] anti-Europeanism', alluding to the politically alienated groups brought together by the Brexit vote and its promise of national self-sufficiency (329).

However, FitzAllen's increasingly problematic valorization of 'the bonds of blood and soil' and distaste for intellectual elites begins to expose her more subversive intentions for the rural community as she systematically exploits this deep attachment to the land by harnessing romantic images of historical nationalism and reinscribing them for fascist purposes (91). Indeed, she begins to champion the British Union of Fascists, attributing the socioeconomic decline of Elmbourne on the corrupting presence of the recent arrival of a local Jewish family. Her exclusionary rhetoric and undisguised process of Othering marks a significant contrast to her initial professed curiosity in English rural tradition as Harrison warns how swiftly fears surrounding the preservation of cultural heritage can be manipulated and recast as commentaries on the present: 'they're not *from* here, and if we're not careful they'll mar the character of England forever' (199; emphasis in original). Though FitzAllen insists her actions are not driven by a nostalgic longing, but rather the aim of forging a new identity for a beleaguered rural England, her rhetoric anticipates more recent calls for a Global Britain which is somehow predicated on an Anglocentric worldview and characterized by isolationist policies.[3] The debilitated condition of Edie's farm community, then, functions as a microcosmic diagnosis of the ailing health of the body politic and the misplaced nationalism and xenophobia that emerges from virulent English nationalist impulses.

Forging a dialogue with the rural nostalgia of *Ghost Wall*, Harrison's examination of English farming traditions reminds us of the 'very real dangers in tying national identity to place [...] because it leaves no room for change' (Harrison 2018b: n.p.). Just as Silvie learns to mistrust her father's ethnonationalist delusions concerning English history, so too does Edie turn her back on FitzAllen's destructive cultural nostalgia by recognizing the futility of preserving – and resurrecting – outdated traditions. In forcing Edie to dissect and critique her halcyon 'vision of a lost Eden to which I longed to return', Harrison delivers a percipient commentary on the deep roots of Brexit rhetoric and the danger in clinging onto an instinctual Englishness as a tonic for cultural decline: 'you can never go back, and to make an idol of the past only disfigures the present, and makes the future harder to attain' (2018a: 324).

Post-truth politics

The ubiquitous nature of 'post-truth' political rhetoric both during and after the referendum led to the term being named the *Oxford English Dictionary*'s word of 2016 (narrowly beating out Brexiteer), denoting circumstances in which appeals to emotion become more influential than objective fact in shaping or guiding public opinion. Tackling the emergence of a post-truth political culture that manipulates the most vulnerable while reinforcing the very structures of neoliberalism responsible for deepening such precarity, Sam Byers's satirical state-of-the-nation novel *Perfidious Albion* (2018) offers a different perspective on this crisis of Englishness, indicating just how easily disenfranchised voters can direct a displaced rage at the wrong targets in an effort to restore socially conservative values. In comparison to Harrison's consoling 'sound of the gone away', we are presented with 'the 'encroachment of the contemporary', which seemingly disrupts the 'ancient, unchanging real' within 'England's visionary soil' and mourns a 'lost England comprised entirely of hedgerows and loam' (2018: 164, 6). Set in the fictional English town of Edmundsbury (a microcosm of post-referendum England) following the Brexit vote, the novel concentrates on the plight of residents in the Larchwood housing estate, their homes targeted by the building company Downton for gentrification. In this post-Brexit climate of uncertainty, Europhobic populist figures have strengthened their authoritarian grip on a politically exhausted electorate and gained further momentum by exploiting the very voters who delivered the Leave vote.

Darkin, an elderly working-class man who feels left behind by contemporary society, resists repeated attempts by Downton to evict him from his home. Rather than positioning the Brexit vote as the root cause of Darkin's plight, Byers accentuates how the dilapidated condition of Darkin's flat signals the longitudinal effects of the erosion of community and the stripping away of the protective shelter of the welfare state, with corporate interests capitalizing on this moment of political transition. In a personal conversation with Byers, he states he was keen to accentuate how Brexit merely brought to the fore a 'deeply unpleasant "little England" sort of nationalism' and 'anti-immigration' rhetoric that were in circulation long before the referendum, citing the erosion of Labour's so-called red wall as a key example (Byers 2020: n.p.). Isolated, atomized and alienated, Darkin derives his opinions from the comforting exclusionary rhetoric of far-right journalist Hugo Bennington, whose aggressive vernacular, 'in a language you didn't need a master's degree in bullshit to understand', speaks to the disenfranchisement felt by disillusioned voters (2018: 25). Byers's cogent remark that Darkin 'read not to have his fears assuaged, but to have them confirmed' speaks to the highly partisan climate of the referendum campaign and the discursive framing of key cultural battles by media outlets (24). Bennington waxes lyrical on the English cultural imaginary in his regular column for *The Record* newspaper, dredging up Wright's concept of a 'Deep England' nationalist mindset, founded on 'an imagined participation immemorial', directing his ire at citizens who dare to question his white masculine authority or destabilize his cherished repository of English signifiers (1985: 79). For Byers, the simplistic politico-media discourses during the referendum campaign

> exacerbated and in the end solidified a growing trend towards polarised positions, and towards polarisation not just as a symptom but as a deliberate political tactic [...] both Remain and Leave became surprisingly inflexible identities for people, around which they shaped other aspects of their lives, and which helped them make more straightforward sense of what up to that point might have been quite complex political positions.
>
> Byers 2020: n.p.

The Leave campaign in particular became quite adept at writing themselves into England's historical narrative.

Realizing the extent of his populist appeal, the Farage-like Bennington becomes an MP for the nativist England Always political party, a darkly humorous version of the United Kingdom Independence Party (UKIP), who struggle to redefine themselves in the wake of the Brexit vote (much like Farage's doomed Brexit Party) but attempt to reignite the bitter vitriol of the referendum campaign:

> chests puffed with post-exit pride, had begun their transformation from a party concerned with redefining England's place in the world to a party preoccupied with people's place in England, and had moved from shaping England's post-Europe future to recapturing its pre-contemporary pomp. Brexit was over, but the energy it had accumulated had to be retained. Fears needed to be redirected. Hatred needed to pivot.
>
> Byers 2018: 119

Bennington positions himself as an ordinary working man in contrast to the deluge of Westminster elites dominating the political class, drawing on the post-war rhetoric of Enoch Powell, employing colonially inflected messaging to criticize an England in which 'equality run[s] riot', and claiming 'for every white Englishman they employ they must also hire three foreigners' (25). In satirizing Bennington's everyman approach and the foundational myths propping up conservative thought, that appeals to disillusioned voters like Darkin, Byers indicates how media rhetoric during the referendum campaign utilized typologies of national sovereignty for political advantage, suggesting a vote for Brexit signified implicit support for national survival rather than a referendum on the specificities of EU membership. As Henderson and Wyn Jones note in their study of contemporary Englishness, 'campaigns led by a series of individuals who, to outside eyes, would appear to exemplify a privileged elite make for a peculiar form of anti-elite politics', but these tactics have proven popular with an electorate tired of the political class (2021: 210). Darkin comes to unintentionally echo the same Brexit-infused phrases Bennington employs in his Europhobic articles. The disillusioned residents of Edmundsbury, 'hitherto ignored by the self-serving shitshow of London-centric political wheeler-dealing' are thus subjected to targeted tactics and have their 'collective, semi-conscious unease' manipulated for further populist gain (25, 66). Bennington's serio-comic attempts to frame 'world events as extended riffs on Harry Potter' – redolent of Boris Johnson's similar tactic with Peppa Pig – and championing of a specifically English nostalgia which contrasts the contemporary moment with the vision of a secure if vague 'historical' England prove to be a consoling panacea for an anxious nation: 'Through simplification, Hugo was selling reassurance. Through nostalgia, he was selling the political equivalent of escapism. And through reductive blame-mongering, he was [. . .] selling a potent combination of the two' (103).

The political force of England Always is bolstered by the emergence of Brute Force, a fascist militia – in the vein of the English Defence League (EDL) – who strong-arm and intimidate voters under the guise of 'Taking Back Control' of Edmundsbury from the imagined threat of undocumented immigrants and instigate a culture war against so-called enemies of the people. As Jan-Werner Müller explains, populism is energized by this 'exclusionary form of identity politics' that promotes the idea of 'the single, homogeneous authentic people' under threat from external forces and unites disenfranchised voters with a single voice (2016: 3, 57). Crucially, this disenfranchisement is not just felt by 'the Darkins of the world' but by elites like Bennington, who harbour a nostalgic 'hankering for a time in which it was felt that they (or people like them) actually mattered: a time in which [...] an England-dominated Britain knew its proper (elevated) place in the world – and naturally, the rest of the world knew it too', strengthening the appeal of England as a viable political community (Henderson and Wyn Jones 2021: 133). For Roger Eatwell and Matthew Goodwin, the national populist phenomenon is also cultivated by deep-rooted fears surrounding 'immigration and hyper ethnic change' due to this desire to re-establish a white voice and these factors are often cited by right-wing politicians as explanatory grounds for current states of decline (2018: 132). Bennington adopts this very approach, admitting Larchwood was home to 'fewer immigrants than almost anywhere else in the country', yet recognizes he can capitalize on the fact that 'anti-immigration sentiment had never been higher' to distract from his own complicity with Downton's gentrifying aims (106). In the 2015 and 2017 general elections, UKIP enjoyed greater success in English constituencies that had seen lower rates of immigration, but in which negative attitudes towards immigration were higher, strengthening the novel's engagement with the political foment of the Brexit moment.

Gesturing to the Facebook-Cambridge Analytica data harvesting scandal and data-mining conspiracies that cast a shadow over the digital tactics of the referendum campaign, Byers introduces the character of Trina, an employee for tech giant Green, who communicates her disdain with the 'tsunami of whitewashed nostalgia and chocolate-box history' England Always advocates through their nativist political oratory (134). When Bennington voices a concern that white men are being marginalized as a result of the ongoing drive for equality, Trina's tweet in response, '#whitemalegenocide. Lol', is seized upon by England Always as a threat to Darkin and fellow working-class men, seemingly validating their fear that the liberal left desire nothing less than the dissolution of historic white English identities (134). Trina, as a black British woman, is not included in Bennington's sacred ethnonationalist fantasy, serving as the personification of the failed 'experiment' of contemporary English society, 'the great politically correct, multicultural, multi-sexual, come-one-come-all melting pot' which actively undermines his homogenous cultural vision (257). As Byers writes, Hugo tries to convince himself that 'he was arguing solely with her in order to hide the fact he was arguing with everyone he thought of as being like her: namely, the swelling, imagined mass of everyone who was not him' (202). *Perfidious Albion*, then, delves into the personal and collective psychological elements underpinning the ethnonationalism of the referendum campaign and politico-media discourses of the post-Brexit moment, with casual attribution bias and confirmation bias affecting the perceived injustices experienced – and grievances held – by diverse groups of voters united under the same umbrella.

Rather than saving Darkin from eviction, England Always and Brute Force contribute to his misery, with his legitimate grievances and anxieties manipulated by Bennington until he is forced to sell his flat to enable the gentrification and redevelopment of his Larchwood estate. Bennington himself falls foul of this unstable, increasingly corporate, political environment; expelled from England Always following a personal scandal, he is unable to restore his beloved country to that nostalgic 'England of his childhood, of his frustrated and bitter dreams, an England in which he once again felt at home' (119). As with Silvie's father in *Ghost Wall*, the English identity Bennington craves is, like Brexit itself, an 'afterlife of dead fantasies' celebrating an unachievable and elusive quintessential Englishness (O'Toole 2018: 213). Meditating on his political downfall, he comes to understand that for:

> all the years he'd spent banging on about how much he loved England [...] he hated England [...] its filthy street markets of foreign tat that babbled with every language except the one Hugo himself spoke; its prancing, marrying queers; its blaring, feral, feminist bitches [...] that was the platform on which he should have stood: not England Always but England Eroded, England Besmeared.
>
> Byers 2018: 316

With this in mind, the cover of *Perfidious Albion*, depicting a post-Brexit corruption of Pieter Bruegel the Elder's infamous painting of Tower of Babel, not only reflects the island mentality at the heart of Bennington's political idealism, but an entrenched fear of cultural infiltration and the erosion of national tradition, capturing 'a near-dystopian vision of England [...] The country was overrun, under threat' (24).

Perfidious Albion thus dissects the same post-truth, populist tactics also evident in Douglas Board's *A Time of Lies* (2017), Michael Paraskos's *Rabbitman* (2017) and Ian McEwan's *Cockroach* (2019). However, unlike these corresponding post-Brexit novels, Byers also takes aim at the liberal left in their 'white-guilt-riddled, virtue-signalling Twitter bubbles' who abandon the conversation surrounding 'working-class maleness' because its parameters make them uncomfortable and who appear incapable of addressing legitimate concerns surrounding class-based immobility and socioeconomic precarity, opting instead to cling to the politics of identity as an ineffectual antidote to the surge in populist thought (200). In this sense, the novel does leave unresolved the question of 'what possible room could there be for a story like Darkin's' in the national narrative, and the failure of successive administrations to protect the most vulnerable, going some way to explaining the subsequent manipulation of such voters by populist forces (141). What the novel does manage to tap into is the very real sense that the Brexit result had very little to do with the machinations of EU bureaucracy; rather, it was the result of rooted social grievances and deeply private wounds, signifying a cultural backlash against perceived inequalities already germinating in the system. Though Byers accepts *Perfidious Albion* is infused with a 'Brexit feeling', he emphasizes that the novel is not so much concerned with the referendum result itself, 'but the viewpoints and policies the referendum so clearly legitimised', as England is forced to confront 'an animating of pre-existing forces, and a change in the landscape through that animation' (Byers 2020: n.p.).

The left behind

In his study of English nationalism, Jeremy Black argues that political elites in the twenty-first century have avoided 'confront[ing] the issue that England exists' (2018: 194). As the previous novels discussed in this chapter indicate, contemporary English nationalism tends to cast its mind back to the historical past for its animating energy and stable sources of identification. Anthony Cartwright's realist fictions, however, sidestep imaginative fiction, drawing their analysis from more sociological forms of storytelling; his detailed examination of the subtle stirrings of a resurgent English nationalism from within his cherished Black Country landscapes offer more substantial commentaries on the present by gesturing to the need for structural reform in correcting regional imbalances. Cartwright's balanced examinations of working-class communities are important interventions in this regard. As Ben Clarke and Nick Hubble note, 'any substantive attempt to examine, disrupt, or extend existing understandings' of working-class voices is somewhat lacking; instead, such voices are 'celebrated' as 'ordinary' and 'hardworking' or 'demonized' as examples of 'dysfunctional' communities hindering the well-being of the body politic (2018: 3).

Cartwright's fascination with the spectral terrain of Dudley, his birthplace and capital of the Black Country, accentuates the importance of historical legacies and the lived experience of communities in providing a stable sense of cultural identification, with their subsequent erasure impacting the political mindsets of his fictional characters. While *Heartland* (2009) insinuates how socioeconomic precarity can give rise to far-right support in regions haunted by the destructive legacies of Thatcherite and New Labour ideologies – anticipating the success of UKIP as an electoral force in this period – *The Afterglow* (2004) and *Iron Towns* (2016) concentrate on the effects of deindustrialization which irrevocably alter the identities and allegiances of working-class communities. Cartwright's fictional landscapes therefore become acutely politicized as he writes the social anxieties and fault lines of class warfare onto his Black Country architecture, revealing the long-tail effects of deindustrialization policies and its influence on the public mood towards European integration. As Michael Sandel comments, working-class voters who held positions in traditional industries 'feel that not only has the economy left them behind, but so has the culture, that the sources of their dignity, the dignity of labour, have been eroded and mocked by developments with globalization, the rise of finance' (qtd. in Cowley 2016). Cartwright's early fictions hold a strong anticipatory logic in narrativizing forms of social disenfranchisement that were to flare up during the EU referendum campaign, as disillusioned English voters perceived Brexit as a salient means of voicing their collective anger, drawing attention to their political marginalization and 'taking back control' of their communal narratives in the absence of alternate governing frameworks. Claire Ainsley's *The New Working Class* (2018) acknowledges how the gradual erosion of traditional class identities and structural changes (which clearly pre-date the referendum) has resulted in a problematic decoupling of class from English political identity; what is required, as former Labour leader Neil Kinnock recognizes, is a narrative of security – 'personal security, employment, education, enterprise, national security' – to overcome the 'identity demarcations that produced the referendum result' (qtd in Payne 2021: 211).

Glen James Brown's *Ironopolis*, set in the deindustrialized Burn council estate of Middlesbrough, is powered by the same socioeconomic pressures and loss of cohesive community evident in Cartwright's novels. Spanning almost seventy years from the 1950s to present day, *Ironopolis* documents how the decline of heavy industry and the dismantlement of Local Authority social housing ensures residents on his fictional estate are denied the continuation of a communal narrative rooted in work and shared culture. For Brown, 'working-class communities have lost the twin anchors of their lives – meaningful employment and a stable home', contributing to 'bubbling grievances which helped to bring about the Leave-vote' (Brown 2020: n.p.). Middlesbrough, referred to as *Ironopolis* on account of its industrial heritage, returned a 65.5 per cent Leave vote in the EU referendum, becoming yet another red wall area that gradually would turn away from Labour and seek new sources of political allegiance. Though 'Brexit as a term didn't exist' while he was writing parts of the novel, he emphasizes how the vote exposed the same issues informing the novel, with these debates over radical inequalities of access and regional imbalances existing 'out in the open for decades' but not being addressed by successive governments. The 'desperation and anger [which] is explicitly tied up with Brexit', as the electorate 'lash out at a government they perceive to be crushing them remotely and dispassionately', not only reveals the legacy of Thatcherite policy in the north-east, but the 'cruel austerity' of the Cameron government in the years leading to the vote: 'I don't even think cruel is the right word because it implies heated emotion and something personal; dispassionate or remote might be closer to it. Just this top-down, cold-blooded, unfeeling bureaucracy' (Brown 2020: n.p.). Through a multi-perspectival, intergenerational narrative, Brown indicates that although the simplistic politico-medial narrative of 'northern' or 'working class' life cannot hold such an incongruity of experience, the ingrained effects of structural unemployment and welfare cuts united communities in their disaffection, with Brexit providing the long-awaited opportunity to remind Westminster of its presence.

Returning to Cartwright, his subsequent novel *The Cut* (2017) reinforces the continuation of uneven development and an incommensurate democratic deficit across England with failed government initiatives, from the Northern Powerhouse and the Midlands Engine to the Regional Growth Fund and plans for high-speed rail networks through HS2, proving ineffective in alleviating social deprivation or bleak economic prospects, resulting in a backlash by the electorate. *The Cut* was commissioned by Meike Zeirvogel of Peirene Press to respond directly to the EU referendum result; Ziervogel comments, the Leave vote 'shocked me. I realized that I had been living in one part of a divided country', hoping that Cartwright could 'build a fictional bridge between the two Britains that have opposed each other since the referendum day' (Cartwright 2017: n.p.). The use of alternating chapters, entitled 'Before' and 'After', to structure the novel indicates the impact of the Brexit vote in deepening the fractures already evident within society. Cartwright's two protagonists, Cairo Jukes, a labourer and representative of the 'left behind' working class, and Grace Trevithick, a filmmaker and archetype of the London-based media, personify the two sides of a divided post-Brexit England. Cartwright's fictional divide aligns with David Goodhart's (2017) 'Somewhere-Anywhere' distinction to explain the two warring camps that emerged from the EU referendum. Whereas 'Anywheres' are younger, university-educated types for whom national attachments hold little merit in comparison to more supranational structures such as the EU, 'Somewheres' are older citizens who hold a deeper affection for local ties and have been denied an 'encouraging narrative of advance' due to widespread deindustrialization, forging a parallel with Cairo's personal stasis (2017: 177).

Cairo barely scrapes by on zero-hour contracts, living amidst the 'wasteland' of canals in Dudley, terrain that his forefathers worked in its prime (Cartwright 2017: 37). As in Cartwright's earlier fiction, the landscape of the Black Country retains a hauntological edge, with the spectral remnants of local tradition and spatial memoranda reducing its inhabitants to a liminal presence, 'here were the ruins, and here were the ghost people among them, lost tribes' (100). Through a paralogical discourse which accentuates the significance of place in the formation of classed identities, a triangular relationship of working practices, space, and identity is established in the novel with any change in one of these co-dependent areas resulting in a subsequent shift in the others, 'there used to be work for all the men [...] There used to be a culture that went alongside the work' (55). Cairo's yearning for the rejuvenation of a region which 'used to be somewhere' impacts his backward-looking inertia; his sporadic melancholic flâneurism through the broken architecture of Dudley's industrial past is a strangely impotent curation for the slow cancellation of his beloved region and its future prospects, but, in an affective sense, also provides psychological protection against socioeconomic decline and a means of securing his cultural identity in the process (44). This bitter resentment therefore not only stems from the erasure of industry, 'tired of the world passing by, tired of other people getting things that you and people like you had made for them', but an insecurity that he no longer contributes to the national narrative and is, like his hallowed architecture, relegated to the past, 'A lot of it is gone, erased. The industrial past [...] Now you act – we act – like there's some sort of shame to it all. The rest of the country is ashamed of us. You want us gone' (101, 111). As studies by Jennings, Stoker and Warren (2018) indicate, such deindustrialized settings outside of major cities struggle to operate under the current economic model and serve as cautionary tales of the decline history of British industry. Travelling from London to produce a documentary on Dudley and the approaching EU referendum, Grace's arrival in the Black Country is signalled by an 'expanse of rubble as the train came out of Birmingham', reinforcing how the psychological trauma of these communities is writ deep on the landscape (22). Just as Bill in *Ghost Wall* salvages the bones of his beloved Ancient Britons, Cairo's decision to become involved with Grace's project – guiding her around deindustrialized sites and participating in interviews – masks his deeper intent of forcing the London media to acknowledge the Black Country's formal industrial glory and bear witness to its current decline, 'He wanted to say something, about the sense of his world being made invisible, mute' (30).

Given the surge in support for UKIP across the West Midlands, 'anchored in a clear social base: older, blue-collar voters, citizens with few qualifications, whites and men', one would expect Cairo to evince some sympathy for anti-establishment parties which espouse messages of self-sufficiency as an escape from socioeconomic decline (Ford and Goodwin 2014: 270). Such destructive nostalgia was undoubtedly exploited by right-wing parties in the run-up to the referendum, with regional and national autarchism promoted as a valid means of reversing socioeconomic disparities and healing cultural wounds; according to Cartwright, the West Midlands, more than other traditional heartlands of heavy industry, has always enjoyed 'more overtly populist leanings' due to the evident decline written across the landscape (Cartwright 2020: n.p.). However, Cairo instead provides the simple forewarning that 'people here will vote against whatever they think the perceived elite will vote', indicating a conflation of faceless EU bureaucracy with the machinations of a remote and dispassionate Westminster (2017: 43). For Timothy Snyder this political perspective comes closer to 'sadopopulism' than simple populism, whereby voters are willing to accept further cultural or socioeconomic decline if it also means their enemies are negatively affected by this outcome, converting 'pain to meaning, and then meaning back into more pain' (2018: 273). Cairo's succinct assessment holds real predictive power, containing the implication that disillusioned voters will not remain impotent bystanders but seek new political allegiances if their socioeconomic marginalization is not addressed or rebalanced, which ultimately led to Brexit being cast as 'a revenge of the places that don't matter' (Rodríguez-Pose 2017: 189).

As David Goodhart succinctly notes in his study on the faultlines within Brexit Britain, *The Road to Somewhere* (2017), 'if people feel the game is stacked against them, they often just refuse to play' (2017: 153). Henderson and Wyn Jones echo this logic, claiming 'the less one believes in an ability to influence politics – the less voice one feels one has – the greater the appeal of this particular vision of England as a political community' (2021: 129). Grace discovers she must re-evaluate her preconceived misconceptions regarding the strength of Leave support in Dudley – which she initially attributes to a pronounced Little Englander or island mentality creating an 'invisible veil between her and these people', buttressed by a xenophobic hostility to post-war demographic shifts or immigration levels – and acknowledge the longitudinal effects of socioeconomic decline and lack of cultural opportunities (2017: 19). As Cairo immediately discerns, such judgements shut down more nuanced discussions of cultural discontent and prevents a deeper examination of prolonged social austerity and regional disparity: 'all you people want to say is that it's about immigration. That we'm all racist [...] You doh wanna hear that its more complicated than that' (24). Robert Saunders rightly argues that 'if we are to be analysts of Brexit, in a commentariat that overwhelmingly backs the other side, we need to interrogate our own assumptions and resist the temptation to project solely onto Leave voters irrational and pathological motives'; in short, 'we should be wary of arguments that play so directly to our own political preferences' (Saunders 2019: n.p.). With this in mind, Cartwright's authorial critique of what Phil McDuff has termed the 'prole whisperer' industry – journalists who report on 'the abstracted wastelands of the north' as if they are a foreign country to the 'Islington values' of Londoners – gestures to lazy attacks on nationalist attachments or place-bound identities to explain away the psychological impulses underpinning the Leave vote and the continued absence of a national conversation on the failure of successive governments to support regional devolution in England (McDuff 2017: n.p.).

As Anthony Barnett notes, in the immediate aftermath of the vote, 'the London media rushed to the North of England, to see if Brexit could be blamed on the lumpen working class missing out on the benefits of economic growth' (2017: 103). After all, it was England-outside-London which secured the overall Leave vote, and 87.6 per cent of constituencies in the Midlands returned Leave majorities (O'Toole 2018). Dudley in particular returned a strong Leave vote of 67.6 per cent. However, studies also reveal that the 'proportion of Leave voters who were of the two lowest social classes was just 24 per cent', complicating the amplification of media claims that an anti-establishment working class delivered the Brexit vote (Virdee and McGeever 2018: 1803).[4] By the same token, Victor Seidler suggests London, as a 'city-state that somehow thrived in ignorance of what was going on' across England, is viewed as 'another country' by voters in 'traditional areas' of the North and Midlands (2018: 23). Accordingly, though Cartwright sets out this apparent divide scarring the face of the country, he also questions the simplistic politico-media narrative which attempted to position the Brexit vote as a culture war between left-behind citizens, 'men from some bygone era' and metropolitan elites: competing discourses that could never be reconciled (2017: 37). Cairo's participation in Grace's documentary as the voice of 'ordinary people' is indicative of this very divide; when his interview is broadcast on the news they place 'subtitles under his words, translated into his own language [...] not making sense at all', pointing to the lack of awareness of the London-centric media to the mood of the nation and the superficial attempts to address the 'English problem' before the referendum (21). By forcing Cairo and Grace to rethink their regional prejudices, Cartwright goes some way to fulfilling his proposed brief of building 'a bridge' between Remain and Leave voters.[5] *The Cut* suggests that to adequately address European integration, England must confront pre-existing political, cultural and socioeconomic grievances that have divided the country long before the events of 2016, with the referendum result ultimately reflecting 'the weight of the past on the present, a sense of betrayal [...] of retribution on some grand, futile scale' (24). Though Cartwright is wary of making any grandiose claims for the power of the 'literary' novel to affect change or alter political perspectives, he believes fictional responses to Brexit open 'a space for nuance, contemplation, reflection [...] which wasn't evident in the political discourse' (Cartwright 2020: n.p.).[6]

Positioning the novel in relation to his earlier work, *The Cut* marks the concluding part of a non-chronological sequence which runs from 1979–2016, with the acrimony of the EU referendum campaign merely 'part of an ongoing political catastrophe that has been playing itself out in this country for 40 years or so (certainly since 1979), but in itself with much longer roots in industry, empire, the class system' (Cartwright 2020). Cartwright thus echoes Ben Wellings in perceiving Brexit as a 'protracted' and 'extended' rupture influenced by events that pre-date the referendum (2018: 147). Whereas his first novel, *The Afterglow*, opens with the fires of the Round Oak Steelworks being extinguished, symbolically and literally, *The Cut* ends with Cairo setting himself on fire as a mark of resistance to the structural decline of his region: 'They voted to relight the fires. He will be the furnace and the flames' (2017: 127). This shocking denouement, unravelling Cairo and Grace's promising relationship, not only reiterates the extent to which Cairo still defines himself through industrial labour and his psychogeographical attachment to the Black Country landscape, but signals the burning resentment still nurtured by left-behind communities and the ongoing failure to establish a productive dialogue between London and England's industrial heartlands. Cartwright explains that his novel's denouement is influenced by an 'invisible epigraph' to *The Cut*, 'as if all that was left was the prospect of setting yourself on fire', which is taken from Mathias Énard's novel *Street of Thieves* (2012), offering a glimpse into the eruption of the Arab Spring. Though he is aware of the dangers of conflating two exceptionally distinct political events, Cartwright is attempting to capture this underlying sense of 'horizons narrowing' for Cairo (his name reinforcing this allusion to the Egyptian crisis) and the 'nihilism' that emerges from entrenched political disenfranchisement and economic underinvestment in deindustrialized regions (Cartwright 2020).

Cartwright is also cognizant of the dangers of writing his own 'emotional and instinctive, rather than analytical' concerns for post-Brexit Dudley into his novel (he comes from a traditional Labour background), maintaining that 'to somehow attempt a kind of ironic detachment from what I've written and the place and people I've written about is probably a worse kind of fraud', paraphrasing Mark Fisher by suggesting such efforts would amount to 'a posture of alleged detachment, a sneer from nowhere' (Cartwright 2020: n.p.).

The cultural and socioeconomic anxieties written into his post-Brexit novel are certainly well founded; the 2019 UK General Election indicated the ongoing impact of the Brexit vote, as the Conservatives took advantage of these geographies of discontent within England to appeal to 'red wall' seats – traditionally Labour-voting, predominantly working-class areas in the North and Midlands – that had voted to 'Get Brexit done'. The result radically redrew the electoral map and indicated the ramifications of the Brexit vote on the political landscape. Labour endured its worst election result since 1935 and the election appeared to sever the historic bond between the party and its traditional heartlands, rupturing the Hampstead-to-Humberside alliance. For Luke Cooper and Christabel Cooper, the Conservatives' new electoral coalition 'is impossible to disaggregate from the Brexit vote and the socioeconomic and cultural factors underlying it', as economically depressed, left-behind regions strive to break the cycle of structural imbalance and unequal economic development (2020: 752). Cartwright interprets the subsequent devastating erosion of Labour's red wall to be a 'self-fulfilling prophecy' of Brexit's potential to 'accelerate division, economic inequality and fragmentation', with his fictional characters not only haunted by the past but 'the alternative futures that have been denied by the politics of this country' (Cartwright 2020: n.p.). The Conservative 'Levelling Up' programme to neutralize the socioeconomic contours of England seemingly responds to the desire for regional reform evident in *The Cut*, and yet this promise to 'Level Up', much like the rallying cry to 'Take Back Control', may become little more than a useful slogan onto which the electorate can project their most cherished hopes and worst fears. It is unlikely the programme will tackle deeply ingrained geographic structures of power troubling an increasingly 'disunited kingdom' or destabilize the financial centrality of London. As Ron Martin (2015) identifies, such spatial economic imbalance is now institutionalized and operates as a core component of national economic policy, meaning the spatial concentration of – and overdependence on – London-centric financial systems will continue to dictate political allocation of power, justifying Cartwright's persistent return to deindustrialized sites of the Black Country which convey the urgent need for political reform.

For Alex Niven, the concept of England has become 'operationally meaningless', reliant on historical debates characterized by their 'mythopoeia, high confusion and self-contradiction'; what is required is a radical reorientation of political thought towards a more egalitarian United Kingdom that moves away from its Anglocentric purview and avoids 'retreating into the false comfort of its enfolding historical shadows' (2019: 13, 20). However, the continued political salience of Englishness in mobilizing disparate groups across the political spectrum, evident in the 2016 EU referendum, complicates such optimistic archipelagic thought. As the introduction theorized, what is telling about these Anglocentric post-Brexit fictions is how little the EU – or even Europeans more generally – factor into the disorientation and disillusionment felt by vast swathes of the populace as authors acknowledge the perils of our inward-looking cultural imaginary and the structural imbalances fracturing the political landscape. The Leave vote within England was not simply a reaction against mass immigration or European bureaucracy; it was a full-throated yawp against the unequal distribution of wealth, resources and political representation, a heartfelt plea for a restructuring of increasingly unjust economic models, and a passionate call for a new social contract. Gary Younge reminds us that if the UK had voted Remain, 'we would already have returned to pretending that everything was carrying on just fine. Those people who have been forgotten would have stayed forgotten' (Younge 2016). In their efforts to continue a well-established literary conversation on the contemporary state of England, these post-Brexit fictions suggest that to answer the European question, we must first address the English problem.

Notes

1 Kingsnorth's *The Wake* (2014), fictionalizing the transition to Norman rule in the eleventh century, forges clear contemporary parallels that gesture to intrusive forms of EU bureaucracy, while King's *The Liberal Politics of Adolf Hitler* (2016), published in the lead-up to the referendum, imagines a dys-EUtopia where European harmonization is just a cover for a nascent neoliberal dictatorship.
2 The ties between the EU and the rural English landscape are more pronounced in Harrison's earlier novel *Clay* (2013), where Jozef, a Polish fast food worker, lost his farm due to strict EU agricultural regulations.
3 Theresa May and Boris Johnson's respective allusions to a 'Global Britain' during their tenures in office were reliant on potential trade deals founded on the bonds of kinship amongst English-speaking peoples only.

4   Dorling and Tomlinson (2017) contend that the strongest Leave support came from more financially stable, middle-class voters in southern constituencies, contradicting the media's focus on the northern backlash. Jonathan Coe's *Middle England* (2018) is an excellent example of how a simmering discontent in leafy Tory shires was also responsible for Britain's act of political withdrawal (see Shaw 2022).
5   The voting intentions of his characters are obscured or elided from the novel, but Cartwright reveals Grace and Cairo would have voted Remain and Leave, respectively (Cartwright 2020).
6   Cartwright cites Ali Smith's Seasonal quartet as providing the most profound post-Brexit response as it explores the elusive nature of personal and collective consciousness and is not 'bound by realism' (Cartwright 2020: n.p.).

Works cited

Ainsley, Claire. *The New Working Class: How to Win Hearts, Minds and Votes*. Bristol: Policy Press, 2018.
Barnes, Julian. 'People Will Hate Us Again'. *London Review of Books* 39(8), 2017: https://www.lrb.co.uk/the-paper/v39/n08/julian-barnes/diary (accessed 29 March 2022).
Barnett, Anthony. *The Lure of Greatness*. London: Unbound, 2017.
Bauman, Zygmunt. *Retrotopia*. Cambridge: Policy Press, 2017.
Black, Jeremy. *English Nationalism: A Short History*. London: Hurst & Company, 2018.
Brown, Glen James. *Ironopolis*. Cardigan: Parthian, 2018.
Brown, Glen James. Personal correspondence, 5 March 2020.
Byers, Sam. *Perfidious Albion*. London: Faber & Faber, 2018.
Byers, Sam. Personal correspondence, 13 March 2020.
Cartwright, Anthony. *The Cut*. London: Peirene Press, 2017.
Cartwright, Anthony. Personal correspondence, 25 May 2020.
Clarke, Ben and Nick Hubble. 'Introduction'. In *Working-Class Writing: Theory and Practice*. Ben Clarke and Nick Hubble (eds). Basingstoke: Palgrave Macmillan, 2018, 1–16.
Cooper, Luke and Christabel Cooper. '"Get Brexit Done": The New Political Divides of England and Wales at the 2019 Election'. *The Political Quarterly* 91(4), 2020: 751–761.
Cowley, Jason. 'Michael Sandel: "The energy of the Brexiteers and Trump is born of the failures of elites"', *The New Statesman*, 13 June 2016: https://www.newstatesman.com/politics/uk/2016/06/michael-sandel-energy-brexiteers-and-trump-born-failure-elites (accessed 12 April 2022).
Dorling, Danny and Sally Tomlinson. *Rule Britannia: Brexit and the End of Empire*. London: Biteback Publishing, 2017.
Eaglestone, Robert. 'Cruel Nostalgia and the Memory of the Second World War'. In *Brexit and Literature: Critical and Cultural Responses*. Robert Eaglestone (ed.). London: Routledge, 2018, 92–104.

Eatwell, Roger and Matthew Goodwin. *National Populism: The Revolt Against Liberal Democracy*. London: Penguin, 2018.

Ford, Robert and Matthew Goodwin. *Revolt on the Right: Explaining Support for the Radical Right in Britain*. London: Routledge, 2014.

Goodhart, David. *The Road to Somewhere: The Populist Revolt and the Future of Politics*. London: Hurst & Company, 2017.

Harrison, Melissa. *All Among the Barley*. London: Bloomsbury, 2018a.

Harrison, Melissa. 'Collective nostalgia, writing in the first person and the worrying resonance of the 1930s'. *Foyles*, 2018b: https://www.foyles.co.uk/Public/Biblio/AuthorDetails.aspx?authorId=85887 (accessed 19 November 2019).

Henderson, Ailsa and Richard Wyn Jones. *Englishness: The Political Force Transforming Britain*. Oxford: Oxford University Press, 2021.

Jennings, W., G. Stoker and I. Warren. 'Towns, Cities and Brexit'. *The UK in a Changing Europe*, 2018: https://ukandeu.ac.uk/towns-cities-and-brexit (accessed 2 April 2022).

Levinger, Matthew and Paul Franklin Lytle. 'Myth and Mobilization: The Triadic Structure of Nationalist Rhetoric'. *Nations and Nationalism* 7(2), 2001: 175–194.

Martin, Ron. 'Rebalancing the Spatial Economy: The Challenge for Regional Theory'. *Territory, Politics, Governance* 3(3), 2015: 235–272.

McDuff, Phil. 'Enough of the patronising myths about the "white working-class"'. *The Guardian*, 7 September 2017. https://www.theguardian.com/commentisfree/2017/sep/07/myths-white-working-class (accessed 23 June 2023).

McEwan, Ian. 'Britain is a one-party state: Ian McEwan talks about his new novel, Europe's moral dilemma and post-Brexit England'. *Neue Zurcher Zeitung*, 26 October 2016: 35–36.

Moss, Sarah. *Ghost Wall*. London: Granta, 2018.

Moss, Sarah. Personal correspondence, 10 March 2020.

Müller, Jan-Werner. *What is Populism?* Philadelphia: University of Pennsylvania Press, 2016.

Niven, Alex. *New Model Island: How to Build a Radical Culture Beyond the Idea of England*. London: Repeater Books, 2019.

O'Toole, Fintan. *Heroic Failure: Brexit and the Politics of Pain*. London: Head of Zeus, 2018.

Payne, Sebastian. *Broken Heartlands: A Journey Through Labour's Lost England*. London: Macmillan, 2021.

Rodríguez-Pose, Andrés. 'The Revenge of the Places that Don't Matter (and what to do about it)'. *Cambridge Journal of Regions, Economy and Society* 11(1), 2018: 189–209.

Saunders, Robert. 'The myth of Brexit as imperial nostalgia'. *Prospect*, 7 January 2019: https://www.prospectmagazine.co.uk/world/the-myth-of-brexit-as-imperial-nostalgia (accessed 2 March 2022).

Seidler, Victor J. *Making Sense of Brexit: Democracy, Europe and Uncertain Futures*. Bristol: Policy Press, 2018.

Shaw, Kristian. 'BrexLit'. In *Brexit and Literature: Critical and Cultural Responses*. Robert Eaglestone (ed.). London: Routledge, 2018, 15–30.

Shaw, Kristian. *Brexlit: British Literature and the European Project*. London: Bloomsbury, 2021.

Shaw, Kristian. 'Performing the Nation: A Disunited Kingdom in Jonathan Coe's *Middle England*'. In *Community in Contemporary British Fiction*. Peter Ely and Sara Upstone (eds). London: Bloomsbury, 2022, 155–176.

Smith, Zadie. 'Fences: A Brexit Diary'. *The New York Review of Books*, 18 August 2016: https://www.nybooks.com/articles/2016/08/18/fences-brexit-diary/ (accessed 1 March 2022).

Snyder, Timothy. *The Road to Unfreedom: Russia, Europe, America*. New York: Crown, 2018.

Virdee, Satnam and Brendan McGeever. 'Racism, Class, Brexit'. *Ethnic and Racial Studies* 41(10), 2018: 1802–1819.

Wellings, Ben. 'Losing the Peace: Euroscepticism and the Foundations of Contemporary English Nationalism'. *Nations and Nationalism* 16(3), 2010: 488–505.

Wellings, Ben. 'Brexit and English Identity'. In *The Routledge Handbook of the Politics of Brexit*. Patrick Diamond, Peter Nedergaard and Ben Rosamond (eds). London: Routledge, 2018, 147–156.

Wright, Patrick. *On Living in an Old Country: The National Past in Contemporary Britain*. London: Verso, 1985.

Wyn Jones, Richard, Guy Lodge, Ailsa Henderson and Daniel Wincott. 'The Dog that Finally Barked: England as an Emerging Political Community'. London: Institute for Public Policy Research, January 2012: https://www.ippr.org/files/images/media/files/publication/2012/02/dog-that-finally-barked_englishness_Jan2012_8542.pdf (accessed 13 March 2022).

Wyn Jones, Richard, Guy Lodge, Charlie Jeffery, Glenn Gottfried, Roger Scully, Ailsa Henderson and Daniel Wincott. 'England and Its Two Unions: The Anatomy of a Nation and its Discontents'. London: Institute for Public Policy Research, 2013: https://www.ippr.org/publications/england-and-its-two-unions-the-anatomy-of-a-nation-and-its-discontents (accessed 13 March 2022).

Younge, Gary. 'Brexit: A disaster decades in the making'. *The Guardian*, 30 June 2016: https://www.theguardian.com/politics/2016/jun/30/brexit-disaster-decades-in-the-making (accessed 14 March 2022).

8

Inexhaustible Literature? Contemporary Experimental Approaches in Literature

Mark P. Williams

... Let's try again: Somewhere in the last three years I stopped reading literature for a while. It crept up on me at the end of a repeated round of ultimately unsuccessful research application processes. The main body of the research I undertook turned on the minutiae of international policy research, meta-analyses of social attitudes, and historical policy documents from Hansard to decades-old interviews and speeches. Literature became the thing I would return to once I had secured the funding. The approach to literature I would take would be an experiment in itself: it focused *through* and *around* the 'literary' – with heavy-handed scare-quotes – and onto the general realm of the fictive at two extremes, the populist and the experimental. The gambit was this: the politics of the time would be revealed either in starkest relief or in clearest congruence through the areas which were the edges of the literary because these would be least subject to the moderations of good taste, education, emphasis on subtlety, style, and what we might term the literary editorial norms of publishing. The hypothesis was that populism should track to general meta-analyses of the politics and social attitudes of the time, whereas experimental fiction should describe the Michael-Fish-moments of literary turbulence, the extreme events not forecast.[1] But then, in the midst of *Coronazeit*, the applications were unsuccessful, the lifestyle of teaching work became a whole alternate universe, and I stopped reading literature. I read articles to teach English, I focused on teaching for several institutions simultaneously, all from one corner of one room while one son tried to homeschool in another room and the youngest had to play in another. I watched lots of Contrapoints, Vaush, Thought Slime, Philosophy Tube, Shaun, F D Signifier and Lonerbox. Between watching video essays, and virtual teaching and virtual job interviews, reading books fell away.

Small things brought me back, but slowly: crossover comic books, some bought for my kids and several for myself because they operate as surprisingly radical or ambitious experiments in narrative-blending, and they're fun; getting a new David Peace book as a birthday present (thank you Martyn Colebrook); reading histories of political groups in Britain and Europe in the 1970s; hearing about a writer recommended by Philosophy Tube; then the chance to write a small piece on *New Worlds* for *Foundation*; reading the recent retranslations of the Turkish and Swedish unauthorized adaptations of *Dracula* back-to-back, *Dracula in Istanbul* (2020, from Kazıklı Voyvoda, 1923) and *Powers of Darkness* (2021, from *Mörkrets makhter*, 1899). All this led to my returning to Modernist literature, instead of just theories of Modernism and modernity, and the idea that modernization periods (re)produce Modernism.

Then I attempted to express the tensions of modernization I could remember from my own childhood, beginning with lists:

> the land of one-p-chews, £1 swimming in the summer holidays, 60p *Judge Dredd* and *Transformer* comics, Garbage Pail Kids chewing gum I never chewed, *He-Man* and *She-Ra*, *ThunderCats* and *Sectaurs*, *Visionaries* and *Supernaturals*, arcade side-scrollers and holidays in Llandudno, white dog shit and winter power cuts with the frost patterns sometimes on the inside of the windows.

All the narrative elements of these things to me represented moments of modernization: tensions of archaism and technology; the *feel* of the time.

Through this I started to think seriously once more about what it was that had always drawn me back to literary analysis. I recognize that in part this goes with the collective experience of enduring the pandemic – fundamental reassessments of the conditions of daily life as noted universally by journalists, analysts, and, more slowly, by employers and governments. But it is also something sharply visible in literary texts which reflexively attempt to represent, reflect, and critically grasp the nettle of contemporary modernity. This impulse to express our tensions with modernity *is* a moment of Modernism. In what follows I will try to outline a selection of those from the 2010s and illuminate through too-too selective sampling some necessary details of what stands out and strikes me from these. Memory and identity are crucial here; the sense of self and other, and of self-as-Other to those around you under the pressure of modernization. Modernity is a funhouse mirror in a ruined castle by the sea: Modernism tells us we're seeing ourselves twisted out of shape but also takes seriously the feeling of being doubled, split and haunted.

History | Aspiring to *The Condition of Muzak*

In 1977, Michael Moorcock published *The Condition of Muzak*, a summation or culmination – or just a climactic moment – of the narrative of Jerry Cornelius. The title mashes, with typical wit and vitriol, Walter Pater's maxim that 'all art aspires to the condition of music' into the transient, liminal form of lift-music, mall-music, store-music, as a comment on the arts of its moment. Moorcock's novel is in its own way a demand for a renewal of art that recapitulates the demands of Modernism, insisting that Modernist impulses be seen as still present in the 1970s. Given that interest in experimentation was apparently in a rather ambivalent phase during this period, resulting in it being bracketed as either intermodernist or proto-postmodernist in subsequent literary periodizations and theorizations, this is an interesting territory to recover and re-cover (where, after all, does the New Wave really stand in relation to Modernism?). As I have argued at length elsewhere, not only have the cultural moments of the 1970s been miscast as supporting roles to the idealistic 1960s and a materialistic 1980s, they have cast longer shadows on our culture today than we have sometimes been led to believe. My failed research proposal aimed to begin with this pivotal ending-beginning period and move forward (over-ambitiously) to the 2010s, it planned to conclude around the time of what proved to be the beginning of the Covid-19 pandemic.

Further, the styles and approaches that Moorcock actively championed during his tenure editing *New Worlds* and beyond – in his general approach to narrative fiction, in his support for friends whose work pushed boundaries, from J.G. Ballard and M. John Harrison through David Britton and Michael Butterworth of Savoy, to Angela Carter, and more recently Alan Moore – tended to be demands for continual recapitulation of the Modernist imperatives. This is an internally riven demand: Make work of the ever-changing *now* but make it authentically from where you are coming from as an individual subject; to make something of *our* collective now from *your* individual history. It also raises the twin issues of what does it mean to be *from* somewhere when writing with an identifiable perspective; identity in dialectic with identification.

Place becomes important, but in contrary ways; as in the Gothic, which Carl Einstein observed was highly significant in the development of the avant-garde, the interplay of space and character takes on a peculiar symbolic set of associations, almost a sub-language, where spatial locations become key characters. In *The Blue Monday Diaries* (2016), Michael Butterworth writes that in the technological developments of postwar Britain 'the future was arriving' and in 'the 1970s it was arriving from a past of grime and smoke: science fiction conjuring industrial Manchester as The Twilight Zone, the experimental and the outré, a place where '[i]ndustrial decay and badly developed modernist housing estates existed side by side' (24). The experimental work of *New Worlds*, and Savoy, and Creation Books etc., are all corpora that reflect this.

In the relation of Modernism to modernization, both periodization and aesthetic evaluation must be understood in respect to the new politico-cultural hegemony which arose since the 1970s; we have to call it by its names: Globally, neoliberalism; in Britain, Thatcherism. And it has a character, with internal contraries all its own: community-grounded but individualist and aspirational, socially traditionalist but economically disruptive of tradition, demanding consumption but also eschewing (and displacing) productive industry, uprooting populations but rejecting cosmopolitanism, and so on. This is the painful transition into semiperipherality of much of Britain in order for London to become a financial, core, city within the global world-system; modernization focused on the City of London as a financial centre, and Greater London and the South East as economic centre. It produces a combined and uneven modernization, where, although through London, Britain operates as a core nation in the world-system, it still contains multiple semi-peripheral (and increasingly semi-peripheralized) regions and cities dependent on reduced manufacturing and extractive industries, such as Manchester and Glasgow, Liverpool and Merseyside, the North East, and Northern Ireland. These semi-peripheries culturally 'register' the 'thresholds marking new class geographies' which this modernization produces (Shapiro and Barnard 2017: 11–20). We see this in the Liverpool of Clive Barker from his quite experimental early plays and the stylized horrors of *The Books of Blood* (1984–86), which deploy a rich variety of ludic narrative strategies in amongst their more generic framing. It certainly includes highly regionalized aesthetic experimentation such as the Manchester of Savoy in the emergence of their *Lord Horror* novels and comic books, or Alan Moore's Northampton-based mosaic novels *Voice of the Fire* (1995) and *Jerusalem* (2016), with their wild shifts of voice and historical period matched by idiosyncratic subjectivities. We see semiperipherality also in the more self-consciously internationalist avant-garde aesthetics of cult publisher, Creation Press/Creation Books, deploying a reflexively eclectic range of classic texts from drug cultures and subcultures alongside less-published classic texts such as Salvador Dalí's *Diary of a Genius* (1998, 2020 [1973]), Artaud's version of *The Monk* and *Heliogabalus, Or the Anarchist Crowned*, beside Pierre Guyotat's *Eden Eden Eden* and *Tomb for 500,000 Soldiers* (all 2003). These sit alongside distinctively British avant-garde texts such as Steven Wells's 'anarcho-commie sex pulp' anti-novel *Tits-Out Teenage Terror Totty* (2000) – and former Young British Artist, Jake Chapman's *Meatphysics* (2003).

Form and formalism | The Johnson–Pratchett Problem

So, what do I mean by form and how does it resonate with content: Does form mean 'structure' or 'genre', and is 'resonate' different from 'reflect'? – and in using the two together does it imply an emergent quality of harmony?

In the Discworld novels of Terry Pratchett the name B.S. Johnson is used as the name of an inventor of that fantasy world's worst inventions, objects which never do quite what they are *designed* to do but instead perform some other function. Obviously originating as a jab at the experimental novels of B[ryan]. S[tanley]. Johnson, notable for experimenting with textual surface in *House Mother Normal,* the book-in-a-box of *The Unfortunates* (1971), the hole in the page to force a proleptic anticipation in *Albert Angelo* (1964), and for breaking faith with the narratives themselves – perhaps most notably with the cry of 'fuck all this lying' (Johnson 2004: 167) addressed directly to the reader at the end of *Albert Angelo*. Such risky formal textual ventures can fail – the omnibus edition of Johnson novels (2004) I first bought had cut the hole slightly too big (see 149) and so spoiled part of the device.

Over the course of Pratchett's Discworld books the inventions and devices of Pratchett's Bergholt Stuttley 'Bloody Stupid' Johnson become a series of increasingly eccentric and dangerous mechanical items, which appear as occasionally useful McGuffins in their stories because although they don't work as intended, they do *work as something else* – such as the Post Office sorting machine containing a wheel where Pi equals exactly three which sorted letters from alternate universes until it was stopped by force (but still manages to save the day near the end). The persistent usefulness of experimental 'device' in the stories stands in for experimentation *with* story; yes, experiment can break a story, but sometimes that breakage is precisely what makes a better story.

Christopher Nosniboor published a comprehensively deconstructive development on the relations of form and story entitled *This Book is Fucking Stupid: Fifty Shades of Shit* (2012). The novel alternates the lives of two old friends, the relatively stable and socially conformist Ben, and the much less economically and romantically stable Stuart – alternating focalization between the two in the mundane details of their lives enables the reader to see they ultimately have more in common than not, and to see the ways in which their material circumstances have circumscribed their outlooks. Interspersed within this are Nosniboor's theoretical exegeses on form and the state of the novel, and also, most experimentally, various online reviews of earlier drafts of the stories which would ultimately form *This Book is Fucking Stupid*. The effect is exhaustively auto-deconstructive and addresses questions of the value of boredom, the drive towards escapism and the pitfalls of attempting to escape through any given outlet with a mercilessly materialist eye. It is a contemporary formulation of Modernism as more realist than mere Realism, by including excerpts from the conditions of its own formulation and its (draft) reception within itself in an expanded edition – with an introduction by Douglas Coupland. It almost negates criticism; it even makes the experience of boredom more interesting, but like most experimental writing, it is also a challenging read which demands a lot. So, the Johnson–Pratchett Problem: experiment may return to story to question the reader's expectations to either reinstate it or to subvert it. The story may be a better story for representing something significant about the world precisely for having its story-ness broken into pieces.

There is nothing outside the text | There is (no)thing outside (the) [con]text | (T)here is no(thing) outside the text

In the early 1980s, Savoy Books had planned to be the first UK publisher to follow African-American SF legend Samuel R. Delany's *Tides of Lust* (1980) with William Burroughs' Western Lands Trilogy and Neo-Hoodoo Surrealist, Ishmael Reed's *Mumbo Jumbo*, *The Last Days of Louisiana Red*, *The Freelance Pallbearers*, and *Flight to Canada*, but were bankrupted by police raids seizing, among others, Delany's novel under the Obscene Publications Act.[2] While James Williamson comments in *Dust: A Creation Books Reader* (1994) that

> Branded in 1992 as 'politically incorrect' and ridiculously linked to a 'satanic underground' by a sadly ill-informed mainstream journal – which resulted in a visit from the plain clothes police – we were in fact already making available the work of fundamentally oppressed 'minorities' – the disabled, black women, AIDS sufferers, alcoholics and 'mad' people[.]
>
> Williamson 1994: 5

Stewart Home's *Suspect Device: A Reader in Hard-Edged Fiction* (1998) provocatively made its case that 'the "marginal" is the foundation on which the "mainstream" is built' and sought to demystify this relationship with an emphasis on wildly divergent fringe writing which was of its moment as 'an unrepresentative sample of what is "out there"' (vii). It's notable that this is a fight that continues to happen and yet continues to be necessary, for assemblages of reasons. The world intrudes on the text...but the avant-garde text intrudes back into the world. That is the tone I want to use to approach the case-study texts that follow, beginning with Deborah Levy's *Swimming Home* (2011).

'Emotional and cerebral choreographies' | Deborah Levy's *Swimming Home* (2011)

Swimming Home is a textual wolf-in-sheep's-clothing; it arrives as a bourgeois domestic novel about a relationship breakdown, but then abruptly begins to manifest breaches in textual expression which, by the final chapter, have become so profound I argue they force a re-reading which upends the entire premise.

The novel is accompanied by a commentary text from Tom McCarthy, and it is perhaps significant to the reading of the text that the original version from the publisher And Other Stories presented McCarthy's essay as an 'Introduction', while the reprint, co-published with Faber and Faber, turned this into an 'Afterword'. Certainly this change of ordering transforms *something* about the way in which we read the text but it is not immediately clear what it alters when reading the text the first time; McCarthy's text doesn't present spoilers for the plot or manifest content of the text. However, it does, perhaps, give a clearer weighting to certain ways of reading it. I suggest that these are not only important to the text, that they are actually its core, and that they make the text more unsettling than it otherwise appears on a first reading – the editors *had* to move the 'Introduction' to the 'Afterword'.

Most reviews of *Swimming Home* note that the plot concerns a famous, philandering poet, Jozef Jacobs, and his disintegrating relationship with his family: his wife Isabel, a successful war correspondent, and their daughter Nina. Their domestic situation is breached by the arrival of the eccentric Kitty Finch, a poetry fan, found swimming naked in the pool of their holiday villa who has brought her poem, 'Swimming Home', for Jacobs to read.

Swimming Home's manifest plot beats for the first few sections appear so predictably middle-class as to cause a creeping feeling of disjunction: starting with a midlife crisis and an older male poet having (another) sudden affair with a young women so manic-pixie-like as to self-consciously echo innumerable cinematic outings. For example, it is important to note that the novel begins with a quotation from *La Revolution surréaliste* number one, introducing both the avant-garde and the idea of the unconscious through dreams. This is accentuated with the cinematically proleptic flashforward to 'A Mountain Road. Midnight.' – and this prolepsis actually introduces Kitty Finch (2012 [2011]: 3).

The mountain road scene recurs three times throughout the book, not as a complete repetition but as iterations where the precise phrases used by the characters, Jozef and Kitty, change, without clear explanation, becoming shorter and more intense with each iteration. In each, Kitty speaks more and more, confronting Jozef more explicitly.

In the first version, the beginning, the paragraph begins

> When Kitty Finch took her hand off the steering wheel and told him she loved him, he no longer knew if she was threatening him or having a conversation. Her silk dress was falling off her shoulders as she bent over the steering wheel. A rabbit ran across the road and the car swerved.
>
> [....] She asked him to open the window so she could hear the insects calling to each other in the forest. He wound down the window and asked her, gently to keep her eyes on the road.
>
> Levy 2012: 3

When, at the end of the sequence, the narrative tells us indirectly that 'He asked her to please, please drive him safely home to his wife and daughter' (4) we establish the narrative of a younger woman disrupting an established relationship – a heavily freighted symbolic triangle of three women in the male protagonist's life. The concluding sentence is the enigmatic pronouncement from Kitty Finch: '"Yes", she said, "Life is only worth living because we hope it will get better and we'll get home safely"' (4). It leads us immediately to assume several things about their relationship and to anticipate tragedy in their story involving at least one of them. However, the iterations of the scene introduce increases in textual complexity more formally significant than simply unreliable narration.

When the same sequence recurs midway through the novel it now begins 'It was getting dark and she told him the brakes on the hire car were fucked, she couldn't see a thing, she couldn't even see her hands' (26). The dress still falls off her shoulders and the rabbit still runs across the road, but things are more intensely sexual:

> He told her to keep her eyes on the road, to just do that, and while he was speaking she was kissing him and driving at the same time. And then she asked him to open the window so she could hear the insects calling to each other in the

forest. He leaned his head out of the window and felt the cold mountain air sting his lips. Early humans had once lived in this mountain forest. They knew that the past lived in rocks and trees and they knew desire made them awkward, mad, mysterious, messed up.

'Yes', Kitty Finch said, her eyes now back on the road. 'I know what you're thinking. Life is only worth living because we hope it will get better and we'll all get home safely. But you tried and you did not get home safely. You did not get home at all. That is why I am here, Jozef. I have come to France to save you from your thoughts.'

Levy 2012: 26

Ambiguity of desire and portentous symbolism of three formulations of femininity (a mother, a child and an implied lover) here gives way to plain sexual demand and the implication of psychological damage, both gendered, simultaneously foregrounded by the brakes of the car Kitty is steering being 'fucked'. The risk of the road stands in for the risks of illicit sex outside of marriage, and the brakes for both Kitty's mental state and the relationship between them. But here Jozef's words about his wife and daughter are absent: there is only Kitty, now more sexually direct, acting to kiss him as they speak – figuratively more in the driving seat as well as still holding the steering wheel. The insects recur, but now the forest itself is an ancient wilderness linking the couple to early humans, who, through the focalization of Jozef's wandering thoughts, are 'awkward, mad, mysterious, messed up'.

The final occurrence is at the very end of the arc of their relationship: they have a confrontation after their sexual encounter in the Hotel Negresco; the affair is now manifest content, they have had the encounter proleptically foregrounded so much earlier and the passage has changed again. It is still getting dark, the first paragraph is identical to the second above, brakes still 'fucked' – Kitty 'couldn't see a thing, couldn't even see her hands' – and Jozef once more 'told her to keep her eyes on the road' but there are no insects and no forest, only Kitty telling him again that she has 'come to France to save you from your thoughts' (146).

Tom McCarthy's 'Afterword' observes that Levy is equally at home with philosophy and dense theoretical material as with aesthetic and literary concepts, comparing it to what he calls the 'emotional and cerebral choreographies' of expressionist theatre on the one hand and the 'Interzone' of Burroughs on the other (159). He also, most tellingly, draws attention to Lacan, and emphasizes that the core of the novel is 'in classical Freudian fashion' desire 'and its inevitable flip side: the death drive' (160). I suggest that this is so close to being an excessive reveal that it produces an almost uncanny theoretical prolepsis – it's not a spoiler, but it's too much. I believe it gives the violent darkness at the heart of the novel a clearer focus: the novel ends with a death in the swimming pool – Jozef Jacobs – reflecting the appearance of Kitty Finch, symbolically naked, at the beginning. The revelation is given an animal-cum-fairytale image: His body is as heavy as a bear. When they arrived at the villa they had been talking about bears invading pools in California and Jozef asks if Kitty is a bear before she gets out of the pool at the beginning: hence, there are three 'bears' in the text, one of whom is also a disruptive Goldilocks-figure.

I have been fortunate enough to be able to teach the text multiple times in multiple institutions and the interpretation of the text I forward here was developed during seminar reading while I was teaching at UEA in Norwich – it owes part of its development from an excellent joint lecture I heard from colleagues Kirsten Haywood, Alex Valente and Karen Schaller, and to probing and thoughtful seminars with highly engaged students following this. The course where we taught *Swimming Home* dealt with aesthetic approaches to textual representation ranging from Romance through Nineteenth Century Realist to Modernist and Postmodernist novels. An openness to diverse theoretical approaches was explicitly welcomed. Levy's text came after reading Prosper Mérimée's *Carmen* (1845), Woolf's *Mrs Dalloway* (1925), and Nabokov's *Lolita* (1955), alternated with Realist texts, Gaskell's *Mary Barton* (1848), Gissing's *New Grub Street* (1891), and Andrew Cowan's *Pig* (1994). Initially then, *Swimming Home* appeared to fit more straightforwardly within the broad vein of realist texts while retaining a distinct impulse of counter-realism; something post-postmodernist, a searching for a register of renewed authenticity via appropriations from cinema. The frequent moments of radical undecidability and the imagery of psychoanalysis obviously troubled this perspective, such as the 'Thing' in a bucket:

> They crowded round the bucket, which was half full with muddy water. A slimy grey creature with a red stripe down its spine clung to a clump of weed. It was as thick as Mitchell's thumb and seemed to have some sort of pulse because the water trembled above it. Every now and again it curled into a ball and straightened out again.
>
> 'What is it?' Mitchell couldn't believe they had bothered to lug this vile creature across the fields all the way back to the villa.
>
> 'It's a thing.'
>
> Levy 2012: 102–103

Different characters perceive the 'thing' as having naturalistically incompatible physiognomic features – a grey slug (invertebrate), something with many legs (arthropod), and something more like an amphibian (vertebrate) – but as Isabel and Jozef's conversation makes clear it is also related to Jozef's past infidelities. The dialogic pun where Jozef comments that his 'thing' is 'freaking you all out' to the other characters (104–105) is then contrasted with Jozef's daughter Nina comparing Kitty Finch to the thing. Then there is the Burroughsean nightmare of the antiquarian-cum-gun dealer, Mitchell, in which he dreams of slicing up centipedes with a cleaver only to see the pieces multiply and continue living. The estrangement these episodes produced seemed initially to be constrained by the intensity of the narrative focalization around the perceptions of the core family, particularly Nina's defensive perspective on her father, Jozef.

However, after a psychoanalytic reading from a colleague above and the three seminar group discussions with students afterwards, it became clear that not only was its realism a stylistic feint, but that the specific duality of psychoanalysis was central – *Swimming Home* is a Surrealist text not just in allusion and themes, but in form as well. The novel invites twin readings: first as a novel of essentially bourgeois relationships with ambiguous and troubling textual details revolving around Kitty Finch which might be resolved by a number of different interpretive strategies, and then second as a form of irresolvable anti-novel. The latter is pointed to by the epigraph, and the 'Afterword' serves to signpost it, but it is never explicit: the final chapter subverts the reading of the whole novel. It does so through the opening of its final chapter, titled 'Nina Jacobs London, 2011':

> Whenever I dream my twentieth-century dream about my father, I wake up and immediately forget my passwords for Easyjet and Amazon. It is as if they have disappeared from my head into his head and somewhere in the twenty-first century he is sitting with me on a bus crossing London Bridge watching the rain fall on the chimney of Tate Modern. The conversations I have with him do not belong to this century at all, but all the same I ask him why he never really told me about his childhood? He replies that he hopes my own childhood wasn't too bad and do I remember the kittens?
>
> Our family kittens (Agnieska and Alicja) always smelt a bit feral and my childhood pleasure was to groom them with my father's hairbrush.
>
> Levy 2012: 155

The passage, indirectly but decisively, pushes us back to the beginning of the novel, with its establishing date of 1994. It also pushes us to return to the precise words of the epigraph: 'Each morning in every family, men, women, and children, *if they have nothing better to do*, tell each other their dreams. We are all at the mercy of the dream and we owe it to ourselves to submit its power to the waking state' (vii). The irreal logic of some passages, the apparent telepathy and odd non-sequiturs that make many scenes sit somewhere between New Wave SF of a Ballardian mode and comedies of manners dislocated from the 1960s are more logically understood when we see the whole of the text through a Surrealist lens. This opens up the latent psychoanalytic violence of the imagery and language juxtapositions and omissions to a darker reading: the penultimate chapter is headed 'Nina Ekaterina' – a name echoed by the name Kitty Finch, and by the two kittens mentioned in the 2011 passage. Nina and Kitty are no longer merely symbolic doubles, rather Kitty is a dream form double for Nina, with a name formed out of her own. The two kittens with echoing names seem to amplify this logic: the twentieth-century dream in question has been that of Nina Jacobs; the entire book up until then is that dream.

As a dream-narrative psychodrama, the recurrence of unreadable texts (we never see the text of the poem 'Swimming Home') and hidden objects (the poem manuscript, a gun, the thing) point towards unsayable concepts, while the recurring and iterating scene of achronological car crash seems increasingly Ballardian. It is not the Ballard of *Crash* (1972) but rather of *The Atrocity Exhibition* (1965) where narrative fragments echo and reflect one another imperfectly to convey emotional content via impression, not narrative logic.

The recurring mention of insects in the repeated proleptic scene, plus the repeated appearance of insects in Kitty Finch's room, and the possibly-insectoid 'thing' in the bucket, coupled with the proliferating centipedes of Mitchell's nightmare produce a multiplying effect of discomforting insect imagery which, in the context of an experimental text, tends to recall the Freudian-Joycean conjugation of 'insects' and 'incest'. What we are left with then is an undecidable suggestion of a dream-work which persistently but never clearly suggests either a sublimated incestuous desire, where Nina creates a narrative of the affair which finally shattered her parents' marriage where the third party weirdly echoes herself, or, alternatively, a darker-still narrative of sublimated incest trauma which is projected on to a fictive alter-ego. The novel can offer no decision between options such as these because it is merely a dream. We know it is trauma and we know it is Surrealist, and there also is the trauma of Nina losing her father, but does that manifest narrative indirectly point to a different latent narrative – we are left profoundly unsettled as the ending suggests (mis)directions but without finality.

Memento mori | Gary J. Shipley and Kenji Siratori's *Necrology* (2012)

Split and dissonant narrative appears in a divergent form in Gary J. Shipley and Kenji Siratori's text *Necrology* (2012). This text an exercise in textual decomposition-recomposition on the subject of life and death – placing subject and form into homologous tension. It performs this reflexivity via two parallel columns on every page, one by Shipley on the right, one by Siratori on the left, which sometimes appear to have related approaches to the subject of death and the study of death and other times appear more incongruous. Attempting to read both texts independently inevitably results in the eye skittering across the column you are not focusing on and attempting to read both together blurs and amplifies the experience of interpretive confusion which is clearly part of the point. Siratori is clearly inspired by cyberpunk while Shipley is somewhat more in line with the postmodernist Gothic.

Siratori's work is notoriously difficult; Dennis Cooper (2018), in an illuminating interview, asks whether his narrative strategies, together with his also-notorious elliptical responses in interview, constitute an attempt to 'code' or conceal his sense of self from the reader, withholding the possibility of a secure grounding in intention but also holding identity out of reach. Siratori's subsequently (also) coded response to Cooper's question is illuminating enough for the reading experience: Siratori is a writer of negation and refusal of story in favour of pattern and feeling – he expresses this to Cooper by likening text production to Techno music, and this makes a great deal of sense of his *technique* of writing through repetition and sample. As *Necrology* indicates, there is a sort of rhythm at work.

Nevertheless, *Necrology* is a particularly hard read because of its structure and form primarily due to Siratori's textual negation. Siratori has for some time made a great deal of use of a sort of word-processor-Burroughsean philosophy of textual production, a cut-up and copy-paste methodology, which tends to produce strange loops of interest embedded in otherwise completely alienating units of text. These are often difficult to term 'novels' or even 'anti-novels' since they largely eschew even the sense of narrative. Somewhere in *Invisible Cities* or in *If On A Winter's Night A Traveller...*, or in slightly different words in both, Italo Calvino makes a comment that different stories by a writer tend to be variations of the same story. Burroughs says something related somewhere; Burroughs wrote in routines, Siratori writes in samples but, ultimately, they undertake a similar process of producing their own megatext. In *Necrology*, what we experience is the pairing of part of Siratori's megatext with another by Shipley, also routine-based, also Burroughs-inspired, but tonally different. In Siratori's terms this clashing unification in parallel columns might be best understood in terms of mixing – literary turntablism. The text itself also presents another guiding metaphor.

In an afterword, titled 'The Corpse-Bride: Thinking with Nigredo', Reza Negarestani then uses an ancient torture-punishment as a suggestive philosophical exploration of the concepts of life and death that Siratori and Shipley's cross-faded experiments play out. Negarestani examines the brutal ancient practice of tying a live person to a corpse, lip-to-lip and hand to hand, until the living and the dead become one, beginning with a quotation from Virgil's Aeneid and progressing through medieval and Early Modern variations. As a metaphor, this also seems to unpack something of the method of this difficult text. Reviewer David Peak (2013) has also commented that viewing Siratori's prose objects as dead text tied to Shipley's makes an effective reading, but perhaps we can take this further still. The twin-column form has been used by various experimental writers to different ends but the three most pertinent here are: Jacques Derrida, Irvine Welsh, and Stewart Home.

Derrida's work *Glas* (1974) is obviously an influential model here. Presenting Derrida's deconstruction of the work of G.W.F. Hegel on the left half of each page and of the autobiographical work of Jean Genet on the right. The disruptions to coherently reading one column independently of the other are magnified – or self-reflexively exacerbated – by changes in size and eruptions of larger quotations. Irvine Welsh also uses twin columns in a story in *The Acid House* (1994), showing two neighbours, a man and a woman, who each fantasize about the other but never quite break the ice, is an effective humorous device for commenting on gender relationships and social isolation which fits with Welsh's own interest in disrupting the visual surface of the page, as evidenced in *Marabou Stork Nightmares* (1995) and *Filth* (1998) – *Filth*'s tapeworm narrative functioning as a dominating, superimpositional column, erasing the narrative of Bruce Robertson. Finally, Stewart Home's 'anti-introduction' to *Suspect Device* is operationally the more pertinent here. Home places two different texts, one largely in a fictive register, the other in a more academic and literary-theoretical mode, side by side with an introductory paragraph which claims 'Stewart Home' is a fictional persona comparable to the Luther Blissett Project,[3] under the heading 'Proletarian Postmodernism'. To add to the disjunctive effect this appeared within the body of the anthology, rather than where an introduction might be expected (he wrote another, different introduction there instead).

As a text, *Necrology* is clearly more focused on impression and echo than on readability, and Siratori's narratives are always the more obstructive of this. However, the publication of such a text implies some sort of framing position or interest, a level at which we might, if not exactly decode, then better appreciate the aims – more akin to Welsh's deliberate juxtaposition – whereby the two columns double one another in a more meaningful way by their precise togetherness. Shipley's text incorporates clear impressionistic narrative elements which act, perhaps as heavily extended metaphors, suggesting interpretive possibilities. Their contents recall the routines of Burroughs: early on, the subtitle 'THE BODY FARM' (2012: 16), appearing all-caps suggests narrativization and therefore interpretive access. It gives a clear, grotesquely violent image, deliberately redolent of a 'torture-porn' aesthetic: 'a doctor enters the room, his skin greenish, his hands galvanised', who is placed opposite 'the girl' and proceeds to remove her skin 'like a swimsuit' but at this point the two characters become pure textual device again and we are no longer operating as if these images are intended to be characters. The vignette concludes:

> She comes to in the middle of the procedure (a standard data-colonization) and begs for the return of her discarded cutis, but the doctor, hardened against these cries from the dead, barely raises his eyes from the warren of ancient tunnels that cringe beneath his scalpel.
>
> Shipley and Siratori 2012: 16

The only literal thing here is the shift back to concept and language, taking us away from the visceral misogynist image and into something altogether more Surrealist; it echoes horror movies but then swerves into other registers. Shipley plays with terms which overlap with those of Siratori: 'incidence of data-molestations are on the increase' (22) sound suggestive of real world cybercrime problems driven into the future, while 'In the cities, cadaverous machines stream through the streets looking only outside themselves for death' (23) might allude equally to Clive Barker's *Books of Blood* or Eliot's *The Waste Land*. This effect repeats, persists as the two narratives present horror re-registrations of fragmentation as a kind of modernization – doctors and bodies and machines return and recur in iterative echoes. Kenji Siratori's de-and/or-re-formed prose fragments repeat and replay motifs of embryos, dogs, ADAM (always all-caps), wombs and blood, DNA and skulls, while Shipley's anti-narratives cycle through more reflexive variations on these themes, where occasionally suggestive phrases leap out at the reader: 'spore specimens of purpose in prose-CURRENT slurry' (119), which becomes 'amputated prose-CURRENT' (149) and, possibly, ultimately 'flat graphomania fertilized by nihil rain of incoherence' (212).

The doubling, I think, is the key here. Negarestani's afterword, originally published in Robin MacKay's *Collapse* journal in a volume on philosophical horror, operates not just as a dislocated introduction – like Home's anti-introduction – it also suggests a modelling. To reach for a suggestive Marxian allusion, there is something about the implied life and death of the concept of Modernism itself at work here which 'weighs like a nightmare' on writing concerned with attempting renewal (Marx 1852).

'In English dreams, their imperial lusts' | David Peace's *Patient X* (2018)

Contrastingly, as another text that bridges British and Japanese cultural contexts, David Peace's *Patient X: The Case-Book of Ryunosuke Akutagawa* (2018) uses nested fictionalizations which appears more conventionally narrative but ultimately takes us to equally strange places. *Patient X* compares itself to classics of literary Modernism, formally and structurally. Subtitled 'The Case-Book of Ryunosuke Akutagawa' it alludes repeatedly to the crime-narrative focus of so much of Peace's oeuvre but takes a vastly more sweeping scope.

Peace takes both the fictions and life of Akutagawa as source material to link together a series or sequence of novella-like episodes up until his eventual suicide. I received *Patient X* as a present from Martyn Colebrook; the combination of style and content, of ideas and expression, plus the fact Martyn got it for me, reminded me so much of the lectures and texts from the courses on 'Modernism', 'European Modernism' and 'Critical Theory' that I took way-back-when at the University of Hull, when I first decided to pursue literary study further, that it was both a remembrance and a return. (Listening to John Hoyles extemporize on Eliot's *The Waste Land*; Brian Rigby on André Gide; Angela Leighton on Woolf; and a performative lecture on silence in Beckett and Pinter from Owen Knowles.) I don't find this emphasis on remembrance coincidental: Peace's method of reconstructive fictionalization provokes such a response and he's spoken in interview about reconstructing history and memory when he writes.

Patient X travels across the world, using stories of stories, and the adaptation and reimagining of some of Akutagawa's most famous images – notably that of Kappa, the Japanese water-demon which is taken from being a creature used to satirically comment on Japanese society to a personal double for Akutagawa which recurs in slightly altered form or by allusion, across the text.

The story or episode set in London is, perhaps inevitably, called 'Jack the Ripper's Bedroom' and is set at the very end of the Victorian era. Like various other narratives in the book, it is a frame narrative of one writer to another, this time Natsume Soseki telling the story of his time in London to Akutagawa as a young student. He explains the misery of his situation at the time and his impressions of Christopher Wren's architecture, the Houses of Parliament, and then, from out of the fog narrates his encounter with a Mr Nemo. When Nemo places a hand on his arm he jumps at the man 'made taller by his hat, dressed all in black' who was 'standing there in that street, on the border between night and fog' (Peace 2018: 62). Noting the meaning of Nemo's name; Nemo says 'It's Latin you know', Soseki replies 'for "no man"' (62). Because of the 'kindness in his eyes' Soseki joins Mr Nemo and agrees to accompany him to his own lodgings; the journey becomes increasingly heavy with suggestion and symbolism from there, from Nemo commenting 'if Monsieur Baudelaire declared [Constantin] Guys to be the Painter of Modern Life, then I declare myself the Painter of Modern Death' (63), to his landlady mistakenly referring to him as Mr Sweeney, only to be told by Nemo 'Sweeney doesn't live here any more. It's only me now, Mrs Bunting' (65).

While the story's structure recalls the subterranean metropolitan imagism of Poe's William Wilson, with its definitively Gothic embedded narrative structure and authorial doubling it also makes allusion to Conrad's *Heart of Darkness*, both in its obsessive focus on darkness and water, especially the river Thames, and in particular at the climax of the narrative when Soseki refers to having come to 'the end, the ends of the earth' (71), recalling Marlowe's speech to his nameless audience of Lawyer, Accountant, Director of Companies, and, of course, us – as reader and fellow traveller. As the story reaches its climactic moment, Mr Nemo takes Soseki to his attic lodgings and the ladder and the metaphor-heavy creaking of the building becomes the sound of a ship.

With gravitational inevitability he invites Soseki to see his work only for Soseki to expect paintings and encounter the private obsessions of an apparent psychopath and possible murderer who attempts to suffocate him with a pillow. Soseki ends his narrative with lines which force the reader to question whether we feel the writer ever really escaped from his portentous double:

> Down, down, the tin against my chest, the pillow pressed into my face, the smell, the stench of oil, of sweat, struggling but falling, falling backwards, falling but

struggling, his weight upon me, body crushing me, in English dreams, their imperial lusts, I was struggling, still struggling, struggling and falling, falling away and falling apart, I was falling apart, I was falling apart, bells tolling one, two, three, four, pealing five, six, seven, eight, ringing nine, ten, eleven, twelve, striking thirteen, thirteen, thirteen – 'Mr Sweeney, please,' came the voice in the dark, in the light, the silhouette in the doorway. 'Her Majesty has breathed her last.'

Peace 2018: 73

The repetition and imagistic approach to expressing violence and danger, and, possibly, the moment of death, or its close approximation, it recalls Peace's *Red Riding Quartet* very strongly. Another pairing, implicitly present here is perhaps with Alan Moore's *From Hell* (1989–99) which made such a powerful case for the concrete imbrication of modernity, murder and the decline of Imperial power in an uneven, cyclonic pattern around the central story of the crimes. In *Patient X*, the constant centre is Akutagawa's ultimate suicide, constantly present by uncomfortable musings on mortality and the presence of repeated instances of literary doubling. Akutagawa's literary interests and life also repeatedly make small parallels with Japanese imperial culture. In this context, the allusion to Conrad's *Heart of Darkness* within Peace's story makes plain both the general historical correlations between the Gothic and Modernism (again, recalling Carl Einstein) while also, coming so early in the text, functioning as a prolepsis to the historical fate of Japan's imperialism – which Peace's Tokyo Trilogy takes on in the post-WWII. It also performs the function of situating Akutagawa within the framework of a world-literary Modernism.

A return to 'Meng and Ecker's Lowly Arts Club (Banned)' | David Britton's novels

I recall encountering the names David Britton and Lord Horror in *Clive Barker's A–Z of Horror* standing in WH Smiths as a kid; there, Britton's Lord Horror novel and comics were paired with Alan Moore's epic deconstruction of Jack the Ripper, *From Hell*, under the heading 'Y is for Year Zero', which quoted Michael Moorcock's legal testimony in defence of Britton's novels and comics as satire. As a post-grad I returned to Savoy and eventually wrote a paper on Britton and Moorcock called 'Meng and Ecker's Lowly Arts Club (Banned)' exploring intertextual interactions between Moorcock's multiverse and Savoy; I considered it a work-in-progress for years, and failed to get it published, now it feels too much in need of revision.[4]

There are three Savoy novels published by David Britton during the 2010s, *La Squab* (2012), *Invictus Horror* (2013), and *Razor King* (2017). The long-running experimental graphic narrative *Reverbstorm* (1996–2013) was also brought to its conclusion with the publication of its final eighth episode within the collected hardback edition *Lord Horror: Reverbstorm* (2013), which included the wordless graphic narrative material from the final edition of the earlier series *Hard Core Horror #5* as a prologue. *Reverbstorm* is a properly experimental narrative but technically belongs more to consideration as a graphic novel, and so I will only note its significance briefly here as a comparative text that is primarily a graphic narrative, where the novels under discussion only make use of graphic accompaniment or appropriations of character from graphic fictions.

There are many succinct versions of the Lord Horror story – here I will appropriate from a legal analytical perspective on them by Martin A Kayman:

> The straightforward account is as follows. As a centre for avant-garde culture, the bookshops founded in Manchester in 1976 by Butterworth and Britton soon became a target for a moral campaign led by the new Chief Constable, James Anderton, a militant Christian and renowned homophobe (see Weeks 2012, 382). First charged with selling obscene material in 1982, the owners of Savoy Books were convicted in 1991 for publishing an obscene novel entitled *Lord Horror* (Britton 1989) and a related comic book, *Meng and Ecker No.1* (Britton and Guidio 1989). Savoy's cause was taken up by the campaigning group, Article 19, and the following year the verdict was overturned in the Crown Court (R. v. Britton & Butterworth 1992).
>
> Kayman 2016: 193

Savoy's status as a distinctively Mancunian avant-garde counter-culture publisher was reinforced most recently with the Michael Butterworth exhibition on 'The Use and Abuse of Books' organized by an independent art collective in conjunction with the Anthony Burgess Foundation in 2014. There, various of Savoy's more controversial and transgressive texts were displayed alongside notebooks and scrapbooks kept by David Britton, and with a screening of the truly disturbing experimental film *Lord Horror: The Dark and Silver Age*. Academic research into Savoy will no doubt be stimulated by the acceptance of their archives as the Michael Butterworth Collection at Manchester Metropolitan University and the David Britton Collection at Oxford's Bodleian Library.

Britton's fictions are extraordinarily controversial even within the contemporary avant-garde for their use of fascistic and Nazi imagery and fascistic characters, therefore it is always necessary to rehearse some of the stated intentions of Savoy in addressing them – here is David Britton in conversation with Andrew Darlington:

> 'They're just scum' explodes Dave Britton. 'Fascists are scum, you just can't deal with them, you can't reason with them or excuse them. They're shit. They are evil, purely evil. But can you name me one novel – just one, which captures that essence of pure evil? C'mon. Name me one…' I flounder, before eventually settling on the only, too obvious candidate – 'Lord Horror' (1990) by Dave Britton.
> 'Right. Ramsey Campbell is promoted as England's answer to Stephen King. [….] He's a great writer, and good luck to him. But I don't see that element of pure evil in what he writes. Thomas Harris' 'Silence Of The Lambs' (1988) is closer [….] Clive Barker comes even closer still, particularly in 'The Books Of Blood' (1984–1986). Clive Barker can be brilliant, also in the way he smears it across the mediums from short stories to movies. But even he rarely gets it exactly right. And that's what I wanted to do with 'Lord Horror' – I wanted to create a character who is that personification of evil.'
> Darlington 2017: n.p.

Through the use of childhood cartoon imagery and the rural idylls of Mole and Ratty in *La Squab* (2012), the local environs of Christmastime in Porchfield Square in *Invictus Horror* (2013), and 1950s-style Western imagery mashed up with childhood confectionary in *Razor King* (2017) Britton's novels of the 2010s continue the strategy whereby, as Barlow puts it, 'Lord Horror does not permit the reader to think they may be somehow beyond fascism [….] Horror's noxious ideals are shown to have the potential to contaminate all human thought' (Barlow 2016: 44). In each, the effect is to produce a distressing reading experience which continues to raise the question Noys identified in his earlier article on the Lord Horror graphic narratives:

> The result is an acute feeling of anxiety for the critic and historian, drawn on the one hand to condemnation but on the other hand, still discerning a complex and ambiguous political and cultural gesture. The lack of closure in the *Lord Horror* graphic novels is evident in the difficulty of coming to the closure of a judgement on the cultural politics of these works.
> Noys, 2002: 317

But, of course, this too is part of the Horror technique, ambiguity remains because, along with the satire, Savoy's legal battles have become part of their own stories.

The fictive mask of the writer is never dropped or can never be dropped, because experimental writing is always more *in the world* than non-experimental writing, because it breaks the story. In *La Squab* Ken Reid's elves Fudge and Speck look at Lord Horror and begin a chapter with 'Hello David', where 'Horror couldn't see him, but who else would be calling him by his real name except a friend with achieved ambition' (2012: 161). He then goes on to say to the elves 'Today I want to talk to you about the slippage of memory [....] and...about whatever Britton intends me to say in fact!' (162). The 'true' voice of the author has broken through the narrative voice but the *masque* continues; the controversial author is enfolded by his characters.

David Britton's Meng and Ecker novel *Invictus Horror* (2013) deploys a two-part structure of offensive and deliberately repellent provocation, which both rely on giant-sized bodies: 'Christmas Eve in Porchfield Square' and 'Christmas Day in Porchfield Square'. In the first, the square is physically overshadowed by Lord Horror manifesting as a glass giant, and the second sees the return of Horror's antagonist Dr Mengele as a sort of Sauron-like version performing a grotesque reunification of Meng and Ecker along with many other Holocaust victims until they also become a single giant overshadowing the area around Deansgate.

The list of names Britton deploys as allusions in the second part in particular is extremely provocative: Dieter Müller; Kristina Zywulska; Mosche Broderzon; Gustav Laudauer; Leo Frank; Baron Moses von Goldschlag; Mani Leib; Rosa Luxemburg; Ben Zion Raskin; Zygmunt Bauman; Leopold Bloom; Isaac Babel; Captain Choter-Ischai; Itzig Wittenberg and so on. This list presents an image of complexity – they range from communists to pacifists, anarchists, liberals to nationalists, members of the Jewish Brigade, resistance fighters to artists and poets and philosophers to, on the farther end of the spectrum, several fictional characters from classics of world literature. It forces the reader to engage with the multiplicity and multidimensionality of Jewish cultures in a manner that creates a counter-pressure against Britton's grotesque characters and their vile anti-Semitic, racist perspective: its effect is moral and aesthetic disjunction. The final section concludes with an extended iteration from a chapter of an earlier book, *Motherfuckers* (1996), recalling Michael Moorcock's use of this technique in the Jerry Cornelius fictions. It concludes with Nietzsche's final lines from *Ecce Homo* (1908) presented as a floating, unattributed spoken quotation, possibly uttered by the characters, possibly by the author: 'Have you understood me? Dionysos versus Christ [*sic*]' (2013: 129) – with the latter phrase in bold type. Reiterated here, it reminds me of Keith Seward's comments of Britton that 'You get the sense there is a wavering line between the author and his creation [....] He grew up in industrial Manchester, the son of a Christian mother and Jewish father. This fact is either trivial – meaning his half-Jewish parentage has no bearing whatsoever on the Horror world in his head – or it's so deeply Oedipal that you hate even to pursue the thought' (2008: 31). It is no coincidence that Britton's other novel of the period *La Squab* (2013), focuses on Meng's daughter Squab, the sometimes-childlike-sometimes-teenage girl, and makes implicit Nabokov allusions throughout while even featuring Sigmund Freud as an anthropomorphic crematorium; the moral and aesthetic problematics of projection are central to the whole sequence: the question of who is projecting what onto whom is uncomfortably persistent.

Britton's authorial voice is theatrically dropped towards the end of the novel *Razor King* (2017) to comment in a more personal-seeming style:

> Do I have to spell it out?
>
> Look at the millions of white trash on Twitter and Facebook, and marvel at their vulgarity. Do you think if they had been there they would not have partied and participated in similar camps in England?
>
> The truth is there for all to see.
>
> England is at once a *Herrenvolk* republic. Its racial subordination hides significant class inequality.
>
> Britton, 2017: 293

The accusation is here more plainly stated than it has been across the Lord Horror sequence, that fascism and antisemitism, and especially Nazism and the horrific crime of the Holocaust, are not so distanced from British culture and identity as we would like to think; Britain's unaddressed and less-addressed Imperial crimes stand in uncomfortable proximity, and Britain's population is riddled with Nazi-and-Far Right sympathies.

Keith Seward comments that Britton's is a 'Boschean method', which holds no appeal to the actually existing far-Right; he writes of the first novel that '[a]s if its anti-anti-semitism weren't obvious enough, the novel continually undermines its own protagonist's hatreds' (Seward, 2008: 16). Seward writes that, compared to infamous texts such as *The Turner Diaries* which have inspired terrorist violence and circulate in far-Right circles 'It is not lauded on skinhead discussion boards or promoted on neo-Nazi web sites' (18). The further inference for the full cycle of texts is that, given their gender-bending (pro-)antagonists Meng and Ecker, their drug-addled and decadent, often physically decaying Lord Horror (sometimes covered in human faeces like a cocoon), as well as the emphasis on extremely dense literary and artistic references to Dada, Surrealism, Cubism, Futurism etc., its aesthetic remains too grotesque and socially transgressive for real world Far Right and reactionary politics. Abel Diaz, who has reviewed Seward's book online, comments on Britton's penultimate novel, *Razor King*, qualifying his own perspective by saying 'For the record, I am half Ashkenazi Jew but agree absolutely with Wilde that there is no such thing as a moral or an immoral book' (Diaz, 2017), because he considers that is precisely the inescapable nature of transgressive experimental literature.

The class orientation of Britton's fictions has been consistently towards the working class and working-class culture in all its messy, uncompromising and often contradictory forms: its multiculturalism and wholehearted embrace of Black American music and culture, together with working-class racist language and tendencies to support ruling-class culture. This manifests in particular in architectural images: Lord Horror becoming a vast oven and consuming himself; Squab and Horror meeting a decidedly predatory watermill, Omoglossipsigo, who eats nymphet-like mermaids while protesting innocence, likely a veiled echo of Operation Yewtree; and, finally, Lord Horror's 'Aetheric' manifestation in *Invictus Horror*. At the beginning of this novel, Lord Horror manifests on Christmas Eve in Porchfield Square as a giant made out of glass, who drops giant fatal splinters down on people below. In this 'routine', he is a personification of Beetham Tower, Deansgate, a 47-storey glass-fronted building, which stands on Porchfield Square and has been notorious since its completion for making a loud humming noise in high wind thanks to a design feature on the roof, a 'blade' with no practical purpose, which is made up of fins which resonate when the wind moves over them (see Stuart 2020). The building has seen a range of controversies since its completion in 2006, from its design to its state of repair, so it is clear that the reasons for it to loom large in Britton's (anti-)narrative are because of what we might call its weight on the mind of the area. Not least of these effects in the minds of ordinary people is the sense of being overshadowed by the lives and lifestyles of the superwealthy who can afford to live in such accommodation, and which has a physical correlate in blocking sunlight out of working people's lives. This implied criticism of the rule of architecture over working people brings me to an unexpected parallel with Stewart Home's anthology *Denizen of the Dead* (2020).

A spectre is haunting the city: Stewart Home's *Denizen of the Dead* (2020)

I was lucky, really, to encounter the work of Stewart Home when I did; I had ambitions to undertake post-graduate study and had thrown myself into a range of Early Modern and Medieval readings under truly inspiring courses from

Lesley Coote and Brian Levy at Hull when Home published *69 Things to Do With a Dead Princess* (2002). I read a review, got curious and read the novel – then I saw he was coming to Hull, to the tiny art space of Red Gallery. I went, with my best friend, and there were a handful of us there. It was an experience: Home recited his work from memory, spinning out his sex-and-violence-and-theory routines with a solid punk attitude. It stuck with me – I grabbed a handful of his books, and two CDs, and leapt in: *Defiant Pose, Suspect Device, Red London*. They, and all his other books, which I've chased down since, gave me an alternate reading list to situate alongside my studies which profoundly expanded my thinking on the relation of text to culture to politics – afterward, Home and I corresponded for a while and he asked me to do some research on his mother's time living near Nottingham (I spent time combing through microfiche but failed to turn up anything; I suspect I may be the source for Ziggy Williams in *Tainted Love* [2005]). Since then, I return to Home's work constantly for its combination of philosophical and political polemic with transgressive, irreverent aesthetics as a dedicated avant-gardist of decades' standing.

Home's project in the anthology *Denizen of the Dead: The Horrors of Clarendon Court* (2020) is a direct political engagement with the phenomenon of 'ghost homes' as it is haunting one specific area of London. Clarendon Court is the current name for a development project which was also named The Denizen, a high-rise, high-end residential space advertised for its proximity to the Barbican and Moorgate tube stations and for being a short walk to The City of London; property sites for the actual location use terms like 'boutique' and 'sophisticated'. It has been extensively protested by artists from across London and around the world for replacing social housing for around 110 families with extreme luxury apartments which stand, predominantly empty but accrue value by their existence in the heart of London's housing market. A highly visible part of this was Spectres of Modernism, an installation project which placed brightly coloured critical slogans on the balconies of neighbouring flats at Bowater House directly opposite Clarendon Court, with contributors including Turner Prize winners and Man Booker nominees.[5]

Home's anthology forms a part of this protest, extending it into print and on the web – with further Gothic stories set in The Denizen/Clarendon Court published online. Home's anthology brings together a host of short experimental texts, mostly specific to this protest or connecting it to wider critiques of inequality. One feature of it is the appearance of a ritualistic spell produced by the w.o.n.d.e.r. coven, conjuring the concept of the occult to resist neoliberal property practices, the CIP page describes it as

Twelve symbols plus one interjected throughout the book. Each individual symbol of this living spell was contributed by one member of the coven. Combined in the correct order they are the lock and key of one complete spell designated to transform the neoliberal project and overdevelopment as represented by Clarendon Court.

Home, 2020: n.p.

Textual interventions include a fragmentary, multi-narrative text from John King, mixing apparent realism with a speculative dystopian near-future which also includes a haunting spectre, while other contributors include Iphgenia Baal, Bridget Penny and Katrina Palmer – who all produced texts for Home's Semina series of experimental novels (2008–2020). The anthology also includes a series of manipulated Gothic texts. These stories are 'plagiarised' in the sense employed by Home in his earlier critical fictions, where key terms, names, places, dates are replaced or updated to make a critical comparison; these modified nineteenth-into-twenty-first century stories are attributed to 'Abraham Stoker', 'Charlotte Stetson' (better known as Perkins-Gilman) and 'Richard Marsh' and all set within the environs of The Denizen, Clarendon Court. It is an approach that Home used to great effect in *Down & Out in Shoreditch & Hoxton* (2004), to juxtapose, for example, contemporary London underworlds with those of Marsh's *The Beetle* and Stoker's *Dracula* (both 1897).

The other two novels Stewart Home published during the 2010s bear quite different relationships to his earlier fictions. *The 9 Lives of Ray the Cat Jones* (2013) concerns the careers in boxing and crime of the Welsh 'gentleman thief' Raymond Jones who was, according to Home the first cousin of his own mother, Julia Callan Thompson – in an epilogue Home frames the novel as an anonymously delivered (likely) ghostwritten autobiography, akin to the old model of criminals narrating and elaborating their lives for a popular audience. This familial and crime connection locates its textuality as a conceptual sequel to his book about his mother, *Tainted Love* (2005) which also incorporated true crime and autobiographical elements.

Home's second novel of the 2010s, *Mandy, Charlie, and Mary Jane* (2013) is an elaborate textual assault on the university, on the issues of cultural studies, and similar to Home's established fictions, on the literary form of the novel. It concerns Charlie Templeton, a university lecturer in cultural studies, his wife Mandy, and Charlie's mistress and student, Mary-Jane Millford. It attacks all sorts of conventions of taste and aesthetics, including the likely audience for Stewart Home novels, as Charlie Templeton quickly reveals himself to be even more grotesquely abusive than the reader might have anticipated, repeatedly drugging his wife and mistress to have sex with them while they are unconscious, dealing unscrupulously with colleagues and strangers, going on increasingly wild drug binges (cocaine, unsurprisingly, featuring prominently), before engaging in violent murder of his wife and mistress in a scene which reflexively parodies *American Psycho* for its coupling of misogynistic murder with a flat, affectless style, and then penultimately committing a suicide attack against Lindisfarne. The surprise of the narrative being that the life of Charlie continues after this in 'Hell', which is similar enough to his life before to raise immediate questions about how much of his obviously fantastic adventures are projections of his disjointed sense of self. As with *69 Things to Do with a Dead Princess* (2002) and *Memphis Underground* (2007) the blur between internal and external life, between living characters and imaginary, dead or unliving ones (such as an animated ventriloquist dummy in *69 Things*) is always revealed to be an aspect of textuality.

Inconclusion | Never odd or even

We remain doubled and split, twisted out of shape and haunted, but perhaps new fictions show us, briefly, that we are just looking at a funhouse mirror in a crumbling castle. Ultimately, then, conclusion is impossible; the world doesn't stop for us and these are texts that are as obsessively *in the world* as possible while fighting to be something (somewhere) else at the same time; funhouse mirrors trying to be windows, and then trying to be doors. An old colleague I studied with once said that you don't really finish a PhD, you just stop – the text never really ends because it's there again, written in a slightly different way in the next one. (Echoes of Calvino and Burroughs.)

With experimental fiction the Johnson–Pratchett Problem is what sets us firmly back into a material understanding of what it is that experimental fiction does for us today; where it reflects the conditions of modernity to reflect upon our assumptions and meaningfully, critically change with our moment. Sometimes breaking the story makes the text do something more powerful, and sometimes it needs to be broken again, a different way, next time. (Echoes of Beckett's injunction to fail again but fail better.)

Separation of the avant-garde work from the life of the author is not only not always practical, but more importantly, it is not always critically appropriate. The experimental text and its author are mutually imbricated, perhaps more intensively than other literary and popular works because of their tense relationship with mainstream culture; consciously and unconsciously they reflect and illuminate something important that 'normal' literary forms cannot. (Echoes of Trotsky's defence of Céline the writer while condemning his fascistic politics.)

Similarly, we cannot separate our reading from our own moment under modernity, under the pressure of modernization. In lieu of any sense of conclusion then I offer a continuation of the core problems, and a return to the era of my introduction. Each expression of Modernist impulses creates its own history, but at the same time it also recreates the histories of Modernisms we have read until *just then* – this, then, is a statement of the purpose of Modernism as new beginning: To re-make literature of our moment... In other words: Let's try again...

Notes

1. BBC weather forecaster, Michael Fish, is famous for saying on 15 October 1987: "Apparently, a woman rang the BBC to say that a hurricane was on the way. Well, if you're watching, don't worry, there isn't, but having said that, it could become very breezy in the Channel." Hours later, the South East of England, the Channel, and Northern France were hit with the Great Storm of 1987 in which 18 people lost their lives in Britain, and four in France, a ship capsized in Dover and a ferry ran aground at Folkstone (see https://www.bbc.com/news/uk-england-kent-41366241). I think that it was a colleague of Fish defending him who said a weather forecaster does not predict for the extremes of possible outcomes; that comment has stuck with me as a useful cultural metaphor.
2. They discuss getting the rights to Burroughs in interviews such as D.M. Mitchell's *A Serious Life* and the promotional material for the Ishmael Reed texts appears in the back pages of their other books of the time such as Michael Moorcock's *My Experiences in the Third World War* (1980).
3. The Luther Blissett Project was an open name by a group of Italian avant-gardists who declared that 'anyone can be Luther Blissett', and under this name they carried out a number of media pranks and published a manifesto – which was even explained on television by the real Luther Blissett, a Black British footballer who used to play for Watford, then A.C. Milan, where he attracted the attention of the avant-gardists.

    Stewart Home has used the name Luther Blissett before, alongside other open names such as Karen Elliot and Monty Cantsin. Four former Blissetts from Bologna published the cult historical thriller *Q* (1998), and were later joined by another collaborator to become Wu Ming (which can mean either 'Anonymous' or 'five people'). Wu Ming published more historical thrillers with a left-wing slant on their historical lenses, including, *Altai* (2009), a sequel to *Q*.

4   I sent a copy to Savoy several years ago and I think the presence of a caricature of Michel Houellebecq and a brief allusion to The Beatles' Sergeant Pepper in *Razor King* (2017) are nods to my paper.
5   See https://spectresofmodernism.wordpress.com/ (accessed 28 May 2023).

Works cited

Barlow, Jonathan. 'New Wave Sword and Sorcery: Jerry Cornelius and Lord Horror'. Jacob Huntley and Mark P. Williams (Guest eds), Paul March-Russel (ed.). *Foundation*, 45.3 (number 125), 2016: 35–47.

Britton, David. *Invictus Horror*. Manchester: Savoy, 2013.

Britton, David. *La Squab*. Manchester: Savoy, 2012.

Britton, David. *Razor King*. Manchester: Savoy, 2017.

Butterworth, Michael. *The Blue Monday Diaries*. London: Plexus, 2016.

Cooper, Dennis, 'Spotlight on Kenji Siratori...', 18 September 2018: https://denniscooperblog.com/spotlight-on-kenji-siratori-human_worms-2004-2/ (accessed 23 February 2023).

Darlington, Andrew. 'Savoy Wars'. *Eight Miles Higher*, 25 July 2017: https://andrewdarlington.blogspot.com/2017/07/radical-publishing-savoy-wars.html (accessed 22 May 2023).

Diaz, Abel. 'From Our Man in Kent, Washington', November 2017: https://www.savoy.abel.co.uk/HTML/may17.html (accessed 25 January 2023)

Home, Stewart (ed.). *Denizen of the Dead: The Horrors of Clarendon Court*. London: Cripplegate Books, 2020.

Home, Stewart. *Suspect Device: A Reader in Hard-Edged Fiction*. London: Serpent's Tail, 1998.

Johnson, B.S. *B.S. Johnson Omnibus: Albert Angelo, Trawl, House Mother Normal*. London: Picador, 2004.

Kayman, Martin A. '"The Law Is a Ass": Obscenity, Blasphemy and Other Literary Offences after Lady Chatterley'. In *Literary Trials: Exceptio Artis and Theories of Literature in Court*. Ralf Grüttemeier (ed.). London: Bloomsbury, 2016: 191–216.

Levy, Deborah. *Swimming Home*. London: Faber & Faber, 2012 [2011].

Marx, Karl, 'The Eighteenth Brumaire of Louis Bonaparte' (1852): https://www.marxists.org/archive/marx/works/1852/18th-brumaire/ch01.htm (accessed 12 February 2023)

McCarthy, Tom. 'Afterword'. In Deborah Levy, *Swimming Home*. London: Faber & Faber, 2012: 159–160.

Noys, Benjamin. 'Fascinating (British) Fascism: David Britton's *Lord Horror*'. *Rethinking History* 6:3, 2002: 305–318, DOI: 10.1080/13642520210164526.

Peace, David. *Patient X: The Case-Book of Ryunosuke Akutagawa*. London: Faber & Faber, 2018.

Peak, David, 'Necrology, a collaborative text by Gary J. Shipley & Kenji Siratori' *Heavy Feather Review*, 6 June 2013: https://heavyfeatherreview.org/2013/06/06/necrology-by-gary-j-shipley-and-kenji-siratori/ (accessed 12 February 2023).

Seward, Keith. *Horror Panegyric*. Manchester: Savoy, 2008.

Shapiro, Stephen and Philip Barnard, *Pentecostal Modernism: Lovecraft, Los Angeles, and World-Systems Culture*. London: Bloomsbury, 2017.

Shipley, Gary J. and Kenji Siratori. *Necrology*. South Carolina: CreateSpace, 2012.

Stuart, Andrew. 'Why does the Beetham Tower hum in the wind?', *Manchester Evening News*, 10 February 2020: https://www.manchestereveningnews.co.uk/news/greater-manchester-news/beetham-tower-hum-wind-14361850 (accessed 25 January 2023).

Weeks, Jeffrey. *Sex, Politics and Society: The Regulations of Sexuality since 1800*, 3rd edn. Harlow: Longman, 2012.

Williamson, James. *Dust: A Creation Books Reader*. London: Creation Books, 1994.

Speculative Fiction of the 2010s

Anna McFarlane

Introduction

British speculative fiction of the 2010s started with a vision of war, and fracture. In Adam Roberts's *New Model Army* (2010) private militias swarm over the English countryside, organized spontaneously and democratically through Wikis that allow the mercenaries to communicate their preferences for strategy in real time. The interconnectivity of the militias and their decision-making process, facilitated through GPS and the internet, is in contrast with the geo-political zones they occupy and fight over. Scotland has long seceded from the political zone once described as the 'United' Kingdom, and the UK in turn has seceded from the European Union. What remains of Europe is a patchwork of lands, protected by any travelling mercenaries that the local rump bureaucracies can engage and afford. A new kind of political and identitarian power foments – the nation state is no more, and the collective power of the body politic, the literal bodies of the soldiers shaping these zones in combat, emerges: 'Now, belatedly, they're realizing that they're not dealing with the flare-up of ancient European intra-belligerence. Or they are dealing with that, but that's not the problem. The problem is that real democracy has come back' (257–258). These issues of fragmentation and the possibility of something new emerging were played out in several other science fiction novels of this period. Christopher Priest's *The Islanders* (2011) imagines a world in which a collection of islands, the Dream Archipelago is sandwiched between two large land masses at the planet's poles. The novel acts as a kind of tour guide to the islands, a gazetteer, including encyclopaedia-style descriptions of the islands interspersed with interlinking short stories, drawing the reader's attention to the themes of borders and connections. In one story, a couple are travelling together and considering a sexual relationship. As they go to bed together, the woman says that she does not want their relationship to become physical and the man should imagine a sheet of glass between them. He thinks:

> I knew about glass, but the glass I knew about was not for looking through, nor was it a barrier. On the contrary it was a medium of transient, non-fixed effect, used to control or enhance an electronic flow at some frequencies, while at others it functioned as an insulator or compressor. Her metaphor did not work for me.
>
> Priest 2011: 260

Through the negotiations of the bodies of these lovers, *The Islanders* draws on the themes of connection and distance, the border as a window to another country, and one that can be read through the body politic of an army, or the bodies of lovers in a different kind of boundary negotiation.

New Model Army and *The Islanders* were published at the beginning of the decade, and many of the themes with which these novels are concerned would come to define the 2010s in Britain. The political fracturing of the land was begun with the (failed) Scottish Referendum campaign that nevertheless made a strong case for Scotland as a separate political entity, a case that continues to be reflected in the starkly different political cultures of Westminster and Holyrood. This episode was followed by the fracturing of Britain's relationship with the EU through 2016's Brexit referendum. These issues were centred around specific events, referenda that anchored the news cycles for long stretches of time, but less easy to quantify was the damage sustained by Britain's communities as a result of the long policy of austerity, officially inaugurated by the Liberal Democrat–Conservative coalition government in 2010, that ate away at the country's infrastructure over the course of this decade. Likewise, the influence of the American culture wars on UK politics and the country's own reckoning with its past – culminating most visibly in the UK Black Lives Matter and decolonization movements – sometimes seemed to result in political polarization often stoked by a news media struggling to keep its head above water in the new attention economy. Finally, the looming existential threat of the climate crisis, (looming because its extant effects are often repressed), provides a terrifying backdrop to these crises. The emergence of new communities and possibilities, linked together by the power of communication technologies, and finding a sense of belonging and shared agency amongst these divisive times, remains hypothetical and experimental but continues to be imagined in speculative fictions.

In response to these circumstances, the speculative fiction of the 2010s has seen a number of trends emerge that I will trace through this chapter. There was already a well-established tradition of weird fiction in the UK, remarked upon in the most significant recent periodization of British sf, known as the 'British Boom' and documented by Andrew M. Butler (2003). Originally including China Miéville and Jeff Noon, in the 2010s this weird tradition shifted ever closer to realism, in the hands of M. John Harrison and Nina Allan among others. The settings for these fictions were largely urban, but a greater focus on rural settings, or at least settings beyond the metropoles, became more commonplace as writers tackled the perceived polarization between the concerns of the urban 'cultural elites' and working-class concerns largely associated with people living in ex-mining communities and rural economies. These class divisions were used as a way of reading the divisions that led to Brexit, and the issues are often conflated to some extent, as in the work of Dave Hutchinson, whose works including the *Fractured Europe* sequence (2014–18) and *Shelter* (2018) draw on these divisions to explore contemporary British politics and masculinity. The fracturing of political collectives and these divisions between the metropoles and the rest of the country, between the different countries of the UK and even between the different regions, resulted in (and were the result of) deep anxieties about the meaning of Englishness in the contemporary world. It sometimes seemed that as the strength of Welsh, Scottish, and Cornish identity grew, English identity was increasingly beset by the lack of a positive identity; the flag of St George had often been associated with racism and an insular 'little England' leaving little room for a positive, democratic vision of what England might come to represent in a time after the empire or, indeed, after the United Kingdom. This manifested in fiction with concerns about the enchantment and disenchantment of the land. Inflected with anxieties about climate change and the threats it poses to the English countryside, this weird literature that seeks to find the magic in the land, the magic that connects landscapes with concepts like 'community' and 'home' also acted as inspiration for Mark Fisher's theorization. A cultural critic and university lecturer, Fisher's best-known work roughly coincides with the decade of the 2010s and in many ways captures the often anxious and pessimistic tone of these debates. The 2010s also saw the US Culture Wars have major ramifications for the UK sf scene, a situation that resulted in the celebration of more diverse perspectives, including a series of texts dealing with the relationship between the individual and the state through the body, and specifically through the experience of pregnancy. Beginning with Joanna Kavenna's *The Birth of Love* in 2010, these texts use more traditional science fictional toolsets, working within dystopia or with technological nova like babies gestated outside of the womb, to engage with healthcare and the body as means of control by the state or by private corporations. Finally, technological anxieties about surveillance technology were in evidence throughout much of 'hard' British sf, but also provided an opportunity for thinking about how new and utopian interconnected collectives might be brought into being. Tim Maughan's *Infinite Detail* (2019) shows the concerns surrounding the misuse of algorithms, surveillance, and social media while exploring the utopian obverse of these issues – the ability to produce new communities. Perhaps ironically, Maughan's utopian vision of the internet is based on another fracturing, the separation of a local internet enclave from the World Wide Web, allowing a local and democratic mobilization of internet technologies. By finding the utopian possibilities in the fractures, sf of the 2010s offers some hope against a backdrop that has often seemed irrevocably bleak.

Mark Fisher and the speculative theory of the 2010s

Alongside the speculative literature of 2010s Britain there was a continuing speculative theoretical and academic engagement with literature and society. There have often been productive crossovers between speculative theory and speculative fiction (see, for example, Donna J. Haraway's literary-theoretical interventions from the 'Cyborg Manifesto' [1984] onwards, or Jean Baudrillard's theoretical evocation of the politics of J.G. Ballard, cyberpunk and simulation in his 'Two Essays', 1991). The most significant figure to be publishing in Britain during this period, with work that straddled the lines between theory and speculative literary practice, was Mark Fisher. Through his blog *K-Punk*, and later through a series of popular theoretical interventions, Fisher theorized the weird and the eerie, the role of genre in thinking through the politics of contemporary Britain, the relationship between the urban jungle and the eerie rural landscape, and the splitting of identity versus the work needing to be done by solidarity. All of these issues are mobilized in the speculative fiction of the decade and make Fisher a crucial figure both for theorizing these works, and as a primary text for literary attention, in that he articulates his political-theoretical positions using the motifs and language of speculative fiction and conveys the despairing pessimism and the dreamlike imaginings of his contemporary era.

Fisher's most significant text, *Capitalist Realism*, was published in 2009 in the immediate wake of 2008's worldwide financial crisis that saw the banks bailed out with trillions of pounds of taxpayers' money as financial institutions were deemed 'too big to fail' by political leaders. Fisher continued to publish, teach, and act as a public commentator until his death by suicide in 2017. Fisher's theoretical project is therefore substantially concurrent with the decade of the 2010s and these years saw him emerge as a major voice for understanding the contemporary economic and cultural situation as his work ranged from literary aesthetics, genre, to the politics of British music production since the 1980s. *Capitalist Realism* framed the problems of 'late' capitalism, or neoliberalism, in genre terms, opening with a reading of Alfonso Cuarón's dystopian film *Children of Men* (2006), and threading speculative readings throughout. Fisher described a compulsory realism as a correlate of the Thatcherite neoliberal dogma that 'there is no alternative' to capitalism. Realism as an aesthetic is therefore aligned with the neoliberal agenda and acts as a means of closing down debate about the utopian possibilities of other futures and other possible communities, or ways of organizing society. While capitalist realism closes down these utopian possibilities, the reality itself is 'fungible' according to Fisher: 'Capitalist realism...entails subordinating oneself to a reality that is infinitely plastic, capable of reconfiguring itself at any moment' (2009: 54), a phenomenon he reads through Ursula K. Le Guin's novel *The Lathe of Heaven* (1971), in which the protagonist remakes reality with his mind as he reveals his subconscious thoughts and desires to a therapist who then harnesses this power to his own ends. The rational approach associated with 'realism' and the demands for campaigners and citizens to 'be realistic' when demanding possible political outcomes turns out to be a precarious state, when the reality they are being asked to conform to is, in fact, built on shifting sands where the premises change regularly to suit the flows of capital and the unforeseen disasters associated with the free market and neoliberalism.

While Fisher's prognosis was that capitalist realism was closing down alternatives to the status quo, he found some alternatives still survived, haunting the late-capitalist machinery. In 2014's *Ghosts of My Life*, Fisher adopted Derrida's concept of hauntology from *Spectres of Marx* (1993), a portmanteau term that evokes beings that are not quite there through drawing on haunting and ontology in the same term. Fisher particularly saw the hauntology of alternative affects and ways of being in certain strains of British music, some of which he described as inhabiting alternative realities where British culture could have turned out differently. Fisher imagines a 1990s Britain culturally defined by Bristolian record producer Tricky's dark and complex trip hop, instead of the mainstream 'Britpop' of rock bands Oasis and Blur, which was promoted by Tony Blair as part of the 'Cool Britannia' rebranding of the country. Fisher calls Tricky, 'the herald of a future for British music that never materialised' (41), and describes the work of Goldie and Tricky together, writing:

theirs was not a music that petitioned for inclusion in any kind of ordinariness. Instead, it revelled in its otherworldliness, its science-fictional glamour. Like art pop's first pioneer, Bowie, it was about identification with the alien, where the alien stood in for the technologically new and the cognitively strange – and ultimately for forms of social relations that were as yet only faintly imaginable.

Fisher 2014: 42

This was music that promised a Britain that might revel in strangeness and difference, rather than seeking to find a bland monoculture to act as a baseline default into which others could be 'included'. Trip hop, jungle, and these other ghostly genres evoked the kind of radical spaces imagined in music subcultures and the unregulated urban spaces to be found in China Miéville and Jeff Noon's British Boom novels and those weird fictions that would follow in the 2010s. While dreaming of these radical spaces, Fisher's tone is funereal. For Fisher, these hauntings are just that – spectres of a past that never was, and of a culture that can never be. These traces of radicalism in the British underground are glowing embers of a long-past possibility that cannot be recaptured, a tone that is tempting to read biographically given the pain of Fisher's life-long experience with a depression that would ultimately end his life. The melancholy of identifying these hauntological cultural figures, moments, and modes is combined with the conviction that they could have led to an alternative culture, an alternative Britain, to the one we currently inhabit. This conviction filters through Fisher's work and places his critique at a juncture between identifying the dystopian tendences in British culture, and recognizing the flickering utopian impulses that have never flourished, but surely may yet offer a vision for a better future.

Fisher most directly dealt with speculative fictions in his sustained analysis *The Weird and the Eerie* (2016) and his essay 'Exiting the Vampire Castle' (2013). *The Weird and the Eerie* mapped out definitions of those titular terms and discussed them predominantly in terms of an English culture, drawing on the ghost stories of M.R. James, perhaps best known for the short story 'The Monkey's Paw' (1902); the titular preserved paw grants the owner a wish, but it will be granted at a cost. The couple who come into possession of the paw wish to have their money problems solved, but it turns out this comes at the expense of their son's death, the windfall arriving in the form of a compensation payment for his workplace accident. Fisher begins by discussing the two terms in the light of Freud's essay on the *unheimlich* (commonly translated as 'the uncanny', but this does not satisfy Fisher and he uses the German). For Fisher, Freud's eventual conclusions do not explain the status this essay has accrued as one of the key interventions in aesthetics of the twentieth century; rather, Fisher points to the theories that Freud picks up and puts down again, his numerous examples and hypotheses, and the ways in which repetition and the figure of the doppelganger circulate throughout. Fisher is positioning the weird and the eerie as distinguishable from, and even opposite to, the *unheimlich*; he sees the *unheimlich* as a view of the outside taken from the inside, whereas, 'the weird and the eerie make the opposite move: they allow us to see the inside from the perspective of the outside' (2016: 10). In Fisher's differentiation, 'the weird is that *which does not belong*' (10), and can be described through the example of a cinematic montage placing incongruous images against each other, as in surrealism. Meanwhile, 'the eerie seldom clings to enclosed and inhabited domestic spaces; we find the eerie more readily in landscapes partially emptied of the human' (11). Therefore, in Fisher's analysis, the eerie raises questions of agency. With humans absent from the scene, the terror comes from the knowledge that something inhuman must be the source of any sounds or activity in the landscape. An example of this might be the M.R. James story 'The Mezzotint' (1904), in which the titular mezzotint (a printed copper plate), features the aspect of a country house, with no human figures present. As the story progresses, a figure does appear, but its inhumanity strikes terror into the viewer.[1]

In 'Exiting the Vampire Castle', Fisher once again uses a motif from fantastic literature to explore contemporary politics, this time using the figure of the vampire to discuss the 'call-out culture' that he identifies among contemporary leftists. The practice of 'calling out' initially began as a well-meaning attempt to give learning opportunities to activists who might be able to 'be better' if informed that their behaviour was harmful, or damaging in some way. It also offered opportunities to root out more damaging behaviours by challenging activist communities to address issues of sexual exploitation or systemic racism. However, driven by the polarizing effects of social media, call-out culture began to police the speech of others, looking for increasingly minor deviations from the political narrative accepted (often implicitly) by a wider group, and pillorying individuals who failed to live up to the standards deemed to be required. Punishment could involve ostracism from online groups, or from in-person activist communities, an atmosphere that made communication – especially communication that might involve disagreement – stressful, and incentivized non-confrontational (and therefore less productive) political conversation. Fisher describes this atmosphere through his own experiences:

> 'Left-wing' Twitter can often be a miserable, dispiriting zone. Earlier this year, there were some high-profile twitterstorms, in which particular left-identifying figures were 'called out' and condemned. What these figures had said was sometimes objectionable; but nevertheless, the way in which they were personally

vilified and hounded left a horrible residue: the stench of bad conscience and witch-hunting moralism. The reason I didn't speak out on any of these incidents, I'm ashamed to say, was fear. The bullies were in another part of the playground. I didn't want to attract their attention to me.

Fisher 2013: n.p.

Fisher saw this as a major barrier to solidarity in leftist movements, and advocated for creating spaces where difficult conversations could be had in a spirit of solidarity. There were some critiques of Fisher's position at the time, and more broadly there has been a public debate about whether 'call-out culture', or arguably its successor 'cancel culture', exist, and if they do about which 'side' of the political divide bears the brunt of the chilling effect (Norris 2021). However, given the affective atmosphere Fisher describes, it is fair to argue that a *belief* in call-out culture would have a chilling effect on speech, regardless of any material evidence or long-term consequences for those who have been 'called out' or 'cancelled' – and, indeed, the online vitriol in response to 'Exiting the Vampire Castle' led to Fisher leaving Twitter permanently. In reference to activists who had dismissed the political interventions of the working-class comedian Russell Brand, partly through focusing on his use of (to use Brand's words) 'proletarian linguistics' (quoted in Fisher) that they found sexist, Fisher analyses what he calls, 'this grim and demoralising pass, where class has disappeared, but moralism is everywhere, where solidarity is impossible, but guilt and fear are omnipresent – and not because we are terrorised by the right, but because we have allowed bourgeois modes of subjectivity to contaminate our movement' (2013: n.p.). The other example Fisher gives is the online pillorying of Owen Jones, a journalist and author responsible for the most successful and mainstream critique of British class politics in the 2010s, a reaction that Fisher simply puts down to a distrust of 'celebrity', or popular culture, and one that would, taken to its logical conclusion, dismiss any left-wing voice unless coming from 'a position of impotent marginality' rendering it useless in affecting any change. Fisher uses the Vampires' Castle as an image to describe this environment, where bourgeois identities are used to deflect from class consciousness:

> the Vampires' Castle was born the moment when the struggle *not* to be defined by identitarian categories became the quest to have 'identities' recognised by a bourgeois big Other… the Vampires' Castle seeks to corral people back into identi-camps, where they are forever defined in the terms set by dominant power, crippled by self-consciousness and isolated by a logic of solipsism which insists that we cannot understand one another unless we belong to the same identity group.
>
> Fisher 2013: n.p., original emphasis

Fisher particularly draws attention to the elision of class in such discussions, and the impossibility of criticizing the Vampires' Castle without being accused of standing with racists, sexists, homophobes and the rest. In using the Vampires' Castle as an image for this politics, Fisher invokes the Gothic, anti-Catholic representation of the priesthood, as seen most quintessentially in Matthew Gregory Lewis's *The Monk* (1796), to describe this new bourgeois politics as a kind of corrupted and anti-democratic zone of power, claiming victimhood while accruing moral superiority. Most importantly perhaps, Fisher identifies the fracturing of the British socialist movement into multiple identities put to work policing each other as serving the interests of capitalism, because call-out culture acts as a deflection from solidarity and class struggle. Writing in 2013, Fisher did not yet see the divisions that would come to the surface in the Brexit referendum campaign, or in the conspiracy theories that spread through social media, becoming prominently visible in the various covid pandemic conspiracies, but Fisher's analysis points to the fracturing of political identity as both a cause and consequence of capital's attack on community, society, and even nationality. Fisher also saw the role of social media as crucial to understanding the methods of the Vampires' Castle and as a potential route out of it:

> We need to think very strategically about how to use social media – always remembering that, despite the egalitarianism claimed for social media by capital's libidinal engineers, that this is currently an enemy territory, dedicated to the reproduction of capital. But this doesn't mean that we can't occupy the terrain and start to use it for the purposes of producing class consciousness.
>
> Fisher 2013: n.p.

The associations of social media with surveillance, advertising, the power of capital and the authoritarianism of the state are taken into account here, but with the acknowledgement that social media may have a role to play in changing the face of British politics, or even being a place to foment political revolution. In finding this grain of hope, Fisher captures the dystopian/utopian tone of much speculative fiction of the 2010s.

The British Boom and weird fiction

For speculative fiction in Britain the most recent significant literary periodization trend is what has been called the 'British Boom' in science fiction, which took place in the late 1990s and early 2000s. The British Boom tapped into the broader phenomenon of weird fiction, one which is part of an American tradition stretching back to H.P. Lovecraft and encompassing the work of significant contemporary authors, particularly Jeff Vandermeer. Vandermeer contributed to the canonization of the genre through his work as an editor alongside Ann Vandermeer, as well as contributing his own writing, including *Annihilation* (2014), which was later made into a significant film (2018) directed by Alex Garland and starring Natalie Portman. However, while this British tradition spoke to the genre of the weird, it did so from a position self-consciously located in Britain. The texts associated with the boom did not simply repackage the American themes and concerns that tend to dominate the science fiction space, but laid claim to an originality based in a serious consideration of the role of Britain (and, more specifically, England) as a potential site of fantasy and subversion, as I have argued elsewhere (McFarlane, 2019: 304–308). Noon showed us a Manchester inhabited by animal-human hybrids on psychedelic drugs while Miéville's London found anthropomorphized rats and jungle music subcultures in the capital's hidden nooks and crannies. The British Boom drew on specific regional areas and their characteristic communities (particularly their music scenes) to create a speculative fiction that refused the cultural tendency to flatten all territory into an American franchise, and created something really new. Politically, these texts implicitly dealt with a post-Thatcher era that had left many urban communities behind, creating the underground worlds of jungle music and club culture that invited weird alternative identities to flourish, hidden from the light of mainstream society. This weirdness and difference provided a tempting milieu for speculative fiction, and the British Boom was born.

Inevitably, the speculative fiction of the 2010s draws on this background as it deals with similar problems in a new context. The financial crash of 2008 brought Reaganite and Thatcherite policies of the free market to an unsurprising apotheosis, and the system was propped up by the public purse so that the perpetrators were largely safe from consequence while insecurity was the order of the day for the precariat and working people. The age of austerity and the so-called gig economy that grew up around it once more created conditions for communities to fall through the cracks and to grow together in unexpected ways. This time, however, people found it ever more difficult to come together physically (due to finances and shift work) and social media stepped into that space. This tendency has only been exacerbated by the global pandemic that began at the decade's end (many would date this from March 2020 when the UK entered the first of its lockdowns). Weird and unexpected communities have grown up around conspiracy theories, and the attention economy that provokes social media companies to prioritize clicks and eyeballs above all else has fuelled political polarization. Politics was quick to capitalize on the proliferation of online voter data; the campaigning company Cambridge Analytica was shown to be scraping user data from social media accounts to target advertising personally and to promote the causes of Brexit and the election of Donald Trump in 2016. British speculative fiction of the 2010s drew on the tradition of region-specific sf to imagine ways to find solidarity in this divided world and to combat the internet monopolies which, once again, threatened to flatten out culture into a homogenous reflection of their own monopolies.

Mark Bould identifies the focus on regionality as a revival in weird fiction: 'In its focus on landscape, rural lifeways, and horrors ancient and modern, supernatural and secular, this revival formulates complex, anxious responses to the destabilizations of globalised modernity, including climate upheaval; it constantly risks, without necessarily falling into, a dangerous nativist essentialism' (2022: 148 n5). He argues that this new weird is related to the English eerie (as identified by Fisher) and the 'pictureskew', a concept developed by China Miéville as 'not a contradiction to the picturesque, but its bad conscience' (Miéville 2018: n.p.). Of course, Miéville, one of the key writers identified in the British Boom, continued to work during this period, publishing *Railsea* in 2012, a weird rewriting of Herman Melville's *Moby-Dick* (1851) set on a planet connected by a sea of intersecting railway lines. The image of the railway is prominent in Miéville's work – his Bas-Lag novel *The Iron Council* (2004) features a group of railway workers gone rogue, building the railway line as they travel, so that they can choose their own path in a kind of Communist-trade union inspired fantastic utopia. In his non-fiction work, *October: The Story of the Russian Revolution* (2017), the railway is also an important symbol as it carries Lenin in and out of exile and bears communications across the vast, quickly-changing landscape of Russia's vast terrains. In Britain, of course, the railway has strong working-class and collectivist connotations as a public transport traditionally staffed with well-unionized workers, while Miéville's use develops this into themes about determinism and the individual or collective's ability to shape the future. The railway connects different parts of the country, and it was subject to savage cuts following the Beeching reports (named for their author Richard Beeching) of the 1960s Conservative government under Harold Macmillan.[2] This event served to shut down a large number of rural stations and many miles of rail line, contributing to the isolation of some communities and the privileging of the metropoles. Therefore, the image of the railway serves to bring together the themes of class war, urban-rural division, and self-determination versus contingency.

Building on the tradition of the British Boom, Nina Allan's work brings the regionality characteristic of British Boom science fiction to life in weird fiction that echoes the work of M. John Harrison in its almost magic-realist intermingling of the mundane and the fantastic. Allan's debut *The Race* (2014) has five distinct sections that rewrite the same stories, acting as a palimpsestuous, and at times hallucinatory, engagement with themes of familial abuse, working-class struggle, and the role of representational art in constructing and maintaining selfhoods and political identities. The first section introduces us to the world of the titular race; a working-class community in an alternate reality Britain is centred around dog-racing that acts as the centre of a gambling economy and as a major focal point for socializing and maintaining community connections. The protagonist, Jenna makes some money crafting bespoke gauntlet gloves for the racers, while her brother Del has effectively wagered his daughter's life on his next race, relying on his unlikely success to repay the loan sharks who have taken her hostage. The next section is told from the perspective of Christy, a writer living in what seems to be the Hastings of our reality. Christy suffers sexual abuse at the hands of her brother, Derek, and their story is a mirror-world version of Jenny and Del's relationship, begging the question of whether Christy is the writer of the story of section one. The following sections add layers and offer different ways of nesting the different narratives together, creating a recursive portrayal of Christy's psychic state, but also a magical realist evocation of Britain and British culture. Jenna/Christy grows up without a mother, with only her emotionally-distant and preoccupied father and her abusive brother. Jenna's work as a gauntlet artisan in the first section reads as a dream of the possibility of the community acceptance and economic productivity that Christy lacks, as social ties for her are almost non-existent and there is very little help forthcoming from the state, no security net to speak of. The book speaks to the loneliness of a contemporary Britain sucked dry by the austerity politics promoted as a response to the 2008 financial crisis from 2010, and a longer history of working-class neglect dating from post-industrialization and particularly the Thatcher era.

Allan followed *The Race* with *The Rift* (2017), which once again walked the line between the everyday and the fantastic to show the bizarre and extraordinary worlds that exist in what appears to be mundane reality. The book is primarily told from the point of view of Selena Rouane, an assistant in a jeweller's shop whose life shifts on its course when her long-lost sister Julie, missing and presumed murdered, reappears after nearly twenty years. Julie returns with a story that mashes up the mundane with both the horrific and the fantastic. She has fallen through a 'rift' in space time, suddenly transported from Lake Hatchmere near Manchester to the planet of Tristane, (the root 'trist/triste' suggesting a planet of melancholy). The novel intricately describes the geography and architecture of this other planet. Julie also got into a car with someone she calls Stephen Barbershop, someone who Selena knows as Steve Jimson, a murderer convicted after Julie's disappearance who always claimed himself innocent of involvement with Julie. The book consists largely of Selena's narrative and Julie's story, but these sections are interspersed with sections from imaginary books, threaded through with intertextual references to *The X Files* and *Picnic At Hanging Rock*, sections from imaginary novels based on Julie's story, newspaper articles and the scripts of conversations between the two sisters. The treatment of the text as a kind of compendium, and the use of 'found' literatures shows the influence of Jeff Vandermeer whose *City of Saints and Madmen* (2001) uses similar techniques to explore an imaginary world from several angles, or Priest's *The Islanders*, but here these techniques are put to use for the darker ends of exploring the (lack of) separation between fantasy and reality. The *Rift* forms a diptych with *The Race*, as both deal with the ways in which the trauma of sexual assault separates people from the others around them, creating isolating worlds within worlds. Allan's use of the fantastic proves the point made in magic realism – that this is a true representation of lived experience rather than an escapist fantasy. The horror of sexual assault snatches Julie from her quotidian experience and she can never return, not unlike an alien abduction, or a fall through an unexpected black hole into another universe.

> Could a story change a place? Selena wondered. It was almost as if Julie's version of Hatchmere [...] had contaminated the real one, bleeding into it through the rift to make it more like itself. The idea was ridiculous, she knew that, and yet that was how it felt to her, standing there at the side of the road where Julie had stood – perhaps – twenty years ago, balanced upon the hair's-breadth dividing line between one version of reality and another.
>
> Allan 2017: 373–374

The influence of narrative on a sense of place shapes it, and Allan characterizes contemporary provincial Britain as a place of dystopia, a scene from a disaster movie:

> Selena thinks of those provincial English cities that become dead zones at night, their precincts and underpasses sinister suddenly, like sets from disaster movies their pavements and car parks flyblown and rain-streaked. Industries laid to waste and workers demonised, history demolished. Racketeering and rent rises, unemployment and bomb damage, decade after decade after decade of governmental neglect.
>
> Allan 2017: 365

The setting is important from a characterization perspective, as the loneliness of contemporary Britain makes it all the more believable that Selena would cling to someone who appears from nowhere claiming to be her long-lost sister, but it also situates the text as a commentary on contemporary Britain, a place in search of new communities, identities and narratives.

Impact of the American culture wars on UK sf fandom

While the UK dealt with the Scottish Independence Referendum and the Brexit Referendum, the 2010s saw the culture wars in US politics become increasingly entrenched. The backlash against Barack Obama, the USA's first black president, and the rise of reality television star and political reactionary Donald Trump saw increasingly bitter divisions between Republicans and Democrats, and these often along lines of social issues such as racism, gun ownership, policing, and abortion. These fed into the political polarization seen more broadly across cultures, fuelled by economic crises and social media communication, but they also had specific impacts in speculative fiction fan communities and sf literature, both in the US and abroad. In the US, the main event around which discussion of the culture wars in sf fan cultures circulated was the Sad Puppies debacle. The Sad Puppies (named ironically for a dismissive and sarcastic way of describing someone upset on the internet), were a group of sf fans who claimed that science fiction fan culture had been monopolized by 'social justice warriors' at the expense of the quality of the literature itself. The group realized that with only a small, coordinated group it was possible to change the nominations on the ballots of the Hugo Awards, the most important science fiction fan awards in the US, awarded annually by the members of the World Science Convention ('Worldcon'). They began in 2013 by trying unsuccessfully to get works written by their organizers onto the ballot, an aim they achieved in 2014, when the Worldcon took place in London. In 2015, they organized full suggested 'slates' of nominations for consideration by members, while an even more extreme group, the 'Rabid Puppies', offered a similar slate that it asked supporters to submit without alteration. These attempts to subvert the award process were defeated by the mobilization of Hugo voters to vote against Puppy nominations, even to the extent of having to vote for 'no award' in cases where the entire shortlist was comprised of puppy nominees (see Walter 2015). The Puppies were similarly defeated in 2016 (see Barnett 2016). Rather than a measure of popularity, or artistic merit, the Hugo Awards were in danger of becoming a proxy zone for political arguments, but the issue was dealt with via a change in the voting regulations in 2017 which made bloc voting of this kind more difficult. The 2010s also saw the rebranding of a number of major awards as fandom took steps to come to terms with some of its difficult history. In 2015, the World Fantasy Awards changed the design of their trophies. Previously these had taken the form of a small bust of H.P. Lovecraft but, in recognition of the racist premises of Lovecraft's writing (particularly fundamental to his famous story 'The Call of Cthulhu', 1926) the design was changed in 2015. The James Tiptree Jr. Award, named for Alice B. Sheldon's nom de plume and given in recognition of science fiction or fantasy exploring gender norms, was renamed The Otherwise Award in 2019. Concerns had been raised about Sheldon's death by suicide after killing her ailing partner, leading to discussions about whether Sheldon's act was an example of 'caregiver murder'. Finally, the Joseph W. Campbell Award for Best New Writer was renamed the Astounding Award following winner Jeannette Ng's critique of Campbell as a fascist in her 2019 acceptance speech in Dublin.

While the Hugos and these other awards bodies have been traditionally based in the USA – although the Worldcon has increasingly taken place outside the US since 2010 – and the Sad Puppies debacle was primarily reflective of US politics, these developments were widely followed and reported, and had a big impact on UK fandom as well. An immediate result was a greater concern for diversity in sf awards and attention to the demographic make up of the nominations. This was primarily discussed through analysis of submissions to, shortlists for, and winners of, the annual Arthur C. Clarke Award for best science fiction novel published in the UK. The Clarke Award is unusual in publishing full lists of the novels submitted, and therefore holds some good data on changes in the diversity of not just the shortlists but also the wider field in the UK over time. The evidence showed that the Clarke Award became more diverse over the 2010s, sometimes exceeding 30 per cent women in the submissions. While this is clearly a long way from gender parity, this was an improvement on the previous decade, which more often saw submissions from women under 20 per cent (Hunter 2019). The Clarke Award also showed diversity in its winners during the decade 2010–20, with six women being honoured and three writers of colour (Tade Thompson, Colson Whitehead, and Namwali Serpell). These are, of course, blunt metrics for assessing diversity, but the trend in UK fandom and awards culture was towards highlighting perspectives that had previously gone unrecognized and, based on the Clarke Award data, this meant a greater award platform for Black writers and women dealing with issues related to gender and power.

The importance of women writing on gender can also be better understood in the context of the American culture wars. As the culture wars stoked up polarization on the issue of abortion in the USA (culminating in 2022 with the US Supreme Court's overturn of the landmark Roe vs Wade ruling that protected the right to abortion at a federal level), a whole genre of feminist dystopias, taking Margaret Atwood's *The Handmaid's Tale* (1985) as an origin text, proliferated. In the US these novels included Hilary Jordan's *When She Woke* (2011), Meg Ellison's *The Book of the Unnamed Midwife* (2014), and Leni Zumas's *Red Clocks* (2018). These dystopias dramatize and explore the threats to bodily autonomy experienced in the contemporary USA through speculative dystopias and have been criticized for using the genre of the slave narrative to do so (Crawley 2018), finding horror in the idea that what has already systematically happened to enslaved Black Americans might one day happen to white women. In the UK, writers built from this genre with a twist, more often situating their writing on reproduction as a critique of eugenics (in the tradition of Aldous Huxley's *Brave New World*, 1932) while also feeding into contemporary anxieties about the threatened National Health Service in the UK as austerity over the 2010s led to substantial cuts and privatization syphoned money ringfenced for healthcare into private profits (McFarlane 2022). It would not be right to say that the moral or religious objections to abortion are settled in the UK – there have been worrying comments in recent years from Conservative Members of Parliament, including Jacob Rees-Mogg and the Health Secretary at the time Jeremy Hunt. It is also the case that abortion has not been decriminalized in the UK, meaning that women are still arrested in some cases of stillbirth and miscarriage (Das 2022). This situation means that there is little room for complacency in UK abortion politics. However, in speculative fiction the issues tend not to be framed in terms of religious fundamentalism to the same extent as the American feminist dystopias, but in terms of healthcare, agency, and control.

Perhaps most significantly is the focus on ectogenesis in these novels. Anne Charnock's Clarke-Award winning *Dreams Before the Start of Time* (2017), Helen Sedgwick's *The Growing Season* (2017), and Rebecca Ann Smith's *Baby X* (2016) all imagine a future where babies are gestated outside of the womb. Furthermore, all three novels imagine this development in technology as an intrusion of private profit into the private world of gestating and birthing babies. Ectogenesis, that is the gestation of foetuses outside the womb, is not currently possible, but there have been advances in this technology during the course of the decade. Lamb foetuses have been gestated in 'bio-bags' with the intention that this technology could be available to premature babies in the near future. The feminist implications of this have primarily been explored by Sophie Lewis (2019), a British commentator living and working in the USA, who sees bio-bags as posing a risk to the (already under threat) availability of abortion. Given that legislation surrounding abortion is often based on the viability of the foetus, the availability of bio-bags could reduce the timescale for abortion and result in more forced parenthood. However, on the other side of this debate, there is a tradition of radical feminist promotion of ectogenesis as a tool for overcoming the biological burden of carrying children, and thereby working towards women's liberation, see for example the work of Shulamith Firestone (1970), and the liberal feminist tradition has continued in this vein to some extent, as Evie Kendal (2015) argues from a bioethics perspective that ectogenesis could lead to gender equality, particularly in granting women greater, more equitable access to the workplace.

Rather than offering women freedom from the literal burden of carrying the next generation (as envisaged by techno-utopian feminisms such as Firestone), I have argued elsewhere that reading these novels:

> shows the difficulties that women in the UK face as they consider the future of reproduction in a society where universal healthcare is under a slow but constant assault. In their different ways, these novels diagnose a bleak situation in which technologies that could change social and political relations might be envisaged, but these technologies will simply move into a pre-existing matrix of social and gender inequality, rendering them tools of oppression.
>
> McFarlane 2022: 39

Joanna Kavenna's *The Birth of Love* also deals with these issues, although in a way that foregrounds the experience of pregnancy and birth as philosophically and existentially important to a greater extent, placing a narrative about the deaths of women from childbed fever (because of the increasing medicalization of birth and the doctors' ignorance of germ theory) against a dystopian future in which the population is controlled as a response to climate change, and childbirth has been fully automated, severed from its affective ties. Jane Rogers's *The Testament of Jessie Lamb* (2011, another winner of the Clarke Award) follows in the footsteps of P.D. James's *Children of Men* (1992), in that a sickness is making it impossible for women to give birth without sacrificing their lives, and is related to Atwood's *Handmaid's Tale* in its use of a personal testimony as a narrative device. Ken MacLeod's *Intrusion* (2012) shows the use of biopolitics via healthcare as a means of controlling the public and reveals the eugenicist assumptions underpinning such authoritarian intrusions into individual liberty, while Paul McAuley's *Austral* (2016) uses miscarriage as a metaphor for an uncertain future in the face of climate change. At first glance, these novels (particularly those authored by women) could be read alongside that tradition of the feminist dystopia coming from the US, but on closer examination there is a long tradition of eugenics discourse and the specific situation of NHS healthcare that gives them a particularly British outlook that is important to consider in their interpretation.

Infinite Detail and surveillance

This chapter has focused to a great extent on the political fractures that became impossible to ignore in the 2010s – between the rural and the metropole, the political polarizations of Brexit and austerity, and the effects of the American culture wars on UK sf culture. A driving factor that I have mentioned regularly, but never tackled directly, is the importance of the internet and social media in finding expression for these divisions and in stoking their fires. Mark Fisher's description of the Vampires' Castle began to engage with social media and its problems as a political tool as it mobilized bourgeois identity categories, and the surveillance potential of communications technologies and the potential for abuse by nation states was revealed by Edward Snowden in 2013 when he showed the extent of the USA's National Security Agency's incursions into the private lives of American citizens. Critique of social media, the internet as a tool for political surveillance, and the danger of unexamined algorithms as drivers for shaping our spaces for communication have been the target of several significant British sf novels of the decade. Tim Maughan's *Infinite Detail* (2019) is an example that builds on the regionality of the British Boom and contemporary weird fiction, while also critiquing the internet and thinking about some utopian paths beyond the current difficulties of finding a commons beyond the attention economy and the polarization stoked by the micro-blogging format used in Facebook posts and tweets. *Infinite Detail* responds to this cultural milieu with a novel in the tradition of the British Boom that remixes those regional and musical tendencies for the occasion. *Infinite Detail* gives a near-future portrayal of a Bristol that has been torn apart by a cataclysmic event; the internet has shut down, leaving the UK as an unmapped terrain where people struggle to survive without the rule of law, basic utilities or supply chains. Bristol is a particularly evocative setting for the novel. Maughan's Bristol is multicultural and defined by cultural exchange and music as a zone of community. Bristol was a key site for the British Black Lives Matter protests that took place in June 2020 following the police murder in the USA of George Floyd. A controversial statue of a Bristolian slave trader, Edward Colston, who had gifted some of his riches to the city for philanthropic projects and given his name to a number of local roads and landmarks, was torn down and thrown into the harbour (Siddique and Skopeliti, 2020). Bristol was also home to the trip hop scene, including Tricky who grew up in the city's Knowle West council housing estate and became emblematic of an alternative Britain in the writings of Mark Fisher. It is also known as the home of guerrilla artist, Banksy, who used the nearby lido at Weston-Super-Mare as the setting for his most significant artistic installation, Dismaland, in the summer of 2015. These radical artistic, cultural, and political roots are drawn upon in Maughan's rendering of a UK broken by infrastructural and political failure.

The novel's alternating chapters give us a 'before' and an 'after'. In the 'before' chapters we learn about the People's Republic of Stokes Croft, an area of Bristol where the internet has been jammed by cyberactivist and hacker Rushdi Manaan and replaced by a localized communitarian network, known as 'Flex', allowing artists to map the area using virtual graffiti and to live together experimentally. Characters wear 'spex', similar to Google Glasses, spectacles that allow them to access the internet and to see virtual reality mapped onto physical reality. In the aftermath, a young girl, Mary, moves through the rubble of Bristol, seeing the ghosts of those who died in the violence and sometimes bringing comfort and closure to their searching families. She draws the faces she sees, pinning them to the wall to make a memorial to the dead in an abandoned retail unit, surrounded by the 'kaleidoscopic mass of debris' (2019: 4) left to her by the believers – gifts from desperate people who have nothing of value to give. If someone recognizes a portrait, she gives it to them for free. It turns out that Mary is able to tap into the Flex network so that she can see those final moments before the network died, the technology haunting the area, the supernatural and the virtual laid over each other indistinguishably.

The before and the after have contrasting tones that align with their affective worlds. In the 'before' there is the rush of busy, multicultural urban living – perhaps more noticeable in a post-2020 reading when the excitement, anonymity, and closeness to strangers that the city can offer has been in short supply, or problematized, during the course of the pandemic. This is dramatized through the motif of hand-holding and of touching things with one's hands. On the New York subway some commuters wear anti-bac gloves to avoid the germs – pointing out that 'you don't know who has been touching what, where their hands have been before' (40) – while Rush holds hands with a homeless man to pay for him to get through the subway barrier. 'The city recognises that they're together'. The 'before', in that rush of urbanism and the communitarian politics of the People's Republic of Stokes Croft, gives the sense of excitement that comes from criticality, the urge to tear down the power structures that restrict the possibilities (for the internet, for identity, for meaning making) and to make something new as a subversive supplement to the mainstream digital-capitalist hegemony. In the 'after', this excitement has abated and the people collectively take on the grim challenge of living onwards. The nostalgia for the 'before times', for the order of the connected world, is combined with solastalgia, a term coined by Glen Albrecht in 2007 to describe the mourning for a world unaffected by climate change and its associated environmental disruptions. This nostalgia and solastalgia are located in the debris of digital capitalism, the plastic throwaway objects brought in via global supply chains from the engine of production that is China. Once these supply chains are shut down, the disposable single-use objects will never be replaced, and they become vessels for longing, representations of a society that contained the seeds of its own destruction, but nonetheless was home.

As well as its evocative and detailed engagement with the city of Bristol as its setting, *Infinite Detail* draws on the British Boom's tradition of engaging with urban, DIY music and associated subcultures. Live music events and raves temporarily make spaces for alternative forms of community and connection. This is disrupted by the cataclysmic event. When we first see Mary walk through the wreckage of Stokes Croft with the grieving parents of a dead boy 'Airborne reggae vibes drift across the street from somewhere, pulses and tones, like the jungle tape stripped of its urgency' (16) – the music is a shadow of its former self, no longer pulsing with a beat that engages the body via vibration as much as the ear, no longer alive with the urgency of counter-culture and community – drifting like the ghost of its former self in an echo of Mark Fisher's hauntologies.

In its evocation of a Bristol painted and overlaid with virtual reality art the home of Banksy is dramatized as a space where the community is trying to take back some agency, although the enterprise of the hackers and art activists is also mooted as a kind of gentrification, causing barriers to local people. In a newspaper article about the People's Republic of Stokes Croft there are interviews with a local shopkeeper who has had to replace his surveillance equipment in order that it can function in the PRSC so that his insurance premiums will not be affected; a delivery driver complains about having to leave the area to pick up the day's jobs while her daughter, employed on a zero hours contract, also has to leave so that she can receive shifts via her mobile phone. The problems caused by the zone highlight the encroachment of digitalization into the working lives of the people in Stokes Croft, making visible the structural inequalities that force them to dance to the tune of the internet and the few giant corporations that occupy what was once vaunted as a commons. This is echoed in New York where the NYC app uses smart bins to return the deposit for a drinks can straight to the user, thereby taking away the livelihood of hundreds, perhaps thousands, of homeless and precarious people who rely on collecting cans for subsistence. Taxi driving jobs have already been taken away thanks to self-driving cars, making the gig economy an obsolescent model not long after its emergence – already the precarious jobs it provided are being colonized by digitization and automation.

Conclusion

Infinite Detail, alongside many other examples of 2010s British speculative fiction, works through the shocks of the last thirteen years, and the threat posed by the systems in which we find ourselves entangled. Artificial intelligence, surveillance capitalism, and the unfettered growth of Silicon Valley monopolies that extend unprecedented influence over our quotidian activities and our political landscape are the subject of the speculative fantasy of conspiracy theory, as well as the critical utopias of sf writers. For example, Nick Harkaway's critique of state surveillance in 2017's *Gnomon* shows an interest in a sense of place, refiguring London as a place created around you as you move, a replica of the city filtered through digital logic. Harkaway's novel ranges over a number of locales, but perhaps most notably the financial markets in post-crash Greece, a country which suffered particular shocks in the crisis aftermath. The possibility that we might be living in a digital simulation is made more real by the mediation of our political and economic structures by internet intrusion and surveillance, and our personal relationships as social media shapes identity. Our behaviour is nudged and changed imperceptibly by the internet's need for clicks and advertising revenue, leading to a feeling that we are not in control of our collective direction. Material landscapes and the remnants of past cultures (industrial, musical), linger beneath the data, haunting contemporary science fiction with the loss of futures that never came to be, what Fisher describes, quoting Franco 'Bifo' Berardi, as 'the slow cancellation of the future' (Fisher 2014: 6). However, while Fisher bemoans the inertia of contemporary culture, British science fiction finds in these mournful hauntings a new style that combines the mulch of rural landscapes with post-industrial, post-Thatcher, post-austerity, post-Brexit politics.

From this negativity emerge utopian expectations in speculative fiction and concerted attempts to find ways to mitigate the power of Silicon Valley, to overcome the fractured politics of the decade and to find a new sense of community. Like Maughan's free internet zone in Bristol, Canadian-British author Cory Doctorow (based in London during the early 2010s) writes prolifically on the potential for freeing the commons of the internet from the private companies who have colonized it over the last decades, perhaps most notably in 2017's *Walkaway* which shows the potential for leaving behind the overdetermined spaces of mainstream digital society and making something new. In *Infinite Detail* the architect of the People's Republic of Stokes Croft, Rushdi Manaan, gives what could be a manifesto for this thread of speculative fiction in the 2010s:

> This is an experiment, a statement. People don't realise how reliant we are on the internet now. If it disappeared tomorrow there'd be chaos. It's not just that you wouldn't be able to Facebook your mates or read the news – everything is connected to it now. The markets would stop trading. The economy would collapse. There'd probably be no electricity, no food in the shops. Vital equipment in hospitals would stop working. It's not just your phone or your spex – cars, busses, trains – everything would grind to a halt. It'd feel like the end of the world. We're just trying to show people how dependent we've all become on something that we don't own, that isn't controlled by us. We're just trying to show people that there are alternatives, different ways of doing things.
>
> Maughan 2019: 84–85

Notes

1 The story was adapted for television by Mark Gatiss and screened over Christmas 2021; in terms of television culture, this English concept of the weird and the eerie is regularly engaged by Gatiss in his television work, and his *League of Gentlemen* collaborators Reece Shearsmith and Steve Pemberton in their anthology series *Inside No. 9* (2014–present).

2 For more on the Beeching Reports and their legacy, see Charles Loft's *Government, the Railways and the Modernization of Britain: Beeching's Last Trains* (2006).

Works cited

Albrecht, Glenn et al. 'Solastalgia: The Distress Caused by Environmental Change'. *Australasian Psychiatry* 15(1), 2007: S95–S98.

Allan, Nina. *The Race*. London: Titan Books, 2016 [2014].

Allan, Nina. *The Rift*. London: Titan Books, 2017.

Barnett, David. 'Hugo awards see off rightwing protests to celebrate diverse authors', *The Guardian*, 21 August 2016: https://www.theguardian.com/books/2016/aug/21/hugo-awards-winners-nk-jemisin-sad-rabid-puppies (accessed 27 May 2023).

Baudrillard, Jean. 'Two Essays'. *Science Fiction Studies* 18(3), 1991: 309–320.

Bould, Mark. *The Anthropocene Unconscious*. London: Verso, 2022.

Butler, Andrew M. 'Thirteen Ways of Looking at the British Boom', *Science Fiction Studies* 30, 2003: 374–393.

Crawley, Karen. 'Reproducing Whiteness: Feminist Genres, Legal Subjectivity and the Post-racial Dystopia of The Handmaid's Tale (2017-)'. *Law and Critique* 29, 2018: 333–358.

Das, Shanti. 'Women accused of illegal abortions in England and Wales after miscarriages and stillbirths', *The Observer*, 2 July 2022: https://www.theguardian.com/world/2022/jul/02/women-accused-of-abortions-in-england-and-wales-after-miscarriages-and-stillbirths (accessed 27 May 2023).

Firestone, Shulamith. *The Dialectic of Sex: The Case for Feminist Revolution*. New York: William Morrow and Company, 1970.

Fisher, Mark. *Capitalist Realism: Is There No Alternative?* Winchester: Zero Books, 2009.

Fisher, Mark. 'Exiting the Vampire Castle', *Open Democracy*, 24 November 2013: https://www.opendemocracy.net/en/opendemocracyuk/exiting-vampire-castle/ (accessed 27 May 2023).

Fisher, Mark. *Ghosts of My Life: Writings on Depression, Hauntology and Lost Futures*. London: Zero Books, 2014.

Fisher, Mark. *The Weird and the Eerie*. London: Repeater, 2016.

Hunter, Tom. 'Gender parity, science fiction, and the Arthur C. Clarke Award'. *Medium*, 9 May 2019: https://clarkeaward.medium.com/yes-more-women-are-publishing-science-fiction-but-so-are-way-more-men-e3cdb91dcb0 (accessed 27 May 2023).

Kendal, Evie. *Equal Opportunity and the Case for State Sponsored Ectogenesis*. London: Palgrave Pivot, 2015.

Lewis, Sophie. 'Do Electric Sheep Dream of Water Babies?', *Logic*, 3 August 2019: https://logicmag.io/bodies/do-electric-sheep-dream-of-water-babies/ (accessed 27 May 2023).

Loft, Charles. *Government, the Railways and the Modernization of Britain: Beeching's Last Trains*. London: Gollancz, 2006.

Maughan, Tim. *Infinite Detail*. New York: Farrar, Straus and Giroux, 2019.

McFarlane, Anna. 'Coded Networks: Literature and the Information Technology Revolution'. In *British Literature in Transition 1980-2000: Accelerated Times*. Eileen Pollard and Berthold Schoene (eds). Cambridge: Cambridge University Press, 2019: 293–308.

McFarlane, Anna. 'Ectogenesis on the NHS: Reproduction and Privatization in Twenty-First-Century British Fiction'. In *Technologies of Feminist Speculative Fiction: Gender,*

Artificial Life, and the Politics of Reproduction. Sherryl Vint and Sümeyra Buran (eds). Palgrave Macmillan, 2022: 21–44.

Miéville, China. 'Skewing the Picture'. *Rejectamentalist Manifesto*, 3 May 2018: https://tentacular.tumblr.com/post/173542023303/skewing-the-picture (accessed 27 May 2023).

Priest, Christopher. *The Islanders.* London: Gollancz, 2011.

Roberts, Adam. *New Model Army.* London: Gollancz, 2010.

Siddique, Haroon and Clea Skopeliti. 'BLM protesters topple statue of Bristol slave trader Edward Colston'. *The Guardian*, 7 June 2020: https://www.theguardian.com/uk-news/2020/jun/07/blm-protesters-topple-statue-of-bristol-slave-trader-edward-colston (accessed 27 May 2023).

Walter, Damien, 'Diversity wins as the Sad Puppies lose at the Hugo awards', *The Guardian*, 24 August 2015: https://www.theguardian.com/books/booksblog/2015/aug/24/diversity-wins-as-the-sad-puppies-lose-at-the-hugo-awards (accessed 27 May 2023).

10

The Neo-mythological Novel: Re-writing the Epic in Contemporary British Fiction

Nick Bentley

Introduction

In 2018, Boris Johnson's position as a trustee of the charity 'Classics for All' was suspended due to his inflammatory remarks on the wearing of burqas by Muslim women (Adams 2018). While perhaps only one moment in Johnson's chequered career, this incident reveals something of the role classical studies has played in the culture wars raging in the first quarter of the twenty-first century. After attending Eton and studying Classics at Balliol College, Oxford, Johnson had been a champion of the classics, but his several references to ancient Greece and Rome can be aligned to his belief in the preservation of class hierarchies based on the limited access of a privileged few to such markers of cultural capital. As Charlotte Higgins has noted, Johnson's classical allusions are actually 'flicks of show-offery, projections of superiority, mere flourishes that remind us that geeky Greekery is part of brand Boris' (Higgins 2019: n.p.). Implicitly recognized in the name 'Classics for All', however, the aim of the charity is to broaden and democratize the subject and make it more accessible to a modern, mainstream audience, an ambition put in jeopardy by Johnson's divisive remarks.[1]

British literary fiction has not been blind to this contest over the cultural positioning of classical literature (and education). Indeed, a discernible trend is the rise of novels that take classical literature as the basis for contemporary rewrites. In particular, ancient Greek literature has provided a popular source for British novelists in works such as Pat Barker's *The Silence of the Girls* (2018) and *The Women of Troy* (2021), Natalie Haynes's *The Children of Jocasta* (2017) and *A Thousand Ships* (2019), Hannah Lynn's *Athena's Child* (2020), Daisy Johnson's *Everything Under* (2018) and Kamila Shamsie's *Home Fire* (2017), all of which have sought to re-examine classical Greek characters, narratives and themes from a modern perspective. This growth is in one respect a response to similar trends in international literature and culture, especially in north America, including Margaret Atwood's *The Penelopiad* (2005), Madeline Miller's *The Song of Achilles* (2012) and *Circe* (2018) and Daniel Mendelsohn's *Odyssey: A Father, a Son and an Epic* (2017). Allied to this is the prominence of popular culture figures who have brought classical literature to new audiences such as Stephen Fry in his series of books: *Mythos* (2017), *Heroes* (2019) and *Troy* (2020); stand-up comedian and author Natalie Haynes in her BBC Radio 4 Show, 'Natalie Haynes Stands Up for the Classics', and Mary Beard in TV documentary series such as 'Meet the Romans with Mary Beard'. It could also be said that the return to a mythical past can be seen as a driving force in other popular television fantasy series of the 2010s such as *A Game of Thrones* (2011–19), itself an adaptation of George R. R. Martin's *A Song of Fire and Ice* series (1996–2011), as well as other series during this period that specifically cite classical narratives such as *Atlantis* (2013–15); *Troy: Fall of a City* (2018); *Britannia* (2017–); *American Gods* (2017–21) and *Domina* (2021–2023).

Of course, classical allusion and intertextual references are nothing new: from Shakespeare's classical history plays to Joyce's *Ulysses* and the reliance on classical reference in much modernist poetry of the early twentieth century (Eliot, Pound, Aldington, H.D.). But there is something distinct about this most recent reconfiguration of contemporary fiction and classical literature. In this chapter, in what is the first sustained study of what I term the neo-mythological novel, I want to read this new category of contemporary fiction with respect to two main areas. First, as a development and combination of a series of other literary-critical trends in the longer contemporary period stretching back to (at least) the 1990s: the neo-Victorian and neo-historical novel; the concept of metamodernism; the focus on historiographic metafiction as a characteristic of postmodern literary practice; the popularity of magic realism; and the intersection of popular genres with so-called 'serious' literary fiction. Second, these novels consciously promote the use of epic and mythological sources as a way to engage with a number of contemporary social, cultural and political concerns of the last decade or so, namely feminist revisions of past classics in the wake of the #MeToo campaign; increased LGBTQ+ awareness and continued campaigns against homophobia as well as a cultural focus on transgender identities and experiences; the popularization of critical race theory in response to movements such as Black Lives Matter, the Windrush scandal, decolonizing the curriculum, and an increased awareness of black history (including British involvement in the transatlantic slave trade); and a renewed interest in working-class culture driven by increased inequalities due to a decade of austerity. These topics have direct relevance to the readings I make in this chapter of four novels that appeared within two years of each other in the latter half of the 2010s: Barker's *The Silence of the Girls* (2018), Haynes's *The Children of Jocasta* (2017), Shamsie's *Home Fire* (2017) and Johnson's *Everything Under* (2018). Before discussing them, however, I want to expand on some of the trends in literary and cultural studies informing the new genre.

One of the key categories of British fiction over the last forty years or so has been the neo-historical novel, itself a development of what Linda Hutcheon (1988) defines as 'historiographic metafiction', a body of writing that has formed distinct sub-categories such as the neo-Victorian, the neo-Georgian, the neo-Edwardian, and the neo-Tudor.[2] The neo-historical is difficult to pin down, but Elodie Rousselot (2014) defines it as a tension in the 'reimagining of the past', which 'on the one hand [...] strives for a high degree of historical accuracy, while on the other [...] is conscious of the limitations of that project. The mode of verisimilitude employed by the neo-historical novel therefore confirms its simultaneous attempt *and* refusal to render the past accurately' (4). Influenced by postmodern suspicions towards truth claims in traditional history writing, she stresses the temporal duality of the new form that is simultaneously aware of its duty to readdress the past while at same time recognizing the limitations of its own textuality. Similarly, Ann Heilmann and Mark Llewellyn (2010), in focusing on the specific category of the neo-Victorian novel, make the distinction that:

> whereas 'historical fiction' encompasses within its title a notion of the fictional imagination, neo-Victorianism is potentially able to be interpreted as offering a different sense of the historical imaginary, and one which can be seen not only as imitating or mimicking an earlier style or mode, but also as seeking to inherit its position and in some senses displace its precursor.
>
> Heilmann and Llewellyn 2010: 15

Rousselot and Heilmann and Llewellyn are keen to stress the potential of neo-Victorian fiction to interrogate the ideologies and structures of feeling of the Victorian period through the lens of contemporary ways of thinking and attitudes to whole series of cultural-political contexts, such as gender, class, race and sexuality. Nick Hubble (2015: 170–176), for example, in the 1990s volume of the Decades series, identifies the ways in which much neo-Victorian fiction of the 1990s was invested in interrogating Thatcherite rhetoric of championing the return of 'Victorian values'. One of the distinctions that all these critics draw attention to is the tension between neo-historical fiction's attempt to replicate the voice, tone, style and structures of feeling of the period in which the fiction is set and a self-conscious sensitivity to the cultural and ideological sensibilities of their moment of publication. It is in this context, that I want to argue the neo-mythological novel has a distinctive contribution to the genre. In many ways, the retellings of ancient Greek narratives represented in the novels discussed in this chapter correspond to the general approach in the neo-historical to readdress and revise the past. As we shall see, the novels discussed here all succeed in critiquing attitudes to marginalized identities in the most famous iterations of the classical myths they draw upon. In a formal sense, therefore, the neo-mythological novel can be seen as another subsection of the neo-historical. The difference, of course, is that the focus in the originating texts on myth rather than history represents a differing ontological position; whereas the neo-historical novel can claim a certain understanding of an actual set of events (however far postmodernism complicated the notion of any sense of authentic access to the 'material reality' of the past) there is no serious recourse to fact against which the neo-mythological can be judged. Indeed, the classical era has since the Renaissance been regarded as a touchstone for permanence and essentialism rather than for historical specificity. Greek drama, epic and poetry still carry a sense of capturing certain essences of humanity that transcend time. This aspect of their cultural reception is intriguing for a period in which, following the credit crunch, fears about the permanence of Western capitalism, and various profound political divisions (such as Brexit in the UK and the Trump presidency in the US) has seen uncertainty and precarity prosper. Indeed, in a contemporary moment when truth seems to be a precarious concept, perhaps there's solace to be found in revisiting older narratives that seem to carry with them some sense of permanence. For the generation on the other side of postmodernism, the mythological, somewhat paradoxically, seems to replace the historical as the repository for truths about the human condition.

However, what is also apparent in the contemporary novels discussed in this chapter is that they combine a fascination with the exalted essentialism of the mythical with the suspicious irreverence of the more mundane modes of realism and/or the comedic. An interesting thing happens when reading these contemporary adaptations of myth: the conventions of the realist novel begins to impinge on the claims to the transcendent made by the epic. Of particular interest are the moments when a destabilizing fracture occurs between the mythic certainties and the attempt to convey a narrative through recourse to verisimilitude with respect to motivation and character. At such moments, a textual fissure destabilizes the reader's position vis-à-vis the characters and events with which they are engaging. This is an ontological rupture: how can we trust these quotidian, reliable narrators when they too are subject to the divine intervention of the gods? Adapting Hutcheon, we can think of these novels as producing a form of 'mythographic metafiction', an attempt to portray a realistic (and modern) set of ethical positions in a form in which the realism is always under threat of slipping into the non-realism of the mythic and supernatural. Hutcheon (1988) describes historiographic metafiction as a form of writing that, 'refutes the natural or common-sense methods of distinguishing between historical fact and fiction [...] by questioning the ground of that claim in historiography and by asserting that both history and fiction are discourses, human constructs, signifying systems, and both derive their major claims to truth from that identity' (93). Mythological metafiction does something similar, but slightly different. It also gestures towards truth claims, but these claims are always couched in metaphoric, rather than literal notions of historical accuracy, thus destabilizing the reader's natural inclination to trust the events and characters to which they are introduced.

In this context, we can identify another cultural influence on the rise of the neo-mythological novel: the metamodern. Metamodernism emerged as a critical theory in the early years of the twenty-first century as a way of accounting for both the demise of postmodernism as a viable and still *avant garde* form of literary fiction, (paradoxically undermined by its popularity in the 1990s) and the subsequent need for a new generation of artists and novelists in the new millennium to move beyond a mode that was increasingly seen as passé.[3] For many theorists of the metamodern, however, this new form had not quite arrived. It is thus defined by Timotheus Vermeulen and Robin van den Akker (2010) as an early twenty-first-century trend in aesthetic practice that 'oscillates between a modern enthusiasm and a postmodern irony, between hope and melancholy, between naïveté and knowingness, empathy and apathy, unity and plurality, totality and fragmentation, purity and ambiguity. Indeed, by oscillating to and fro or back and forth, the metamodern negotiates between the modern and the postmodern' (5–6). In their formulation, the metamodern registers an attitudinal cultural and aesthetic shift that rejects the radical scepticism and irony of postmodernism while retaining some of its questioning attitudes to received discourses of power. In this formulation, the metamodern retains the power to distinguish between sincere and broadly accurate accounts of the past and the nihilistic excesses of an abandonment of all truth claims. This promise of a new sincerity is always under threat of buckling under poststructuralist textuality and the constructedness of all discourses, but it can carve out an authentic foothold in the movement between the sincere and the ironic: 'Metamodernism moves for the sake of moving, attempts in spite of its inevitable failure; it seeks forever for a truth that it never expects to find' (5). This power to oscillate between truth and scepticism is particularly conducive to the way in which myth operates in the neo-mythological novel in its ready acceptance of timeless, essential poetic truths revealed through a set of narratives and characters that also resonate in a realist frame. This looking backwards to myth in order to reveal truths in the present is also at play in David James and Urmila Seshagiri's (2014) identification of metamodernism as a discernible trend in contemporary fiction that circumvents postmodernism's scepticism through a return to modernist techniques associated with the early part of the twentieth century. As they argue 'Metamodernism's value [...] lies in the ambition that unifies its otherwise varied artistic and historical positions: to reassess and remobilize narratives of modernism' (89). This remobilization is registered in a focus on both the stylistic and historical concerns of modernism in that it offers: 'a critical practice balanced between an attention to the textures of narrative form and an alertness to the contingencies of historical reception'.[4] This is reminiscent of attitudes to the mythopoetic adopted in much modernist writing of the early twentieth century, for example, in Eliot's celebration of classical allusions as fragments 'shored against [the] ruins' of the fallen present, and Joyce's mock-heroic transubstantiation of the epic Odysseus myth to the quotidian streets of turn-of-the-century Dublin. One of the key features of modernist literary practice is the use of intertextual references to classical and mythical characters and narratives as a way to critique a debased modernity. The recent trend for the neo-mythological novel can then in some ways be seen as a subcategory of James and Seshagiri's neo-modernism. However, as we shall see in the discussion of the selected examples in this chapter, the neo-mythological novel is not interested in merely maintaining a reverence for the cultural capital of its classical intertexts or of holding up a classical golden age to a tawdry present. It is also keen to interrogate the ideological discourses embedded in those classical precursors.

Indeed, as suggested at the opening of this chapter, it is in the context of the culture wars of the 2010s that the neo-mythological novel is provided with some distinctive angles of intervention. All of the novels discussed in this chapter address, to differing degrees, aspects of identity politics that have been at the heart of these culture wars over the last decade or so. This is achieved through interrogation of and confrontation with the lived ideologies of characters as they bump up against prevailing power structures. Barker's and Haynes's novels, for example, offer feminist revisions of the classical paradigms established in Homer and Sophocles respectively. Barker's text is also interested in class formations, as is Johnson's *Everything Under*. Barker also examines LGBTQ+ relationships most prominently in the relationship between Achilles and Patroclus (perhaps taking the lead here from American author Madeline Miller in her *Song of Achilles*). Johnson explores transgender identities through figures associated with Tiresias and her configuration of the character most associated with Oedipus in her contemporary re-telling. Kamila Shamsie offers her retelling of the Antigone narrative through a concentration on race and ethnicity; areas which can also be identified in Barker's examination of slavery in an ancient Greek context. The novels' relationships to their respective mythical intertexts are, therefore, ideologically complex and rich. Clearly the authors are fascinated by the stories in the sources they refer to – Sophocles, Homer, Euripides – but they are also keen to challenge many of the ideological assumptions embedded in their narrative structures and themes. In many ways they adhere to another concept developed by Linda Hutcheon in respect to postmodern historiographic metafiction, that of the 'complicitous critique' in that they celebrate the forms, feel and mood of the classical intertexts, while simultaneously critiquing much of the content (Hutcheon, 1989). This is achieved by defamiliarizing the originating narratives and highlighting aspects of the texts the originals overlooked. For example, in *The Silence of the Girls*, the description of the violence presented in *The Iliad* as part of a heroic structure of feeling is defamiliarized through Barker's refraction through a contemporary feminist and class-based lens. This produces an interesting tension between being faithful to the original and wanting to convey a set of ideological considerations that are focused on our own times and therefore speak to contemporary inequalities of gender, class, race and sexuality.

Pat Barker, *The Silence of the Girls* (2018)

Pat Barker's 2018 novel, *The Silence of the Girls*, revisits some of the events contained in Homer's *Iliad* with particular attention to Achilles' feud with Agamemnon. It does so, however, by focalizing through a character that is barely mentioned in Homer's text, Briseis, the queen of Lyrnessus, who becomes Achilles' 'prize' when the Greeks sack her city. Although central to the plot, Briseis is primarily a silent figure in Homer, operating merely as a token in the homosocial rivalry between the two Greek warriors. Through the reclamation of this lost female figure, the novel aims to challenge the concept of the heroic as presented in the original. As Catherine Lanone (2020) has noted, 'Rather than romance, Barker is interested in the politics of power' (n.p.). This is a formal shift as well as one of content. As part of the examination of the patriarchal and homosocial frameworks of power, Barker replaces the epic with a contemporary realism in her vivid descriptions of the horror and violence of war especially as it is visited on women.

The opening of the novel clearly sets out Barker's aim to shift the modes: 'Great Achilles. Brilliant Achilles, shining Achilles, godlike Achilles ... How the epithets pile up. We never called him any of those things; we called him "the butcher"' (2019 [2018]: 3). Much of the novel is told through Briseis' first-person narrative, which acts as a counter-narrative to the official mythologizing of Homer. One scene exemplifies this shift in mode well: Book 9 of *The Iliad* includes a description of Achilles 'giving pleasure to his heart with a clear-voiced lyre [...] singing tales of men's glory. Patroklus alone sat opposite him in silence' (Homer 1987: 137).[5] In Barker's version, Briseis and Iphis (Patroclus' wife) are audience to Achilles' performance and occasionally contribute to the conversation (2019: 55–57). Achilles' songs, which 'were all about deathless glory, heroes dying on the battlefield or (rather less often) returning home in triumph' and are 'stirring tales of courage and adventure' (56) are specifically gendered; as Briseis notes, she remembers many of them from her childhood, but 'the songs belonged to my brothers' (57). Later, Alcimus and Automedon play songs to Achilles during a drinking party which are all 'about battles, about the exploits of great men. These were the songs Achilles loved, the songs that had made him' (296). These songs are designed to romanticize war and to carry to future generations the codes of masculinity embedded in heroic deeds. While listening to them, Briseis reflects: '*We're going to survive* – our *songs*, our *stories. They'll never be able to forget us.*' (296, italics in the original). It would seem, therefore, it is the very power the songs have to convey the heroism of war that allow them to transcend their historical moment.

However, Briseis' narrative is invested in trying to undermine that power. Towards the end of the text, she writes, '*We need a new song.*' (314, italics in the original). This sense of newness is about form as much as content, and Briseis' narrative is presented in a form of realism that attempts to wrest control over the narrative away from the (masculine) epic tradition. The possibility of achieving a mark of relative freedom within the narrative, however, is fraught and Briseis seems to admit defeat towards the end of the novel: 'Looking back, it seemed to me I'd been trying to escape not just from the camp, but from Achilles' story; and I'd failed. Because make no mistake, this was his story – *his* anger, *his* grief, *his* story' (297). Achilles' narrative proves to be difficult to resist, but it is significant that Briseis survives, while Achilles does not. As Lanone argues, 'Briseis becomes the voice of communal memory, retrieving the tales of silenced women, both famous and forgotten ones' (2020: n.p.). It is in this textual freedom that Briseis' narrative stands as testimony against the raw patriarchal power of the epic precursor.

Barker's narrative, then, although ostensibly *about* Achilles, serves to deconstruct the image of the nobility and honour of war on which his reputation is built. She does this by bearing testimony to the physical (and, in particular, sexual) violence on which this 'heroic' narrative is dependent. Briseis' role is to de-romanticize the narratives by providing a realist counter-narrative to the mythologizing aspects of Achilles' songs and stories. As Emilie Walezak (2021) has noted, the modes of epic and realism are broadly divided between the passages that describe Achilles and Briseis' first-person narrative respectively. There is, however, slippage between these two modes, especially in the later sections of the novel when the balance between the everyday and the supernatural moves Barker to a contemporary form that her previous novels have rarely approached, that of magic realism.[6] After the realistic frame has been firmly established through Briseis' account, the existential frame shifts when Achilles' mother, the goddess Thetis, returns to soothe the guilt-stricken Achilles after the death of his lover Patroclus. This point occurs around two-thirds into the text and is presented through a third-person narration focalized through Achilles, in a break from the first-person account of Briseis. This intrusion of the supernatural into what the reader has come to accept as a predominantly (secular) realist mode captures the sense of wonder at the appearance of the mythopoetic into the quotidian lives of the soldiers:

> What do they [the Greeks] see? A tall man standing on a parapet with the golden light of early evening catching his hair? No, of course they don't. They see the goddess Athena wrap her glittering aegis round his shoulders; they see flames thirty feet high springing from the top of his head. What the Trojans saw isn't recorded. The defeated go down in history and disappear, and their stories die with them.
>
> Barker 2019: 206

Often the descriptions of the supernatural are left ambiguous; for example, when Achilles encounters Patroclus' ghost, it is left unclear whether this is a real intrusion into the ontological frame of the narrative, or a projection of Achilles' guilty imagination. There are moments, however, when Briseis' realism corroborates the existence of the divine in what we might think of as the material or lived experience of all the characters in the novel, for example, in the sections that describe Briseis preparing Hector's body after he has been killed by Achilles, where she too accepts the effects of the supernatural. The repeated renewal of Hector's body after each occurrence of the severe damage inflicted upon it by Achilles sets out the magic realist parameters of the text. As Briseis notes, 'I was still finding it difficult to believe in the miraculous preservation of Hector's body' (271). This cognitive dissonance is caused by the tension between the narrative modes of realism and the epic, a tension that lies at the heart of the text's exploration of the relationship between modernity and the ancients.

A key theme in the novel that also foregrounds the tension between the realistic and the epic is Barker's de-mythologizing of the romance of war. One of her approaches in this context is to show how violence is normalized during war, and how barbaric behaviour is incorporated into the everyday lived realities of those caught up in it. This can be seen in the several matter-of-fact descriptions of violence, such as when Briseis summarizes a recent campaign by the Greeks: 'Another successful raid, another city destroyed, men and boys killed, women and girls enslaved – all in all, a good day' (26–27). Or when on her first night in captivity, Briseis comments, 'He fucked as quickly as he killed, and for me it was the same thing' (28). Achilles is particularly immersed in this lived ideology of nonchalant violence; as Odysseus tells Achilles when trying to coax him back to the battlefield, 'Fighting. You know you can't get enough of it. It's who you are' (155). Lanone has argued that in this aspect of the novel, Barker draws parallels between the fighting in *The Silence of the Girls* with her depiction of the First World War in her earlier Regeneration Trilogy (1991–1995). During the height of battle, Briseis engages in helping the wounded in scenes that are certainly redolent of her descriptions of the First World War in her earlier work. In this section of *The Silence of the Girls*, the heroism and valour of war is undercut by references to its horror and brutality registered in the field hospitals where 'there was a constant buzzing of bluebottles [...] and shouts and screams from some of the patients' and where 'more men died of infection [...] than from loss of blood' (138). The context of war, here, is framed with respect to an essentialist recognition of the perpetual power dynamics in terms of age, youth and patriarchy; as Breisis notes: 'so many of these men were very young, some of them hardly more than boys – and for every one who was gung-ho and desperate to fight there was another who didn't want to be there at all' (139). Later in the text Achilles meets Lycaon, Priam's son, in an encounter that references Wilfred Owen's 'Strange Meeting': 'one springs up and stares with piteous recognition in fixed eyes [...] *Friend*, it says' (243).⁷ The novel also registers modern attitudes amongst the rank and file of soldiers to the wars; as one of the wounded notes 'How many generals do you see here? [...] *No*, they're all too bloody busy leading from the rear' (141). As well as linking between the Trojan Wars and the First World War, the neo-mythological frames of the text also gesture towards the contemporary moment, and discussion of the non-heroic realities of war must be taken in the context of the 2010s, especially as more and more (filmic and textual) accounts of the experiences of the wars in Afghanistan and Iraq began to circulate in the Western cultural consciousness.⁸

One of the other ways the novel undermines the epic is in reading the experience of war against modern medical and psychological knowledge about trauma. There are two specific examples in the novel of characters suffering from what contemporary psychiatrists would identify as Post-Traumatic Stress Disorder, the first after Briseis and the other women are subjected to watching their family members being killed before being enslaved by Agamemnon's forces; the second, in the description of Achilles' response to watching the death of his lover Patroclus. Indeed, much of the first sections of the novel are taken up describing Briseis' experiences of her city being sacked by the Achaeans, including witnessing her fourteen-year-old brother being killed by Achilles. In the period after this, she is presented as suffering from psychological symptoms associated with PTSD including depression, 'to my exhausted mind everything sounded like a battle, just as there was no colour in the world but red' (30); and nightmares, 'Again and again, behind my closed lids, I watched my youngest brother die' (31). Reminiscent of Cathy Caruth's identification of the way trauma is intimately related to memory and repetition, Briseis suffers from flashbacks and a disorientation of time. Caruth (1996) argues that the 'double wound' in trauma narratives of the initial experience and its repetition disrupts a forward trajectory and locks sufferers into an endless cycle. As she writes: 'At the core of these [trauma] stories [...] is thus a kind of double telling, the oscillation between a *crisis of death* and the correlative *crisis of life*: between the story of the unbearable nature of an event and the story of the unbearable nature of its survival' (7). This chimes with aspects of Briseis' experience; in the immediate days after the violent attack on her city, she notes, 'Time played curious tricks too; expanding, contracting, burrowing back into itself in the form of memories more vivid than daily life' (37), and she laments, 'I wish I could forget it, but I can't' (14). However, Caruth's model only takes us part way into the representation of trauma in Barker's novel. Caruth's understanding of trauma fixates on the difficulty for the sufferer in moving beyond the traumatic experience because of its repetition. For Briseis, however, memory can also provide a point of escape. For example, at the moment of her capture she forces her mind back to times in her 'favourite place', an inner courtyard in the palace where 'the sounds of lyres and flutes would drift out on the night air and all the cares of the day would fall away' (21). Ultimately, her memories are used by Briseis to fuel her desire for testimony and resistance; in relation to her brothers she notes, 'As long as I lived and remembered, they weren't entirely dead' (41). The mental resistance to the male violence perpetrated on her is thus a key feature of the novel's feminist revisioning of power and a resistance to the debilitating power of trauma to return the sufferer to the position of victim.

Briseis' narrative can, therefore, be read as a point of resistance against the heroic narrative. Briseis becomes the chronicler of this resistance, formed through her solidarity with her fellow sufferers. When first captured she notes, 'I felt responsible for every woman and child in that room, not to mention the slaves crammed together in the basement' (12). Later, when Chryseis is about to be returned to her father she notes, 'Gazing around, I was filled with warmth – with love, in fact – for all these women who had come to see her off' (104). This solidarity includes everyday acts of resistance and Carnivalesque humour, for example, in the bawdy discussions the women have about sex. As she notes, 'It seems incredible to me now, looking back, that we laughed' (49) when, for example, discussing Agamemnon's preference for the 'back door'; and when the women mock Myron's dead body by waggling his 'poor limp penis [...] at the rest of us' causing the slave women to 'hoot with laughter' (87). Later, in response to Tecmessa's ironic reference to the stock phrase 'Silence becomes a woman', she and Briseis suddenly 'burst out laughing, both of us together – not just laughing either, whooping, screeching, gasping for breath, until finally, the men turned to stare at us and Tecmessa stuffed the hem of her tunic into her mouth to gag herself. The laughter ended as abruptly as it had begun [...] we were back to our normal selves' (294). This moment of shared, Carnivalesque resistance to the patriarchy, ineffectual of itself, serves to cement a solidarity between the powerless and exploited women. This can again be approached in terms of literary modes where the epic masculine narration is undercut by the comic mode. This realist aspect of the novel connects to a modern audience in a way the epic model is unable to do and also cements Briseis' narrative as testimony to the experiences of the marginalized and unrepresented (mortal) women silenced in Homer's text. As Briseis notes, 'I met a lot of the women, many of them common women whose names you won't have heard' (217). Briseis' narrative steps out of time, here, a feature of much neo-historical fiction. The 'you' she addresses is the 'you' of modernity, a reader placed after the events, and in its slippage of time, presumably a contemporary audience that, like Walter Benjamin's angel of history, is able to take the long view backwards.

Natalie Haynes, *The Children of Jocasta* (2017)

Intrusion into the epic mode by realism and comedy as part of a feminist revisionism is also at play in Natalie Haynes's work. Haynes's fiction is only one aspect of her career and she became a public figure in the 2010s as a champion of the classics, a comedian and radio broadcaster alongside her work as a novelist. Her fiction, therefore, is part of a wider project to promote a love of the classics in a culture that often sees the academic discipline as a luxury enjoyed by a privileged few secreted away in their ivory towers. Indeed, her novels intervened in a public discourse on the place of classical studies in a twenty-first century British higher education system that has witnessed the subject's removal from many post-92 and plate-glass universities in the UK, leaving the discipline predominantly the reserve of the UK's G5 and Russell Group universities. Control over accessibility to the study of classical literature and culture can also be seen as part of a broader conservative agenda to maintain class hierarchies within British culture. Novels such as Haynes's *The Children of Jocasta* (2017) and *A Thousand Ships* (2019) are attempts, then, to resist this cultural narrative by combining classical literary references with popular fiction and addressing the seriousness of the epic with irreverence of realism and comedy.

One of the consequences of this aim is that Haynes's fiction can be accused of a certain amount of presentism in its attempt to identify (or construct) connections between the structures of feeling revealed in the classical texts and the emotional and intellectual responses from a contemporary audience. Much of Haynes's radio comedy show, *Natalie Haynes Stands Up for Classics*, relies on attempts to de-mythologize the classics with several jokes turning on the ludicrous presentation of women in classical texts observed from a contemporary audience grounded in an awareness of gender equality. *The Children of Jocasta* is an interesting example of this approach and in this section of the chapter I aim to show how the novel works hard to promote knowledge of classical stories to popular audiences by examining contemporary issues including, in particular, gender politics and the debates circulating around nationalism, and the Brexit crisis of the latter half of the 2010s.

Haynes's novel is divided between two storylines, a generation apart, which are alternated as the novel moves forward. The earlier (chronologically) takes

Sophocles' *Oedipus Tyrannus* as its intertext and describes Jocasta's narrative from being first married to Laius, losing her first born son, and then, after Laius' death, her relationship with Oedipus, who, of course is ultimately revealed to be her lost child. This narrative is told in the third person, but primarily focalized through Jocasta. The second narrative is the first-person account of one of Jocasta's daughters, Ismene, and broadly follows the events in Sophocles' *Antigone* charting the feud between Jocasta's two sons with Oedipus, Polyneices and Eteocles, their deaths and the subsequent conflict between Antigone and Creon the siblings' uncle (and Jocasta's brother). In both narratives, Haynes is keen to tell the well-known stories from the perspective of characters who are only given minor parts in Sophocles' original plays by giving centre stage to Ismene and Jocasta.

Ismene is described in terms that resonate with contemporary sensibilities: she has a desire to learn and to have access to levels of education usually associated with men only in the classical sources. Ismene tells us that she has a tutor Sophon (whom Haynes explains in an afterword to the novel is a modern addition) and that she likes to find the 'perfect place to read [...] the parchment roll I had taken from my tutor's office' (2018 [2017]: 6). Similarly, Jocasta is given a modern rationality that cuts through the belief in superstition that pervades the classical texts. This can be seen, for example, when she says of her husband Laius after his death, 'It can't make the slightest difference to him now, whether he travels in state or not'. This modern attitude to the departed stands in stark contrast to Antigone's outrage that Eteocles's body is left on the battlefield. This is not just a matter of distinction between character, it is a marker of the text's ability to combine responses to the structures of feeling from two distinct times and cultures.

It is in the context of this historical slippage that the novel's feminist revisionism resides. The text encourages the reader to reflect on the gendered power frameworks embedded in Sophocles, and presumably in the culture from which he emerges, from the perspective of an audience au fait with twenty-first-century feminism. Jocasta is thus outraged by the fact that her father has arranged her marriage to an old man without consulting her in ways that it would be difficult to corroborate from the evidence we have of texts from the period. Jocasta is not told how her marriage was arranged but suspects it was by 'a group of men in a room lit by smoky candles, drawing lots to decide whose daughter would be elevated to royalty' (2018: 13). This image of patriarchy in action is supported by the ideological apparatus that cements power in the form of religious discourse as she is, 'pledged by her father to a man she had never met, before the eyes of a goddess who had ignored her prayers' (13). Indeed, Jocasta is given a healthy modern scepticism towards the place of religion and superstition in supporting the frameworks of patriarchal power; when presented with the prophecy of the Oracle about her son, she questions it on rational grounds: 'if the Oracle was all knowing, it should really have predicted her dramatic change in circumstances [...] she knew that oracles were riddlers, only to be understood by those versed in their opacity, like the priests' (133).[9] As with Barker's *The Silence of the Girls*, there is some slippage here between the modes of a rational realism and the mythological structures of feeling of the classical intertext. It is that she is reluctant (rightly so to a modern secular eye) to believe the Oracle's prophecy that leaves her open to the inevitable trajectory of her tragic narrative.

It is, however, her daughter Ismene who has more agency over the way her story is told establishing her resistance to the absolute patriarchal power to which she is subjected. As she explains to her tutor, Sophon, 'I want to keep a record [...] Of what's happening. When we talked before about history, you said I must always bear in mind who composes it' [...] So I should compose my own history, shouldn't I? Or it will be lost forever' (73–74). Ismene's role in the narrative is in part to become 'a historian, an astute chronicler of events' (215). It is in this context that Haynes decides to jettison the Sophocles narrative at the end of the text by having Antigone survive Creon and become queen of Thebes, and by portraying Jocasta's suicide as an a act of bravery in order to save her family from the plague she realizes she has contracted rather than from the shame of discovering the secret of her incestual relationship with Oedipus. In this way, Haynes's narrative circumvents the tragic mode of Sophocles' version and by analogy shows the strong female characters evading the patriarchal structures imposed upon them. Comedy overcomes tragedy in this retelling, allowing positive futures for Antigone and Ismene and a resistance to the silence they inhabit in Sophocles' text.[10]

Alongside the feminist revision, *The Children of Jocasta* also obliquely comments on the rhetoric of nationhood and isolation at the forefront of public discourse due to the Brexit vote and subsequent crises in play during the period in which the novel was written and published. Haynes develops this contemporary counter-narrative through the theme of plague and how the city has to close its gates and disallow free movement. The return of the 'Reckoning', as the plague is called, makes people nervous of outsiders: 'Thebans wondered if they had made a mistake all those years ago, when they unlocked their gates after closing the city against the first plague to ravage their world' (239). This narrative of isolationism and fear of the outsider echoes rhetoric supporting the Brexit campaign, as does the focus on market forces (cheap labour) as the cause of immigration. Oedipus, as an outsider from Corinth, is identified as a reason for the decline in the health of the body politic of Thebes: 'He had changed Thebes from fortress to market' (240). This parallel between contemporary contexts and classical references is also echoed in the place of populism in the text. Brexit rhetoric in the latter half of the 2010s was often accused of a politics of populism and the response of the Theban crowd to the political speeches of its rulers in Haynes's novel is reminiscent of this kind of appeal to the mob. The novel also offers an implicit reference to the fact that Brexit had still not been implemented (or fully rejected) at the time the novel was published as suggested in the fact that 'Thebes never did reopen her gates, after two summers of the Reckoning' (323). This aspect of Haynes's narrative is part of her wider strategy to reclaim classical literature for twenty-first-century audiences by making associations to contemporary anxieties and concerns, and in doing so she is sensitive to the contexts against which the classics, like her Antigone, can be resurrected.

Kamila Shamsie, *Home Fire* (2017)

Like Haynes, Kamila Shamsie is keen to revisit the Antigone myth from a contemporary perspective. Indeed, given its focus on the tension between state power and divine justice, *Antigone* is a text that readily transfers to different political situations. In Jean Anouilh's adaptation of the play, first performed in Paris in 1944, there are clear references in its questioning of state authority to the occupying Nazi government as well as to the active resistance movement in France. Similarly, Athol Fugard, Jonn Kani and Winston Ntshona's *The Island*, set in the Maximum Security Prison on Robben Island used for political prisoners during the height of the Apartheid laws in South Africa, helped to promote (especially to an international audience) the injustices of the Apartheid system. The drama focuses on the staging of Antigone in the prison and uses the play within the play to champion moral right above the unjust laws of the state. After its premier in The Space, a theatre in the black townships of Cape Town, it travelled to London and New York and was particularly important in galvanizing international objection to the South African government in the call for the implementation of sanctions.

Kamila Shamsie, in her 2017 novel, *Home Fire* also uses the plotline and characterization of Sophocles' play to explore power relationships associated with race and ethnicity and in particular the ways in which British Muslims are represented in political discourse and the media in the period after 9/11, the War on Terror, and the rise of ISIS. As Ankhi Mukherjee argues, the novel foregrounds 'questions of citizenship, colonialism, and race, in particular in the insider-outsider, civilized-barbaric dichotomies determining paradigms of humanity and modernity in global cities today' (2021: 219). *Home Fire* presents its pressing political concerns through a narrative of family relationships in a way that strikes a balance with *Antigone*'s exploration of the personal with the political and philosophical. In five sections, each told from the perspective of the five main characters, it tells the story of Parvaiz who travels from Britain to Syria to join ISIS, and, after he is killed when trying to leave the group, his sister Aneeka's (the novel's modern equivalent to Antigone) campaign to have her brother's body brought back to Britain. It also gives narrative sections to Aneeka's sister, Isma who has a central role in the affair, Karamat Lone, the newly appointed British Home Secretary (the equivalent of Creon in Sophocles' play), and his son Eamonn (Haemon) who develops a sexual relationship with Aneeka. Through the use of these different (and competing) perspectives the novel draws attention to its mode of telling and thus, as perhaps befitting a 2010s adaptation, offers a metafictional re-engagement with the play's central themes. Shamsie's novel is particularly interested in examining the way in which cultural, political, racial and religious identity is constructed and performed through contemporary media platforms, a theme enhanced by the novel's formal structure.

Although the characters in *Home Fire* can be broadly mapped across to Sophocles' play, there are distinctions; for example, Shamsie's text devotes sections to the characters who parallel Polyneices (Parvaiz) and to Ismene (Isma), both of whom only have minor roles in *Antigone*. True to Sophocles' play, however, Shamsie is keen to emphasize the ambiguous characterization of the Antigone figure and her challenge to state power. The novel opens with a clear distinction in character between the passionate Aneeka and her older sister, the more measured Isma, with Aneeka described as someone who 'knew everything about her rights and nothing about the fragility of her place in the world' (2018 [2017], 6). The 'place' referred to involves Aneeka and Isma's double-marginalization, to use Gayatri Spivak's (1988) concept, as Muslim women brought up in Britain and anticipates Aneeka's resistance to that unjust positioning in contrast to Isma's reluctant acceptance. Indeed, one of the key themes in the novel is the differing attitudes taken by each of the central characters to the ways in which Muslim people face prejudice in twenty-first-century Britain. Focalizing the five sections though each character allows the presentation of the self-justification of each to the ways in which they navigate the social, political and cultural othering of the dominant media representations of Muslims in contemporary Britain. Aneeka's contradictory nature, in particular, is foregrounded; she is 'sharp-tongued and considerate, serious-minded and capable of unbridled goofiness' (23) and it is this mixture of commitment and naivety that is revealed in her display of resistance to the authorities based on her belief in a sense of higher moral right above the laws of state. The novel opens with the two sisters rehearsing imagined encounters with state authorities and it is clear that whereas Isma is willing to comply, Aneeka stresses her desire to show 'at least a tiny bit of contempt for the whole process' (6). It is this courage to stand up for what she thinks is right that eventually makes Aneeka a powerful advocate for the return of her brother's dead body to Britain. As she argues, it is 'because the nation to which they first belonged had proven itself inadequate to the task of allowing them to live with dignity' (215). Here she extends the justification from her personal situation to draw attention to the circumstances that have led to Parvaiz's decision to join ISIS.

In contrast to Aneeka and Parvaiz, Karamat Lone, (the UK Home Secretary) and his son Eamonn champion an integrationist approach to their experience of being a Muslim and living in Britain. Initially father and son are aligned in their attitudes to multiculturalism, summed up in Karamat's advice to British Muslims not to 'set yourselves apart in the way you dress, the way you think, the outdated codes of behaviour you cling to [...] Because if you do, you will be treated differently – not because of racism, although that does still exist, but because you insist on your difference to everyone else in this multi-ethnic, multi-religious, multitudinous United Kingdom of ours' (87–88). This advice is based on his belief in the possibility of advancement for someone of Muslim heritage in the United Kingdom, where he could imagine that 'the grandson of the colonised [could] take his place as Prime Minister' (214).[11] However, he is aware that in order to achieve such social mobility he has had to navigate the vicissitudes of the British press with respect to his Muslim identity and how that intersects with his national context. In one example, he describes how 'the tabloids that had previously attacked him' now rebrand him as 'a LONE CRUSADER taking on the backwardness of British Muslim' (35).

It is this integrationist position that has persuaded Eamonn to anglicize his name from Aymon, and to adopt a broadly apolitical nature, as seen when he first meets Isma in the US. Eamonn's position towards his father shifts, however, when the latter's policies come into direct conflict with Aneeka's desire to retrieve

Parvaiz's body. This element of the text parallels the speech in Sophocles' play in which Haemon attempts to temper Creon's decision to punish Antigone's transgression of the edict not to bury the body of Polyneices. Haemon argues, 'No, it's no disgrace for a man, to learn many things and not be too rigid' (Sophocles 1984: 96). This attempt to appeal to a leader's power to revoke a harsh decision is transfigured in Eamonn's meeting with Karamat, during which he also appeals to his father's desire to be seen to do the right thing; as the son argues, 'A government that sends its citizens to some other country when they act in ways we don't like. Doesn't that say we can't deal with our own problems?' (217–218). It is interesting in the context of the mid-2010s that this is the very argument that was brought into play in the campaign to allow Shamima Begum, a British Muslim teenager to return to Britain, when she and two friends from the same school in West London went to Syria to join ISIS in 2015. As Urszula Rutkowska (2022: 872) has noted, the affair bears an 'uncanny resemblance' to events in Shamsie's novel. Indeed, *Home Fire* entered a live public debate with Shamsie explaining in interview that: 'I wanted to connect it to a story that was very much in the news at the time, that of young British Muslims and their relationship with the British state' (Heriyanto 2018: n.p.). The Shamima Begum incident was at the forefront of this media furore and Shamsie seems to combine the British teenager's experience across the characters of Parvaiz and Aneeka. Parvaiz is shown to have been attracted to the propaganda that was attempting to draw British youth to ISIS. Shamsie's novel is, indeed, invested in portraying the appeal of ISIS in Britain during the period as a kind of subculture aimed at youth. Claire Chambers (2018) has picked up on this aspect of Shamsie's novel and, following work by Marc Sageman (2004), identifies the way in which group dynamics can be a strong driver towards radicalization. Parvaiz decides to leave Britain because he is groomed by Farooq, an older agent of ISIS working to recruit people form the UK, whose 'faux-Arabised accent of a non-Arab Muslim' provides 'an instant glamour' (123). Farooq appears at just the moment when Parvaiz is coming to terms with his own identity as the son of a jihadi terrorist who has been killed in Bagram and the identification of his father as either a courageous freedom fighter or national traitor. Farooq utilizes Parvaiz's identity crisis and combines it with propaganda about the promised land of the ISIS Caliphate being built in Syria, 'A place where migrants coming to join are treated like kings [...] Where schools and hospitals are free, and rich and poor have the same facilities. Where men are men' (144). This appealing narrative is a powerful antidote to the mainstream media presentation of British Muslims as disruptive to the sense of the nation. The presence of competing narratives fought out in individual responses to lived experience is a key theme of the novel and this is presented especially in Aneeka's section which is formally fractured into different kinds of texts including TV, radio and newspaper reports (201), and Tweets (190). As Chambers notes, '*Home Fire* is deeply concerned with texts: sacred texts and secular, texting, online texts and the various typographies of texts' (Chambers 2018: 202). This attention to the forms and (platforms) in which information is circulated foregrounds the mediatized context of the debates over identity. It is significant, in this context, that Aneeka also uses the media to communicate her sense of injustice. When Parvaiz is eventually taken to Pakistan, she choreographs a scene in which his dead body is laid in a public park during a high wind which swirls rose petals and leaves around it, causing her to cry with 'a howl that came out of the earth and through her and into the office of the Home Secretary' (224). This Debordian political spectacle is specifically framed through the context of visual media as 'The cameras panned, then zoomed'. Karamat's one word response – 'Impressive' – shows that he appreciates the powerful symbolism and the manipulation of the mediated public discourse that this scene effects more than any recognition of her genuine pain. The use of modern technology to enhance her claim that 'All these things happen according to the law, but not according to justice' neatly contemporizes Antigone's address to the polis in Sophocles as a cry to a higher level of justice than Creon's manmade power.

The novel, then, is precisely neo-mythological in its combination of using an established 'classic' narrative to explore contemporary political contexts and ethical dilemmas. Its foregrounding of the narrative structures and techniques against which the political debates are framed supply a metafictional aspect to the narrative that draws attention to the ways in which identities are performed and contained within already prescribed parameters that people must negotiate in order to claim some degree of individual agency. One of the key themes of the retellings of the *Iliad*, *Oedipus* and *Antigone* we have discussed so far is the tension between free will and determinism framed through the imposition of a prophecy or an unavoidable outcome. This is a tension related to mode as much as a genuine set of choices individual characters might take. In the original, characters are locked into the rigid trajectories of the epic and tragic modes. However, the neo-mythological rewriting of the myths juxtaposes this trajectory with a modern realism in which characters' lived experiences offer the possibility of evading or escaping those determined outcomes. This thematic and modal tension is also at the heart of Daisy Johnson's 2018 novel, *Everything Under*.

Daisy Johnson, *Everything Under* (2018)

Daisy Johnson's innovative and intriguing *Everything Under* captures the mood of the Oedipus myth, but the correlation of its characters to the figures in the epic tale is at first difficult to identify. Like *Home Fire*, *Everything Under* transfers its classical intertext – *Oedipus Tyrannus* – to a contemporary setting and, in a complicated set of non-linear narratives, tells the stories of Sarah (the character associated with Sophocles' Jocasta) and her daughter Gretel (Antigone); Margot/Marcus (Oedipus) who comes to live with Sarah and Gretel on their riverboat; Roger (Polybus) and Chloe (Merope) who have brought up Margot, and a number of other important characters in the Oedipus narrative such as Charlie (Laius) and Fiona (Tiresias). In this section, I will argue that the novel picks up from its classical intertext the relationship of free will and determinism, the importance of riddles and the inscrutability of language, and, in a Lacanian sense, language's fundamental importance to an individual's psychosexual development.

The main settings for the events are on (or near to) secluded waterways, which places the characters outside of mainstream society in evoking the experiences of marginalized people in a contemporary setting. We are told, for example, that 'River people aren't like other people. You won't see the police down here. You won't see child services or priests' (2019 [2018]: 165), and as Sarah and Gretel explain to Margot, 'We don't call the police here. We don't call the fire engines or the ambulances. It's always been that way' (2019: 194). This secluded setting contributes to the hidden and mysterious nature of the plot and like the Oedipus narrative, it has, at its heart, a riddle that needs to be solved. This riddle is primarily linguistic, and the ambivalent power of language to both reveal and conceal meaning is indeed one of the main themes of Johnson's novel. Sarah and Gretel develop their own private language system which has the positive effect of cementing their close connection, but also locks them into a personal relationship that isolates them from others. We are told, for example, that 'They had cut themselves off from the world linguistically as well as physically' (190) and occasionally that they are 'undone' by their shared vocabulary (6). That Gretel has become a lexicographer in her adult life also stresses the intimate connection between her sense of self and the language games that form her identity. As she explains to her mother, 'If – in any sense – language determined how we thought then I could never have been any other way than the way I am [...] It was in my language. It was in the language you gave me' (136). For Gretel, language determines thought and consequently it also determines fate.

It is significant, therefore, that when Gretel rediscovers her mother after a number of years apart, Sarah is suffering from Alzheimer's disease and language and meaning have become volatile and precarious. As Gretel explains in her second-person address to her mother, 'For you memory is not a line but a series of baffling circles' (5). This is echoed in Charlie's belief that, 'life is a sort of spinning thing. Like a planet or moon going round a planet' (81), which connects thematically to the difficulties Gretel has in unravelling the mystery that surrounds her mother's past. As we are also told 'There is degeneration at work', a term that connects the sense of breaking down with the idea of heredity in the form of the convoluted generational relationships between the characters. Degeneration also refers to the way that meaning is becoming precarious and that connections need to be deciphered like the riddles. In this sense, Gretel and Sarah are compelled to 'endlessly, excavate, exhume what should remain buried' (6). The riddle that is set up at the beginning of the novel is how does Sarah's story connect Gretel's father, Marcus/Margot and Gretel herself; a story that will include 'some lies, some fabrications' (9).

As with the novels we have looked at so far in this chapter, *Everything Under* is also interested in the play between differing modes, in particular the realist frame of the scenes and interactions between characters, and the non-realist (or magic realist) incorporation of the supernatural. Gretel, herself, is imbued with something of a mythical quality; we are told that, as a child, she has in her notebook, 'Next to the riddles [...] strange, spindled drawings of misshapen creatures with the head of one animal and the body of another' (141). These drawings of uncanny creatures are projections of Gretel's otherness, her non-human characteristics, which, like her mother, configure her as a partly mythic figure; when Marcus first encounters her, for example, she was 'covered in a thin film of dirt, as if she'd been dug out of the earth' (114). Gretel, and indeed all the characters seem to hover between a material (realist) existence and supernatural symbolism. The supernatural, however, is registered most obviously in the figure of the Bonak, a creature that stalks the characters at different moments in the narrative. The Bonak is described variously, often in terms of its smell or its 'slow, almost-bovine digestion' (23). Its materiality is fluid and ephemeral; Gretel describes how it can take the form of 'anything' and explains, 'Last summer it was this stupid dog that was so hungry [...] but ages ago it was a storm that nearly wrecked the boat and another time it was a fire that burned a lot of the forest and that we thought would burn us too' (148). From this description, it is evident that the Bonak does not have an ontological existence but is projected by Sarah and Gretel onto external events and situations that induce fear. Later she describes how it 'runs on self-imposed paranoia' (164) and that 'It meant a lot of different things over the years but it was always whatever we were afraid of' (168). At one point it is also described as 'prehistoric, cragged, dappled gold' with a 'long thoughtless face' (132). Its monstrous qualities are combined here with its timelessness, or specifically its pre-historic nature, in that it precedes human writing. The mythic qualities of the Bonak, then, also reflect something of the pre-verbal, which is consequently allied to a psychoanalytical significance. The Bonak represents something deep in the earliest memories of the individual, in what Lacan (1977) would identify as the imaginary or pre-mirror stage; the period before the child enters the symbolic realm of language and social interaction, breaking the primary relationship of child and mother. The Bonak combines something of this Lacanian lack with an embodiment of the deep sense of fear and guilt that is generated by the incest myth at the heart of both the classical tale and Johnson's retelling. This combination of psychosexual fear and the return of the repressed is combined in Gretel's final encounter with the monster in which it and Sarah seem to become the same entity. The locus of the fear, or what Lacan (1992) terms the unknowable 'Thing' of the unconscious, is thus located specifically for Gretel in her mother's body. The only way that it can be defeated is through knowledge about it (or rather knowledge over it); by drawing it out of the emptiness of the semiotic and into the systems of the Symbolic. The Bonak is (almost) destroyed through ingestion, a process that draws it inside the body and thus contains it; Gretel and Sarah 'took turns holding each of the organs, weighing them with the same kind of wonder with which we used to read the encyclopaedia' (250). To be eaten, of course, it has to have a physical substance but this passage gestures to the fact the constitution of Bonak, its very materiality, is indeed located in language. It is conceived as a master signifier that needs to be controlled both through the intellect and through the physical and the final act of feasting on its organs, which represents the same wallowing in the private language that the mother and daughter have shared. Gretel's conclusion on the nature of the trauma is specifically centred in language: 'Again and again I go back to the idea that our thoughts and actions are determined by the language that lives in our minds' (256). Language here is given an ontological quality; although it is of the mind and the intellect, it nevertheless 'lives', and has a corporeal status that is as fearsome as any objective reality. But in this sense it can never be defeated and continues to roam in the recesses of the mind; even after Gretel has rediscovered Sarah, the Bonak lurks, 'rattling through the rooms above our heads' (257). Given the Bonak's status as an internally created monster that is assumed to have external materiality, removing it similarly takes an act of will. However, the belief in the Bonak's demise is something that needs to be sustained and indeed, we are told that the monster returns to haunt Gretel after it has supposedly been killed off by Sarah.

This returns us to the point about language determining life, and, that if the belief is powerful enough, language can determine the actions of the characters. The prophecy that lies at the heart of the Oedipus myth, thus takes on an inevitability that is driven by the will but is no less determined in its material effects than a supernatural system imposing its already-written, fixed model of the future. Sarah tells Gretel (in reported speech) that 'there is no escaping, that the way we will end up is coded into us from the moment we are born and that any decisions we make are only mirages, ghosts to convince us of free will' (47). Gretel tries to resist this deterministic structure of feeling; however, the power of language overcomes her belief in the possibility of any free agency: 'I'd always felt that our lives could have gone in multiple directions, that the choices you made forced them into turning out the way they did. But maybe there were no choices; maybe there were no other possible outcomes' (76). The inevitable trajectory of the prophecy in Johnson's novel is not related to some fixed supernatural law, but to Gretel's inability to escape from the epic mode (where events are set in stone) into a modern realism, where actors have individual agency. As she concludes, 'Again and again I go back to the idea that our thoughts and actions are determined by the language that lives in our mind' (256). The inevitability of the end is also evident in Margot's unflinching belief in Fiona's prophecy that is both a predictor and cause of the tragedy. Of course, this is a novel that follows the classical intertext, so it inevitably drives towards Margot's killing of her father and sleeping with her mother. However, the tragic flaw that the novel inscribes is more related to Margot's inability to view the future as undetermined; for her, the prophecy is 'certain as iron, certain as the seasons, unbendable as stone' (174). The theme of prophecy offers a way, therefore, to compare determinism and free will. This opposition correlates in part to the distinction between the mythical (timeless) qualities of the Oedipus narrative and the sense of modernity that points to more individual agency. Where Barker and Haynes allow their heroines a modern (realist) escape from their epic narrative trajectories, Johnson's text draws them back into the inevitable void at the heart of the Oedipus myth; the blinded father and the hanged mother.

Conclusion

This chapter has examined a number of examples of what I have called the neo-mythological novel. After identifying similarities (as well as differences) between them we can thus define the genre as a category of neo-historical fiction that draws together cultural-political revisionism, historical metafiction, and magic realism honed with a metamodern sensibility that combines postmodern irony with a sincere (modernist) celebration of mythopoeia. Indeed, in such fiction classical myths occupy a particular cultural significance in the post-postmodern potentiality of an authentic belief in the possibility of reclaiming truths from the noise of contemporary multivocality and perspectivism. Unlike the major religions, whose truth claims have come under sustained scrutiny, classical myth, precisely because it is not taken seriously for its religious importance, paradoxically achieves a certain kind of cultural gravitas and probity. The fact that the contemporaries no longer believe the literal veracity of classical heroes and gods, means these stories are able to circumvent postmodern scepticism of claims to historical truth, which (perhaps ironically) allows them to carry privileged cultural weight based on their 'metaphoric' or 'essentialist' truths about the human condition. In this way, the suspicion towards fixed belief systems in the present creates nostalgia for past systems that still carry within them the potential for continuing certainties, a desire that might explain the recent popularity of the form. However, what we also see in the examples discussed in this chapter is that the truth claims embedded within the mythical imagination still carry ideological flaws and fissures that can be put under pressure in the name of drawing attention to the scaffolds on which their power hangs. The recent phenomenon of the neo-mythological novel could be seen as a recurring cultural phenomenon rather than historically specific to the early twenty-first century; however, as with all aspects of the neo-historical, the mode is always Janus-faced, looking back to the strangeness of our ancestors' beliefs in order to throw light on the strangeness of our own.

Notes

1 True to form, Johnson reached for a reference to Cincinnatus in his prime ministerial resignation speech in 2022, with the allusion that he would, like the Roman senator, return for a second term of office after a period of tending his farm. Such a reference implicitly embeds a hierarchical power relationship to those whose educational background might not readily recognize such allusions and it is not difficult to see how this rhetoric is revealing of deeper social divides and culture wars.

2 Critical works in this area (in addition to the ones discussed directly in this chapter) include Louisa Hadley, *The Neo-Victorian Fiction and Historical Narrative: The Victorians and Us*. Houndmills: Palgrave, 2010; Jakub Lipski and Joanna Maciulewicz

(eds). *Neo-Georgian Fiction: Reimagining the Eighteenth Century in the Contemporary Historical Novel*. New York: Routledge, 2021; and the essays included in *Exoticizing the Past in Contemporary Neo-Historical Fiction*, Elodie Rousselot (ed.). Basingstoke: Palgrave, 2014.

3   One of the ironies of this metamodern turn is that the very definitions of postmodernism were couched by Fredric Jameson (1991) in terms of the need for 1950s and 1960s cultural practitioners to distance them from their modernist progenitors of the early part of the century.

4   James and Seshagiri identify a number of twenty-first-century novels that include aspects of this return to modernism, including Julian Barnes's *The Sense of an Ending* (2011), J.M. Coetzee's *Youth* (2002), Tom McCarthy's *Remainder* (2006), Ian McEwan's *Atonement* (2001), Taiye Selasi's *Ghana Must Go* (2013), Zadie Smith's *NW* (2012) and Will Self's *Umbrella* (2012).

5   The Oxford edition of Homer cited here uses the spelling 'Patroklus'.

6   Most of Barker's previous novels deal in a grounded, working-class realism coming out of the 1950s Angry Young Man and kitchen sink narratives, for example, in her early novels, *Union Street* (1982), *Blow Your House Down* (1984) and *Liza's England* (1986).

7   Owen's poem has 'one sprang up, and stared/ With piteous recognition in fixed eyes,/ [...] "Strange friend", I said, "here is no cause to mourn"' (Owen 1988). Wilfred Own's convalescence under the care of the psychiatrist W. H. R. Rivers after suffering PTSD from his experience in the trenches in the First World War is one of the subjects of Barker's *Regeneration* trilogy of novels (1991–1995).

8   For example, Jon McGregor's novel *Even the Dogs* (2010) and acclaimed films such as *Hurt Locker* (Kathryn Bigelow, 2008), *American Sniper* (Clint Eastwood, 2014), *War Dogs* (Todd Phillips, 2016), and *Lone Survivor* (Peter Berg, 2013).

9   It should be noted that Jocasta's doubt is not an example of modern presentism but is in Sophocles' original. It does seem, however, that a contemporary audience is more likely to accept her reasoning in Haynes's formulation, than a classic audience would have towards Jocasta's doubt in the Oracle.

10 It should be noted, of course, that Sophocles' is only one version of the Antigone myth. Euripides, for example, in a lost play has Antigone survive Creon and marry Haemon.

11 As several critics have noted (Mukherjee, Rutkowska), Shamsie's text anticipates the appointment of Sajid Javid as the first Home Secretary of Muslim heritage in Britain, in 2018.

Works cited

Adams, Richard. 'Classical scholars turn backs on Boris Johnson over burqa comments'. *The Guardian*, 14 August 2018.

Barker, Pat. *The Silence of the Girls*. London: Penguin, 2019 [2018].
Caruth, Cathy. *Unclaimed Existence: Trauma, Narrative, and History*. Baltimore: The Johns Hopkins University Press, 1996.
Chambers, Claire. 'Sound and Fury: Kamila Shamsie's *Home Fire*'. *The Massachusetts Review* 59(2), 2018: 202–219.
Haynes, Natalie. *The Children of Jocasta*. London: Picador, 2018 [2017].
Heilmann, Ann and Mark Llewellyn. *Neo-Victorianism: The Victorians in the Twenty-First Century, 1999–2009*. Basingstoke: Palgrave, 2010.
Heriyanto, Devna. 'Interview: Kamila Shamsie talks about "Home Fire", minorities and terrorism'. *The Jakarta Post*, 4 April 2018: https://www.thejakartapost.com/life/2018/04/04/interview-kamila-shamsie-talks-about-home-fire-minorities-and-terrorism.html (accessed 3 July 2023).
Higgins, Charlotte. 'Boris Johnson's love of classics is about just one thing: himself'. *The Guardian*, 6 October 2019: https://www.theguardian.com/commentisfree/2019/oct/06/boris-johnson-classics-prime-minister-latin-greek (accessed 2 July 2023).
Homer. *The Iliad*. Martin Hammond (trans.). London: Penguin, 1987.
Hubble, Nick. 'Historical Representations'. *The 1990s: A Decade of Contemporary British Fiction*. Nick Hubble, Philip Tew and Leigh Wilson (eds). London: Bloomsbury, 2015: 149–179.
Hutcheon, Linda. *The Politics of Postmodernism: History, Theory, Fiction*. New York: Routledge, 1988.
Hutcheon, Linda. *The Poetics of Postmodernism*. New York: Routledge, 1989.
James, David and Urmila Seshagiri. 'Metamodernism: Narratives of Continuity and Revolution'. *PMLA* 129(1), 2014: 87–100.
Jameson, Fredric. *Postmodernism; Or, The Cultural Logic of Late Capitalism*. London: Verso, 1991.
Johnson, Daisy *Everything Under*. London: Vintage, 2019 [2018].
Lacan, Jacques. 'The Mirror Stage as Formative of the I'. In *Ecrits: A Selection*. Alan Sheridan (trans.). New York: Norton, 1977: 1–7.
Lacan, Jacques. *The Seminar. Book VII. The Ethics of Psychoanalysis, 1959–60*. Dennis Porter (trans.). London: Routledge, 1992.
Lanone, Catherine. 'Pat Barker's *The Silence of the Girls* and the state of exception'. *Études britanniques contemporaines* 58, 2020: https://journals.openedition.org/ebc/8286.
Mukherjee, Ankhi. 'On Antigone's Suffering'. *Cambridge Journal of Postcolonial Literary Enquiry* 8(2), 2021: 214–231.
Owen, Wilfred. 'Strange Meeting'. In *Wilfred Owen: Selected Poetry and Prose*. Jennifer Breen (ed.). London: Routledge, 1988: 65–66.
Rousselot, Elodie. 'Introduction: Exoticizing the Past in Contemporary Neo-Historical Fiction'. In *Exoticizing the Past in Contemporary Neo-Historical Fiction*. Elodie Rousselot (ed.). Basingstoke: Palgrave, 2014, 1–16.
Rutkowska, Urszula. 'The Political Novel in our Still-Evolving Reality: Kamila Shamsie's *Home Fire* and the Shamima Begum Case'. *Textual Practice* 36(6), 2022: 871–888.

Sageman, Marc. *Understanding Terror Networks*. Philadelphia: University of Pennsylvania Press, 2004.
Shamsie, Kamila. *Home Fire*. London: Bloomsbury, 2018 [2017].
Sophocles. *The Three Theban Plays*. Robert Fagles (trans.). London: Penguin, 1984.
Spivak, Gayatri Chavravorty. 'Can the Subaltern Speak?' In *Marxism and the Interpretation of Culture*. Cary Nelson and Lawrence Grossberg (eds). London: Macmillan, 1988: 271–313.
Walezak, Emilie. *Rethinking Contemporary British Women's Writing: Realism, Feminism, Materialism*. London: Bloomsbury, 2021.
Vermeulen, Timotheus and Robin van den Akker. 'Notes on Metamodernism'. *Journal of Aesthetics & Culture* 2, 2010: 1–14.

Timeline of Works

2010

Jonathan Coe, *The Terrible Privacy of Maxwell Sim*
Joanna Kavenna, *The Birth of Love*
Jon McGregor, *Even the Dogs*
Adam Roberts, *New Model Army*
James Robertson, *And the Land Lay Still*

2011

D.D. Johnston, *Peace, Love & Petrol Bombs*
Deborah Levy, *Swimming Home*
Christopher Priest, *The Islanders*
Jane Rogers, *The Testament of Jessie Lamb*
Ali Smith, *There But For The*

2012

David Britton, *La Squab*
James Kelman, *Mo Said She Was Quirky*
John Lanchester, *Capital*
Ken MacLeod, *Intrusion*
China Miéville, *Railsea*
Christopher Nosniboor, *This Book is Fucking Stupid: Fifty Shades of Shit*
Will Self, *Umbrella*
Gary J. Shipley and Kenji Siratori, *Necrology*
Ali Smith, *Artful*
Zadie Smith, *NW*

2013

David Britton, *Invictus Horror*
David Britton, *Lord Horror: Reverbstorm*
Jonathan Coe, *Expo 58*
Niall Griffiths, *A Great Big Shining Star*
Stewart Home, *Mandy, Charlie, and Mary-Jane*
Christopher Priest, *The Adjacent*

2014

Nina Allan, *The Race*
M.R. Carey, *The Girl with All the Gifts*
Bernadine Evaristo, *Mr Loverman*
Stewart Home, *The 9 Lives of Ray the Cat Jones*
Will Self, *Shark*
Ali Smith, *How To Be Both*
Rebecca Ann Smith, *Baby X*

2015

Jonathan Coe, *Number 11*
Kazuo Ishiguro, *The Buried Giant*
Tom McCarthy, *Satin Island*
David Peace, *Red or Dead*
Sunjeev Sahota, *The Year of the Runaways*
Ali Smith, *Public Library and Other Stories*

2016

Tahmima Anam, *The Bones of Grace*
Paul McAuley, *Austral*
Christopher Priest, *The Gradual*
Alex Scarrow, *Plague Land*
Ali Smith, *Autumn*
Zadie Smith, *Swing Time*

2017

Nina Allan, *The Rift*
David Britton, *Razor King*
Anthony Cartwright, *The Cut*
Anne Charnock, *Dreams Before the Start of Time*
Cory Doctorow, *Walkaway*
Mohsin Hamid, *Exit West*
Nick Harkaway, *Gnomon*
Natalie Haynes, *The Children of Jocasta*
Justina Robson, *The Switch*
Helen Sedgwick, *The Growing Season*
Will Self, *Phone*
Kamila Shamsie, *Home Fire*
Ali Smith, *Winter*
Olivia Sudjic, *Sympathy*

2018

Glen James Brown, *Ironopolis*
Sam Byers, *Perfidious Albion*
Jonathan Coe, *Middle England*
Guy Gunaratne, *In Our Mad and Furious City*
Melissa Harrison, *All Among the Barley*
Simon Ings, *The Smoke*
Daisy Johnson, *Everything Under*
Sarah Moss, *Ghost Wall*
John Osmond, *Ten Million Stars Are Burning*
David Peace, *Patient X*
Christopher Priest, *An American Story*
Olivia Sudjic, *Exposure*

2019

Bernadine Evaristo, *Girl, Woman, Other*
Niall Griffiths, *Broken Ghost*
Natalie Haynes, *Ten Thousand Ships*
Tim Maughan, *Infinite Detail*
Ali Smith, *Spring*

2020

Jonathan Coe, *Mr Wilder and Me*
M. John Harrison, *The Sunken Land Begins to Rise Again*
Stewart Home, *Denizen of the Dead*
Christopher Priest, *The Evidence*
Ali Smith, *Summer*

Timeline of National Events

2010

- 8 April: The 2010 Equality Act gained royal assent, coming into force later in the year in September.
- 6 May: UK General Election in which the Conservative Party under David Cameron won 306 seats, while Labour under Gordon Brown won 258 seats, and Nick Clegg's Liberal Democrats won 57. A coalition government was formed between the Conservatives and the Liberal Democrats, with Cameron as Prime Minister and Clegg as Deputy Prime Minister.
- 15 Sep: The Fixed-term Parliaments Act 2011 received royal assent and came into immediate effect.
- 25 Sep: Ed Miliband narrowly defeated his older brother David to win the Labour Party leadership after Brown's resignation.

2011

- 27 Feb: At the 83rd Academy Awards, the British film *The King's Speech* won the Oscar for Best Picture.
- 3 March: The Referendum on the Law-making Powers of the National Assembly for Wales (turnout: 35.63%) in which 517,132 (63.49%) people voted yes/ie and 297,380 (36.51%) voted no to the question: 'Do you want the Assembly now to be able to make laws on all matters in the 20 subject areas it has powers for?' As a result, Wales did gain primary legislative powers.
- 5 May: In the Scottish Parliament Election, Alex Salmond's SNP won a landslide majority of 69 out of 129 seats. The size of the victory led to the UK Government agreeing to the Independence Referendum that would take place in September 2014.
- 5 May: In the Welsh National Assembly Election, Labour under Carwyn Jones won 30 out of 60 seats, and was able to form a minority government.
- 5 May: The United Kingdom Alternative Vote Referendum saw 13,013,123 (67.9%) vote no to introducing a form of proportional representation for UK general elections.
- 4 Aug: 29-year-old Mark Duggan, a black British man, was shot dead by police in North London, triggering widespread civil unrest and rioting for four days, not just in London, but also other cities such as Birmingham, Manchester, Liverpool, and Bristol.

2012

8 Mar: The Welfare Reform Act 2012 introduced Universal Credit as a unified replacement to a number of existing benefits and tax credits.

3 May: Boris Johnson won re-election as Mayor of London.

4–7 June: A Bank Holiday on 5 June to celebrate the Queen's Diamond Jubilee was combined with the movement of the late May Bank Holiday to 4 June, to create a four-day weekend.

27 July: The Summer Olympic Games in London begin. Great Britain and Northern Ireland won 29 golds, 18 silvers, and 18 bronzes and finished third in the overall medal table, a feat they would surpass by coming second in the table at the 2016 Summer Olympics, held at Rio de Janeiro, Brazil.

2013

1 Apr: The so-called 'Bedroom Tax' – introduced as an 'under-occupancy penalty' in the previous year's Welfare Reform Act – came into effect. Having one or two bedrooms more than the calculated allowance (which assumed, for example, that children of the same gender under the age of 16 would share a bedroom) resulted in a reduction in housing benefit of respectively 14%, and 25%.

23 May: Off-duty soldier Lee Rigby was murdered in the street by Islamist terrorists Michael Adebolajo and Michael Adebowale near the Royal Artillery Barracks in Woolwich.

2014

13 Mar: Legislation to allow same-sex marriage in England and Wales, which had been passed by the UK Parliament in July 2013, came into effect. The first same-sex marriages took place on 29 March. Equivalent legislation by the Scottish parliament came into effect on 16 December.

22 May: UKIP under Nigel Farage won the largest share of the vote (26.6%) in the 2014 Election for the European Parliament, electing 24 members, ahead of Labour (24.4%, 20 seats) and the Conservatives (23.1%, 19 seats).

18 Sep: Scottish Independence Referendum (turnout: 84.59%), in which 1,617,989 (44.7%) people voted yes and 2,001,926 (55.3%) voted no to the question, 'Should Scotland be an independent country?' As a consequence, Scotland remained in the UK.

14 Nov: Nicola Sturgeon became leader of the SNP after standing uncontested in the leadership election following Alex Salmond's resignation.

2015

7 May: UK General Election in which the Conservative Party under Cameron won 330 seats, while Miliband's Labour Party won 258 seats, Sturgeon's SNP won 56 seats,

and Clegg's Liberal Democrats only 8. This resulted in a surprise overall majority of 10 for Cameron.

12 Sep: Jeremy Corbyn was elected the new leader of the Labour Party following Miliband's resignation.

17 Dec: The EU Referendum Act 2015 received royal assent, giving effect to a Conservative Party manifesto commitment by requiring a referendum to be held before 31 December 2017 on whether Britain should leave the EU.

2016

20 Feb: Cameron announced that the EU Referendum would take place on 23 June 2016.

21 Feb: Boris Johnson, Mayor of London and (since the 2015 General Election) MP for Uxbridge and Ruislip, declared that 'after a huge amount of heartache' he would be backing the leave campaign for the upcoming EU referendum.

5 May: In the Scottish Parliament Election, Sturgeon's SNP won 64 seats, just short of an overall majority, and formed a minority government.

5 May: In the Senedd (Welsh Parliament) Elections, Jones's Labour won 29 seats, Plaid Cymru won 12, the Conservatives won 11, UKIP won 7 and the Liberal Democrats only1. Jones was able to form a viable minority government by offering the sole Liberal Democrat member a seat in his cabinet.

16 June: Jo Cox, the Labour MP for Batley and Spen, died after being shot and stabbed multiple times in the street by Thomas Mair, a far-right activist who shouted 'Britain First' as he stabbed her.

23 June: United Kingdom European Union Membership Referendum (turnout: 72.21%), in which 17,410,742 (51.89%) people voted to leave the EU and 16,141,241 (48.11%) voted to remain. There was a marked national and regional variation in the vote. Scotland (62%), Northern Ireland (55.78%), and Greater London (59.93%) all voted to remain in the EU. Wales voted narrowly (52.53%) to leave the EU but within the country, Cardiff and the Welsh-speaking rural counties of Ceredigion and Gwynedd voted to remain. In England, the South East (51.78%), South West (52.63%) and North West (53.65%) regions voted narrowly to leave, but in other regions, especially the West Midlands (59.26%), the East Midlands (58.82%), Yorkshire and the Humber (57.71%) and the North East (58.04%), the majority for leaving the EU was much greater.

24 June: Cameron announced that he would resign as Prime Minister before the start of the Conservative Party Conference in October, thus triggering a leadership election.

26–28 June: Hilary Benn, the Shadow Foreign Secretary, was sacked by Jeremy Corbyn after it became clear that he was organizing a mass resignation of Shadow Cabinet members to force Corbyn to stand down. Over the following day and a half, two thirds of Corbyn's Shadow Cabinet resigned in support of Benn. On 26 June, Corbyn lost a vote of no confidence amongst Labour Party MPs by 172–40, thus triggering another leadership election.

30 June: Boris Johnson, the frontrunner to become the new Conservative Party leader, gave a press conference in which, rather than announcing his candidature, he instead declared that he was not going to run after all.

11 July: Theresa May became leader of the Conservative Party following the withdrawal of her remaining rival, Andrea Leadsom, from the leadership contest.

13 July: May became Prime Minister. One of her first acts was to appoint Johnson as Foreign Secretary.

24 Sep: Corbyn was re-elected as leader of the Labour Party after winning over 60% of the votes cast by the membership.

2017

24 Jan: The UK Supreme Court ruled that Article 50 of the Treaty of the European Union, which set the withdrawal process in motion, could not be invoked by the Government without an Act of Parliament, which would require majority support in the Commons. The European Union (Notification of Withdrawal) Act 2017 was quickly introduced and passed, with Corbyn whipping Labour MPs to support it.

29 Mar: Article 50 was formally invoked, setting a withdrawal date on 29 March 2019, two years after the date of notification as specified in the Treaty on the European Union.

8 June: UK General Election in which the Conservative Party under May won 317 seats, Corbyn's Labour Party won 262 seats and Sturgeon's SNP won 35. May was forced to agree a 'confidence and supply' agreement with the Democratic Unionist Party (DUP) of Northern Ireland, in order to secure a parliamentary majority.

14 June: 72 people died in the Grenfell Tower fire.

19 June: Brexit negotiations formally opened when David Davis, UK Secretary of State for Exiting the European Union, arrived in Brussels to meet with Michel Barnier, the Chief Negotiator on behalf of the European Commission.

2018

26 June: The European Union (Withdrawal) Act 2018 came into effect, removing the competence of EU institutions to legislate for the UK, while enabling existing EU law to be incorporated into UK law as 'retained EU law'. It also, as a result of Government defeat by an amendment authored by Conservative MP Dominic Grieve, made future ratification of a withdrawal agreement dependent upon the prior enactment of another Act of Parliament approving the final terms following completion of the ongoing Brexit negotiations.

9 July: Johnson resigned as Foreign Secretary, after the resignation of Davis a day earlier, following a Cabinet meeting at Chequers on 6 July in which Theresa May set out her support for a 'facilitated customs arrangement' with the EU.

13 Nov: The text of a deal between the UK and the EU, comprising the Withdrawal Agreement and a non-binding Political Declaration on the future relationship, was

agreed. The inclusion of a Northern Ireland Protocol effectively meant that Great Britain would remain aligned with the EU's rules for state aid and labour and environmental standards. Eurosceptic Conservative and DUP MPs feared that this would make the UK a 'vassal state'.

12 Dec: May survived a confidence vote of Conservative MPs by 200 votes to 117.

2019

15 Jan: May's Brexit deal went down to a crushing defeat in the House of Commons by 432 votes to 202. The consequence was that the Government effectively lost control of Parliament, allowing MPs to take matters into their hands, raising fundamental questions about the validity of the British democratic system.

18 Feb: Seven Labour MPs held a press conference to announce that they were leaving the party to form The Independent Group (TIG). The group was subsequently joined by another Labour MP, and then on 20 February by three Conservative MPs.

27 Feb: The UK Government accepted an amendment from Labour MP Yvette Cooper to a Brexit motion requiring an Article 50 extension if the Commons rejected May's Brexit deal again and a no-deal exit.

22 Mar: The European Council agreed that Brexit be postponed until 12 April if no deal was agreed by UK, and 22 May 2019 if the UK accepted the negotiated deal before 12 April.

25 Mar: A People's Vote march, calling for any Brexit deal to be put to the public in another referendum, took place in central London, involving between 300,000 to a million people, depending on estimates.

27 Mar: With MPs having wrested control of the Commons agenda for the day from the Government, a series of eight indicative votes was held representing a range of options from a no-deal exit to a revocation of Article 50. None gained a majority, although Conservative MP Ken Clarke's proposal of a permanent customs union between the UK and the EU fell just six votes short.

1 Apr: MPs took control of Commons agenda for a second round of indicative votes. In this case, there were four options: a permanent customs union, 'Norway plus', confirmatory referendum and revocation. All four were rejected, with 212 out of 312 Conservative MPs opposing all of them, leading Nick Boles MP to announce his departure from the party at the end of the debate in frustration at their refusal to compromise. The customs union option fell by the narrow margin of 276 votes to 273, with the SNP abstaining and TIG voting against. The SNP did support the Norway plus option (moved by Boles) but this fell by 282 votes to 261, with TIG, some Liberal Democrats and the one Green MP voting against.

3 Apr: A third day of MPs controlling the Common agenda resulted in a private member's bill, forcing the Government to apply for another extension to Article 50, brought forward by Cooper with support from Conservative MP Oliver Letwin. Against almost all precedent, this was rushed through on a series of very narrow

votes before moving on to the Lords the next day, where attempts to filibuster the bill were defeated by repeatedly proposing closure motions. As an indication of the irregularity of these proceedings, the number of these motions approved within seven hours was only one less than the seven instances which had previously been approved since 1900.

10 Apr: The European Council agreed that the final deadline for Brexit be postponed until 31 October 2019, by which time the UK had to accept the negotiated deal; a condition attached to the extension prohibited any renegotiation. This meant that the UK had to hold 2019 European Parliament elections in May in order to be allowed to remain in the EU after 1 June.

23 May: Farage's Brexit Party won the European Elections, taking 29 seats.

24 May: May announced she would resign, triggering a Conservative Party leadership election.

24 July: Johnson became Prime Minister following his election the previous day as leader of the Conservative Party after winning the final run-off with Jeremy Hunt. One of his first significant acts was to reopen negotiations with the EU, with David Frost leading the talks for the UK.

28 Aug: Before the end of its summer recess, the UK Parliament was ordered to be prorogued (suspended) by the Queen on the advice of Johnson; advice which was later ruled unlawful on 24 September by the UK Supreme Court. In the event, therefore, Parliament was suspended for only two weeks from 10 September, during which time a number of street protests and demonstrations occurred protesting what was seen in some quarters as a form of coup.

4 Sep: Another unorthodox deployment of parliamentary procedure enabled a cross-party bill requiring a new Article 50 extension, which saw the Government defeated by 328 votes to 321. Johnson's response was to strip the whip from all twenty-one Conservative MPs who voted against him and declare that he would rather be 'dead in a ditch' than agree a further extension.

15 Oct: Bernadine Evaristo's *Girl, Woman, Other* was named joint winner of the Booker Prize alongside Margaret Atwood's *The Testaments*. Evaristo is the first black woman to win the Booker.

17 Oct: Johnson and then European Commission President, Jean-Claude Juncker, announced the details of a revised Withdrawal Agreement. The main difference to May's deal lay in a revised Northern Ireland Protocol removing the all-UK elements and in effect leaving Northern Ireland in a different customs regime to the rest of the UK. While there would be no need for customs checks on the land border with the Republic, there would need to be checks on the sea border between Northern Ireland and Britain.

19 Oct: The UK Parliament sat on a Saturday for the first time since 1982 in order to approve the deal. However, an amendment by Letwin was passed which withheld Commons support for the deal until the implementing legislation had first been passed. The net result of this was that Johnson grudgingly sent an unsigned letter to the EU requesting another extension. In response, the European Council agreed a

third extension to the Article 50 period notice, postponing Brexit until 23:00 on 31 January 2020, at which point the UK did in fact finally withdraw from the EU.
- 29 Oct: Johnson introduced the Early Parliamentary General Election Act 2019 to circumvent the Fixed Term Parliaments Act and called an early election on Thursday, 12 December.
- 12 Dec: UK General Election in which the Conservative Party under Johnson won 365 seats, while Corbyn's Labour won only 202 and Sturgeon's SNP won 48. This gave Johnson a parliamentary majority of 80.
- 13 Dec: Corbyn announced that he would be standing down as soon as a successor was elected.

2020

- 13 Jan: Legislation to allow same-sex marriage in Northern Ireland came into effect after having been passed by the UK Parliament (during a period when the Northern Ireland Assembly was suspended) in July 2019.
- 23 Jan: The European Union (Withdrawal Agreement) Act 2020 received royal assent paving the way for the UK Government to ratify the negotiated withdrawal treaty and leave the EU.
- 24 Jan: The treaty agreeing the withdrawal of the UK from the EU was formally signed by Johnson and the new President of the European Commission, Ursula von der Leyen.
- 31 Jan: The UK formally withdrew from the EU at 23:00 GMT.
- 23 Mar: First 'Covid lockdown' began. Due to the Covid-19 pandemic, the British people were directed to stay at home except for essential purchases, essential work travel (if remote work was not possible), medical needs, one exercise per day, and providing care for others. Non-essential retail businesses were closed during this period. At the peak of the pandemic, the daily fatality rate was over 1,000. As the wave of infections subsided, restrictions became eased gradually from May and then more significantly in June.
- 4 Apr: Keir Starmer became leader of the Labour Party after winning the leadership contest.
- 7 June: The statue of trans-Atlantic slave trader, Edward Colston (1636–1721) was toppled, defaced, and pushed into Bristol Harbour during a Black Lives Matter protest.
- 31 Dec: The 'transition period', in which the previous EU rules on trade, travel and business continued to apply to Britain, ended at 23:00 GMT, meaning the UK had completed its formal separation from the EU.

Timeline of International Events

2010

April   Apple released the first iPad in the US, before rolling it out globally over the rest of the year.

April   Julian Assange leaked footage of a 2007 airstrike in Iraq titled 'Collateral Murder' on the website WikiLeaks. Over the course of the year, WikiLeaks went on to release over 90,000 internal reports about the US-led involvement in the War in Afghanistan from 2004 to 2010 and more than 250,000 American diplomatic cables, including 100,000 marked 'secret' or 'confidential'.

Oct   The photo-sharing social networking app Instagram was launched for use with Apple's mobile operating system. After reaching ten million registered users within a year, it was bought by Facebook in April 2012. At the same time, the Android version was released, leading to another massive expansion in the number of users.

Nov   Sweden issued a European Arrest Warrant for Assange over allegations of sexual assault.

2011

Jan   Tunisian street vendor Mohamed Bouazizi dies after setting himself on fire a month earlier, sparking anti-government protests, known collectively as the Arab Spring, which quickly spread through Egypt, Libya, Syria and other countries.

May   President Barack Obama announces that the US has killed Osama bin Laden, leader of Al Qaeda, at his compound in Abbottabad, Pakistan.

July   In Norway, Anders Behring Breivik kills 8 people in a bomb blast which targeted government buildings in central Oslo, then kills 69 at a massacre at a Workers' Youth League camp on the island of Utøya.

Sep   Occupy Wall Street protests begin in the US. This develops into the Occupy movement which spreads to 82 countries by October

2012

June — Assange lost his extradition battle with Sweden and sought refuge in the Ecuadorian Embassy in London, where he was granted asylum that was eventually withdrawn in April 2019.

Nov — The incumbent Democratic President, Barack Obama, won a second term in office against the Republican Mitt Romney in the US elections.

Nov — Xi Jinping assumed office as the General Secretary of the Chinese Communist Party, also becoming President of the People's Republic of China in the following March. Since then, Xi has imposed a more authoritarian rule at home – removing term limits for his presidency in 2018 – and an assertive foreign policy abroad.

2013

Jan — Following trial of the beta version in the previous year, the first full version of the video conferencing system, Zoom, was released, which allowed up to 25 participants to simultaneously participate in a meeting (it currently allows up to 1,000 concurrent participants). Although the software was immediately successful, it rose to global prominence during the Covid-19 pandemic of 2020, when it became one of the most downloaded mobile apps in the World.

July — The Black Lives Matter (BLM) movement began in the US with the use of the hashtag #BlackLivesMatter on social media after the acquittal of the Neighbourhood Watch coordinator, George Zimmerman, for the fatal shooting of the African-American teenager, Trayvon Martin in the previous year. The movement became associated with street protests following the deaths of two more African Americans in 2014, Michael Brown and Eric Garner. Brown was shot and killed by a police officer in Ferguson, Missouri, which became the site of a series of protests. Garner was killed in Staten Island, New York, after an NYPD officer put him in an illegal chokehold.

2014

Feb — Following the deposition of Ukrainian President, Viktor Yanukovych, earlier in the month, which sparked pro-Russian demonstrations, Russian troops captured strategic sites across Crimea. Following the installation of a pro-Russian government and a rapidly held referendum, Crimea declared independence on 16 March 2014, allowing it to be incorporated into Russia two days later. These events are now seen as the opening salvo of the Russo-Ukrainian War, which is now an armed conflict following Russia's invasion of Ukraine in 2022.

2015

June — Donald Trump announced his candidacy for the 2016 US presidential election. Despite being initially considered an outsider, he rose to the top of the opinion polls relatively quickly and was declared the Republican nominee in May 2016.

Dec — The (at the time) non-profit organization OpenAI was founded in San Francisco to research artificial intelligence (AI). It became widely known globally following the release of the AI chatbot, ChatGPT, in December 2022.

2016

Sep — The Chinese short-form video hosting service, Douyin, was launched by ByteDance, gaining 100 million users within a year. In September 2017, the app was launched on the international market as TikTok. By July 2020, TikTok, excluding Douyin, was reporting around 800 million monthly active global users.

Nov — Despite winning a smaller share of the popular vote, Donald Trump beat Hillary Clinton in the US election to become the 45th President of the United States.

2017

Oct — The #MeToo movement rose to global prominence as a hashtag on social media following the publicization of numerous allegations of sexual abuse against the film producer Harvey Weinstein. Since then it has become a social movement against sexual harassment and rape culture.

2018

May — The EU's General Data Protection Regulation (GDPR) came into effect imposing strict privacy controls for European citizens.

Oct — The Intergovernmental Panel of Climate Change (IPCC) published its Special Report on Global Warming of 1.5°C, which found that if global warming could be limited to 1.5°C above pre-industrial levels rather than 2°C, the impacts on ecosystems and human health and well-being would be reduced to manageable effects. In March 2023, the IPCC's latest report noted that global warming is now on course to reach 1.5°C in the first half of the 2030s and that only immediate and massive reductions in carbon reductions will stop it accelerating beyond that level.

2019

April Assange arrested by British police in the London Ecuadorian Embassy, where he had lived within a small room for nearly seven years, and held in Belmarsh prison (where he currently remains) pending the result of a request to extradite him to the US to face charges of espionage.

Dec A cluster of cases of pneumonia of unknown origin were detected in Wuhan, China. By early the following month, Chinese scientists had isolated the sequence of a new coronavirus, which was labelled severe acute respiratory syndrome coronavirus 2 (SARS-CoV-2). The disease caused by this virus was named coronavirus disease 2019 (Covid-19).

2020

Jan The rapid spread of Covid-19 from China led to the World Health Organization (WHO) declaring a Public Health Emergency of International Concern (PHEIC) on 30 January.

Mar The WHO declared Covid-19 to be a global pandemic on 11 March. By the beginning of May 2023, there had been over 750 million confirmed cases of Covid-19 globally and nearly seven million deaths.

May African-American George Floyd was murdered in Minneapolis as a result of a white police officer, Derek Chauvin, kneeling on his neck for nine minutes while Floyd was handcuffed and lying face down in the street. The following BLM protests across the US involved between 15 and 26 million people, therefore making it one of the biggest movements in US history.

Nov The Democratic nominee and former Vice President, Joe Biden beat Donald Trump in the US election, after receiving over 81 million votes, more than cast for any candidate previously.

Biographies of Writers

Nina Allan was born in Whitechapel in 1966 and grew up in the Midlands and West Sussex. She has studied at the Universities of Reading, Exeter and Oxford. She has worked as a bookseller and as a buyer for an independent chain of record stores, an experience which informs the job of the protagonist in her 2021 novel, *The Good Neighbours*. Her first novel, *The Race* was published in 2014 by the independent NewCon Press and then republished in a longer version by Titan Books in 2016. Sandwiched between those two editions, was a novella, *The Harlequin* (2015). *The Rift* (2017) won the British Science Fiction Award for Best Novel. Her third novel, *The Dollmaker* (2019) is an uncanny love story. *Stardust: The Ruby Castle Stories*, which originally appeared in 2013, was republished by Titan as *Ruby* in 2020. One of the protagonists of *Ruby* ponders whether 'it was possible to take a wrong turning and end up living a life that was not your own' – a question that repeatedly occurs in slightly different variations throughout Allan's fiction. Following the EU referendum, Allan moved with her partner Christopher Priest to Scotland to the Isle of Bute, which is the setting for most of *The Good Neighbours*. A short story collection, *The Art of Space Travel and Other Stories* was also published in 2021. Her latest novel, *Conquest* (2023), is a mundane and elliptical story of alien invasion, set to the repeating patterns of Bach's Goldberg Variations.

Pat Barker was born in Yorkshire in 1943. She studied at the London School of Economics, graduating in 1965. She began to write in her mid-20s. Her first novel, *Union Street*, was published by Virago Press in 1982, after being rejected by many publishers as too depressing. This novel and the next two, *Blow Your House Down* (1984) and *Liza's England* (1986) (originally published as *The Century's Daughter*) depict the lives of working-class women in the north of England. *Blow Your House* down alludes to the serial killer Peter Sutcliffe, known as the Yorkshire Ripper, who murdered thirteen women around Leeds between 1975 and 1980. In the 1990s, Barker published the Regeneration Trilogy – *Regeneration* (1991), *The Eye in the Door* (1993) and *The Ghost Road* (1995) – which explores the history of the First World War. The final novel in the trilogy won the Booker Prize. Other works include *Another World* (1998), *Border Crossing* (2001), *Double Vision* (2003), *Life Class* (2007), *Toby's Room* (2012) and Noonday (2015). *The Silence of the Girls* (2018) tells the events of the *Iliad* from the point of view of Briseis and was followed by a sequel, *The Women of Troy* (2020).

Anthony Cartwright was born in Dudley, West Midlands, in 1973. He studied English and American Literature at the University of East Anglia and worked in factories, meatpacking plants, pubs, warehouses and on the London Underground before training as an English teacher in 1998. Cartwright's fiction often centres around his hometown, dealing with the collective trauma of the Thatcher years, deindustrialization, and working-class culture in the post-industrial context. His first novel, *The Afterglow* (2004), is a novel in the realist mode and won the 2004 Betty Trask Award. It follows the Wilkinson family, telling the story of how the closure of a local steelworks affected the wider working-class community. *Heartland* (2009), which was adapted by BBC Radio 4 for its *Books at Bedtime* series, is set in the fictional multicultural area of Cinderheath and deals with increasingly fractured inter-ethnic relations in a period when older forms of working-class political culture (and the industrial base which underpinned it) have significantly diminished. *Heartland* was also translated into Italian and his increased profile in Italy led to the 2015 publication of *Il Giorno Perduto* ("The Lost Day"), co-authored with the Italian writer Gian Luca Favetto, about the Heysel stadium disaster. Following the 2016 referendum, Cartwright was commissioned by Peirene Press to write a novel responding to the decision to leave the European Union, which was eventually published as *The Cut* (2017). He has also written a number of scholarly articles on postwar working-class writer, Alexander Baron, and on pedagogical and creative practice. He is currently a lecturer at the University of the West of England.

Jonathan Coe was born in Bromsgrove in 1961. He was educated at King Edward's School, Birmingham, which is the one of the key settings of his 2001 novel, *The Rotters' Club*, and Trinity College, Cambridge, before studying for a PhD in English Literature at the University of Warwick. His first novel, *The Accidental Woman*, was published in 1987. He came to prominence with the publication of his fourth novel *What a Carve Up!* (1994), a savage satire on Thatcherism, which won the John Llewellyn Rhys Prize, and the Prix du Meilleur Livre Étranger in France. This was followed by *The House of Sleep* (1997), whose protagonists Robert and Terrance take their names from the popular British TV sitcoms, *The Likely Lads* and *Whatever Happened to the Likely Lads?*. *The House of Sleep* won the Writers' Guild of Great Britain Best Novel award and, in France, the Prix Médicis. The title of *The Rotters' Club*, which centres on the character Benjamin Trotter, is taken from another of Coe's pop culture enthusiasms, the title of an album by the experimental rock band Hatfield and the North. Trotter also features in two sequels, *The Closed Circle* (2004) and *Middle England* (2018), which concerns the events surrounding the 2016 referendum on membership of the EU. Coe's 2004 biography of experimental novelist B.S. Johnson, *Like a Fiery Elephant*, which itself is experimental in form, won the Samuel Johnson Prize in 2005. Coe's most recent novels are *Mr Wilder and Me* (2020) and *Bournville* (2022).

Niall Griffiths was born in Toxteth, Liverpool, in 1966 into a family with Welsh roots. In 1976 the family emigrated to Australia only to return three years later. His non-fiction book, *Ten Pound Pom* (2009), records his experiences of returning to Australia and reflecting on his childhood memories. After gaining a degree in English, Griffiths worked in a number of short-term jobs before starting a PhD at Aberystwyth University. However, he ended up dropping out and accumulating experiences around the town, which fed into his first novel, *Grits* (2000). His second novel, *Sheepshagger* (2001) was a compelling account of the revenge that Ianto from the West Wales mountains takes on those he sees as desecrating his homeland. *Kelly + Victor* (2002), set in Liverpool, describes how a passionate sexual relationship tips into destruction with visceral detail, and was subsequently filmed in 2012. His fourth novel *Stump* (2003) tells the intersecting stories of a one-armed man from Liverpool hiding out in a Welsh seaside town and two men on the way from Liverpool hunting for a one-armed man somewhere in Wales. *Stump* won both the Welsh Books Council Book of the Year and the Arts Council of Wales Book of the Year Award. After two more novels, *Wreckage* (2005) and *Runt* (2007), he wrote the travel guides *Real Aberystwyth* (2008) and *Real Liverpool* (2008). *The Dreams of Max and Ronnie* (2010) was Griffiths's take on *The Dream of Rhonabwy*, a contribution to the Welsh publishing imprint Seren's series *New Stories of the Mabinogion*, in which modern authors rewrote the stories from that Welsh classic. Griffiths's most recent novels are *A Great Big Shining Star* (2013) and *Broken Ghost* (2019).

Guy Gunaratne is a contemporary, non-binary British writer, filmmaker and journalist, who moves between London, England and Malmö, Sweden. They studied film and journalism at Brunel University and subsequently, current affairs journalism at City, University of London, and held the role of Fellow Commoner in Creative Arts at Trinity College, Cambridge between 2019–2022. Their first novel, *In Our Fast and Furious City* (2018), won three major literary awards: the Jhalak Prize, the Authors Club Award, and the International Dylan Thomas Prize, as well as being shortlisted for the Goldsmith's Prize and longlisted for the Orwell Prize for Political Fiction, as well as the Booker Prize. Their second novel, *Mister, Mister* is due for release in 2023.

Mohsin Hamid is a British Pakistani writer, who often speaks of his hybrid identity and transnational residence. He has lived for substantial periods of his life in Pakistan, America, and Britain, and likewise, his novels, essays, and articles often reflect transnational anxieties, connected to post-9/11 politics, global technology, and migration. He has written five novels to date, all of which have been published within the twenty-first century. These include *Moth Smoke* (2000), *The Reluctant Fundamentalist* (2008), *How to Get Filthy Rich in Rising Asia* (2013), *Exit West* (2017), and most recently, *The Last White Man* (2022), as well as a collection of essays, entitled *Discontent and Its Civilizations: Dispatches from Lahore, New York and London* (2014). His work has won numerous prominent literary prizes, including the Betty Trask Award for *Moth Smoke* in 2001, the Asian American Literary Award for *The Reluctant Fundamentalist* in 2008, and the Aspen Words Literary Prize for *Exit West* in 2018, as well as being shortlisted for the Hemingway Foundation/PEN Award in 2001, the Booker Prize in 2007 and 2017, the James Tait Memorial Prize in 2008, and the National Book Critics Circle Award in 2018.

M. John Harrison was born in Rugby in 1945. Following publication of his first short story in *Science Fantasy* magazine in 1966, he relocated to London, where he met Michael Moorcock, the editor of *New Worlds*, the magazine centrally associated with the science fiction New Wave. Harrison began writing reviews and short fiction for *New Worlds*, becoming books editor in 1968. His early novels include *The Committed Men* (1971) and *The Centauri Device* (1975). *The Pastel City* (1971) was the first work in the Viriconium sequence (1971–84). *In Viriconium* (1982), the third novel of the sequence, began life as work commissioned by David Britton and Michael Butterworth of Savoy Books. The Kefahuchi Tract trilogy consists of *Light* (2002), *Nova Swing* (2006), which won the Arthur C. Clarke Award, and *Empty Space* (2012). The collection, *Settling the World: Selected Stories 1970-2020*, came out in 2020. *The Sunken Land Begins to Rise Again* (2020) was an offbeat post-Brexit state-of-the-nation novel that received wide critical acclaim and won the Goldsmiths Prize for fiction which 'breaks the mould or extends the possibilities of the novel form'. His most recent book is the anti-memoir, *Wish I Was Here* (2023).

Simon Ings was born in 1965 in Hampshire and educated at Churcher's College, Petersfield and at King's College London and Birkbeck College. His first novel, *Hot Head* (1992), was shortlisted for the British Science Fiction Association Award for Best Novel, as were his fourth and ninth novels, *Headlong* (1999) and *Wolves* (2014). His most recent novel, *The Smoke* (2018) is a complex post-Brexit alternate history of a Britain in a world in which America never became a global power due to a nineteenth-century volcanic eruption and there was no Second World War. Ings has edited a collection of 100 of the best science-fiction short stories on artificial intelligence from around the world, *We Robots* (2020). Ings is also a journalist and the former culture editor of the *New Scientist*. He has also written two non-fiction books: *The Eye: A Natural History* (2007) and *Stalin and the Scientists: A History of Triumph and Tragedy 1905–1953* (2016). A third, *Engineers of Human Souls: Four Cautionary Tales of Political and Literary Megalomania* is due to be published in 2024.

D. D. Johnston was born in Central Scotland. For a number of years he worked in fast food, during which time he co-founded McDonald's Workers' Resistance, a collective of radical McDonald's workers who grew to international notoriety through the use of (often crude) humour to promote an awareness of workers' rights and direct action among their colleagues. This led him into the early-2000s anti-globalization movement, with his experiences in fast food and protest forming the basis for his first novel, *Peace, Love and Petrol Bombs* (2011). The novel was chosen by author, Helen Fitzgerald, as a *Herald* newspaper 'Book of the Year' and was translated into Spanish in 2013. In 2011, Johnston completed a PhD in Creative Writing. His thesis was published as the 2013 novel, *The Deconstruction of Professor Thrub*, in which a young postgraduate attempts to write a thesis on free will by researching the life of a Belfast woman whose life traverses some of the major revolutionary upheavals of twentieth-century Europe, all while his disillusioned PhD supervisor (the eponymous Professor Thrub) is trying to avoid him. In 2015, he published *The Secret Baby Room*, a Manchester-set crime novel, which explores themes of poverty, abuse and childhood trauma. His most recent novel, *Disnaeland* (2022), is a piece of speculative fiction imagining how a working-class Scottish community responds to the end of the world. Johnston's work frequently draws on humorous self-reflexive irony and bathos to depict the extraordinary power of ordinary people to survive in, and change, the world they live in. He is currently a Senior Lecturer in Creative Writing at the University of Gloucestershire and lives in Cheltenham Spa where he looks after his young son, Hart.

James Kelman was born in Glasgow, Scotland, in 1946. A prolific author since the late-1970s, his work frequently draws on modernist and European existentialist traditions while rooting them within a distinctly working-class Scottish context. His first published novel, *The Busconductor Hines* (1984), depicts the alienation of a young Glaswegian bus conductor as he strives to imagine a more exciting life. His third novel, *A Disaffection* (1989), was shortlisted for the Booker and won the James Tait Black Memorial Prize. It is written in Kelman's typical stream-of-consciousness style and follows an embittered Glasgow school teacher estranged from those around him. His 1994 novel, *How Late It Was, How Late*, about a heavy-drinking ex-convict recently made blind after an incident of police brutality, won the Booker Prize. He has also won numerous other prizes, including the 1998 Stakis Prize for 'Scottish Writer of the Year' for his collection of short stories *The Good Times*, and both the Saltire Society and Scottish Arts Council Book of the Year for *Kieron Smith, Boy* (2008). However, despite critical acclaim, Kelman has remained a controversial figure due to his uncompromising approach to literary form and the Scots language. *How Late It Was, How Late* was branded 'literary vandalism' and his Booker victory 'a disgrace' while a Booker judge for *The Busconductor Hines* expressed incredulity at a novel 'written entirely in Glaswegian!' Kelman is also a veteran activist, participating in the Workers' City group critical of Glasgow's 1990 'City of Culture' celebrations. He has also been a supporter of the Edinburgh Unemployed Workers Centre (including its renamed incarnation, the Autonomous Centre of Edinburgh), speaking at its opening. More recently, he has been active in Kurdish solidarity activism, speaking in support of imprisoned Kurdish leader, Abdullah Ocalan.

Deborah Levy was born in Johannesburg in 1959. After her father, Norman Levy – a member of the African National Congress – was placed under a banning order by the Apartheid government, the family moved to London in 1968. A playwright, a poet and a novelist, Levy has also written several non-fiction books, including three volumes of autobiography: *Things I Don't Want to Know* (2013), *The Cost of Living* (2018) and *Real Estate* (2021). Her first novel, *Beautiful Mutants*, was published in 1989. This was followed by *Swallowing Geography* (1993) and *Billy and Girl* (1996). During the 2010s, *The Man Who Saw Everything* (2019) was longlisted for the Booker Prize, while *Swimming Home* (2011), in which the summer holiday of a poet and his family is interrupted by a fanatical fan, and *Hot Milk* (2016), concerning the trip of an anthropologist and her mother to southern Spain, were both shortlisted.

Christopher Priest was born in 1943 and grew up in Cheshire; he left school at 16 when his family relocated to Essex. For the next seven years, he worked unhappily with a firm of chartered accountants in Central London but found consolation when a colleague introduced him to science fiction. Priest began writing his own stories from the mid-1960s and published his first novel *Indoctrinaire* in 1970. *Fugue for a Darkening Island* (1972), *Inverted World* (1974), *The Space Machine* (1976), *A Dream of Wessex* (1977) and *The Affirmation* (1981) followed before his inclusion among 'The Best of Young British Novelists 1983'. Priest's characteristically acerbic memoir of the photo shoot and launch party marking the announcement of this list, 'Where Am I Now?' (2008), mercilessly condemns the whole process as a charade and is scathing about the behaviour of some of his peers. Priest's ninth novel *The Prestige* (1995), winner of both the James Tait Black Memorial Prize and the World Fantasy Award, was filmed by Christopher Nolan in 2006. *The Separation* (2002) won the Arthur C. Clarke Award. Of his later novels, *The Islanders* (2011), *The Adjacent* (2013), *The Gradual* (2016) and *The Evidence* (2020) are all set wholly or partially in the Dream Archipelago setting of *The Affirmation* and related short stories written from the 1970s onwards. *An American Story* (2018), partially set on the Isle of Bute where Priest now lives, revolves around 9/11 conspiracy theories; while *Expect Me Tomorrow* (2022) is a typically idiosyncratic climate-change novel featuring two sets of identical twins. A volume of short stories, *Episodes*, came out in 2019. His most recent novel is *Airside* (2023), in which a film critic retrospectively investigates the disappearance of a 1930s Hollywood star.

James Robertson was born in 1958 and grew up in Bridge of Allan, Stirlingshire. Educated at the independent co-educational boarding school, Glenalmond College, Robertson went on to complete a PhD on the novels of Walter Scott at the University of Edinburgh. He subsequently worked in various roles in the book trade. Robertson became a full-time author in the early 1990s, initially publishing poems and short stories, and from 1993 to 1995 was the first writer in residence at Hugh MacDiarmid's house in Lanarkshire. His first novel, *The Fanatic* (2000), combined settings in contemporary Scotland in the months surrounding the 1997 election with a story of Scotland in the 17th century, and was followed by the historically set *Joseph Knight* (2003). In November 2004, Robertson was the first, and to date, only writer-in-residence at the newly opened Scottish Parliament building, where he gave three masterclasses on different aspects of the relationship between Scottish literature and politics. These were later published as essays alongside a set of sonnets in *Voyage of Intent: Sonnets and Essays from the Scottish Parliament* (2005). *The Testament of Gideon Mack* (2006), longlisted for the Booker Prize, was set in Scotland between the 1950s and the present day, as was *And the Land Lay Still* (2010). His more recent novels are *The Professor of Truth* (2013), *To Be Continued...* (2016), and *News of the Dead* (2021), which won the Walter Scott Prize for historical fiction.

Justina Robson was born in Leeds in 1968 and educated at the University of York. Both her first and second novels, *Silver Screen* (1999) and *Mappa Mundi* (2001) were shortlisted for the Arthur C. Clarke Award. *Natural History* (2003) and *Living Next-Door to the God of Love* (2005) were set in a shared universe. *Keeping It Real* (2006) was the first of what would become five novels in the very successful *Quantum Gravity* series, featuring the cyborg Lila Black. In 2011, she published, *Heliotrope*, a short story collection. *Transformers: The Covenant of Primus* (2013) was a tie-in to the well-known media series that came 'encased in an interlocking Autobot emblem that when pulled open emits Transformer sounds'. *Glorious Angels* (2015) was shortlisted for the British Science Fiction Association Award for Best Novel. Her next novel, *The Switch* (2017), includes elements of homage to Iain Banks, who had died earlier in the decade, in what is a sophisticated work of queer political science fiction. In 2018, Robson collaborated with Adrian Tchaikovsky on a series called *After the War* for which he wrote the first volume *Redemption's Blade* (2018) and she wrote the second, *Salvation's Fire* (2018). In 2020, Robson edited a volume of stories, *The Tales of Catt & Fisher: The Art of the Steal*, set in the *After the War* universe. Her most recent book is a novella telling the story of an evolving AI tasked with saving humanity from itself, *Paper Hearts* (2020).

Kamila Shamsie is a British Pakistani writer based principally in the UK, but with homes also in the US and Pakistan. She has written eight novels to date, shifting in her early fiction from largely South Asian settings to more wide-ranging and transnational panoramas in recent novels. Both her first and third novels, *In the City by the Sea* (1998) and *Kartography* (2002) were shortlisted for the John Llewellyn Rhys Prize, while her second novel, *Salt and Saffron* (2000), was listed on Orange's '21 Writers of the 21st Century'. In 2013, she was placed on Granta's list of 20 best young British writers, while her fifth novel, *Burnt Shadows* (2009), won the Anisfield-Wolf Book Award, and her seventh novel, *Home Fire* (2017), won the 2018 Women's Prize for Fiction. Shamsie's writing also raised controversy when she had the Nelly Sachs Prize rescinded in 2019 due to her involved in the pro-Palestinian Boycott, Divestment, and Sanctions Movement. Following this, numerous authors joined together to protest this decision in a letter to BDS. Shamsie's most recent novel, *Best of Friends* (2022) has received praise from reviewers, and her writing continues to attract widespread critical and popular attention into the 2020s. Apart from her fiction, she is also a well-recognized and often polemic cultural and critical commentator, and in 2009, she wrote *Offense: The Muslim Case* to address contemporary political and media representations of Muslim extremism.

Ali Smith was born in Inverness, Scotland in 1962. She studied at the University of Aberdeen, and Newnham College, Cambridge, where she began a PhD. She lectured at the University of Strathclyde, before becoming ill. Following that she began to write, first publishing short stories collected as *Free Love and Other Stories* (1995) and then *Other stories and other stories* (1999). Her first novel, *Like*, was published in 1997 and the second, *Hotel World*, was published in 2001 and shortlisted for numerous prizes, winning the inaugural Scottish Arts Council Book of the Year Award. She has published four more novels – *The Accidental* (2005), *Girl Meets Boy* (2007), *There But For The* (2011), *How To Be Both* (2014) – and two more collections of short stories. Smith's work is formally inventive, often narrated from a number of positions, and often suggestive of life and experience as mysterious, explanations just outside the field of vision. A number of her works have used their formal explorations to think about the identities and possibilities open to women and about the construction of sexuality, and in this she has been seen as reviving and rethinking the experiments of Virginia Woolf. In 2013 Smith published a series of lectures given by her at Oxford University in the previous year, and these, like Woolf's essays, combine literary critical work with fictional scenarios and voices. Her post-Brexit *Seasonal Quartet* of novels comprises *Autumn* (2016), *Winter* (2017), *Spring* (2019) and *Summer* (2020).

Zadie Smith was born in the London Borough of Brent in 1975. She went to Hampstead Comprehensive School before studying English Literature at Cambridge. Her first novel, *White Teeth* (2000), finished during the final year of her degree, was the subject of much anticipation, having been auctioned before completion. On publication, it quickly became a bestseller and was critically praised, winning many awards including the James Tait Black Memorial Prize and the Commonwealth Writers First Book Prize. A long, complex but often comic tale of postwar London, featuring a cast of characters from different ethnic and class backgrounds, the novel was at first viewed in some quarters as celebrating a multicultural London before further consideration and the author's own statements suggested that it was expressing a more nuanced viewpoint. *White Teeth* was adapted for television in 2002, the same year as Smith's second novel, *The Autograph Man* was published to mixed reviews. During the academic year 2002–2003, Smith studied at Harvard and her third novel, the Orange Prize winning *On Beauty* (2005) is set mainly in the Greater Boston area. She published a collection of essays, *Changing My Mind* in 2009. After teaching at the Columbia University School of the Arts, Smith took up a permanent post at New York University in 2010. Her fourth novel, *NW* (2012), is set in Kilburn and follows the trajectories of several characters who grew up in the same housing estate. It is more brutal than *White Teeth* but also evokes a modernist temporality and a sense, at least, of what is at stake in thinking about the future rather than the past. A futuristic short story 'Meet the President' was published by the New Yorker in August 2013. Since then, she has published a novella, *The Embassy of Cambodia* (2013) and her short story 'Miss Adele Amidst the Corsets' (2014) was shortlisted for the BBC National Short Story Prize. Her most recent novel is currently *Swing Time* (2016), but *The Fraud* is scheduled to come out in 2023.

Olivia Sudjic, whose family background was originally from Yugoslavia, was born in London in 1988 and educated at the City of London School for Girls before reading English Literature at Cambridge. She was named among the 20 best British novelists aged under 40 on the latest ten-yearly *Granta* Best of Young British Novelists list published in 2023. Her first novel *Sympathy* (2017) employs an experimental structure to explore how a twenty-something woman visiting New York becomes obsessed with an older woman through Instagram. Her second book, *Exposure* (2018), is a non-fiction essay on the anxiety epidemic, autofiction and internet feminism. Her most recent novel is *Asylum Road* (2021).

Index

2008 financial crash 248

Abbas, Madeline-Sophie 81, 83
Ahmed, Sara 139–140, 141, 142, 150
Ainsley, Claire 197
Alberti, Fay Bound 170–171
Aldiss, Brian 23, 28
Allan, Nina 8, 12, 241, 250, 307
  The Race 250
  The Rift 250–252
Anam, Tahmina
  The Bones of Grace 17
Atwood, Margaret
  The Handmaid's Tail 254, 255
  The Penelopiad 264
awards 252–254

Ballard, J.G. 28, 242
  The Atrocity Exhibition 234
  Crash 234
  Kingdom Come 28
  Millennium People 28
  Wind from Nowhere, The 23
Banerjee, Debjani 86
Banks, Iain 40, 41, 47 n.3
Barker, Clive 212, 223, 226
  Clive Barker's A-Z of Horror 226, 228
Barker, Pat 10, 288 n.6, 307
  The Silence of the Girls 19, 263, 265, 269–275, 277
  The Women of Troy 263
Barnes, Julian
  'People Will Hate Us Again' 184
Barnett, Anthony 200
Baudrillard, Jean 242
Bauman, Zygmunt 186, 229
Begum, Shamima 83, 101, 281
Benjamin, Walter 146
Bennett, Alice 18
Bentley, Nick 19

Bhabha, Homi 98
Black Lives Matter 1, 17, 240, 256, 264, 301, 304, 306
Botha, Mark 137, 138
  Future Theory: A Handbook to Critical Concepts 138
Bould, Mark 249
Bound, Douglas
  A Time of Lies 195
Bourdieu, Pierre 16
Brand, Russell 246
Brexit 3, 4, 6, 8, 11, 17, 26, 33, 36, 37, 39, 44, 45, 55, 66, 67, 80, 81, 174, 175, 177, 178, 179, 183, 191, 192, 193, 196, 197–198, 201, 247, 252, 266, 297–301
  see also European Union (EU) Membership Referendum
'Brexlit' 6, 174, 176, 177, 183–184, 189
British Boom (of science fiction) 241, 244, 246–252, 258
Britton, David 226, 229–230
  Invictus Horror 227, 228
  La Squab 227, 228, 230
  Lord Horror books 212, 226, 231
  Lord Horror: Reverbstorm 227
  Razor King 227, 228, 230
Brown, Craig 174, 177
Brown, Glen James 185, 197
  Ironopolis 185, 197–198
Butler, Andrew M. 241
Butler, Judith 17, 84
Butterworth, Michael 211, 227
  The Blue Monday Diaries 211
Byers, Sam 189–196
  Perfidious Albion 6, 184–185, 189–196

Calvino, Italo 128, 221, 234
Cameron, David 2, 3, 5, 81, 183, 198, 295–297

Carey, M.R.
  The Girl with All the Gifts 15, 16
Carr, Nicholas 70
  The Shallows 51–53, 59, 69
Cartwright, Anthony 11, 113–114, 119, 123, 196–203, 205, 307–308
  The Afterglow 197, 202
  The Cut 6, 129–132, 185, 196, 198–203
  Heartland 196
  How I Killed Margaret Thatcher, 113–118, 120
  Iron Town 197
Caruth, Cathy 273–274
Castel, Robert 15, 16
Charnock, Anne
  Dreams Before the Start of Time 254
Christopher, John 28
Citton, Yves 54, 58, 75
Clarke, Ben 196
Clegg, Nick 2, 5, 295–297
Coe, Jonathan 11, 153–179, 308
  The Accidental Woman 153
  Expo 58 11, 153, 157, 163–167, 178, 179, 205
  Middle England 11
  Number 11 153, 157, 167–173
  The Terrible Privacy of Maxwell Sim 11, 153, 157–163
  use of parody 153–5, 165, 166, 177, 178–9
  What a Carve Up! 153, 174, 178
Colebrook, Martyn 210, 224
Connell, Liam 9
Corbyn, Jeremy 27, 297–301
Coupland, Douglas 204
Covid-19 pandemic 1, 23, 51, 211, 248, 306
Crary, Jonathan 13
Crawford, Robert 30
Crews, Brian 161, 162
Crowhurst, Donald 160–161
Cusk, Rachel 73

Derrida, Jacques 222, 242
  Glas 222
  Spectres of Marx 242
Doctorow, Cory 260
  Walkaway 260
Drabble, Margaret
  The Ice Age 25

Eaglestone, Robert 186
Edgerton, David
  The Rise and Fall of the British Nation 27
Edwards, Caroline 146
Esty, Jed 114
European Union (EU) 2, 28, 36, 44, 107, 113, 239, 297–301
European Union (EU) Membership Referendum 1, 3, 4, 80, 84, 107, 109, 129, 175, 183, 185, 199, 204, 297
  see also Brexit
Evaristo, Bernadine 107
  Girl, Woman, Other 17

Farage, Nigel 192, 296, 300
Firestone, Shulamith 254
Fisher, Mark 13, 241, 242–247, 249, 256, 259
  Capitalist Realism 242
  'Exiting the Vampire Castle' 245–247, 256
  Ghosts of My Life 242
  The Weird and The Eerie 245
Fordham, John 124
Freud, Sigmund 28, 244–245

Gantea, Jean-Michel 169
Ghosh, Amitav 14
Gibbon, Lewis Grassic 32
  A Scots Quair 31, 32, 125, 126
Gibbons, Alison 66
Goodhart, David 198–199, 200
  The Road to Somewhere 200
Gray, Alistair 10, 30
Great British Class Survey, 8–9, 20, 108, 112, 121
Greene, Graham
  Brighton Rock 34
Grenfell Tower 99, 298
Griffiths, Niall 10
  Broken Ghost 10, 16, 33–34, 35, 36
  A Great Big Shining Star
Guignery, Vanessa 153
Gunaratne, Guy 17, 82, 308–309
  In Our Mad and Furious City 17, 94–100

Hames, Scott 31, 124
Hamid, Mohsin 17, 82, 309
  Exit West 17, 88–94

Hamilton, Patrick
  Hangover Square 34
Haraway, Donna 242
Harkaway, Nick 259
  Gnomon 259
Harrison, Melissa 189–191
  All Among the Barley 184, 189–191
  Clay (2013) 56, 204 n.2
Harrisson, M. John 8, 12, 42, 241, 309–310
  The Sunken Land Begins to Rise Again 28, 44–46, 47
Hayles, N. Katherine 54, 57, 59, 75
Haynes, Natalie 264, 268
  The Children of Jocasta 263, 268, 275–278
  Ten Thousand Ships 19, 263, 275
Heilmann, Ann 265
Henderson, Ailsa 4, 6, 187, 193, 200
Hinton, James
  Seven Lives from Mass Observation 25–26, 27
Hobsbawm, Eric
  'The Forward March of Labour Halted' 25
Hogg, Emily 9, 16
Home, Stewart 214, 223, 224, 231
  The 9 Lives of Ray the Cat Jones 233
  69 Things to Do with a Dead Princess 232
  Denizen of the Dead 231, 232–233
  Mandy, Charlie, and Mary Jane 233–234
  Suspect Device: A Reader in Hard-Edged Fiction 214, 223, 232
  Tainted Love
Homer, 268, 269–270
  The Iliad 269–282
  The Odysssey 282
Hubble, Nick 7, 24, 28, 120, 125, 196, 265
Hudson, Kerry 110–111, 131
  Lowborn 110
Hutcheon, Linda 153, 155, 156, 179, 265, 267, 269
  The Politics of Postmodernism 155
Hutchinson, Dave 12, 241

Ings, Simon 310
  The Smoke 30, 38–40, 42, 46

Ishiguro, Kazuo
  The Buried Giant
  Klara and the Sun 15

James, David 268
James, M.R. 245
  'The Monkey's Paw' 245
  'The Mezzotint' 246
Jameson, Fredric 39
Johnson, B.S. 160, 161, 213
  Albert Angelo 213
  Christie Malry's Own Double-Entry 160, 161–162
  House Mother Normal 213
  Unfortunates, The 213
Johnson, Boris 24, 26, 36, 44, 193, 204, 263, 287
Johnson, Daisy 10
  Everything Under 263, 265, 269, 282, 283–286
Johnson-Pratchett problem, the 19, 213–214, 234
Johnston, D.D. 129, 310–311
  Peace, Love and Petrol Bombs 125–129
Johnston, Jennifer 28
Jones, David Martin 177
Jones, Owen 246

Kavenna Joanna
  The Birth of Love 241, 255
Kayman, Martin A 226
Kelman, James 10, 11, 30, 31, 311
  Mo Said She Was Quirky 11, 118, 119, 123–125, 132
King, John 184
  The Liberal Politics of Adolf Hitler 204 n.1
Kingsnorth, Paul 184
  The Wake 204 n.1
Knepper, Wendy 121, 122
Kostka, Violetta 153, 155, 156
Kristeva, Julia 155–156
Kundnani, Arun 86, 90

Lanchester, John
  Capital 13, 14
Lanone, Catherine 270, 271, 272
Lasch, Christopher 162–163
  The Culture of Narcissism 158

Le Guin, Ursula
    The Lathe of Heaven 242
Levy, Deborah 215, 311
    Swimming Home 215–220
Liao Pei-chen 80
Lindsey Oil Refinery strikes (2009) 109
Llewellyn, Mark 265
Lovecraft, H.P. 248, 253
Lynch, Mick 132
Lynn, Hannah *Athena's Guild*

McAuley, Paul
    Austral 15, 255
McCarthy, Tom 56, 62, 119, 215, 217
    Satin Island 14
McCrudden, Chris 110
McEwan, Ian 185, 195
    Cockroach 195
McGill, Hannah 165
McGregor, Jon 10, 12
    Even the Dogs 12, 288 n.8
    Reservoir 13 56
MacIlvanney, William 7, 28
McIntyre, Vonda 39
    The Exile Waiting 39, 42
MacLeod, Ken
    Intrusion 15, 255
Mahdavi, Pardis 144–145
Maugham, Tim 10, 260
    Infinite Detail 16, 242, 256–259
May, Theresa 81, 83, 141, 204, 298–300
Metamodernism 267–268
#MeToo 1, 264
Miéville, China 241, 244, 249
    Iron Council 249
    October 249
    Railsea 249
Miliband, Ed 5, 296, 297
Miller, Madeline 264, 269
Moorcock, Michael 226, 229
    The Condition of Muzak 211
Moore, Alan 212, 226
Morey, Peter 79, 95
Morrison, Jago 83
Moseley, Merritt 153
Moshfegh, Ottessa
    My Year of Rest and Relaxation 69

Moss, Sarah 10, 189–189
    The Fell 15
    Ghost Wall 6, 184, 185–189, 190, 195, 199
Mukherjee, Ankhi 80, 279

Nairn, Tom 27
Negarestani, Reza 222, 224
New Wave (of science fiction) 211, 234
New Worlds 210, 212
Newland, Courttia
    A River Called Time 17
Niven, Alex 204
Nolan, Val
    'Cofiwch Aberystwyth' (2020) 33
Noon, Jeff 241, 244, 248
Nosniboor, Christopher 213
    This Book is Fucking Stupid: Fifty Shades of Shit 213
Noys, Benjamin 228

O'Brien, Phil 110, 114, 116
Orwell, George 9, 146
Osmond, John
    Ten Million Stars Are Burning 33, 34–36, 46
O'Toole, Fintan 186

Paraskos, Michael
    Rabbitman 195
Peace, David 224–226
    Patient X 224–226
Pratchett, Terry 213
Priest, Christopher 42, 251, 311–312
    The Evidence 28, 42–44
    The Islanders 239–240
proletarian postmodernism 222

Richards, I.A. 143
Rigby, Lee 94, 97, 98, 101, 177, 296
Roberts, Adam 12
    New Model Army 239, 240
Robertson, James 30, 312
    And the Land Lay Still 7, 30–32, 34, 46
Robson, Justina 47, 312–313
    The Switch 30, 40–42, 46

Rogers, Jane
  The Testament of Jessie Lamb 254
Rousselot, Elodie 265
Rowling, J.K.
  Harry Potter and the Chamber of Secrets 62
  Harry Potter and the Deathly Hallows 62
Rutkowska, Urzula 85, 281

Sadaf, Shazia 91
Sahota, Sunjeev
  The Year of the Runaways 14, 17
Sandel, Michael 197
Saunders, Robert 201
Scarrow, Alex
  Plague Land 15
Scottish Independence Referendum 1, 17, 32, 240, 252, 295, 296
Sedgwick, Helen
  The Growing Season 254
Self, Will 15, 51, 57, 71
  Grey Area 61
  Phone 57, 58–62, 68
  The Quantity Theory of Insanity 58
  Shark 58
  Umbrella 58, 60, 61
Seward, Keith 229–230
Shallcross, Michael 153, 155
Shamsie, Kamila 17, 82, 269, 278–282, 283, 313
  Home Fire 17, 82–88
Shaw, Kristian 36, 129, 184
Shipley, Gary J. 221
  Necrology 221
Sillietoe, Alan 10
Siratori, Kenji 221
  Necrology 221
Smith, Ali 11, 18, 67, 137–150, 205, 313–314
  as a political writer 137–138
  Autumn 16, 66, 147
  Companion Piece 138–139
  How To Be Both 145
  Public Library and Other Stories 142, 143
  Spring 140, 147, 148
  Summer 15
  There But For The 138
  The Whole Story and Other Stories 142
  Winter 139, 147, 148, 149–150
Smith, Rebecca Ann
  Baby X 254
Smith, Zadie 11, 107, 118, 120–122, 124, 184, 314
  'Fences: A Brexit Diary' 184
  NW 11, 118, 119–122, 124, 125, 132
  'Two Paths for the Novel' 119, 122
Sommerfield, John
  May Day 125
Sophocles 269, 276, 282
  Antigone 84, 88, 276, 278, 279, 282
  Oedipus Tyrannus 276, 283
Standing, Guy 16
Stiegler, Bernard 54, 57, 60, 75
Sudjic, Olivia 18, 51, 57, 68, 314
  Exposure 57, 68, 69, 73, 74
  Sympathy 57, 68–73, 74

Tew, Philip 11, 12
Thatcher, Margaret 24, 47, 114, 117, 159, 178
Thirlwell, Adam 18, 51, 62–63, 67
  Kapow! 57, 63–66, 67–68, 74
Tressell, Robert 126
  The Ragged Trousered Philantrophists 126
Trexler, Adam 14
Trump, Donald 1, 80, 249, 252, 266, 305, 306

van den Akker, Robin 267
Vandermeer, Ann 248
Vandermeer, Jeff 248, 251
  Annihilation 248
  City of Saints and Madmen 251
Vermeulen, Timotheus 267
Virdee, Satnam 114

Walsh, Joanna
  Girl Online 71–72
Watson, Rebecca
  Little Scratch 69
Waugh, Patricia 137, 138
  Future Theory: A Handbook to Critical Concepts 138

Welsh, Irvine 30, 224
　Filth 224
　Marabou Stork Nightmares 224
White Review, The 62–63, 66
Williams, Mark P. 19, 20
　on modernism and the tensions of modernization 209–210
Williams, Raymond 24, 27, 28, 35, 108, 111–112, 116, 117
　Keywords 108, 110
　Towards 2000 24
Williamson, James 214
Wilson, Nicola 110
Wright, Patrick 187

Wyndham, John 28
　The Day of the Triffids 23
Wyn-Jones, Richard 4, 6, 187, 193, 200

Yeo, Colin 81
Young, Tory 18
Younge, Gary 204
Yuval-Davies, Nina 85, 96

Ziervogel, Meike 129
Žižek Slavoj
　Welcome to the Desert of the Real 37–38
Zrari, Imad 174, 175, 176, 177

www.ingramcontent.com/pod-product-compliance
Lightning Source LLC
Chambersburg PA
CBHW071801300426
44116CB00009B/1165